翻译讲堂

Twenty Lectures on Translation of Legal Terms

法律术语翻译二十讲

李长栓 著

商务印书馆

### 图书在版编目(CIP)数据

法律术语翻译二十讲 / 李长栓著. —北京:商务印书馆,2020(2022.6 重印)
(翻译讲堂)
ISBN 978-7-100-18248-5

Ⅰ. ①法⋯ Ⅱ. ①李⋯ Ⅲ. ①法律—名词术语—翻译—文集 Ⅳ. ①D90-055

中国版本图书馆 CIP 数据核字(2020)第 049004 号

**权利保留,侵权必究。**

## 法律术语翻译二十讲

李长栓　著

商 务 印 书 馆 出 版
(北京王府井大街36号　邮政编码100710)
商 务 印 书 馆 发 行
北京市十月印刷有限公司印刷
ISBN 978-7-100-18248-5

| 2020 年 6 月第 1 版 | 开本 880×1230 1/32 |
| --- | --- |
| 2022 年 6 月北京第 2 次印刷 | 印张 12½ |

定价:62.00 元

# 前言

本书收录了我从 2014 年底至 2018 年初在《东方翻译》杂志发表的一系列文章，主题是辨析中英文常见法律术语的含义，提供译文；如有必要，改进现有译文。

过去 20 年，本人作为口译员，参加了数百次中外法律领域的交流研讨活动，聆听了数千次专家发言，对国内外司法和法律制度有了较多了解；同时，本人也为联合国翻译了不少法律和人权类文件，积累了一些心得体会，感到有必要写出来，与学习法律、翻译和外语的同学分享。

本书包括 20 篇文章，每篇涵盖一个专题领域。文章以常见的法律概念为切入点，提供背景知识，解释中外差异，提示热点问题，探讨翻译方法，以帮助外语学习者了解法律，帮助法律学习者学习外语，帮助翻译学习者更准确地翻译。本书的目标读者为：

- 口笔译译员
- 英语学习者
- 法学专业学生
- 法律英语学习者

从事任何领域的翻译，都需要了解专业知识，最好成为这个领域的专家。因此，我鼓励学习法律的同学从事法律翻译。对于学习外语的同学来说，可以通过大量的翻译实践，不断积累法律知识，最后达到"以假乱真"的程度。

本书主要分析法律概念的含义，探讨相关译法，但这还远远达不到系统介绍法律知识的目的。如果需要对法律有深入理解，还必须阅读相关中外文法律教科书。

本书不同于双语词典。双语词典不按知识体系排列词条，本书则按法律领域分类讲解，对于上场之前需要"恶补"专业知识的读者，可能会有一些帮助。另外，词典力求客观，本书不乏个人观点。

本书不同于分类词典。分类词典在宏观上分类，但在微观上仍然是词条的罗列，并不阐述概念的含义和概念之间的联系。本书在宏观上分类，微观上注意分析概念之间的联系。

本书不同于翻译教材。翻译教材讲字词句篇的翻译方法，本书仅限于法律概念的翻译，包括查证方法。不仅给出翻译结果，还提供解决问题的思路和方法。

本书不同于法律教材。教科书提供完整的知识系统，本书只是选取个别核心概念，进行与翻译相关的剖析。另外，教科书通常为单一语言，本书则在行文中，尽量括注重要概念的英文。还有，教科书使用专业语言，本书则尽量使用日常语言，便于非法律专业的读者理解。

法律是一个广阔的领域，涉及众多部门法和多如牛毛的概念。鉴于笔者的视野有限，本书收录的概念偏重于司法制度、诉讼法和国际人权法。读者在翻译工作中，必定还会遇到很多专业和翻译问题。但本书提供的思路和方法，可能有助于读者解决这些问题。

本人不是学法律出身，对中外司法和法律制度的了解，大部分来自"道听途说"（hearsay），所提翻译建议，也不一定专业，请读者批判地看待。对某些制度的评论，也是一孔之见。不当之处，敬请批评指正。

希望本书提供的资料，能对外语学习者起到法律扫盲的作用，对法律工作者，起到补习外语的作用，对翻译工作者，起到借鉴译法的作用。

　　最后，感谢中国政法大学杨宇冠教授从专业角度为本书把关并欣然作序。杨教授的序里原本有大段论述《刑事诉讼法》英文本翻译的内容，编辑认为放在序言里篇幅较长，但是这部分内容又极有价值，删去实在可惜。经过考虑和协商，最后决定将这部分内容抽取出来，放在附录，以飨读者。

李长栓<br>
2018 年 8 月 21 日

# 序

## ——读《法律术语翻译二十讲》体会

李长栓教授的大作《法律术语翻译二十讲》即将由商务印书馆出版。他来信嘱我作序。我说"我既荣幸且惶恐，恐怕不够格作序。"因为李教授是翻译大家，每次聆听他的翻译，我都是很佩服的；而我不是英语专业的，虽然懂一点英语，也翻译过一些作品，如英国学者洛克的《政府论》、密尔的《论自由》等，但皆属于业余之作。我的本行是法律，主要研究刑事诉讼法和国际人权法。然而，我又很高兴能够有机会先行拜读李教授的大作，并承诺写篇体会，不敢称序。

这本书收录了李长栓教授从 2014 年底至 2018 年初在《东方翻译》杂志发表的一系列文章，主题是辨析中英文常见法律术语的含义，并提供了详细的解释和译文。读后受益匪浅。我学习法律近 40 年，对英语也非常感兴趣，深知翻译不容易，好的翻译更不容易，精通外语和法律专业的翻译更是非常珍贵。我多次聆听李长栓教授在国际学术研讨会上的翻译，他翻译得很准确，很用心，看得出对专业词汇理解细致入微。听他的翻译是一种享受。他的这本书总结了他数年来从事法律翻译的心得，供大家参考，这是非常有意义的。作为先睹为快者，我谨向作者表示感谢和敬意，并愿意把此书介绍给大家。

这本书包括了李教授的 20 篇文章，每篇涵盖一个专题领域，偏重于司法制度、诉讼法和国际人权法。这些也正是我的兴趣所在。作者说，他这本书的目的在于："以常见的法律概念为切入点，提供背景知识，解释中外差异，提示热点问题，探讨翻译方法，以帮助外语学习者了解法律，帮助法律学习者学习外语，帮助翻译学习者更准确地翻译。"我以为，此书意义还不止于此：法律交流是中外交流的重要组成部分，交流需要准确，双方探讨的是同一概念才行，否则容易引起误解；对一些词语概念的准确理解不仅是学习法律或外语的人应当注意的事情，法学界人士也需要对一些概念准确把握才行，例如司法的概念、逮捕的概念、法制和法治的概念等不仅涉及翻译问题，还是事关司法改革的重大问题。所以，这本书不仅可以对外语学习者起到法律扫盲的作用，对法律工作者起到补习外语的作用，对翻译工作者起到借鉴译法的作用，而且对司法改革的倡导者，可以起到开阔视野的作用。

李教授很谦虚，他说："本人不是学法律出身，对中外司法和法律制度的了解，大部分来自'道听途说'（hearsay），所提翻译建议，也不一定专业，请读者批判地看待。"我以为，他本书中的阐述和建议并非来自"道听途说"，而是他工作经验的总结和认真钻研的结晶。

李教授在此书中阐述的问题都是司法领域内一些重大的和根本性的问题，例如，第一讲是关于"judiciary / 司法部门"。"司法"在中文语境下有多种含义，中国哪些部门属于司法部门，并无统一的认识。最显著的是中国的"司法部"并不主管司法。有人认为中国的司法机关包括法院和检察院。对于检察院是否为司法机关也有不同认识，说它是司法机关的理由是中国的检察院有批捕权，而在国外和根据国际人权公约和刑事司法准则，批捕通常属于司法权。然而，中国检察院的批捕与国外和国际公约中的批捕有巨大不同。我国检察院的批捕通常是对侦查部门已经抓捕并羁押的人批准继续羁押；而国外和国际公约中的"批捕"指具有审判权的部门对抓捕个人、限制个人自由的理由进行审查，发布抓捕令。所以并不能以检察院有批捕权证明检察院是司法机关。国外负责提起公诉的部门通常对审查起诉阶段的被指控人也有决定是否关押的权力，有提起公诉并关押相关人员和撤销案件并释放相关人员的权力，但是这并不是说它们也是司法机关了。

李教授认为："在翻译 judiciary 的时候，为了避免在中国的语境下引起混淆，可以直接翻译为'法院'"，我觉得比较妥当。当然，也不可一概而论，还要看具体情况，译为"司法部门"或者"法院"。在中文中，"司法"通常有四种含义：第一种含义指国家有关部门的立法、侦查、起诉、审判等一系列活动。例如，"联合国刑事司法准则"就包括在联合国主持下各国一起建立或者是制定有关刑事司法的一系列规则，这就相当于立法行为和对侦查、起诉和审判工作的规制。我国的司法改革，也包含了法律的制定和修改等立法活动。第二种含义指国家专门机关所进行的执法行为，包括刑事诉讼中的侦查、起诉、审判、执行等活动和民事、行政诉讼中的审判活动。第三种含义仅指法院的审判。第四种指法院审判人员处理案件的各种活动。这四种含义在不同的语境下使经常交错使用。所以，在翻译 judiciary 的时候，还要看讲话者在什么语境下使用这个概念，可以译为"司法"，也可以译为"法院"。

李教授在此书中对"jury / 陪审团"作了详细的阐述。我不知道是何人何时第一次把 jury 这个词翻译成"陪审团"，这实际上是不准确的，容易引起人们误解。因为中文里"陪审"常给人以"陪而不审"的感觉，但英美法律的 jury 却不只是陪着审判而已，它是真正有权决定案件判决的审判组织。诚如李教授指出："陪审团是一组普通的公民（刑事案件一般为 12 人），全程参与审理，听取控辩双方的开场陈述（opening statement）、控辩双方对双方证人的询问（examination）和交叉询问（cross-examination），以及控辩双方的总结辩论（closing argument）。陪审团根据双方证人的表现和控辩双方的推理论证，结合法官（finder of law，法律的认定者）提供的法律指导，作出被告人有罪（guilty）或无罪（not-guilty）的裁决（verdict）。"据此，英美法系中的 jury 并非陪着法院审理案件，而是实实在在地对案件有决定权，这是由人民参与司法审判、由人民决定被告人是否有罪的具体机制。jury 译为"陪审团"，juror 译为"陪审员"，这种译法已经约定俗成了，要改也难。但是李教授在此书中的解释对于我国同胞了解国外的陪审制度有很重要的意义。

李教授不仅辨析了陪审团的概念，在此书中，他还分析归纳了陪审团审判的优越性。他认为："陪审团的决定基本可靠。……除此之外，陪审团制度还有其他作用。一是普法宣传作用。通过参与审理，普通公民对于诉讼程序有了切身的体验，对实体法也会有局部的了解，这比抽象的普法宣传更为有效。二是提高公民的责任意识。陪审团负有重大的责任，被告人的身家性命可能掌握在自己手上。所以，陪审团会非常重视这样的机会，不会任意裁判。三是陪审团的裁决容易被各方认可，不会出现申诉（petition）、缠诉（endless petition）、闹访（aggressive petition）的现象。因为陪审团是双方共同选定的，双方都会信赖陪审团的决定，且社会大众因为有陪审的经历，更容易接受陪审团裁决。四是培养公民的司法主人翁态度。"这就超越了翻译的意义，而是对相关法律制度的论述，属于法学研究的范畴了。这对于理解国外相关制度，进行我国陪审制度的改革都有重大的参考价值。

李教授此书中对于"attorney-at-law／法律代理，律师"这个概念的辨析同样具有重大意义。他告诉我们：attorney-at-law 这个词的本义是"法律代理人"。中文虽然经常翻译为"律师"，但在美国不仅指私人开业律师，还指法官和公诉人。在美国，他们都属于美国律师协会（American Bar Association）。相对而言，中国的律师范围较窄，仅限于为社会提供法律服务的职业法律工作者（私人开业律师）。在美国的刑事诉讼中，公诉人（prosecutor）也可以称为 prosecuting attorney（公诉律师），他们是代表人民或国家的律师。辩护律师可以称为 defense attorney。如果英文里仅仅使用 attorney(s) 一词，没有明确说明是代表国家的律师还是代表被告人的律师，译者要根据情况明确翻译为"公诉人""辩护人"或"控辩双方律师"。书中还告诉我们：美国的律师享有充分的调查取证权（right to investigate and collect evidence）、会见当事人的权利（right to interview the client）和阅卷权（right to access case files）；可以雇用私人侦探（private detective）；可以随时会见当事人，且不受监听；可以在审前充足的时间内获得全部证据材料（evidentiary material）；可以在法庭进行热忱的辩护（zealous defense）而不必担心受到公诉人的报复。美国没有所谓"律师伪证罪"（the crime of falsifying or assisting the client to falsify evidence）的提法。当然，律师伪造证据或协助证人作伪证，要受到律师协会的纪律处分，包括吊销执照（to be disbarred）。另外，与 attorney-at-law（法律代理）相对的说法，是 attorney-in-fact（事务代理）。这对于我国法律从业人员的管理①、律师的职能等方面的问题

---

① 在美国,法官、检察官、律师都属于法律从业人员,都必须通过司法考试,都受美国律师协会的管辖,例如无论是法官、检察官或律师在职业道德或纪律方面发生问题时,皆由律师协会的相关部门进行调查、听证、处理。如果问题属实,律师协会可以吊销相关人员的法律从业人员资格,则相关人员就不能继续从事法律职业。

之解决都有启发。

　　李教授此书对"法系"也作了详细分析。学法之人常见到"英美法系""大陆法系"这样的词。此书中对这些概念也有精辟的解释。"英美法系"（Anglo-American Law）又称"普通法系"（common law）。"普通"为"普遍通行"的意思，也就是说"普通法系"之渊源在于大众，在于人民的风俗习惯。与"普通法系"相对应，人们把欧洲大陆的法律制度称为"大陆法系"（continental law，又译"欧陆法系"），也称为"市民法"（civilian / citizens' law）、"罗马法系"（Roman law）、"民法法系"（civil law）①。称"大陆法系"是从它的地域特点而言，因为相对英国而言，法国、德国、意大利等国家地处欧洲大陆；称"罗马法系"主要指这些国家是受罗马法影响；称"民法法系"（civil law）者也是从法律性质而言，古罗马市民法很发达，"民法法系"当指"公民的法律"，而不仅指狭义的民法。

　　难能可贵的是，该书中，作者还对美国的刑事诉讼程序作了详细的说明，这对于了解美国刑事诉讼有很大帮助。特别是作者对 arrest warrant（拘留证）这个概念进行了辨析，他指出：在美国，拘留证是由法院签发的；拘留之后两三天，要到法院初次到庭（initial appearance），由法官决定先放回去（保释），还是继续关押（remand，还押）。在美国，法院从拘留就开始介入；在中国，法院直到审判阶段才介入。这不仅对于厘清相关概念的差异有作用，而且对于了解司法权力配置有参考作用。

---

　　① 注意：civil law 这个词组，在英语中也指世俗的法律的总和，包括刑法、诉讼法等，而汉语中的"民法"仅指调整民事关系的法律。参见洛克《政府论》、密尔《论自由》对该词组的用法，往往指国家制定的法律，特别是刑事法律，作为与神法、自然法相对的概念使用。

此书中对"standards of proof / 证明标准"也有详细的阐述。在国外的刑事司法活动的不同阶段，存在不同的证明标准，不都是排除合理怀疑。比如，在美国，警察只要有 reasonable suspicion（有合理犯罪嫌疑），就可以拦住一个人进行简单搜查；但警察若要更仔细地搜查或拘捕（arrest）一个人，就要达到更高的标准：probable cause。probable cause 是指有一定的可能性（a fair probability），一般翻译为"合理根据"，即进行或提请拘捕、搜查的警员所掌握的证据要达到使一个智力正常的普通人相信有一定的事实根据怀疑某人实施了、正在实施或将要实施某种犯罪，或者相信在某地能找到与犯罪有关的物品。这对于了解相关常识，特别是证明标准的概念有重要意义。

此书中对"hearsay evidence / 传闻证据"及其原理有详细阐述。作者指出：根据传闻证据规则的原理，证人作证时，不能以转述别人的陈述来证明一件事的真实性。原来是谁说的，谁要来作证，否则就违反了被告人有权与指控者当面对质（right to confrontation，right to confront the accuser）的权利。排除传闻证据的基本原理是，证人只能证明自己的所见所闻（perception，感知），比如听到、看到、感到了什么，而不能证明别人的所见所闻。因为别人不到庭作证，无法接受交叉询问（cross-examination，对方律师的询问），因此别人未经质疑的证言被认为不可靠。我们事先固定、在法庭使用的证人证言，在美国法院被认为是"传闻证据"。这些知识对于完善我国的法庭质证制度有参考价值。

此书中还介绍了"deposition / 庭外录取证言"的制度。如果一个证人将来无法到庭作证，可以提前把他的证言以录音、录像或逐字记录的形式记录下来，供将来在法庭使用。庭外录取证言需要双方的律师参加，通常在一方的律师事务所进行。录取证言叫 take deposition，作证的人叫 deponent。deposition 也指以这种方式录取的证言。deposition 与 affidavit（宣誓陈述）意思不同。后者是指证人在宣誓状态下自愿提供的书面证言，需要由司法官员或公证员主持证人宣誓并在证言上签字，还要注明作证地点。作 affidavit 不需要通知对方律师，但作 deposition（庭外作证）需要双方在场。oral testimony（口头作证）则是指在法庭现场作证。作者指出：deposition 不同于中国法庭使用的证人证言。证人证言是指证人就其所了解的案件情况向公安司法机关所作的陈述。证人证言一般是口头陈述，以笔录加以固定；办案人员同意由证人亲笔书写的书面证词，也是证人证言。中国的证人证言是单方面提供的，可以在法庭使用，接受律师的"质证"（指出其中的瑕疵）。在美国，这种证言只能用于反驳证人当庭的证言，即证人出庭作证时，律师发现所述内容与先前的书面证言不一致，才能把先前的证言拿出来证明证人不可信。在中国，律师可以针对文件质证；在美国，只能 challenge a witness（通过交叉询问质疑证人）。美国遵循口头审理原则（orality principle），所有证据必须通过证人之口进入法庭。这些知识对于完善我国的证人作证制度，特别是司法人员和律师在庭外取证的制度有特别重要的参考价值。①

此书中还对"examination and cross-examination / 询问和交叉询问"作了详细的解释。在英美法律的刑事审判中，公诉人（或辩护人）逐一传唤自己的证人到庭后，首先通过自己的提问，让证人把自己感知（看到或听到）到的（有利于本方的）事情经过说一遍。这个过程叫"询问"（examination）；询问本方证人时，叫作 direct

---

① 我国刑事诉讼中，相关人员在法庭外取证尚未有具体程序规制，辩护律师接触证人和取证出现不少问题。此书中对司法人员庭外取证的方式介绍很有启发。

examination（直接询问）或者 examination-in-chief（主询问）。直接询问只能用开放性问题（open-ended questions），即以 W 和 H 开头的问题；不允许用诱导性问题（leading questions）。但如果询问过程中发现自己的证人不配合，可以要求法官确认该证人为 hostile witness（敌对证人），从而准予使用诱导性问题。交叉询问（cross-examination）是控方或辩方对对方传来证人的询问。因为询问指向对方证人，彼此交叉，故名。交叉询问通常使用诱导性问题，因为对方的证人被默认为"敌对证人"，不会与询问者配合。经过第一轮直接和交叉询问后，还可以针对交叉询问中出现的问题，进行第二轮直接询问，叫作 redirect（examination），以及第二轮交叉询问，叫作 recross（examination）。中国传统的庭审方式没有直接询问和交叉询问，由法官主导查明事实，对被告人/证人的询问由法官来做，而不像英美法系那样由法官维持秩序，让控辩双方提问。现在虽然在向对抗制靠拢，但法律实务工作者并不熟悉直接询问和交叉询问的技巧，甚至对于什么是交叉询问存在误解。作者指出：当我们听到有人谈"交叉询问"时，一定要明白是不是真的"交叉询问"，否则直译出来，听众可能会产生困惑。李教授这段论述不仅介绍了"交叉询问"的真正含义，而且分析了我国刑事诉讼法庭审理方式与英美法律的差别。我完全赞同李教授的意见，在法律交流中，中文说到"交叉询问"时一定要注意语境，不能见到这个词就直译过去，否则很容易引起困惑。这充分反映了作者对翻译的认真负责精神。

关于询问证人，问题很多，需要进行一些普法活动。例如我国大陆市面上通行的《公民权利和政治权利国际公约》[①]（以下简称"公

---

[①] 我国大陆通行的《公民权利和政治权利国际公约》并非中文作准本，参见杨宇冠、甘雨来：《〈公民权利和政治权利国际公约〉中文本问题研究》，载《社会科学论坛》2009 年第 10 期。

约")中文通行本第十四条第三款第戊项规定：刑事诉讼中被告人有权"讯问或业已讯问对他不利的证人，并使对他有利的证人在与对他不利的证人相同的条件下出庭和受讯问"。"讯问"在汉语中是严厉盘问的意思，通常是指司法机关对犯罪嫌疑人、被告进行的盘问，对证人不应当使用"讯问"一词，而应当改为"询问"。"业已讯问对他不利的证人"这种表述令人费解。与该条款对应的英文为："To examine, or have examined, the witnesses against him"，通行中文本将英文中"have the witnesses examined"理解为"have examined the witnesses"，也就是把"have examined"理解为完成时，以至将其表述为"业已询问"。本条款的英语原意应当理解为"have the witnesses examined"，因此本条款应为："亲自询问或由他人询问对他不利的证人"。我国市面上所用的"公约"这一句就属于典型的误译了。"业已讯问"这种误译不仅是外语理解和翻译的错误，而且是会产生误导，使人们认为该国际公约中被告人的此项权利是"业已讯问"证人，实际上该项权利是要求将证人带到法庭上，接受被告人的询问或者由被告人的代理人（辩护律师）进行询问。在西方刑事诉讼中，通常是由辩护律师代表被告人对证人进行询问；如果要强调被告人自己询问的权利，通常用"confrontation"这个词，意为与证人当面对质。李教授在该书中对这些问题的阐述对于正确理解交叉询问、法庭作证的含义具有重要意义。

以上略举数例说明李教授此书不仅对翻译的人员有用，而且对正确理解法律，特别是外国法和国际法也有很大的作用。

李教授此书中还探讨了一些拉丁语的词汇的翻译问题。国内通拉丁语者很少。李教授介绍了许多拉丁语法律术语的意思，可以帮助读者理解法律原意，省去许多查找的困难，对于学习法律和外语的人都很有意义。

我好像扯远了，就此打住吧。再次说明，我的这些文字实在不敢称序，只是读李教授的大作《法律术语翻译二十讲》后的一些感想和体会而已，不当之处，请李教授和读者批评指正。

杨宇冠<br>2018 年 8 月 25 日<br>于北京中国政法大学蓟门桥校园

# 目　录

第一讲　司法部门、法院及其他相关概念的翻译 …………… 1
第二讲　世界两大法系简介 …………………………………… 14
第三讲　美国的刑事诉讼程序及相关术语的翻译 …………… 28
第四讲　司法独立等概念的含义及其翻译 …………………… 41
第五讲　与证据法相关的术语及其翻译 ……………………… 55
第六讲　十八届四中全会文件翻译举例评析 ………………… 70
第七讲　陪审团制度及相关术语的翻译 ……………………… 91
第八讲　美国刑事案件庭审过程及相关术语的翻译 ………… 107
第九讲　劳动法中的几个概念及其翻译 ……………………… 120
第十讲　"职务犯罪"等罪名译法探讨 ……………………… 138
第十一讲　与税收相关的几个概念及其翻译 ………………… 156
第十二讲　刑法学中的几个概念及其翻译 …………………… 174
第十三讲　法律援助中的几个概念及其翻译 ………………… 185
第十四讲　国际人权法中的几个概念及其翻译 ……………… 198
第十五讲　青少年司法中的几个术语及其翻译 ……………… 212
第十六讲　Court of Cassation 等相关概念及其翻译 ……… 228
第十七讲　几个拉丁语法律术语及其翻译 …………………… 244

| 第十八讲 | Merits of a Case 等法律概念的翻译 | 263 |
| 第十九讲 | Summary Execution 等联合国术语的翻译 | 281 |
| 第二十讲 | 法律翻译中的咬文嚼字 | 304 |

**附录** 杨宇冠：《刑事诉讼法》英译本指瑕 …………… 325

**汉英索引** ………………………………………………… 340

**英汉索引** ………………………………………………… 361

# 第一讲

## 司法部门、法院及其他相关概念的翻译

### Judiciary 司法部门

美国实行三权分立，行政（the Executive Branch）、司法（the Judiciary）、立法部门（the Legislature）相互独立，相互制约。英语中谈到 the judiciary，就是指法院，不包括公诉机关（the prosecution service / the prosecutors' office）、警察部门（the police）、国家安全机关（national security agency，如 CIA），后者属于行政机关。而在中国，对于哪些部门属于司法部门并无统一的认识，基本看法是司法机关包括法院和检察院。对于公安机关、国家安全机关和司法行政机关（司法行政机关指司法部系列）是否属于司法机关，大家有不同认识。全国人民代表大会官方网站上的一段话，反映了司法机关这一概念的模糊性：

> 一般理解，我国的司法机关包括"公检法司安"机关。"公"指公安机关，"检"指检察机关（人民检察院），"法"指审判机关（人民法院），"司"指司法行政机关，"安"指国家安全机关。"公检法司安"机关根据职能依法履行不同职责。在我国，公安机关、国家安全机关和司法行政机关虽然是行政机关，但也承担部分司法方面的职能，人民法院和人民检察院是专门行使审判权和检察权的司法机关。由于各机关的性质和产生方式不同，因此在人民代表大会会议上，人民法院、人民检察院直

接向人大报告工作；公安机关、国家安全机关和司法行政机关的工作情况则体现在政府的工作报告当中。①

所以，在翻译 judiciary 的时候，为了避免在中国的语境下引起混淆，可以直接翻译为"法院"②。而翻译中国的"司法机关"时，需要根据讲话人的具体所指，翻译为 the courts，或 the courts and the prosecutors' offices / procuracies，或 the judicial and law enforcement departments in general，或 justice administration organs 等。当然，如果条件许可，也可以翻译为 the judicial authorities，然后予以解释（同传的时候甚至无法解释）。

另外须注意，"司法"作为一个动宾结构，可以译为 the administration of law / justice，不译为 judicial administration（法院管理、司法行政）："Judicial administration consists of the practices, procedures and offices that deal with the management of the system of the courts."。③

"执法机关"是 law enforcement agency，就是指警察，属于行政部门："In North American English, a law enforcement agency（LEA）is a government agency responsible for the enforcement of the laws. Outside North America, such organizations are called police services."。④

---

① 《我国司法体制的基本构成是怎样的？》，引自中国人大网（http://www.npc.gov.cn/npc/sjb/2013-02/19/content_1755111.htm，读取日期 2014-07-21）。

② 话又说回来，如果看到介绍英美法系司法制度的文献，其中提到"司法"的时候，应当理解为"法院"，因为英美法系"司法"的概念专指法院。

③ "Judicial Administration"，引自 Cornell Law School Legal Information Institute 网站（http://www.law.cornell.edu/wex/judicial_administration，读取日期 2014-07-21）。

④ 维基百科 Law Enforcement Agency 条（http://en.wikipedia.org/wiki/Law_enforcement_agency，读取日期 2014-07-21）。

# Courts 法院

北美的英国殖民地成立"合众国"(United States)之前,是13个互不隶属的殖民地(colonies)。每一个殖民地都有自己的宪法、一套独立的行政、立法、司法体系。后来成立了联邦制的合众国,各"国"(states,汉语译为"州",其实就是成立联邦之前的colonies)的一套体制继续保留;在此基础上,又增加了一套联邦制度,负责各州交由联邦政府管理的事务。没有交给联邦政府管理的事务,仍由各州来管理。美国的联邦制,是历史发展的结果。

具体到司法体系,各州原本就有自己的 district court(地区法院,一审法院)、appellate court / court of appeals(上诉法院)和 supreme court(最高法院)这样一个三级法院体系。district court 也叫 trial court(审判法院),是指 court of first instance(一审法院)。这里须要注意的是,各州各级法院的名称各不相同:有的法院叫 superior court,实际上是一个 trial court 或 appellate court;纽约州有一类法院叫 the Supreme Court,其实是一审法院。州法院命名体系混乱,原因很简单:美国立国之前是多个殖民地,各殖民地想怎么叫就怎么叫。这些法院,现在都属于州法院(state courts)。在翻译中涉及各州法院时,译者一定要先去查一查该州的法院体系图,便于理解各法院之间的关系,从而给出可以理解的译文。

在州法院体系之上,美国设立了一套联邦法院系统,包括 1 个联邦最高法院(the Supreme Court of the United States)[①]、13 个联邦上诉法院(Federal Courts of Appeals)和 94 个联邦地区法院(United States District Courts)。联邦最高法院设在华盛顿。联邦上诉法院和联邦地

---

① 在美国,凡是冠以 the United States 的机构,都是联邦机构,可以译为"联邦",而不是"美国"。

区法院分布在全国各地。一个联邦上诉法院管好几个州，叫一个巡回区（circuit）。过去法官办案，不是常驻一个地方，而是骑在马背上巡回办案。因此联邦上诉法院也叫巡回法院（circuit courts）。在13个联邦巡回区，有11个巡回区是编号的（1st-11th Circuit）。另2个不编号的巡回区：一个是District of Columbia Circuit，只管华盛顿特区；一个是the Federal Circuit，相对应的法院叫作United States Court of Appeals for the Federal Circuit（美国联邦巡回区上诉法院），管理全国联邦地区法院上诉过来的特定类型的案件（如专利）。这里要指出的是，华盛顿特区巡回法院和11个编号的巡回法院（United States Court of Appeals for the ＿＿＿ Circuit，第＿＿＿巡回区上诉法院）都是分地域管辖（各管几个州），但美国联邦巡回区上诉法院是按事项管辖（即只管特定的事项，如专利），权力横跨全国各州。①

　　根据以上安排，一个州平均有两个联邦地区法院，负责一审；当事人不服判决，需要上诉时，可能还需要到设在其他州的联邦上诉法院，因为全国才有13个。联邦法院的管辖权（jurisdiction）包括涉及联邦法律的诉讼（Federal Question Jurisdiction，联邦问题管辖权）和涉及跨州事项的诉讼（Diversity Jurisdiction，多样性管辖权）等。有些案件联邦法院和州法院都有管辖权。不过，百姓生活中的大多数诉讼都在州法院进行，不必跨州奔波。

---

① The Federal Circuit is unique among the courts of appeals as it is the only court that has its jurisdiction based wholly upon subject matter rather than geographic location. The Federal Circuit is an appellate court with jurisdiction generally given in 28 U.S.C. § 1295. The court hears certain appeals from all of the United States District Courts, appeals from certain administrative agencies, and appeals arising under certain statutes.（维基百科 United States Court of Appeals for the Federal Circuit 条，http://en.wikipedia.org/wiki/United_States_Court_of_Appeals_for_the_Federal_Circuit，读取日期2014-07-21。）

上文提到的美国联邦巡回上诉法院属于专门法院，除此之外，还有其他专门法院。如破产法庭（bankruptcy court）、税务法庭（the United States Tax Court）、国际贸易法庭（the Court of International Trade）、联邦索赔法院（the Court of Federal Claims，受理向联邦政府索赔的诉讼）、美国军事上诉法院（the United States Court of Appeals for the Armed Forces）、美国退伍军人权利上诉法院（Court of Appeals for Veterans Claims）等。

中国的法院体系简单明了。在中央一级是最高人民法院（the Supreme People's Court）；各省、自治区、直辖市有高级人民法院（high people's court）①，区级市有中级人民法院（intermediate court），县区有基层人民法院（basic-level people's court）。中国也有各种专门法院，如军事法院、海事法院等。

## Judge 法官

法官主持审判。在对抗制（adversary system，英美法系的审判方式）和纠问制（inquisitorial system，大陆法系的审判方式）体制下，法官的角色不尽相同，但有共同之处，那就是不受他人影响，秉公办案。

在大陆法系国家（civil law jurisdictions/countries），刑事审判采用纠问制②，法官的作用比较积极，在诉讼中会主动地调查案件，盘问证人和当事人，质疑证供的可信性③。法官职业一开始就和检察官或律师分开，即通过司法考试后，可选择做法官、检察官或律师，彼

---

① 这里的"高级"不要翻译为 higher。
② 中国的包公断案的方式就是典型的纠问制。
③ 近些年，大陆法系的审判制度也在改革，总体趋势是向普通法系靠拢。

此之间的流动性很小。但在法国，检察官办公室附属在法院内，检察官和法官经常流动。

在普通法系国家（common law jurisdictions/countries），人们普遍认为，只有德高望重的人才能担当法官。因此，法官一般是从经验丰富的律师、检察官甚至是法学教授中选拔出来的，一般必须得到立法机构的批准。他们在法庭审判中的角色比较消极，不会主动地调查案件或盘问证人和当事人；他们的角色犹如比赛中的裁判（referee），确保诉讼双方有平等的参与机会，并在聆听双方的理据后作出裁判。普通法国家的法官可以通过具体的案例，确定法律规则，这些规则就叫判例法（case law），具体的规则称为 common law principles。判例法相对于成文法或制定法（statutory law，国会制定的法律）而言。判例法可能被立法机关吸收，成为成文法的一部分。比如，knock-and-announce（敲门告知）就是由法官确立的规则，意思是警察到家里搜查之前，要先敲门告知，不能破门而入。因此，在普通法系国家，法官不只是应用法律，其判决在某种程度上延伸了法律。

前些年，中国的最高法院实施了案例指导制度（case guidance system），由最高法院发布一些典型案例（typical cases），供下级法院判案时参考，但这些案例里面体现的规则，对下级法院没有约束力，与英美法系的"判例"或"先例"（precedents）有相当大的差别。

中国法院审判通常采取合议庭制度，美国法院采用独任法官审判制度（如果不用陪审团的话）。"合议庭"可以译为 a panel of judges；有的法律词典上翻译为 collegiate bench，可是这个短语国外法律工作者听不懂。

另外，中国还有"司法官"的称呼，兼指法官和检察官，可以翻译为 judicial officers。

# Jury 陪审团

陪审团是一组普通的公民（刑事案件一般为 12 人），全程参与审理，听取控辩双方的开场陈述（opening statement）、控辩双方对双方证人的询问（examination）和交叉询问（cross-examination），以及控辩双方的总结辩论（closing argument）。陪审团根据双方证人的表现和控辩双方的推理论证，结合法官（finder of law，法律认定者）提供的法律指导，作出被告人有罪（guilty）或无罪（not-guilty）的裁决（verdict）。

很多人觉得，陪审团成员是普通公民（lay persons），不懂法律，怎么能够使用法律？实际上，陪审团的主要任务是认定哪方所说的事实属实（finding the fact）；只要认定了某个事实，就必须套用相关的法律规定（由法官提供），作出有罪或无罪的裁决。比如，被告人被控醉驾或酒驾（drunk driving or driving under the influence of alcohol），陪审团需要做的就是认定被告人是否存在酒后或醉酒驾驶行为；如果存在，就必须作出有罪的裁决，因为法官已经告诉陪审团，酒（醉）后驾车是犯罪行为。

笔者认为陪审团审判有很大优越性。首先，陪审团的决定基本可靠。据美国法官和律师介绍，绝大多数情况下，他们也会做出同样的决定。除此之外，陪审团制度还有其他作用。一是普法宣传作用。通过参与审理，普通公民对于诉讼程序有了切身的体验，对实体法也会有局部的了解，这比抽象的普法宣传更为有效。二是提高公民的责任意识。陪审团负有重大的责任，被告人的身家性命可能掌握在自己手上。所以，陪审团会非常重视这样的机会，不会任意裁判。三是陪审团的裁决容易被各方认可，不会出现申诉（petition）、缠诉（endless petition）、闹访（aggressive petition）的现象。因为陪审团是双方共同选定的，双方都会信赖陪审团的决定，且社会大众因为有陪审的经历，更容易接受陪审团裁决。四是培养公民的司法主人翁态度。虽然陪审团制度是历史的偶然——由过去的 trial by ordeal[①] 发展而来——但它的确是司法民主的最佳体现。当然，司法民主是法治下的民主，陪审团的决定不能逾越法律。如果法官发现陪审团不顾法律任意裁判，可以无视陪审团的决定，独立作出裁决。这叫作 judgment *non obstante veredicto*（JNOV），日常英语是 judgment notwithstanding the verdict（不顾陪审团裁决的裁判；*non obstante* 的意思是 notwithstanding）。还有一种对陪审团的制约，叫 directed verdict（指令裁决），意思是在公诉人举证完毕之后，法官觉得公诉人的证据甚至达不到最低证明标准（minimum standard of proof），任何讲理的陪审团（reasonable jury）都不会作出有罪裁决，这时，法官就会直接指令陪审团作出无罪裁决，不用再听取被告人的证据。相对于大陪审团（grand jury）而言，陪审团也叫小陪审团（petit jury）。小陪审团是针对个案临时挑选的一组人；大陪审团是由普通公民组成的常设机构，决定是否起诉一个嫌疑人。近来，国内一些法院在试点引进类似陪审团的制度，以减轻法官面临的巨大社会压力。英美的陪审团制度不同于我国的人民陪审制度（people's assessors system 或 lay judges system）。美式的陪审团制度能否在国内生存，还需拭目以待。据一位德国法官说，德国历史上曾经引进美式陪审团，结果很不理想。当时流传一句话：有罪就选择陪审团审判，无罪就选择法官审判。意思是：陪审团不够客观公正，认定是否有罪，有一定的随意性，所以，如果被告人真的有罪，就选择陪审团审判，运气好的话，有可能被无罪释放。法官更加客观公正，不会乱来，所以，如果被告人无罪，选

---

① 通过让嫌疑人经受某种磨难而作出判决，如将嫌疑人手臂灼伤，若伤口在几日内痊愈，则定为无罪；否则就是有罪。常译为"神判"。

择法官审判，法官更有可能还你清白。后来该制度被废除。

## Finder of Fact 事实认定者

接受陪审团审判是美国公民的宪法权利（可以放弃）。如果有陪审团参加审判（jury trial），陪审团就是事实的认定者（finder of fact）；如果没有陪审团审判（bench trial），法官既是事实认定者，又是法律认定者（finder of law）。"认定者"在英文里面是"发现者"（finder）。陪审团负责在证人证言和证据中"发现"事实真相，法官"发现"应当适用的法律。

## United States Attorney / Federal Prosecutor 联邦律师 / 联邦公诉人

在美国联邦地区法院和联邦上诉法院代表政府从事诉讼活动的人叫 United States Attorneys（联邦律师）或者 federal prosecutors（联邦公诉人），他们隶属于司法部（Department of Justice）。司法部部长叫 Attorney General（律师长，首席律师），是政府的首席法律顾问。副部长叫 Solicitor General，代表政府到联邦最高法院从事诉讼（特殊情况下司法部长去代理）。全国共有 93 个联邦律师，每个司法辖区（judicial districts）一个（关岛和北马里亚纳群岛共用一个）。每人都有自己的办公室，叫 District Attorney's Office（地区公诉人办公室）。各州司法部设立的公诉人办公室叫 State's Attorney's Office[①]。

prosecutor 这个词经常被翻译为"检察官"，笔者认为不准确。该词在英文中的定义是："a government official who conducts criminal prosecutions on behalf of the state"[②]（在刑事案件中代表国家提起诉

---

[①] 那是另外一个系统。

[②] WordNet 3.0，转引自 The Free Dictionary 网站（http://www.thefreedictionary.com / prosecutor，读取日期 2014-07-21）。

讼的政府官员），其职能不包括我国检察官所肩负的"法律监督"（"检察"）职能（对公安、法院、监所等活动的监督），所以翻译为"检察官"不如翻译为"公诉人"准确。

我国的"检察官"一般翻译为 procurator 或者 public procurator。该词来自拉丁语动词 *procurare*，意思是"take care of, manage"。*pro-* 的意思是 on behalf of（代表），*curare* 的意思是 see to（保证），直译就是"代管人"。这个词仅在大陆法系国家使用。历史上，是指古罗马帝国代表皇帝掌管地方财务的官员。今天，这个词多在社会主义（包括前社会主义）国家使用，如苏联（俄罗斯）、中国、越南。非社会主义国家偶尔也有使用，如苏格兰的检察官叫作 procurator fiscal。有一次笔者遇到苏格兰的检察官到中国开会，看到中国使用 procurator，感到十分亲切和兴奋。中国的检察院叫 procuracy 或 procuratorate，检察长叫 Procurator-General。苏联的检察长，俄语叫 Генеральный Прокурор СССР（苏联检察长），现在俄罗斯的检察长叫 Генеральный Прокурор Российской Федерации（俄罗斯联邦检察长），乌克兰的检察长叫 Генеральний Прокурор України（乌克兰检察长），其词源和发音都类似于英语的 Procurator General。

有趣的是，在苏联时代，检察长翻译为英语是 Procurator General[1]，到俄罗斯时代，同样一个俄语称呼，却翻译为 Prosecutor General[2]。这也反映了一个国家司法理念的变迁。这使笔者思考中国的检察官到底该如何翻译。

在国际交往中，笔者发现多数外国人都不认识 procurator 这个

---

[1] 维基百科 Procurator General of the Soviet Union 条（http://en.wikipedia.org/wiki/Procurator_General_of_the_Soviet_Union，读取日期 2014-07-21）。

[2] 维基百科 Prosecutor General of Russia 条（http://en.wikipedia.org/wiki/Prosecutor_General_of_Russia，读取日期 2014-07-21）。

词，更读不出来 procuratorate（检察院）一词（['prɒkjʊəˌreɪtərɪt]）。所以，笔者的做法是一律翻译为英语的 prosecutor，以避免解释的麻烦。"检察院"翻译为 the prosecutors' office，最高人民检察院翻译为 The Supreme People's Prosecutors' Office。当然，如果出于准确性的考虑，需要使用 procurator，则相应的"检察院"建议用 procuracy，而不是用 procuratorate（procurator + -ate）。因为后缀 -acy 和 -ate 都可以表示办公机构，用 procuracy 显然容易读一些。越南的最高人民法院，就叫 The Supreme People's Procuracy of Vietnam[①]。

## Attorney-at-law 法律代理，律师

attorney-at-law 这个词的本义是"法律代理人"。中文虽然经常翻译为"律师"，但在美国不仅指私人开业律师，还指法官和公诉人，他们都属于美国律师协会（American Bar Association）。相对而言，中国的律师范围较窄，仅限于为社会提供法律服务的职业法律工作者（私人开业律师）。在美国的刑事诉讼中，公诉人（prosecutor）也可以称为 prosecuting attorney（公诉律师），他们是代表人民或国家的律师。辩护律师可以称为 defense attorney。如果英文里仅仅使用 attorney(s) 一词，没有明确说明是代表国家的律师还是代表被告人的律师，译者要根据情况明确翻译为"公诉人""辩护人"或"控辩双方律师"。在英语中，attorney-at-law 与 counselor、counselor-at-law、lawyer 是同义词。还有一个词 counsel，也用来指辩护人，可以是一个律师，也可以是律师团。这个词的用法有些奇怪，即不用定冠词，如"The client acted on advice of counsel."。

---

① 维基百科 The Supreme People's Procuracy of Vietnam 条（http://en.wikipedia.org/wiki/Supreme_People%27s_Procuracy_of_Vietnam，读取日期 2014-07-21）。

美国的律师享有充分的调查取证权（right to investigate and collect evidence）、会见当事人的权利（right to interview the client）和阅卷权（right to access case files）。可以雇用私人侦探（private detective）；可以随时会见当事人，且不受监听；可以在审前充足的时间内获得全部证据材料（evidentiary material）；可以在法庭进行热忱的辩护（zealous defense）而不必担心受到公诉人的报复。

美国没有所谓"律师伪证罪"（the crime of falsifying or assisting the client to falsify evidence）的提法[①]。当然，律师伪造证据或协助证人作伪证，要受到律师协会的纪律处分，包括吊销执照（to be disbarred）。另外，与attorney-at-law（法律代理人）相对的说法，是attorney-in-fact（事务代理人）。

## Defendant 被告（人）

在英语中，刑事案件公诉人（prosecutor，代表国家）的相对人和民事案件原告（plaintiff）的相对人都叫defendant。在中国法律体系中，"被告"一词用于民事案件，"被告人"一词用于刑事。

另外，在中国，在刑事侦查和审查起诉阶段，即公诉机关向法院起诉前，受到刑事指控的人被称为犯罪嫌疑人（suspect）；在公诉机关向人民法院起诉后，被称为刑事被告人（criminal defendant）；被定罪量刑后，才可以称为"罪犯""犯人"（criminal, convict, prisoner）。在美国，称呼被告人可以用defendant或the accused。

辩护人（为被告人提供辩护者）叫作defender，一般由律师担任

---

[①] 1996年《中华人民共和国刑法》第三百零六条规定：在刑事诉讼中，辩护人、诉讼代理人毁灭、伪造证据，帮助当事人毁灭、伪造证据，威胁、引诱证人违背事实改变证言或者作伪证的，处三年以下有期徒刑或者拘役；情节严重的，处三年以上七年以下有期徒刑。

(defense lawyer/attorney)。中国也允许被告人的监护人、亲戚朋友等人来担任。

## Expert Witness 专家证人

专家证人是在法庭就某个专业领域的问题提供证言的专家。中国不用"专家证人"的概念,但法庭上可以使用司法鉴定机构的鉴定意见①,鉴定人也可以出庭接受询问。"鉴定机构"可以译为 forensic examination centers、forensic assessment centers、forensic laboratories 等。"鉴定意见"可以译为 forensic science opinions,鉴定人可以译为 forensic examiner。有些译员直接把"鉴定人"翻译为 expert witness。这在前几年是可以的,因为当时中国法律中的鉴定人与美国法律中的 expert witness 最为接近。但 2012 年刑诉法中作出了新的规定:

第一百四十四条 为了查明案情,需要解决案件中某些专门性问题的时候,应当指派、聘请有专门知识的人进行鉴定。②

这里面出现了一个说法,叫"有专门知识的人",学者称之为"专家证人"(类似于西方的专家证人制度),不同于该法律其他地方规定的"鉴定人"。那么,再把"鉴定人"翻译为 expert witness,便无法翻译真正的"专家证人"了。因此,建议把"鉴定人"直译为 forensic examiner,把"专家证人"译为 expert witness。

---

① 过去叫"鉴定结论",后来人们提出质疑:既然是结论,何必再让法官认定? 遂改为"鉴定意见"。
② 《中华人民共和国刑事诉讼法(2012 年修正版)》。

# 第二讲

## 世界两大法系简介

像做任何专业的翻译一样，译者必须对相关专业知识有基本的了解。本文通过对世界两大法系的简要介绍，为译者提供最基础的法律知识和一些基本概念的译法，帮助译者构建法律方面的知识框架，提高译者的宏观驾驭能力。

### 一、法系

法系是按照法的形式特征和源流关系对世界各国法所作的分类，通常把具有某种特征的某国法和效仿这一国法而制定的其他国家的法划分为一个法系。① "法系"在英语中可以说 legal families、legal systems、legal traditions，但 legal systems 还有狭义的解释，即一个国家的法律制度。② 不同的研究者对世界的法系有不同分类。我们经常见到的有大陆法系和英美法系。此外还可以见到中华法系（Chinese Law）、印度法系（Hindu Law）、伊斯兰法系（Islamic Law）、社会主义法系（Socialist Law）等提法。③④

---

① 曾庆敏：《法学大辞典》，第6版，上海辞书出版社，1998年，第1073页。

② "Comparative law and hybrid legal traditions: an introduction"，引自 Academia 网站（http://www.academia.edu/2078774/Comparative_law_and_hybrid_legal_traditions_an_introduction, 读取日期 2014-08-14）。

③ 黄震：《中华法系与世界主要法律体系》，引自价值中国网（http://www.chinavalue.net/General/Article/2012-10-20/200688.html, 读取日期 2014-08-14）。

④ 维基百科 Comparative law 条（http://en.wikipedia.org/wiki/Comparative_law, 读取日期 2014-08-14）。

## 二、英美法系

"英美法系"（Anglo-American Law）又称"普通法系"（common law）。"普通"为"普遍通行"之义（如"普通话"中的"普通"）①。《牛津法律词典》（*Oxford Dictionary of Law*）对 common law 的解释如下：

> The part of English law based on rules developed by the royal courts during the first three centuries after the Norman Conquest (1066) as a system applicable to the whole country, as opposed to local customs.②

英国、美国、澳大利亚、中国香港等国家和地区，都属于英美法系。

国内学者在会议发言和文章中，还把"英美法系"称为"海洋法系"，因为英美两国均为海洋国家。③笔者尝试查找"海洋法系"这个概念是否来自英文，但几经努力，没有找到，因此怀疑是国内学者因应"大陆法系"创造出来的一种说法。尽管国内有学者撰文称，美国比较法学者威格摩尔（John H. Wigmore）1923年把世界法系划分为16个，其中包括海洋法系④（又译海事法系⑤），但因为与"海洋法

---

① 更确切的译法应当是"共同法""普遍法"（见《common law 是不是普通法》，中国教育文摘，http://www.eduzhai.net/yingyu/615/765/yingyu_247644.html，读取日期2014-08-14），但事到如今，似乎已无力回天，只能重新解释"普通"的含义；更多解释见《元照英美法词典》"Common law"词条。

② E. A. Martin: *Oxford Dictionary of Law* (London: Oxford University Press, 2003), p.93.

③ 《陆法系和海洋法系》，引自自由飞翔的博客（http://blog.sina.com.cn/s/blog_4c1c53f3010009fi.html，读取日期2014-08-14）。

④ 黄震：《中华法系与世界主要法律体系》，引自价值中国网（http://www.chinavalue.net/General/Article/2012-10-20/200688.html，读取日期2014-08-14）。

⑤ 何勤华：《关于大陆法系研究的几个问题》，《法律科学》2013第4期，第5页。

系"并列的还有英国法系，因此，威格摩尔所称"海洋/海事法系"必定不是与"大陆法系"相对应的概念（可能来自 maritime law）。所以，即使能够准确还原威格摩尔的"海洋法系"，也不能用以翻译国内学者的同名概念。依笔者判断，与大陆法系相对立的"海洋法系"，翻译为 Oceanic Law 恐怕无人能够听懂。因此，笔者建议，讲话人谈到"英美法"，无论用哪种说法（英美法、普通法、海洋法、不成文法），一律翻译为 common law，因为这一说法最为简单；尤其是同传的时候，最节约时间。

common law 在英文中其实有不同的意思。与"大陆法系"相对时，翻译为"普通法系"；与 statutory law（成文法/国会制定法）相对时，翻译为"判例法"；此时的 common law 就等于 case law（判例法）或者 precedent（先例）；与衡平法（equity law）相对应时，翻译为"普通法"。① common law 还被翻译为"习惯法"，但因与 customary law 的翻译相冲突，在大陆地区已不多用。至于两者的关系，*the Pop-up Oxford World Encyclopedia* 在词条 customary law 中这样解释：

> Unwritten rules generally accepted as binding by a community as a result of long use. All legal systems recognize custom as a source of law, although the authority ascribed to it and the extent to which it is recognized in legislative measures and case law varies. <u>In English law, custom is at the root of much of the common law, but it is rarely recognized by case law today, whereas in Japan, where the adoption of codified laws is very recent, courts have given effect to older customs</u>

---

① 维基百科"英美法系"条（http://zh.wikipedia.org/wiki/ 英美法系，读取日期 2014-08-14）。

(relating, for example, to marriage), even where they conflict with the civil code.①

"衡平法"（equity law）是与"普通法"（common law）相对的概念。1066年诺曼人征服英格兰（Norman conquest）之前，英格兰各地各自按照当地的习惯解决纠纷。诺曼征服之后，国王并没有主动去统一英格兰法律；国王感兴趣的只是收税，所以就派人到各地巡视，包括参与当地法院工作。同时，从国王的咨询机构（the *curia regis*，御前会议）中分离出来一个常设法院（Court of Exchequer，财税法院），审理财税纠纷。亨利二世（1154—1189在位）时期，国王派人定期到各地巡视，主要进行司法审判。这些人叫作 *justiciae errantes*（跑腿的法官/巡回法官），巡视一圈叫作一个 circuit（时至今日，美国的上诉法院仍叫作 circuit court，巡回法院）。同一时期，国王又成立了第二个常设法院 Court of Common Pleas（普通民事法院）。The Court of Common Pleas 在各地习惯法之上，形成一套通行全国的制度（common law）。亨利二世的以上两项举措是普通法的真正起源。在普通法的发展过程中，原来的 Court of Exchequer（后来也在税收事项之外受理普通民间纠纷）以及后来逐渐发展起来的第三个常设法院 Court of King's Bench（王座法院）也发挥了作用。②

但是，由于按照普通法起诉需要令状（writ），而令状种类和范围有限，许多争议往往由于无相应令状而无法在普通法院起诉寻求法律保护，即使有的诉讼普通法院受理了，又因普通法内容刻板和

---

① *The Pop-up Oxford World Encyclopedia* (London: Oxford University Press, 1998).

② E. A. Martin: *Oxford Dictionary of Law* (London: Oxford University Press, 2003), pp. 93-94.

补救方式（remedies）有限①而难以获得公正处理，于是当事人就到国王那里"上访"（petition），国王根据 chancellor（大臣，一般为神职人员，非法律工作者）的建议，按照公平公正的原则（equity）来判案。后来案件太多，就直接交给 chancellor 处理。审理案件的地方叫 Court of Chancery（译为"御前大臣法庭""大法官法院""枢密大臣法院""衡平法院"等）。本来两类法院相互补充，但到了17世纪时，普通法院（common law court）法官和 chancellor 之间出现个人不和，对于两个法院的规则出现冲突时哪个优先，两者相持不下。詹姆斯一世出面调停，赋予衡平法院规则优先权。衡平法院在审判实践中，逐渐发展出一系列的原则，作为普通法原则的补充。② 下面这段话，简练地概括了衡平法的发展：

> A branch of English law which developed hundreds of years ago when litigants would go to the King and complain of harsh or inflexible rules of common law which prevented "justice" from prevailing. For example, strict common law rules would not recognize unjust enrichment (不当得利), which was a legal relief developed by the equity courts. The typical Court of Equity decision would prevent a person from enforcing a common law court judgment. The kings delegated this special judicial review power over common law court rulings to chancellors. A new branch of law developed known as "equity", with their decisions eventually gaining precedence over those of the common law courts. A whole set of equity law principles were developed based on the predom-

---

① 比如，在房屋买卖中，卖方毁约，买方到普通法院只能起诉要求金钱赔偿，但到衡平法法院，可要求具体履行（specific performance）。

② E. A. Martin: *Oxford Dictionary of Law* (London: Oxford University Press, 2003), pp. 178-179.

inant "fairness" characteristic of equity such as "equity will not suffer a wrong to be without a remedy" or "he who comes to equity must come with clean hands"[1]. Many legal rules, in countries that originated with English law, have equity-based law such as the law of trusts and mortgages.[2]

英国根据 Judicature Acts[3]（司法法，1873—1875），成立了 High Court of Justice（高等法院），将普通法和衡平法的司法职能并入一个法院，废除了 Court of Chancery。但 High Court of Justice 下设一个 Chancery Division，继承 Court of Chancery 的职能。Judicature Acts 还规定，在普通法规则和衡平法规则出现冲突时，以衡平法规则为准（The Judicature Acts also provided that in cases in which there was a conflict between the *rules of law and equity*, the rules of equity should prevail.）[4]。注意：rules of law 和 rules of equity 作为对立概念，应当翻译为"普通法规则"（不是"法律规则"）和"衡平法规则"。

美国继承和发展了英国的法律制度。像英国一样，美国联邦法

---

[1] 其他衡平法原则还有："equity follows the law; he/she who is first in time takes precedence; where the equities are equal, the law prevails; equity assists the diligent, not the tardy; equity is equality; equity looks to the intent, rather than to form; equity looks on that as done which ought to be done; equity imputes an intention to fulfill an obligation"；以及"equity acts in personam"。

[2] "Why it Equity replace the common law?"，引自 Kenyaplex 网站（http://www.kenyaplex.com/discussionforum/7191-why-it-equity-replace-the-common-law.aspx，读取日期 2014-08-14）。

[3] 注意：Judicature Acts 是复数，指有关司法的一系列法律，而不是一部单行法（Act）。

[4] E. A. Martin: *Oxford Dictionary of Law* (London: Oxford University Press, 2003), pp. 178-179.

院和纽约州等，也取消了普通法法院（courts of law）和衡平法法院（courts of equity）的区别，但有些州，如新泽西州，两类法院时至今日仍完全分离。在宾夕法尼亚等州，一位法官会轮流在两类法院审判。①

两类法院的区别已经过时，但即使两类法院已经合并，两者适用的原则还是要区分开。原因是，美国联邦和各州宪法规定，只有按普通法原则提出的民事案件，才有权利得到陪审团审判（宪法还规定重罪案件有权得到陪审团审判）。过去英国的 Court of Chancery 作为适用衡平原则的法院，不用陪审团；即使今天，使用衡平法的案件也不用陪审团。②

汉语"衡平"（equity）作为一个外来观念，似乎难以理解。但其实 equity 的本意是"公平""合理"（the quality of being impartial or reasonable; fairness）。衡平法院追求的是自然公正（natural justice）、合情合理。而在中国，无论是古代还是现代，法官除了考虑法律规定之外，情理也是法官断案的重要依据。似乎可以认为，中国法院所遵循的情理原则，就相当于英美法系的衡平原则。只不过中国自古以来就把情、理、法融为一体进行裁判，而没有发展成为适用不同原则的法院。《名公书判清明集》汇集了古代法官平衡情法进行审判的案例，称法官审判就是"酌情用法，以平其事"，"酌情用法"就是平衡情理与法律。③ 而现代法官运用情理判案的例子也不胜枚举。④

---

① 坎平：《盎格鲁-美利坚法律史》，第 3 版，法律出版社，2001 年。

② 同上。

③ 周明勇：《论司法衡平传统及当代的价值》，引自朝阳法律评论（http://www.law.ruc.edu.cn/cyflpl/ShowArticle.asp?43236.html，读取日期 2014-08-14）。

④ 杜翠：《司法实践中法理与情理的掂量拿捏》，引自阜阳市中级人民法院网（http://fyzy.chinacourt.org/article/detail/2014/03/id/1227469.shtml，读取日期 2014-08-14）。

情（love）、理（reason）、法（law）综合运用，才能达到社会效果（social effect）和法律效果（legal effect）的统一。

## 三、大陆法系

大陆法系（continental law，又译"欧陆法系"），也称为市民法（civilian/citizens' law）、罗马法系（Roman law）、民法法系（civil law）、法典法系（codified law）、罗马-日耳曼法系（Romano-Germanic law），是受罗马法影响而成立的法律系统，当今世界与英美法系并列的两大重要法系之一，覆盖区域广大，德国、法国、意大利、日本、中国（未包括香港特别行政区）等均为大陆法系地区。

之所以称为"大陆法系"，是因为该法系起源于欧洲大陆；称为"罗马法系"，是强调罗马法对它的重要影响；称为"民法法系"，是指这些法系的国家通常都有完整、独立的民法典；称为"法典法系"，是因为这些国家的法律都存在于法典之中，不承认判例法；称为"市民法"（*jus civile*），是因为这些法律通行于作为罗马征服者的公民之中（通行于被征服者的法律被称为 *jus gentium*，"万民法"，调整异邦人相互之间以及罗马人与异邦人之间的关系）。①

对于译者而言，知道了同一法系的不同名称，翻译时就可以使用任一说法而不必担心出错。根据笔者的经验，common law 和 civil law 是两种最常见的说法，音节也最少。

---

① 维基百科"欧陆法系"条（http://zh.wikipedia.org/zh/欧陆法系，读取日期 2014-08-14）。

## 四、普通法系与大陆法系的差异

大陆法系和英美法系的区别主要包括[1]：

（一）**法律渊源**（sources of law）**不同**。英美法系承认不成文法（unwritten law）[2][3]、习惯法（customary law）尤其是判例法（case law）的法律地位，强调"遵循先例"（*stare decisis*）原则；在大陆法系中，制定法（statutes、statutory law，国会通过的法）是正式的法律渊源，而判例（precedent）不是正式的法律渊源，不能作为司法判决的直接根据，法官与无权通过判例创造法律规范。

（二）**法官权限不同**。大陆法系强调法官只能援用成文法中的规定来审判案件，法官对成文法的解释也须受成文法本身的严格限制，故法官只能适用法律（apply the law）而不能创造法律（create law）。英美法系的法官既可以援用成文法，也可以援用已有的判例来审判案件，而且，在一定的条件下还能运用法律解释（legal interpretation）和法律推理（legal reasoning）的技术创造新的法律规则，法官从而不仅适用法律，也在一定的范围内创造法律。法官创造的法律（judge-made law）可以被立法机关吸收，成为制定法的一部分。立法机关如不同意法官对法律的解释，可以通过立法做出具体规定。

（三）**法典编纂**（codification）**不同**。大陆法系的一些基本法律往往采用较系统的法典（code）形式，在它的主要发展阶段上，几乎都有代表性的法典。而在英美法系国家，尽管制定法也在不断增多，

---

[1] "The Common Law and Civil Law Traditions"，引自 UC Berkeley School of Law Library 网站（https://www.law.berkeley.edu/library/robbins/pdf/CommonLawCivilLawTraditions.pdf，读取日期 2014-08-14）。

[2] 曾庆敏：《法学大辞典》，第 6 版，上海辞书出版社，1998 年，第 126 页。

[3] 注意："成文""不成文"并非指有无文字记载而是指是否通过立法机关制定为法条。

但其制定法一般采用单行法形式,不采取包罗万象的法典形式。另外,在许多普通法国家,刑法及民法的许多领域也法典化,如美国各州都有刑法典,加利福尼亚州制定了民法典,英国1906年制定了《海上保险法》。[①]

(四)**法律分类不同**。大陆法系的国家一般都将公法(public law)与私法(private law)的划分作为法律分类的基础,私法主要指民法(civil law)和商法(commercial law),公法主要指宪法(constitution)、行政法(administrative law)、刑法(criminal law)、诉讼程序法(procedure law);进入20世纪后又出现了社会法(social law)、经济法(economic law)、劳动法(labor law)等具有公、私两种性质的法律;而英美法系则是以普通法与衡平法为法的基本分类,无公法和私法之分,普通法是在普通法院判决基础上形成的全国适用的法律。衡平法是从大法官法院受理的申诉案件中形成的法律规则。

(五)**诉讼程序的不同**。由于历史的原因,大陆法系的诉讼程序以法官为中心,法官既要帮助双方当事人理清争议的焦点(issues),积极指导取证(evidence taking)活动,还要在法庭上主动询问(question)双方,积极影响案件审理的过程。这种诉讼程序突出法官的职能,叫作纠问式诉讼制度(inquisitorial system)。英美法系的诉讼程序则以原告(plaintiff)、被告(defendant)及其辩护人(defender)、代理人(attorney-at-law)为中心,法官只是双方争论的"仲裁人"(arbitrator),不能参与争论。因此,英美法系的诉讼程序又被称为对抗制诉讼制度(adversarial/adversary system)。这两种诉讼模式又分别被称为"职权主义"/"干涉主义"和"当事人

---

[①] 维基百科 Codification (law) 条(http://en.wikipedia.org/wiki/Codifica-tion_(law),读取日期2014-08-14)。

**大陆法系和英美法系的区别一览表**

| | 大陆法系 | | 英美法系 | |
|---|---|---|---|---|
| 定义 | 大陆法系强调成文法作用，结构上强调系统化、条理化、法典化和逻辑性，并将全部法律分为公法和私法。 | | 也称普通法系，在以往判决（判例）的基础上逐步形成的通行全国的法律，分为普通法和衡平法两部分。 | |
| 形成 | 西欧 | | 英国 | |
| 主要代表 | 法国和德国 | | 英国和美国 | |
| 其他代表国家和地区 | 瑞士、意大利、比利时、卢森堡、西班牙、葡萄牙、荷兰、日本、整个拉丁美洲、非洲近东一些国家、美国路易斯安那州、加拿大魁北克省、苏格兰 | | 加拿大、澳大利亚、马来西亚、爱尔兰、新加坡、巴基斯坦，以及中国香港地区等 | |
| 法律结构 | 公法 | 指与国家状况有关的法律，包括宪法、行政法、刑法、诉讼法和国际公法。 | 普通法 | 通过国王法院的判例逐步形成的一种全国普遍适用的法律。 |
| | 私法 | 指与个人利益有关的法律，包括民法和商法。 | 平衡法 | 14世纪时为补充和匡正普通法的不足，由英国枢密大臣法院发展起来，不受普通法约束，按公平与正义原则作出判决的判例法。 |
| 法律渊源 | 作为成文法国家，宪法、法典以及其他的法律条例等是大陆法系国家的主要渊源，判例在原则上不作为法的正式渊源。 | | 判例曾是英美法的主要渊源，其基础是"先例约束力"原则，即法院在判决中所包括的判决理由必须得到遵循。但19世纪末20世纪初成文法在英美法系国家的比重和作用不断上升，成文法也成了英美法的重要渊源。 | |
| 内部分歧 | 大陆法各国都主张编纂法典，但各国在法典的编制体制上却不完全相同。以民商法而言，即分为民商分立和民商合一两种编制体例。 | | 作为英美法系的国家，美国比英国更重视成文法。美国不但有联邦成文法还有州成文法。还专门在商法领域，修订了《美国统一商法典》以及一系列的反托拉斯法。它们对于规范公司尤其是大公司的行为有重要影响。 | |

（推进）主义"。（几种主义的说法似乎为中国人自己的创造，笔者没有找到对应的英文说法，较为接近的说法为：court/judge-driven inquisitorial system 和 party-driven adversary system。"干涉主义"，必要时可以翻译为 interventionism。）

## 五、中国的法系

以《唐律》为代表的中国古代法律制度，对东亚诸国如日本、朝鲜、琉球、安南等的古代法制产生过巨大影响，被称为中华法系。但近代随着欧洲的兴起，东亚国家纷纷变法图强，学习西方的典章制度。日本明治维新（Meiji Restoration）之后，仿照西欧国家，制定了一整套法律制度，称六法全书（六种基本法，代指所有法律）。中国的戊戌变法虽然没有成功，但变法前后却翻译出版了大量的西方和日本法律，如1880年官办北京同文馆刻印的《法国律例》和清光绪三十三年（1907年）民办上海商务印书馆出版的《新译日本法规大全》。[①] 中华民国建立之后，参照德国、日本的立法，制定了中国的《六法全书》，分为宪法、民法、刑法、商法、诉讼法和法院组织法（一说为宪法、民法、刑法、商法、民事诉讼法和刑事诉讼法）。1949年后，我国废除了《六法全书》，全面引进苏联的社会主义法律制度，因此中国的法律制度也称为社会主义法系。但苏联的制度基础是大陆法系，因此中国的法律体系也属于大陆法系。香港特别行政区属于英美法系，澳门特别行政区则属于大陆法系的葡萄牙分支。同样由于历史原因，美国的路易斯安那州、加拿大的魁北克省，以及大不列颠的苏格兰，在国家整体上属于英

---

[①] 王兰萍：《〈新译日本法规大全〉点校本札记》，引自法史网（http://fashi.ecupl.edu.cn/article_show_full.asp?ArticleId=276，读取日期2014-08-14）。

美法系的情况下，局部属于大陆法系。①②

## 六、普通法的影响

第二次世界大战之后，美国的影响不断扩大，其法律制度也在不断向外传播。大陆法系国家纷纷借鉴英美法系的一些法律理念和做法。比如，在审判方式上，日本结合美国的对抗制和自己的纠问制，形成了折中主义的审判模式。其主要特点有：1. 在诉讼进行方面，主要由控辩双方推动，注重控诉辩护双方平等对抗。2. 在证据的提出和调查方面，保留了法官主动依职权进行调查证据的权力，注重发挥法官在调查案件事实方面的能动性。3. 在价值目标上，注重正当程序和实体真实。③

中国自20世纪90年代开始进行审判方式改革（trial method reform），引进了英美法系对抗制因素。但这种引进是不完整的：中国法官还保留了一定的调查取证权；证人出庭作证的制度还有待完善；非法证据排除得还不够彻底，等等。最高人民法院推行的案例指导制度（guiding cases system）也是对判例制度的模仿，旨在发挥判例制度统一司法、保证相似的案件得到相似判决结果的功能。但最高人民法院发布的这些案例，对下级法院没有约束力，仅仅供下级法院办案时参考，因此并非英美法系所谓的判例制度。

可以说，现今各国的刑事诉讼法已经找不到纯粹的"职权主义"

---

① 王少普：《明治维新何以仿德国不学英国》，引自人民网（http://theory.people.com.cn/BIG5/49157/17487199.html，读取日期 2014-08-14）。

② 夏征农，陈至立：《辞海》，第 6 版，上海辞书出版社，2010 年，第 1428 页。

③ 尹玄海，伍玉联：《犯罪控制视野下的我国刑事审判方式改革》，引自北大法律信息网（http://article.chinalawinfo.com/Article_Detail.asp?ArticleId=48924，读取日期 2014-08-14）。

或"当事人主义"模式。更不用说,国际司法机构的诉讼程序,基本上也是采取大陆法系和英美法系的混合制。①

　　了解世界法律体系的基本情况,对于理解相关的文本和议题十分重要,是做好法律翻译的基础,故译者应予以充分重视。

---

① L. Carter & F. Pocar: *International Criminal Procedure: The Interface of Civil Law and Common Law Legal Systems* (Cheltenham, U.K.: Edward Elgar Pub. Ltd., 2013).

# 第三讲

## 美国的刑事诉讼程序及相关术语的翻译

做好任何领域的翻译,都必须对该领域有一定了解,熟悉相关概念及概念之间的联系。本文将以美国司法统计局(the Bureau of Justice Statistics)制作的刑事司法制度流程图[①]为基础,结合中国的刑事司法制度,系统介绍美国刑事司法制度及相关术语,为读者提供框架性知识和翻译参考,并为今后中外制度的对比打下基础。

### Entry into the System 进入刑事司法体系

该术语意思是指犯罪嫌疑人(criminal suspect)[②]进入刑事司法体系。该阶段相当于我国刑事诉讼中的侦查阶段(investigation stage)。在有些国家和地区,采取检警一体化(an integrated operation model)的模式,即检察机关(公诉机关)监督/指挥警察开展侦查活动(如德国和中国台湾地区);有些国家采用检警分立模式(如美国、中国)(a separated operation model),警察机关和检察机关的职能相

---

[①] "The Justice System: What is the Sequence of Events in the Criminal Justice System?",引自 Bureau of Justice Statistics 网站(http://www.bjs.gov/content/justsys.cfm,读取日期 2014-10-07)。

[②] 1979年的中国刑事诉讼法称被追诉者(the accused)为"人犯"(criminal),1996年刑事诉讼法修改后改称"犯罪嫌疑人"(criminal suspect)。在移送审查起诉(prosecution review)后称为"被告人"(defendant)。修改的理论依据是,一个人在被法院依法认定有罪之前,被推定为无罪(the accused is presumed innocent before he is found guilty by the court),即无罪推定原则(presumption of innocence)。

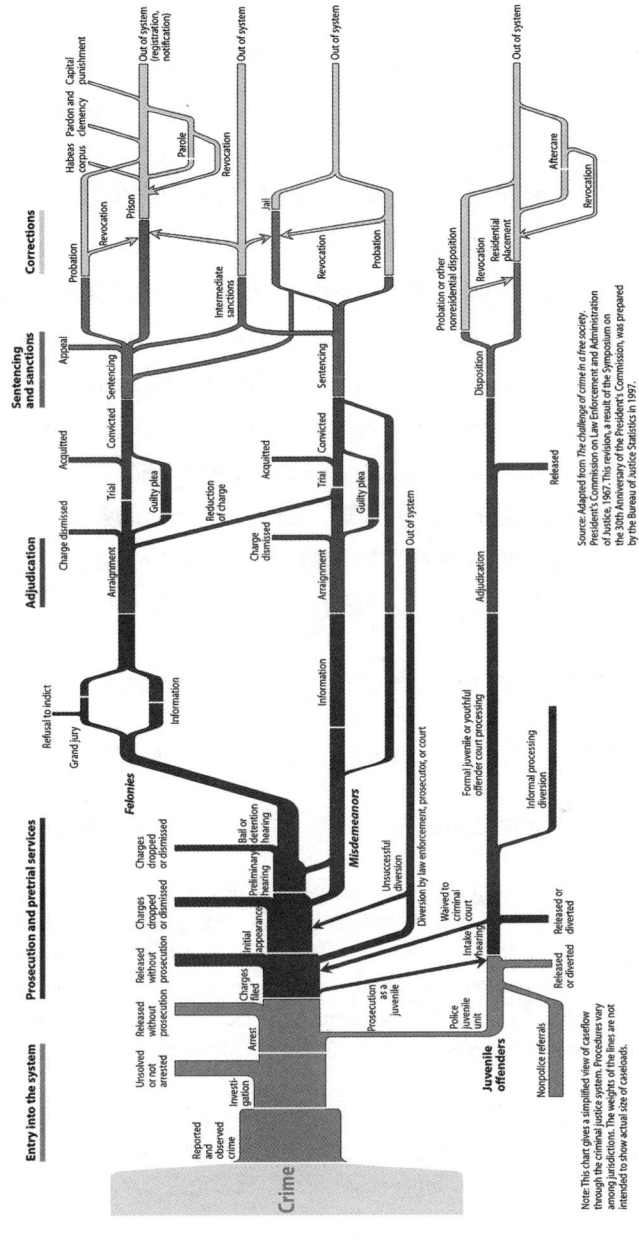

图1 美国刑事司法制度流程图

对独立。但美国一些州，如加利福尼亚州的检察官也参与案件的侦查。

在我国，检察机关对公安机关的监督限于批准警察的逮捕申请（"批捕"）和审查起诉期间对案卷的审查（review）：审查中如果发现公安机关提供的证据不充分，可以退回警察机关补充侦查（return the case to the police for more investigation）。

在美国，拘留证（arrest warrant）是由法院签发的；拘留之后两三天，要到法院初次到庭（initial appearance），由法官决定先放回去（保释），还是继续关押（remand，还押）。在中国，拘留证由公安机关直接签发；拘留之后3天（最多30天），公安机关要请检察院决定是先放回去，还是继续关押（法律上叫"逮捕"）。① 在美国，法院从拘留就开始介入；在中国，法院直到审判阶段才介入。

顺便提及，美国警察实施拘留之后，便进入公诉阶段；但在中国，审查起诉阶段需要侦查终结后才开始。

## Prosecution and Pretrial Services 起诉和审前服务

公安机关（警察）② 经过初步调查，认为确有犯罪发生，也抓到

---

① 词典上通常把 arrest 与"逮捕"作为对等词，在中外交流中引起极大混乱。从中美两国的刑事诉讼流程看，英语的 arrest，相当于中国的"抓捕"；中国的"逮捕"，相当于英语的 remand（或 detention）。因此，英语的 arrest warrant 要翻译为拘留证；中国的逮捕证是 remand/detention warrant。remand warrant 在英文中也存在，remand 的解释为 "Court ordered temporary detention of a person, pursuant to a *Remand Warrant*, while awaiting trial or sentencing, or prior to commencement of a custodial disposition."。（Definitions，引自 Statistics Canada 网站，http://www.statcan.gc.ca/pub/85-002-x/2012001/definitions-eng.htm，读取日期 2014-10-07）。

② 公安机关即警察机关，正式文本中译为 public security organs，日常交往中可以直接说警察机关（the police）。注意不要把公安机关（public security）与国家安全机关（state security organ）混淆。前者负责公众的安全，后者负责国家的安全（反间谍）。

了嫌疑人，就会请公诉部门决定是否指控（charge）；如决定指控，就带嫌疑人见法官（initial appearance），让法官决定继续侦查期间是否有合理根据（probable cause）继续关押（remand / detention），否则要保释（bail）。如获得保释，嫌疑人要遵守保释条件（bail conditions），如宵禁（curfew）、参加戒毒（drug rehabilitation program）、心理辅导（counseling）、定期向审前服务部门汇报情况等，保证审判时按时到庭（appear in court）。很多州接下来还有个初步听证（preliminary hearing）的程序，控辩双方各传证人，法官决定是否有合理根据相信发生了犯罪。如果认为无合理根据便驳回起诉（dismiss the case）。在交给法院审理前，有些州还有一个大陪审团审查证据的程序，看如果起诉的话，证据是否充分（sufficient）。

这个阶段大致相当于中国的审查起诉阶段。中国取保候审/保释的情况很少，审前服务不发达，所以没有专门的审前服务机构。① 在审查起诉阶段，美国的法院广泛介入，中国的法院不介入。可以说，中国的三个诉讼阶段（侦查、审查起诉、审判）公检法三个部门各司其职，但在美国，法院的干预无处不在。这与以司法控制行政部门滥权的制约思想密不可分。

## Adjudication 定罪审判

adjudication 通常翻译为"审判""裁判"，但此处应作狭义解

---

① 审前的羁押不是为了惩罚，而是为了保证诉讼的正常进行（防止嫌疑人脱逃或给社会带来危害），所以，审前羁押是一种强制措施（compulsory measure），不是惩罚（penalty）；惩罚是被法院定罪之后的监禁或其他处罚。在普通人眼中，如果一个人被警察抓了又释放（保释/取保候审），似乎是放纵了犯罪。其实应该理解为正常现象：一个人在被法院定罪之前被推定无辜，所以不该提前接受惩罚；如果对社会无害、也不会逃跑，应当允许嫌疑人在家等候审判。在这样的观念形成之前，恐怕保释难以被大众接受。

释，即只包括定罪与否的裁判，不包括量刑，因为流程图中还有一个环节叫 sentencing and sanctions（量刑和制裁）。在中国，定罪（conviction）和量刑（sentencing）合并进行（统称审判阶段）：在同一次审理（hearing）中，控辩双方（the prosecution and the defense）既出示有无犯罪（incriminating and exonerating evidence）的证据，也出示犯罪轻重（mitigating and aggravating evidence）的证据，法官最后宣判（pronouncing sentence）时（可能不是当天宣判），既确定有罪无罪（guilty or not guilty），也确定处罚（punishment / penalty / sanction）。

在美国，审判阶段仅决定是否有罪〔可以是被告人认罪，或经独任法官（single judge）或陪审团（jury）认定有罪〕，量刑在另外一次听证（量刑听证，sentencing hearing）中确定。中国采用审（trial）、判（sentencing）合一的方式有个弊端：辩护人可能作无罪辩护，但最后法院认定被告人有罪，这时如果辩护人改口说我的当事人罪轻（时刻考虑客户利益最大化），便会出现自相矛盾。（刚说无罪、现在又说罪轻，到底有无犯罪？）如果审、判分离，量刑听证的时候，再换个律师，面子上会好一点。当然，律师也可以说：即使按控方说的，我的当事人有罪，罪也没那么严重。目前，中国已经有一些法院进行审判分离改革（separation of trial and sentencing）试点。

## Sentencing and Sanctions 量刑和制裁

在被告人认罪或经法官或陪审团认定有罪之后，隔一段时间会再举行一次听证，叫量刑听证，决定处罚方式。处罚的种类有死刑（capital punishment / death sentence）、终身监禁（life imprisonment）、监禁（imprisonment）、社会考察（probation，有的词典上译为"缓刑"，不够准确）、罚款（fine）、返还财物

（restitution）等。量刑听证的时候，法官会听取考察部门（probation officer）的量刑前报告（pre-sentencing report），了解被告人成长的历史、犯罪的背景等，作为量刑参考。有的司法辖区（jurisdictions）有量刑指南（sentencing guidelines），里面有详细的计算公式，规定什么情况加几个月、减几个月，法官的自由裁量权（discretion）很小；有的司法辖区给法官较大自由裁量权。

在中国，刑罚的种类和美国差不多，有些叫法不同，如有期徒刑（fixed term imprisonment），相当于美国的 imprisonment；无期徒刑（non-fixed term imprisonment），相当于美国的 life imprisonment (with parole)，即可以获得假释（parole）的终身监禁。

中国的法官自由裁量权很大，比如，有些犯罪的法定刑期是 2—10 年有期徒刑，最低刑期和最高刑期差别很大，法官要根据法定或酌定从轻或减轻（从重或加重）处罚的情节，来确定具体刑期。所谓法定从轻情节（statutory mitigating circumstances），就是法律具体规定的一些情况下，必须从轻处罚；所谓酌定从轻情节（discretionary mitigating circumstances），就是在法律规定的具体情况下，法官可以酌情决定是否从轻。从轻和减轻的区别，在于前者是指在法律规定的量刑幅度内（如 3—5 年），就低不就高；后者是指在法定量刑幅度外，继续降低，如法律规定 3—5 年，实际判 2 年甚至缓刑。

笔者虽经多次查找，还是没有发现"从轻""从重""减轻""加重"处罚的完美英文对应。如属于一般性交流，无区分必要，则"从轻"和"减轻"处罚都可以译为 leniency 或 mitigated/reduced punishment；"从重"和"加重"处罚都可用 aggravated punishment / aggravation。必要时，加上 within (outside) the sentencing range 的说明。

# Corrections 矫正

矫正，是量刑后的执行（enforcement）阶段。对于判"实刑"[①]的人来说，就意味着坐牢（serve their sentence in jail/prison）。关押的地方可能是 jail（看守所），也可能是 prison（监狱）。刑期减去审前羁押时间（叫作刑期折抵）后不到 1 年的罪犯，关押在看守所（中美都一样）；否则关押到监狱。[②] 监狱分为不同安全级别（security level）。从 maximum security 到 minimum security，通常为五级。级别不同，看管的严密程度不同。在监狱表现好，就会获得减刑（goodtime），服刑够一定时间后，可以提前释放（parole，假释，有条件释放）。被假释的犯人，接受考察人员（probation officer）的监管。服刑人员还可能通过别的方式（pardoning、commutation/

---

[①] "实刑"是中国特色的说法，即实际需要在监狱服刑的刑罚，可以直接译为 incarceration；相对于缓刑。中国的"缓刑"是指刑罚的执行方式，如"判二缓三"（判处 2 年有期徒刑，缓期 3 年执行），意思是只要 3 年之内不再犯罪，2 年有期徒刑便不再执行。国外的 probation，尽管常翻译为"缓刑"，实际上是一种刑罚方式（punishment），按这个单词的本义（与 prove 同源，相当于"考验""证明"，所以还有"见习""试用"的意思），应该翻译为"考察"。

[②] jail（看守所）和 prison（监狱）的区别，在于前者是审前羁押机构，被关押的是"未决犯"（defendants pending trial），即被刑事拘留和逮捕者；prison 是量刑后的羁押场所，关押的是"已决犯"（convicts），即被判处死缓、无期徒刑和有期徒刑者。但实践中，前者也关押 1 年以下有期徒刑或余刑在 1 年以下的已决犯。英语中，jail 和 prison 有时候也被混用，尤其是非专业人士。另外请注意：中文语境下的拘留所（custody/detention center），是关押被行政拘留的人（administrative detainees）。这些人违反了治安管理处罚法（Administrative Sanctions Law），还没达到犯罪的程度（其行为属于 administrative offense，不是 criminal offense），公安机关处罚一下就行了。公安机关的处罚如果是行政拘留，就关在拘留所，最多 15 天。拘留所也关押被司法拘留者。如果行为严重，违反了刑法（criminal law），就属于犯罪，公安机关就要走司法程序（不是行政程序），将来被告人被判刑后，关在监狱。监狱是司法部管理的（不是公安部）。

remission、reprieves）获得宽大（clemency）。[①] 对于判"缓刑"（probation，社会考察）的人来说，要接受考察人员（probation officer）的监管，提供社区服务（作为处罚）或遵守一定的条件。

## 词语详解

crime：犯罪。各国规定的犯罪门槛不一样。美国法律把犯罪分为三类：infractions（微罪）、misdemeanors（轻罪）和 felonies（重罪）[②]。infraction 指交通违章（如超速驾驶）之类的轻微犯罪行为，处罚方式为罚款。这类犯罪在中国不属于犯罪行为，属于治安违法（违反了治安管理处罚法），所以中国有犯罪记录的人大大少于美

---

[①] 以上各术语解释如下：pardon 是指"特赦"，意为"forgiveness of a crime and the cancellation of the relevant penalty; it is usually granted by a head of state (such as a monarch or president) or by acts of a parliament or a religious authority"；clemency 是指"宽大"，意为"forgiveness of a crime or the cancellation (in whole or in part) of the penalty associated with it. It is a general concept that encompasses several related procedures: pardoning, commutation（减刑）, remission（减刑）and reprieves"；commutation 或 remission 是指"轻判"，意为"lessening of a penalty without forgiveness for the crime; the beneficiary is still considered guilty of the offense"；reprieve 是指"缓期执行"，意为"the postponement of punishment, often with a view to a pardon or other review of the sentence (such as when the reprieving authority has no power to grant an immediate pardon)"；amnesty 是指"大赦"，意为"a pardon extended by the government to a group or class of persons, usually for a political offense; the act of a sovereign power officially forgiving certain classes of persons who are subject to trial but have not yet been convicted"。参见（维基百科 Pardon 条，http://en.wikipedia.org/wiki/Pardon；Amnesty 条，http://en.wikipedia.org/wiki/Amnesty；读取日期 2014-10-07）

[②] P. Bergman: "Felonies, Misdemeanors, and Infractions: Classifying Crimes: Learn about Crime Classifications"，引自 Nolo Law for All 网站（http://www.nolo.com/legal-encyclopedia/crimes-felonies-misdemeanors-infractions-classification-33814.html，读取日期 2014-10-07）。

国。misdemeanor 是指可能被判处 1 年以下有期徒刑的犯罪；felony 是指可能被判1年以上有期徒刑的犯罪。按照美国的划分方法，中国刑法中规定的所有犯罪，基本都属于 felonies。中国刑法中的轻微犯罪，一般是指法定最高刑为 3 年以下的犯罪，比如轻伤害、数额较大的盗窃诈骗等。所以，汉语讲到"轻微犯罪行为"，不能翻译为 misdemeanor，只能说 less serious crimes。严重犯罪行为，最好说 serious crimes，不说 felonies。

reported/observed crimes：前者指普通人（受害者、目击者等）向警察报告的犯罪，后者是指警察自行发现的犯罪。

investigation：调查或侦查。在中国，警察查明事实的活动用"侦查"或"调查"描述。"侦查"使用的技术手段比较多，是对未知问题的查明；而"调查"可能是问题已明，只是需要其他证据的支撑。翻译为英语无法区分，都是 investigation。

unsolved or not arrested：没有破案或没抓到人。这些案子无法进入司法系统。

arrest：拘留、拘捕、抓人。相当于中国的"刑事拘留"；注意不要翻译为"逮捕"。"逮捕"在中国法律中有特别的含义。翻译为"逮捕"，中国的法律工作者会产生严重误解。如果被抓的人是青少年，转交给警察的青少年犯罪科处置，进入青少年司法系统（与成年人的系统程序有所不同）。

released without prosecution：经过进一步调查，如果警察发现被抓的人没有犯罪，就会释放。释放没有国家赔偿（state compensation）。中国的逮捕，如果后来发现错了，释放后要给国家赔偿。

charges filed：如果警察认为需要处罚，会向公诉人提出指控（charges），公诉人据此决定是否起诉。这就进入"审查起诉"阶段。决定不起诉者，予以释放。中国的检察院在这个阶段也可能作出不起诉的决定。在中国，不起诉决定分为法定不起诉（statutory non-prosecution，符合《刑事诉讼法》第十五条规定情形者）；酌定不起诉（discretionary non-prosecution，适用于犯罪情节轻微，可以免除刑事处罚，对社会没有危险性的案件）；证据不足不起诉（non-prosecution for lack of evidence，适用于检察院发回公安机关两次补充侦查后证据不足的案件）。根据新刑诉法，对于未成年人犯罪，符合条件的，检察院可以决定附条件不起诉（conditional non-prosecution）。

initial appearance：初次到庭。在美国，嫌疑人被拘留后两三天之内就要面见法官，法官当面告诉嫌疑人被指控的罪名，决定是否有继续羁押的合理根据（probable cause）。如法院认为有必要羁押，就继续羁押，否则取保候审（保释）。决定是否继续羁押或恢复羁押（因保释后违反条件）的听证（bail or detention hearing），也可能在稍后的阶段进行，各州的做法不尽一致。按美国的做法，保释是原则，继续羁押是例外。中国也有取保候审（保释）制度，但羁押（"逮捕"）是原则，保释是例外。这个阶段公诉人可撤回指控（drop the charge），法院可以驳回指控（dismiss the charge）。如果是轻罪认罪案件，案件这个阶段就可能处理掉；如果是重罪，又是贫困被告，请不起律师，法院会给被告指派一位律师（public defender，公设辩护人）。

preliminary hearing：初步听证。在这个听证中，法官主要决定是否有合理根据（probable cause）相信嫌疑人在该司法辖区犯罪了。须注意的是，认定的标准是"合理根据"，不是"排除合理怀疑"，所以，不是认定犯罪；认定犯罪需要以后由陪审团或法官来作。如无合理根据，公诉人撤诉或法官驳回起诉。嫌疑人也可以选择放弃初步听证，直接进入大陪审团（grand jury）起诉程序。

grand jury：大陪审团。大陪审团是一个法院的常设机构，由普通百姓组成，任期可达3年。大陪审团独立于法院运作，法官不主持其活动。它的职能包括控诉和调查（accusatory and investigatory functions）。调查职能包括查阅相关证据文件、听取证人证言，控诉职能确定是否有充足的证据（sufficient evidence）提起公诉。如果回答是肯定的，它会发出一个 indictment（起诉书）。注意：大陪审团不定罪；审判阶段临时针对个案组成的小陪审团（petit jury）决定有罪无罪。有些州不用大陪审团，直接由公诉人签发公诉书，这个公诉书叫 information，区别于大陪审团使用的 indictment。中国的公诉书可以借用 indictment 一词（information 一词意思实在太泛）。

　　arraignment：认罪程序。有的词典上翻译为"传讯"，但"传讯"在中国是指传唤取保候审、监视居住者过来问话，是公安部门做的事情。美国的认罪程序包括三项内容：1. 法院将被告人传唤到庭；2. 向其宣读起诉书的内容；3. 由被告人就起诉书所指控的罪行作出答辩。在美国，被告人一般可以作有罪答辩、无罪答辩或不愿争论的答辩（plea of *nolo contendere*）。如果被告人作了有罪答辩（guilty plea，即认罪），就不需要举行听审/庭审（trial）了，会直接进入量刑阶段（sentencing）。如果作无罪答辩，则会进入听审程序；听审可以使用陪审团。如果被告人放弃陪审团审判/听审的宪法权利，则由一个法官（美国通常不用合议庭，a judicial panel）听审。进入听审（trial）的案件很少，大概只占全部起诉案件的 5%。其余的 95%，在听审之前都通过辩诉交易（plea bargaining，或译"认罪协商"）达成认罪，直接进入量刑。辩诉交易，就是公诉人和辩护人协商，以被告人认罪换取公诉人以较轻或较少的罪名起诉。这样公诉人不用担心听审时陪审团认定无罪；被告人也不用担心听审时陪审团按照起诉的罪名定了很重的罪。法官要确认认罪出于自愿、没有受到胁迫

（coercion）。

acquitted：无罪释放。经过法官或陪审团审理，如被认定无罪，便会释放。有罪者，进入量刑程序。量刑程序没有陪审团。量刑后，被告人不服，可以上诉（appeal）。一般有2次法定的上诉机会（appeal as a matter of right），上诉法院必须受理；再往上走，一般是到了最高法院，上诉就不一定被受理。只有遇到重要法律问题（宪法问题）需要解决时，法院才会受理。这时法院会发一个 *writ of certiorari*（调卷令），对案件进行复查。注意：上诉可以针对定罪进行，也可以针对量刑进行。但上级法院不会对下级法院的事实认定重新复查；只复查法律适用是否错误，是书面审查。在中国，每次上诉都是一次重新审理（*de novo* trial），需重新出示证据、进行辩论，与美国很不相同。中国实行两审终审制（two-instances system），与美国相同；两审完结之后，再上诉，就叫申诉。申诉经常翻译为petition，但petition也可以用来翻译"上访"。如果某个情境下"申诉"和"上访"同时出现，英文也需要区分。有些国家把两审之外的上诉称为extraordinary appeal，我们不妨拿来使用。

intermediate sanctions：中间性制裁。量刑可能是社会考察（probation）、有期徒刑或介于两者之间的处罚（intermediate sanctions）。

probation：考察。考察过程中违反监管条件的，可以撤销考察（revocation），重新关到监狱。关在监狱里的人可以申请人身保护令（*habeas corpus*）、特赦（pardon）、宽大（clemency）；被判死刑的，不会立即执行，但最终可能被执行死刑。犯人也可能被假释；假释后不遵守条件者，可能被重新收监（revocation，撤销假释）。

misdemeanor：轻罪。轻罪的处理程序相对简化，尤其是可能判处6个月以下的或单处罚金的，没有接受陪审团审判的权利。

diversion by law enforcement, prosecutor, or court：公检法分流。

为了减轻公检法的负担、改善处置成效、避免给违法者留下污点，警察、公诉部门和法院都开办一些分流项目，对违法者进行帮教，避免走正式的司法程序。如果分流不成功（unsuccessful diversion），还会重新纳入正式司法途径处置。

juvenile offenders：青少年违法者。美国有专门的青少年司法系统（法院），程序与成人司法系统有所区别，侧重于对青少年的帮助教育。青少年司法使用的词汇与成人有所不同。如犯罪不用 crime，用 juvenile delinquency（青少年违法）；"量刑"不使用 sentencing，而是用"处置"disposition；关押青少年犯的地方不叫监狱，叫作 residential facility（寄宿设施）。当然，名称的不同，反映对青少年犯罪的不同态度和处置方式。

青少年的案件来自不同地方。除了警察转过来的（police referrals，转处），还包括其他地方（学校、社会服务机构、邻居等）转过来的（non-police referrals）。intake hearing 是指少年法院决定受理与否的听证。它可以放弃管辖权，把案件交给成人刑事法院处理（waive jurisdiction to criminal court）。也可以决定处置、释放或分流到非正式处置程序（informal processing）。aftercare 是指从寄宿性安置场所放出来之后，要经过一段时间的"后续观护"。

# 第四讲

## 司法独立等概念的含义及其翻译

### Judicial Independence 司法独立

美国实行三权分立（separation of powers），法院独立于行政和立法部门。立法部门负责制定法律（making laws）；行政部门负责执行法律（enforcing laws）；司法部门（专指法院）负责解释和适用法律（interpreting and applying laws）。行政和立法部门对司法部门的制约，止于法官的任命：在联邦系统，法官的任命经由参议院（或众议院）推荐人选，总统提名，参议院再予以确认。① 之后法官就独立办案，不受任何机构或个人的影响，总统也不能打招呼。法官甚至不能单独与一方当事人接触（exparte communications），即办案过程中，一方律师要和法官谈实质内容，另一方律师必须在场。

法官的独立通过一系列制度得到保证，如终身任职（life tenure），不用担心丢工作；国会发工资，且不得减薪，所以不用担心扣工资；还有新闻媒体的监督等。

司法独立包括法院独立（independence of the court）和法官独立（independence of judges）。这两个方面在美国是统一的。在中国，司法独立限于法院独立。依照《中华人民共和国宪法》第一百二十六条的规定，"人民法院依照法律规定独立行使审判权，不受行政机关、

---

① "Frequently Asked Questions"，引自 United States Courts 网站（http://www.uscourts.gov/Common/FAQS.aspx，读取日期 2014-12-31）。

社会团体和个人的干涉。"人民法院独立审判，是指人民法院作为一个整体行使审判权，不是审判员独立。这是因为中国的审判采用合议庭（judicial panel）①的方式（美国是独任法官审判），还设有审判委员会（adjudication committee）②。重大疑难案件，负责审理的合议庭难以做出决定，便提交审判委员会决定。这样审判员（法官）便不是独立审判。鉴于这种制度导致"审者不判，判者不审"（Triers do not decide.），遭到人们诟病，也是一个改革的议题。

另外，现行《宪法》规定法院不受"行政机关、社会团体"的干涉，而1954年《宪法》第七十八条规定，"人民法院独立进行审判，只服从法律。"两相比较，学界认为，政党和权力机关（人大）可以干涉法院的审判工作，因为政党和人大不属于"行政机关、社会团体"。③这样，法院作为一个整体，也不完全独立。

党的十八届中央委员会第三次全体会议发布了《中共中央关于全面深化改革若干重大问题的决定》，提出重要的司法改革举措：改革司法管理体制，推动省以下地方法院、检察院人、财、物统一管理（司法"省级统管"），探索建立与行政区划适当分离的司法管辖制度。

这些举措就是为了加强司法独立，避免法院受到地方利益（政府、党委、人大）的干涉。"省级统管"这个说法，笔者听到国外专家使用 delocalization，觉得很好。该译法尽管没有体现出全

---

① 合议庭，辞典上通常翻译为 collegiate bench，但据笔者的口译经验，这个说法并不为英语国家的人接受。

② 注意不要译为 trial committee，因为 trial 是指一审的审理，而审判委员会不负责审理，只负责裁判。

③ 王幼君：《人民法院依法独立行使审判权的宪法解读》，引自中国政法大学法治政府研究院网站（http://law.china.cn/features/2014-10/29/content_7332411.htm，读取日期 2014-12-31）。

部意思，但用起来很方便，尤其在口译的时候；而且经过解释，也不会引起误解。当然，直译为 unified judicial administration at the provincial level 也没问题。将来改革到中央统管的时候，则可以使用 centralization。

另外，中国讲"独立行使审判权"（independent exercise of judicial power），英文讲 judicial independence（司法独立）。通常情况下，"独立行使审判权"可以笼统翻译为 judicial independence，但在有政治敏感性的环境下，须按字面翻译。

## Prosecutorial Discretion 公诉人的自由裁量权

警察侦查结束后，会把案卷交给公诉机关，公诉机关决定是否起诉，以什么罪名起诉。在美国，公诉人的自由裁量权（discretionary power）很大，几乎不受限制。公诉人可以作出的决定包括：不起诉（drop the charge / dismiss the charge / discontinue the case）、起诉（bring criminal charges）、减少起诉罪名（reduce charges）、分流（diversion）、推迟起诉（deferred prosecutions）、进行认罪协商（negotiate guilty pleas / plea negotiation / plea bargaining）。①

公诉人决定是否起诉时，通常考虑以下因素：一、证据是否充足（sufficiency of evidence），有无可能定罪；二、是否有利于维护社会利益（public interest）；三、犯罪的严重性（seriousness of the case）。因为案件太多，司法和执法部门资源有限，所以要优先起诉重要的案件；四、嫌疑人是否配合（cooperation of the defendant）。如果嫌

---

① "Selective Prosecution: Plea Negotiations and Charging Decisions by Prosecutors"，引自 UNC School of Government 网站（http://defendermanuals.sog.unc.edu/sites/defendermanuals.sog.unc.edu/files/pdf/20140457_chap%2005_Final_2014-10-28.pdf，读取日期 2014-12-31）。

疑人配合，检举揭发更多的犯罪①，公诉人可能终止对他的起诉；五、被告人是否有犯罪前科（criminal record）；六、被告人的罪责（culpability）。

在中国，检察院同样有决定起诉和不起诉的裁量权。中国的不起诉决定分为三种：绝对不起诉（又称法定不起诉）、相对不起诉（又称酌量不起诉）和存疑不起诉（又称证据不足不起诉），可以分别翻译为：statutory non-prosecution、discretionary non-prosecution 和 non-prosecution for insufficient evidence。"绝对""相对""存疑"直译出来不易理解，故采用另一种说法作为翻译的基础。"不起诉"也可以译为 dismissal。所谓"法定不起诉"，就是在法律规定的几项具体情形下不起诉。

一个相关的概念是"免于起诉"，翻译为英文是 exemption from prosecution。这是 1979 年刑诉法的概念，现在已经不用。"免于起诉"的情形已经纳入不起诉。为什么要把"免于起诉"改为"不起诉"？因为"免于"的说法隐含了由检察机关定罪的概念：先认定有罪，再予以免除。这不符合由法院定罪量刑的精神。

## Attorney-client Privilege 律师与当事人的保密特权

在美国，律师和当事人之间的沟通受法律保护，不受侵犯，除非当事人同意，律师不能透露给他人，国家也不能强迫律师或当事人透露沟通的情况。这条原则是为了消除当事人的后顾之忧，促使其与代

---

① 配合警方调查，中国叫作"立功"，词典上通常翻译为 render meritorious service。据笔者经验，外国听众听不懂，也不认为配合警察调查是一种 meritorious service。辞典上的"立功"，是指军人立功，不是犯罪嫌疑人的配合。美国有个军功奖，叫 The Meritorious Service Medal (MSM)，颁发给有杰出贡献的军人。因此，遇到嫌疑人"立功"，直接翻译为 cooperation 即可。

理人充分交流，使代理人更好地保护其权利。但在美国，并非所有的州都保护这项权利。华盛顿州的法律仅仅保护当事人发出的讯息，律师发出的讯息只有在披露了当事人的情况时，才受保护。教士与教徒之间的谈话、医生和病人之间的沟通、心理咨询的内容等，也同样受法律保护，教士和医生不能揭发或透露。作这种规定是为了保护更大的社会价值。

配偶之间也有保密特权，叫作 spousal privilege、marital privilege 或 husband-wife privilege。包括两方面的意思：一是夫妻之间的沟通受法律保护，公诉人不得以此作为证据指控一方，称为 communications privilege；二是国家不得要求夫妻一方在法庭上作证指控对方，称为 testimonial privilege。这样规定是为了保持家庭的稳定与和谐。对于父母和子女之间是否也应享有同样的保密特权（parent-child privilege），尽管有学者持肯定态度，但美国只有个别州在法律上予以确认。中国古代的"亲亲相隐"（建议译为 kinship privilege，解释为 privilege among family members），正是这样的保密特权。即亲属之间有罪应当互相隐瞒，不告发和不作证的不论罪，反之则要论罪。

2012 年的《刑事诉讼法》第四十六条新增了辩护律师的保密特权——"辩护律师对在执业活动中知悉的委托人的有关情况和信息，有权予以保密。但是，辩护律师在执业活动中知悉委托人或者其他人，准备或者正在实施危害国家安全、公共安全以及严重危害他人人身安全的犯罪的，应当及时告知司法机关。"这一条文标志着律师保密特权制度在我国刑事诉讼领域的正式确立。但其他人员之间的保密特权，在中国似乎还没有得到承认，主要是担心妨碍侦查机关查办案件。

# The Presumption of Innocence 无罪推定

也称为"无罪假定"。意思是,在一个人被国家证明有罪之前,被假定无罪(innocent until proven guilty)。在中国《刑事诉讼法》中有一句话:"未经人民法院依法判决,对任何人都不得确定有罪。"许多人认为,这是无罪推定原则在中国的表述。与此相对的一个概念是"有罪推定",即 the presumption of guilt。"有罪推定"的意思是,在嫌疑人证明自己无罪之前,被推定为有罪。"无罪推定"意味着国家要证明嫌疑人有罪,而不是让嫌疑人证明自己有罪("自我归罪",self-incrimination);换言之,嫌疑人有权保持沉默,警察不能通过刑讯逼供(torture)等方法逼迫嫌疑人认罪。然而,中国的《刑事诉讼法》规定,"犯罪嫌疑人对侦查人员的提问,应当如实回答",这就否定了嫌疑人的沉默权,与无罪推定的原则矛盾。所以,无罪推定的原则在我国的适用是不完整的。

与"无罪推定"意思相通的一个概念是"谁主张,谁举证"(*Ei incumbit probatio qui dicit, non qui negat*,"the burden of proof rests on who asserts, not on who denies")。当然,谁主张谁举证是一个通用的举证原则,既适用于刑事案件,也适用于民事案件。个别情况下有举证责任倒置(shift of burden of proof)的情况。

无罪推定的原则体现在许多具体的规定和实践中。比如,联合国《囚犯待遇最低限度标准规则》(Standard Minimum Rules for the Treatment of Prisoners)中关于被拘捕或候审囚犯(prisoners under arrest or awaiting trial)[①]的规定中有这样内容:

---

[①] prisoners under arrest or awaiting trial 转换为中国的法律用语就是"被刑事拘留和逮捕的犯罪嫌疑人"。这两类人统称为 untried prisoners(未经审判的囚犯)。这些人在中国是关在看守所里(看守所也关押剩余刑期较短的已决犯)。对他们的关押属于"强制措施"(compulsory measures),目的是为了便于侦查、防止逃脱、预防再次犯罪,不属于惩罚改造(punishment and rehabilitation)。

87. Within the limits compatible with the good order of the institution, untried prisoners may, if they so desire, have their food procured at their own expense from the outside, either through the administration or through their family or friends. Otherwise, the administration shall provide their food.①

既然是无罪，当然不能限制其饮食。愿意吃外卖，看守所不能阻挡。

88. (1) An untried prisoner shall be allowed to wear his own clothing if it is clean and suitable.

(2) If he wears prison dress, it shall be different from that supplied to convicted prisoners.②

既然是无罪，理应不限制其衣着；但出于管理方便，可以穿"号衣"（prison dress），但未决犯的号衣应该区别于已决犯。

89. An untried prisoner shall always be offered opportunity to work, but shall not be required to work. If he chooses to work, he shall be paid for it.③

既然是无罪，就不能强迫劳动；如果愿意劳动，要给报酬。同一文件关于已决犯劳动的规定是这样的：

71. (1) Prison labour must not be of an afflictive nature.

(2) All prisoners under sentence shall be required to work, subject

---

① "Standard Minimum Rules for the Treatment of Prisoners"，引自 United Nations Human Rights 网站（http://www.ohchr.org/EN/ProfessionalInterest/Pages/TreatmentOfPrisoners.aspx，读取日期 2014-12-31）。

②③ 同上。

to their physical and mental fitness as determined by the medical officer.①

就是说，已决犯必须参加劳动，但参加劳动不能作为一种惩罚的手段使用（must not be of an afflictive nature），而是为了满足人的内在需求。

中国的法院在审判时，被告人通常会穿着黄马甲受审。但按照无罪推定的原则，在被法院定罪之前，被告人无罪，就不应该区别对待。法庭之上也不存在便于管理的问题。所以，有些法院在改革，允许被告人穿自己的衣服受审。这也是一种司法文明的表现。同样，除非出于安全考虑，在看守所和法院也不应该给被告人戴戒具（instrument of restraint）。即使对于已决犯，也不应该以戒具作为惩罚的手段。丧失自由即最大惩罚。

## The Benefit of the Doubt 疑罪从无

"疑罪从无"的意思是在证据不足的情况下，法院要作出有利于被告人的判决。这一理念的基础是，两害相权取其轻（the lesser of two evils principle / lesser evil principle）。即在无法判断一个人是否犯罪的时候，是错放一个坏人值得，还是枉杀一个好人值得？不同的社会在不同时期可能作出不同的价值判断。有的认为宁可错杀一千，不可放过一个；有的认为宁可错放一千，不可枉杀一个。现代西方的司法理念是宁可错放坏人，不可冤枉好人。

在中国，还不能完全做到疑罪从无，所以衍生出"疑罪从轻"

---

① "Standard Minimum Rules for the Treatment of Prisoners"，引自 United Nations Human Rights 网站（http://www.ohchr.org/EN/ProfessionalInterest/Pages/TreatmentOfPrisoners.aspx，读取日期 2014-12-31）。

的说法（即法官认为证据有疑点，不敢轻易判无罪，于是就从轻判决，如该判死刑的判死缓，给被告人翻案的机会）。"疑罪从轻"在英语中并无现成的对等说法。既然 the benefit of the doubt 意思是"疑点的好处"，并没有说疑点（"疑罪"）的好处就是"从无"（acquittal，释放），可以考虑采用 partial benefit of the doubt。

中国学者经常探讨疑罪"从轻"还是"从无"的问题。两者在同一语境中出现时，可以把"疑罪从无"译为 the full benefit of the doubt，区别于 partial benefit of the doubt。例如："应当疑罪从轻，还是疑罪从无？"可以译为："Should the defendant get partial benefit of the doubt or the full benefit of the doubt?"，或者"Should we give the defendant partial benefit of the doubt or the full benefit of the doubt?"。

## Right to Silence 沉默权

在美国，嫌疑人在接受警察讯问时以及在审判中有权保持沉默。这项权利基于美国《宪法》上任何人不得被要求"自证其罪"（self-incrimination）的规定。警察拘捕嫌疑人后，在进行讯问之前，必须告知嫌疑人这项权利（称为米兰达警告，Miranda warning），否则获取的口供无效（但拘捕之前问话，不必告知权利）。米兰达警告的内容可以概括为以下几点[①]：

- You have the right to remain silent when questioned.
- Anything you say or do may be used against you in a court of law.
- You have the right to consult an attorney before speaking to the

---

① 维基百科 Miranda warning 条（http://en.wikipedia.org/wiki/Miranda_warning，读取日期 2014-12-31）。

police and to have an attorney present during questioning now or in the future.

- If you cannot afford an attorney, one will be appointed for you before any questioning, if you wish.
- If you decide to answer any questions now, without an attorney present, you will still have the right to stop answering at any time until you talk to an attorney.
- Knowing and understanding your rights as I have explained them to you, are you willing to answer my questions without an attorney present?

法庭审理中，被告人一般都会保持沉默。被告人也可以放弃沉默权，选择当庭作证。如果嫌疑人保持沉默，陪审团不应由此作出不利于嫌疑人的推断。但沉默权并非绝对权利。

在中国，尽管个别地方采用"零口供"起诉规则（non-confession based prosecution），被视为引入"沉默权"概念，但总的来说，嫌疑人和被告人不享有沉默权，必须如实回答警察的问话。坦白从宽，抗拒从严（Leniency for self-confession and severity for resistance.）。法庭审理中，被告人要接受控辩双方和法官的问话，有最后陈述的权利。我们看美国的审判，被告人一言不发，由律师代言，便是被告人沉默权的表现。

## The Principle of Legality 罪刑法定原则

"罪刑法定"来自于拉丁语 *Nullum crimen, nulla poena sine praevia lege poenali*，翻译为英文是 No crime and no penalty without a previous penal law。不知道是哪位翻译高手译为"罪刑法定"这么简洁达意的说法。它的意思是如果刑法没有事先规定一个行为是犯罪及应受处罚，就不应该因为这个行为处罚一个人。拉丁语太长，难以记忆，所以通常简化为：*nullum crimen sine lege* (no crime without a law)，或者 *nulla poena sine lege* (no penalty without a law)。但毕竟懂拉丁语的人不多。即使译者能说出来，听众也不一定懂。所以，尽管有拉丁语，我们也可以用英语表达，比方说：No criminal offence or punishment without law。"罪刑法定"是大陆法系的说法，英美法系用 the principle of legality 或者 the legality principle（合法性原则）来表达这一概念，为口译特别是同传赶时间提供了极大方便。

从罪刑法定原则可以派生出 4 个原则：法律规定的犯罪行为和处罚要十分明确（确定性原则，the principle of certainty）；法律不回过头来追究以前没有规定为犯罪的行为（禁止溯及既往，non-retroactivity）；法无明文规定不能根据类推决定某一行为是犯罪（禁止类推适用，the interdiction of analogy）；不承认习惯法犯罪（no common law crime，即禁止通过判例规定犯罪行为；犯罪行为应由国会通过的成文法决定）。

中国《刑法》于 1997 年修订时，完全确立了罪刑法定的原则。之前的 1979 年《刑法》没有明确罪刑法定原则，而且还保留了类推制度："本法分则没有明文规定的犯罪，可以比照本法分则最相类似的条文定罪判刑，但是应该报请最高人民法院核准"。

## Proportionality 罪刑相当

在所有领域，proportionality 都可以翻译为"相称原则""比例原则""均衡原则"等。在刑事司法领域，又称"罪刑相适应""罪罚相当""罪刑相当"。它是指根据罪行的大小，决定刑罚的轻重。罪重的量刑则重，罪轻的量刑则轻（The punishment of an offender should fit the crime.）。

《联合国青少年司法最低限度标准规则》（北京规则）〔United Nations Standard Minimum Rules for the Administration of Juvenile Justice （the Beijing Rules）〕有这样的规定：

5.1 The juvenile justice system shall emphasize the well-being of the juvenile and shall ensure that any reaction to juvenile offenders shall always be in proportion to the circumstances of both the offenders and the offence.①

## Due Process of Law 正当法律程序

美国《宪法第五修正案》规定，未经法律的正当程序（due process），不得剥夺任何人的生命（life）、自由（liberty）或财产（property）②。正当法律程序是犯罪嫌疑人（the criminal suspect）和被告人（criminal defendant / the accused）享有的一套程序性权利或保障。正当程序的含义并不确定，但总的要求是法律程序中应保证基本的公正。

due process目前形成共识的译法是"正当程序"。根据 due process 的解释："the conduct of legal proceedings according to established rules and principles for the protection and enforcement of private rights, including notice and the right to a fair hearing before a tribunal with the power to decide the case"。③

## Double Jeopardy 避免双重危险原则

double jeopardy（guarantee against being "twice put in jeopardy"）是

---

① "United Nations Standard Minimum Rules for the Administration of Juvenile Justice (The Beijing Rules)"，引自 United Nations Human Rights 网站（http://www.ohchr.org/EN/ProfessionalInterest/Pages/BeijingRules.aspx，读取日期2014-12-31）。

② "Bill of Rights"，引自 Archives 网站（http://www.archives.gov/exhibits/charters/bill_of_rights_transcript.html，读取日期2014-12-31）。

③ B. A. Garner: *Black's Law Dictionary*, 8th ed. (St. Paul, Minnesota: Thompson West, 2004).

英美法系的叫法，大陆法系类似的原则叫"一事不再理"（*non bis in idem; ne bis in idem*），意思是禁止就同一犯罪事实对被告人进行两次以上的追究。它包括三层意思：一审被宣告无罪后不得以同样的罪名再次起诉；一审定罪后不得再次起诉；不得因同样的犯罪事实多次受到处罚。这就意味着，如果被告人在一审时因为证据不足被陪审团无罪释放，即使警察后来发现了确定无疑的有罪证据，同一司法管辖区域的起诉部门也不能提起上诉或要求重新审理——至少不能以同样的罪名或基本相同的罪名重新审理。但这个原则有两个例外，一是一审陪审团的无罪裁定是欺诈的结果；二是一审陪审团本来认定有罪，但一审法官推翻陪审团裁决，认定被告人无罪（这是允许的，叫 judgment notwithstanding the verdict，也叫 judgment *non obstante veredicto* / JNOV）。

《公民与政治权利国际公约》（International Covenant on Civil and Political Rights）第十四条第七款规定：

> No one shall be liable to be tried or punished again for an offence for which he has already been finally convicted or acquitted in accordance with the law and penal procedure of each country.①

## The Rights of the Accused 被告人的权利

被告人的权利是指被指控犯罪的人从被警察拘捕（arrest）到审判结束期间享有的一系列公民和政治权利（civil and political rights）。这些权利的基础是无罪推定（innocent until proven guilty / presumption of innocence）的原则，体现在正当程序（due process）之中。

---

① "International Covenant on Civil and Political Rights"，引自 United Nations Human Rights 网站 http://www.ohchr.org/EN/ProfessionalInterest/Pages/CCPR.aspx，读取日期 2014-12-31）。

在美国，这些权利通过宪法修正案中的《权利法案》（Bill of Rights）（即宪法的前十个修正案）得到保障，特别是第四、五、六、八修正案。被告人的权利总是和受害人的权利相冲突。

被告人享有的权利包括：

- 正当程序权利（right of due process）
- 不受非法搜查和扣押的权利（protection from illegal search and seizures）
- 接受大陪审团指控的权利（the right to indictment by a grand jury）
- 免受双重危险的权利（protection from double jeopardy）
- 不自证其罪的权利（protection against self-incrimination）
- 得到公正、及时、公开审判的权利（right to a fair and speedy public trial）
- 得到陪审团审判的权利（right to trial by jury）
- 被告知指控罪名的权利（notice of accusations）
- 与指控者当面对质的权利（right to confront one's accuser）
- 获得律师帮助的权利（right to counsel）
- 免于过高保释金和罚款的权利以及免受残忍和非常刑罚的权利（protection from excessive bail and fines, and from cruel and unusual punishment）[①]

尽管这是美国的宪法，但这些权利在世界各国影响很大。联合国关于刑事司法的公约、标准、准则、指南等基本上围绕这些权利展开，国内刑事司法改革的许多议题也与此有关。熟悉这些权利对于译者来说十分重要。

---

① "Bill of Rights"，引自 Archives 网站（http://www.archives.gov/exhibits/charters/bill_of_rights_transcript.html，读取日期 2014-12-31）。

# 第五讲

## 与证据法相关的术语及其翻译

### Burden of Proof 证明责任，举证责任

burden of proof（证明责任，举证责任）也叫 *onus* of proof 或 *onus probandi*。司法活动中，谁提出了一项主张（allegation, assertion, claim），谁就要负责证明这项主张，即所谓"谁主张，谁举证"。这一说法来自拉丁语谚语 *Necessitas probandi incumbitei qui agit*。翻译为英文是 "The necessity of proof lies with he who complains."，也可以说 "The burden of proof rests on who asserts, not on who denies."。更简单的说法是 "He who asserts must prove."，或者 "He who alleges a fact has the burden of proving it."，或者 "He who alleges must prove his allegation."。

有人认为，burden of proof 包括两个不同的方面，即 burden of production（举证责任，提出证据的责任）和 burden of persuasion（说服责任）。有人认为 burden of proof 就是 burden of persuasion，与此相对的是 burden of production（burden of going forward）。还有人认为 burden of proof 分为"初步证明责任"（initial burden of proof = burden of production）和最终证明责任（ultimate burden of proof = burden of persuasion）。可见，这些概念在英文中的使用比较混乱。① 在汉语

---

① The U.S. Supreme Court has defined "the burden of proof" as the "burden of persuasion." In so doing, the Court has distinguished it from the closely related but separate burden of production, sometimes referred to as the "burden of going

中，"证明责任"和"举证责任"的使用也不严谨，很多时候该用"证明责任"的时候，也说成"举证责任"。

## Shifting the Burden of Proof 举证责任转移

有些情况下，要求提出主张的一方举证比较困难，为了维护公平正义，平衡双方责任，法律会规定"举证责任倒置"（reversing the burden of proof，即把本来应当由原告承担的举证责任改为被告承担）或"举证责任转移"（shifting the burden of proof），"转移"和"倒置"意思相同。但此时原告应当先提出"初步证据"（*prima facie* evidence）①，再由被告提出反证；如被告无法提出反证，则原告提出的主张被认为成立。

比如，刑事被告人提出在羁押期间受到刑讯逼供，有身上的伤痕为证，这就是显然成立的证据（*prima facie* evidence）。这时，举证责任转移（shift）到控方，控方需要证明这些伤痕不是刑讯逼供的结果，而是其他原因造成的（因为被告人在其控制之下）。如果不能证明，则被告人的指控成立。

A *prima facie* case（证据显然成立的案件），是指原告的证据已经相当充分，除非被告有相反的证据，原告就会胜诉的案件。比如，

---

forward." Some courts nonetheless use the term burden of proof without further description when referring to either the burden of persuasion or that of production, which they consider separate "elements" of the burden of proof. Yet still other courts distinguish between the two by referring to the burden of persuasion as the "ultimate burden of proof" and that of production as the "initial burden of proof." 〔J. P. McCahey: "The Burdens of Persuasion and Production", *Proof*, 3（2008），7-10（p. 8）〕.

① *prima facie* evidence 也可译为"一看便成立的证据"或"显然成立的证据"。*prima facie* 是拉丁语，意思是 on its first appearance（一看便）或 by first instance（初次）。

你是一个女生，和一个男同学一起参加招聘面试。男同学各方面条件都不如你，他却被录取，你遭到拒绝。这就是一个 *prima facie* case of employment discrimination based on gender（显然的基于性别的就业歧视案件）。除非雇主能够证明最后的录取决定是出于别的原因，否则，法院应当判原告胜诉。

## Standards of Proof 证明标准

在确定了哪一方负有证明责任之后，就是证明标准问题，即负有证明责任的一方要把自己的主张证明到什么程度：是做到法院基本相信，还是确信无疑。大多数国家采用两种证明标准：优势证据标准（preponderance of evidence）和排除合理怀疑标准〔beyond (a) reasonable doubt〕。优势证据标准主要用于民事案件，是较低的证明标准，意思是原告和被告谁的证据更有说服力（哪怕只差 1%），谁就会胜诉。排除合理怀疑标准主要用于刑事案件，是最高的证明标准，意思是公诉人要证明到法官（陪审团）几乎无可置疑地相信被告人犯了罪，才能定罪，否则要放人（acquittal）。除此之外，美国还有第三个证明标准，叫 clear and convincing evidence（证据清楚可信），是一个中等水平的证明标准，用于某些种类的案件，如国家剥夺父母监护权的案件。

刑事司法活动的不同阶段，存在不同证明标准，不都是排除合理怀疑。比如，在美国，警察只要有 reasonable suspicion（有合理犯罪嫌疑），就可以拦住一个人进行简单搜查；但警察若要更仔细地搜查或拘捕（arrest）一个人，就要达到更高的标准：probable cause。probable cause 是指有一定的可能性（a fair probability），也许是 30%，也许是 50%。一般翻译为"合理根据"，即有一定的事实根据怀疑某人实施了犯罪。

中国刑事诉讼中的定罪标准是"犯罪事实清楚，证据确实充分"，可译为"clear facts, accurate and complete evidence"。也有人把"证据确实充分"译为 reliable and sufficient evidence。如果翻译为句子，就是"The facts of the case are clear, the evidence is accurate and complete."，相当于排除合理怀疑的标准。逮捕（审前羁押）的标准低于定罪的标准，不要求证明犯罪嫌疑人实施犯罪行为的所有证据都已查证属实，只要求有（一些）证据已被查证属实即可。

## Disclosure / Discovery 证据开示

律师在出庭辩护之前，可以提出正式申请（motion），要求公诉人提供相关证据。提供的过程叫 disclosure（证据开示）或者 discovery（证据发现）。有人认为 discovery 是指民事诉讼中的证据交换，但实际上刑事诉讼中也有人使用。有些证据，如嫌疑人的供述、书证、照片、体检结果、专家证人的姓名资历和主要作证内容，公诉人必须提供；有些内容，如对案件的证明思路（theory of the case，指控辩双方的论点；就辩方而言，可以称为"辩护策略"），则不必提供。控方不仅要提供嫌疑人有罪的证据（incriminatory evidence），还要提供罪轻（mitigating）或无罪证据（exculpatory evidence）（控方也可能掌握无罪或罪轻的证据，但庭审的时候不拿出来），并且要不断提供后续发现的证据。另一方面，只有在辩方先提出开示请求的情况下，控方才可以向辩方提出开示请求。① 辩方开示多少内容，各州规定不同。

证据开示有利于控辩双方进行充分的审前准备，避免审判中的突

---

① "Criminal Law: Right to Evidence Disclosure. Frequently Asked Questions"，引自 Lawyers 网站（http://criminal.lawyers.com/criminal-law-basics/criminal-law-right-to-evidence-disclosure.html，读取日期 2015-02-25）。

然袭击（surprise attack），从而节省司法资源，提高庭审效率（如遇突袭，被袭击方有权要求休庭准备，导致拖延诉讼）。实际上，经过证据开示，被告人往往十分清楚控方证据的力度，从而可能决定放弃庭审，直接认罪（plead guilty），换取控方较轻的指控。控辩双方这种协商，叫作 plea bargaining（辩诉交易）或 plea negotiation（认罪协商）。学者认为，在中国语境下，"认罪协商"的说法更容易被人接受。

诉讼中的"发现手段"（discovery devices）有很多，比如向对方发送 interrogatories（质询书），要对方在宣誓状态下书面回答某些重大问题；deposition（庭外取证，见后面的词条）；request for admission（确认请求，要求对方确认一些事实，这样开庭时就不用再证明这些事实）；request for physical examination（体检请求，如事关身体状况）；request for production of documents（要求提供文件）；request for inspection（要求查验）。[1]

中国的刑诉法没有证据开示的规定，但有律师阅卷权（right to access case files）的规定。2012 年刑诉法第三十八条规定，辩护律师自人民检察院对案件审查起诉之日起，可以查阅、摘抄、复制本案的案卷材料。1996 年规定的是"自人民法院受理案件之日起"。新法提前了查阅案卷的时间。

## Admissible Evidence 可用证据

在审前证据开示的过程中，如果控辩双方对一项证据（证言、书证、物证等）是否可以展示给陪审团或法官（无陪审团审判时）有异

---

[1] "Discovery dispositions"，引自 US Legal 网站（http://definitions.uslegal.com/d/discovery-depositions，读取日期 2015-02-25）。

议（如认为证据是非法取得的，或可能导致偏见），可以通过 motion（请求、动议），要求在审前举行证据听证（evidentiary hearing）。由法官主持，听取双方辩论，把非法取得或违反证据规则的证据提前排除在外，剩余的证据可以进入法庭。这些进入法庭的证据就叫 admissible evidence，可以译为"可用证据"。主持证据听证的法官通常不是主持庭审的法官。

有人把 admission（动词，admit）翻译为"采信"。尽管"采信"是中国法律界常用的术语，但与 admission 意思不同。

"采信"是"采纳"和"相信"的合称，是指已经进入法庭的证据，被法官（中国无陪审团）采纳和相信，用作定案依据。而 admit 则是指证据能否进入法庭，让庭审的法官或陪审团看到，是在"采信"之前发生的动作，意思是"采用"或"采纳"。

同样，把 admissibility〔相当于大陆法系的"证据能力"（competence）〕译为"可采性"，也只能理解为"可（采）用性""可采纳性"，而不能理解为"可采信性"。笔者建议把 admissibility 译为"可用性""可接受性"，以便和动词 admit / admission 的翻译"采用""接受"协调起来。

追根求源，admit（admission）在日常英语中的意思即"允许进入""接纳"，（如 no admission after 10 pm 意为"晚上 10 点后不得进入"），与法律上的意思没有差别。

美国法院对可用证据的界定和判断标准是：

> Admissible evidence, in a court of law, is any testimonial, documentary, or tangible evidence that may be introduced to a fact finder—usually a judge or jury—to establish or to bolster a point put forth by a party to the proceeding. For evidence to be admissible, it must be

relevant, without being unfairly prejudicial, and it must have some indicia of reliability. The general rule in evidence is that all relevant evidence is admissible and all irrelevant evidence is inadmissible.①

所谓 without being unfairly prejudicial，这里举个例子：血腥的杀人现场照片可能具有很高的证明价值，但可能对陪审团产生不当影响，这时如有其他办法来证明同样的事实，法官可能会排除这些照片。

中国法院判断证据是否可用的标准是"三性"：客观真实性（truthfulness）、关联性（relevancy）、合法性（legality）。庭审中的举证（双方出示证据，production of evidence）、质证（双方相互质疑证据，contestation of evidence）、认证（法官认定证据，acceptance of evidence），围绕证据的三性展开。由于美国有审前的证据听证，在证据进入庭审之前，已经解决了关联性、可靠性等问题，法庭的质证主要围绕证人的可信度（credibility）进行。

## Exclusionary Rules （非法证据）排除规则

警察通过非法搜查或拘捕取得的证据、通过强迫嫌疑人供述获得的证据，以及由此衍生出来的证据（fruit of poisonous tree，毒树之果），不得在法庭使用。这就是非法证据排除规则（直接说 exclusionary rules 即可，不必译为 rules excluding illegally obtained evidence）。该原则的目的是为了保护公民享有的某种宪法权利，如免遭不合理的搜查和扣押（unreasonable search and seizure）的权利，不自证其罪（no compelled self-incrimination）的权利以及被剥夺自

---

① 维基百科 Admissible evidence 条（http://en.wikipedia.org/wiki/Admissible_evidence，读取日期 2015-02-25）。

由、生命和财产时享有正当程序（due process）的权利。非法证据排除规则可以有效地限制公权力（警察和检察机关）对私权利的侵害。虽然可能使有些罪犯逃脱惩罚，但不会冤枉好人。冤枉好人被认为是更大的不公。

该原则有一些例外，例如，"发现不可避免"（inevitable discovery）的原则，即警察只要能证明，即使使用正常侦查手段，这项证据也会被发现，那么非法获得的证据也可以使用。1960 年以前，还有一个例外，即银盘理论（Silver Platter Doctrine），意思是联邦法院可以接受州警察在没有联邦参与或授权的搜查中非法获得的证据。"银盘"比喻受到玷污的证据，用干净的盘子托给联邦，就变成了干净的证据。①现在这个理论已经废弃，很少有人知道。

在审前的证据开示过程中，如果辩护人发现公诉人提供的证据（证言、物证等）涉嫌以非法手段获得（illegally obtained），可以向法院提出"排除动议"（motion to suppress，或译"禁用动议"），法官通过开一个控辩双方参加的 motion to suppress hearing 来决定是禁用（suppress）还是采用（admit）控方的证据。②③ 如果辩方认为某个证据与案件无关或可能导致陪审团对被告人的偏见，也可以提出一个动议，要求在庭审前（pre-trial）或庭审的过程中（during the trial）排除，这种动议叫作 motion in limine（"门槛动议"，in limine = "at the start", literally, "on the threshold"）。如果是在庭审过程中提出，则

---

① 维基百科 Elkins v. United States 条（http://en.wikipedia.org/wiki/Elkins_v._United_States，读取日期 2015-02-25）。

② 维基百科 Motion to suppress 条（http://en.wikipedia.org/wiki/Motion_to_suppress，读取日期 2015-02-25）。

③ suppression (of evidence) 除了"证据的禁用"之义外，还有一个意思是"隐匿证据"，即公诉人非法隐藏对被告人有利的证据。如被发现，审判会被宣告无效，需重新审理，并可能导致解除公诉人的职务。

关于该证据的讨论要避开陪审团进行，以免陪审团受到不当影响。①

## Hearsay Evidence 传闻证据

hearsay evidence（传闻证据）是指道听途说或二手证据。证人作证时，不能以转述来证明一件事的真实性。原来是谁说的，谁要来作证，否则就违反了被告人有权与指控者当面对质（right to confrontation, right to confront the accuser）的宪法权利。排除传闻证据，并非禁止证人说自己听到了什么，而是禁止以所听到的内容证明该内容为真。比如，证人听到两口子吵架，其中一个人说"你真是个蠢猪"，证人可以作证自己听到这句话，说明骂人者当时很愤怒，因此不是传闻证据，但不能用这句话证明某人是蠢猪。

排除传闻证据的基本原理是，证人只能证明自己的所见所闻（perception，感知），比如听到、看到、感到了什么，而不能证明别人的所见所闻。因为别人不到庭作证，无法接受交叉询问（cross-examination，对方律师的询问），因此别人未经质疑的证言被认为不可靠。

从这个意义上讲，一个人的书信、日记、备忘录、口头陈述、笔记、计算机文件、法律文件、收据、合同，如果别人拿来证明其本身所述内容的真实性，则都属于传闻证据②。要认定这些内容的真实性，必须由其作者亲自到庭接受直接询问和交叉询问。

如果证人作证时出现传闻证据，对方律师会提出"反对"（objection）。但传闻证据有很多例外，具体可参见维基百科的

---

① 维基百科 Motion in limine 条（http://en.wikipedia.org/wiki/Motion_in_limine，读取日期 2015-02-25）。

② "Hearsay"，引自 The 'Lectric Law Library（http://www.lectlaw.com/def/h007.htm，读取日期 2015-02-25）。

Hearsay 词条。

中美法律里面都有"传来证据"的概念。传来证据（secondary evidence，二手证据）不是来源于案件事实的证据，而是经过传抄、复制、转述等中间环节后形成的"第二手材料"。它是通过原始证据（original/primary evidence）派生出来的证据。比如物证、书证的复制品，证人转述他人告知的案情，视听资料的复制品等等。传来证据相对于原始证据而言。①

从"传闻证据"和"传来证据"的概念来看，两者虽然都被界定为二手证据，内容上有一定重合，但并不完全相同。因此 hearsay 不能"归化"为"传来证据"。

## Deposition 庭外录取证言

如果一个证人将来无法到庭作证（如即将出国或去世），可以提前把他的证言以录音、录像或逐字记录的形式记录下来，供将来在法

---

① Secondary Evidence: A reproduction of, or substitute for, an original document or item of proof that is offered to establish a particular issue in a legal action. Secondary evidence is evidence that has been reproduced from an original document or substituted for an original item. For example, a photocopy of a document or photograph would be considered secondary evidence. Another example would be an exact replica of an engine part that was contained in a motor vehicle. If the engine part is not the very same engine part that was inside the motor vehicle involved in the case, it is considered secondary evidence. Courts prefer original, or primary, evidence. They try to avoid using secondary evidence wherever possible. This approach is called the best evidence rule. Nevertheless, a court may allow a party to introduce secondary evidence in a number of situations. Under rule 1003 of the Federal Rules of Evidence, a duplicate is admissible unless a genuine question is raised as to its authenticity or unless it would be unfair to admit the duplicate in place of the original piece of evidence. (*West's Encyclopedia of American Law* 第 2 版，转引自 The Free Dictionary 网站，http://legal-dictionary.thefreedictionary.com/secondary+evidence，读取日期 2015-02-25）

庭使用。庭外录取证言需要双方的律师参加，通常在一方的律师事务所进行。一般有法庭工作人员到场，主持证人宣誓，并逐字记录全部谈话或录音录像。录取证言叫 take deposition，作证的人叫 deponent。deposition 也指以这种方式录取的证言。①

deposition 与 affidavit（宣誓陈述）意思不同。后者是指证人在宣誓状态下自愿提供的书面证言，需要由司法官员或公证员主持证人宣誓并在证言上签字，还要注明作证地点。做 affidavit 不需要通知对方律师，但做 deposition（庭外作证）需要双方在场。oral testimony（口头作证）则是指在法庭现场作证。②

deposition 不同于中国法庭使用的证人证言（witness statements）。证人证言是指证人就其所了解的案件情况向公安司法机关所作的陈述。证人证言一般是口头陈述，以笔录加以固定；办案人员同意由证人亲笔书写的书面证词，也是证人证言。中国的证人证言是单方面提供的，可以在法庭使用，接受律师的"质证"（指出其中的瑕疵）。在美国，这种证言只能用于反驳证人当庭的证言，即证人出庭作证时，律师发现所述内容与先前的书面证言不一致，才能把先前的证言拿出来证明证人不可信。在中国，律师可以针对文件质证；在美国，只能 challenge a witness（通过交叉询问质疑证人）。美国遵循口头审理原则（orality principle），所有证据必须通过证人之口进入法庭。

另外，汉语中的"调查取证"可以译为 investigation and evidence taking。取证的内容不限于口头证言。

---

① "Discovery dispositions"，引自 US Legal 网站（http://definitions.uslegal.com/d/discovery-depositions/，读取日期 2015-02-25）。

② "Affidavits"，引自 US Legal 网站（http://definitions.uslegal.com/a/affidavits/，读取日期 2015-02-25）。

## (Evidentiary) Privilege 免证权，作证特权

在司法活动中，一些人有权拒绝作证。最常见的是律师和当事人之间的免证权（solicitor-client privilege）。即律师不得（或不能强迫律师）揭发当事人向其吐露的实情，即使当事人披露警察没有发现的犯罪事实——除非当事人透露的信息可能导致即刻危险。这样规定的目的是为了保证当事人与律师之间的自由交流，保证司法体系的健康运转。

其他作证特权还包括："避免自证其罪的特权"（privilege against self-incrimination）。即如果一个证人说，"我如果作证检举某个人，就会把我自己牵连进去"，这个证人则不必就此作证。"无不利影响的特权"（without prejudice privilege），即为了鼓励通过协商解决法律争议，一方在协商过程中的言行，不得在随后可能进行的诉讼中被另一方用作不利证据。夫妻免证权（marital privilege）即不得强迫夫妻之间相互指证；医生免证权（medical professional privilege）即医生不得指证病人；神职人员免证权（clergy-penitent privilege）即不得强迫神职人员指证信徒；等等。这些特权是为了维护更大的社会价值，如家庭的和谐稳定和虔诚信仰。①

中国现代立法中没有规定免证权，甚至鼓励大义灭亲，而古代则有"亲亲相隐"（kinship privilege）的规定，即亲属之间有罪应当互相隐瞒。不告发和不作证的不论罪，反之要论罪，其目的是维护宗法伦理和家族制度。当前有学者主张在中国引进免证权。

## Principle of Free Evaluation of Evidence 自由心证

自由心证原则（principle of free evaluation of evidence, principle of

---

① 维基百科 Privilege (evidence) 条（http://en.wikipedia.org/wiki/Privilege_(evidence)，读取日期 2015-02-25）。

unfettered consideration of evidence）是指法律不预先设定机械的规则来指示或约束法官，而由法官针对具体案情，根据经验、逻辑和理性良知，对证据的取舍和证明力进行判断，并最终形成确信的原则，因此又称为内心确信原则（inner conviction）。①

"自由心证"的译文来自日语，应理解为"自主心证"。与其相对的证据原则是法定证据主义（legalistic theory of evidence），又称为形式证据制度（formal theory of evidence）。这种制度盛行于中世纪，以法律规定了证据的证明力（probative value），法官不需动脑筋，只需要套用公式即可计算出哪一方的证据较强。例如：被告的供述（confession）被认为是"证据之王"；男子证言的可信度优于女子；达官贵人优越于普通人；僧侣优越于世俗人。

法定证据主义的优点是可避免法官的武断，缺点是有害于人权，这是因为警察可能会对嫌疑人施以刑讯，以从其口中取得被认为是"证据之王"的口供。②

中国的证据制度仍然有法定主义的残留，比如规定直接证据证明力大于间接证据，原始证据优于传来证据，实物证据优于言词证据，而不是由法官根据情况自由判断。

## Classification of Evidence 证据的分类

学术界按不同标准把证据分为原始证据（original evidence）和传来证据（secondary evidence）、直接证据（direct evidence）和间接证据（indirect/circumstantial evidence）③、言词证据（verbal evidence）和

---

① 曾庆敏：《法学大辞典》，第6版，上海辞书出版社，1998年，第532页。

② 维基百科"自由心证"条（http://zh.wikipedia.org/wiki/自由心证，读取日期2015-02-25）。

③ Circumstantial evidence is evidence that relies on an inference to connect it

实物证据（real/physical evidence）①、本证（positive evidence）与反证（negative evidence）等。②

证据的"种类"则是法律规定的证据表现形式，不属于法律上规定的证据种类不能作为证据使用。根据我国《刑事诉讼法》第四十八条的规定，刑事诉讼中的证据共有8种，它们是：（1）物证（physical evidence）；（2）书证（documentary evidence）；（3）证人证言（testimonies by witnesses）；（4）被害人陈述（statements by the victim）；（5）犯罪嫌疑人、被告人供述和辩解（admissions/confessions and justifications by the criminal suspect or defendant）；（6）鉴定意见（forensic examiner's opinions）；（7）勘验、检查、辨认、侦查实验等笔录（documentation of observations, inspections,

---

to a conclusion of fact—like a fingerprint at the scene of a crime. By contrast, direct evidence supports the truth of an assertion directly—i.e., without need for any additional evidence or inference. On its own, circumstantial evidence allows for more than one explanation. Different pieces of circumstantial evidence may be required, so that each corroborates（印证，补强）the conclusions drawn from the others. Together, they may more strongly support one particular inference over another.（维基百科 Circumstantial evidence 条，http://en.wikipedia.org/wiki/Circumstantial_evidence，读取日期 2015-02-25）

① The term "real evidence" describes any evidence that is a tangible object, as opposed or oral testimony or documentary evidence, which records information that is offered as evidence. "Real evidence" is often used interchangeably with "physical evidence" to describe objects that are used to prove or disprove arguments in trial or at a hearing. Real evidence is used to prove a fact based on the characteristics of all or part of an object.（"What is 'real evidence'? Is it the same thing as 'physical evidence'?"，引自 Rottenstein Law Group 网站，http://www.rotlaw.com/legal-library/what-is-real-evidence-is-it-the-same-thing-as-physical-evidence，读取日期 2015-02-25）应当注意的是，material evidence 是指实质性证据、关键证据，指可能影响法院判决的证据，不要翻译为"物证"。

② 樊崇义：《证据法学》，法律出版社，2000 年。

identifications, investigative experiments, etc.）；（8）视听资料、电子数据（audiovisual materials and electronic data）。

英文中常见到的 demonstrative evidence（展示性证据），是为了说明一个有争议的事实而向法院展示的物品，如照片、X 光片、录音、录像、电影、模型模拟、地图、挂图等，是相对于物证、证人证言等其他形式的证据[1]。展示性证据本身在案件中没有发挥作用，是为了说明问题。

exhibit（证物）是指庭审过程中控辩双方在法庭出示的文件或物件，既包括物证、书证，也包括在法庭上临时示意的草图。证物经证人确认后，如果双方无异议，会被法院接受，并标上序号，如 Exhibit 1（证物 1 号）。证物都由法院保管，直至审判结束。在证据的分类中，"证物"并不是一种证据类别。[2]

---

[1] *West's Encyclopedia of American Law* 第 2 版，转引自 The Free Dictionary 网站（http://legal-dictionary.thefreedictionary.com/Demonstrative+Evidence，读取日期 2015-02-25）。

[2] 维基百科 Exhibit (legal) 条（http://en.wikipedia.org/wiki/Exhibit_(legal)，读取日期 2015-02-25）。

# 第六讲

## 十八届四中全会文件翻译举例评析

笔者最近学习了中央编译局翻译的《中共中央关于全面推进依法治国若干重大问题的决定》①英译本，从中选出一些句子和段落进行分析，提出商榷意见，总结翻译规律，介绍法律知识，希望进一步提高党政和法律文件的翻译质量，服务于中国对外开放的大局。

本文例句按其在《决定》中出现的顺序排列，没有归类；说明中的要点以粗体显示，最后作归纳总结。

例1：

原文：健全有<u>立法权的人大</u>主导立法工作的体制机制……

译文：We need to improve the systems and mechanisms through which <u>those people's congresses with legislative power</u> lead legislative work...②

建议：We need to improve the systems and mechanisms through which the people's <u>congress, which exists to legislate,</u> will dominate legislative work...

说明：尽管级别低的人大无立法权，但此句的关注焦点并非有立法权

---

① 《中共中央关于全面推进依法治国若干重大问题的决定》，引自新华网（http://news.xinhuanet.com/politics/2014-10/28/c_1113015330.htm，读取日期2014-10-28）。

② 例1—例11译文均引自 *Resolution of the Central Committee of the Communist Party of China on Certain Major Issues Concerning Comprehensively Advancing the Law-Based Governance of China*, (Beijing: Central Compilation and Translation Press, 2015).

的人大和无立法权的人大,而是全国人大立法权旁落的问题:

> 从应然角度看,享有立法权的人大及其常委会在立法中发挥主导作用是人大作为立法主体依法履职的题中之义。然而,从实然角度看,现有立法体制下近八成的法律、法规是由作为执法机关的行政机关起草的。党的十八届四中全会通过的《决定》,在针砭一些法律法规未能全面反映客观规律和人民意愿、针对性与可操作性不强、立法工作中部门化倾向及争权诿责现象较为突出等现象的同时,明确提出"健全有立法权的人大主导立法工作的体制机制,发挥人大及其常委会在立法工作中的主导作用"。①

因此,此处"有立法权的"是一种强调性用法,应翻译为非限定性定语从句。

教训:**译者不仅要知道作者说了什么,还要知道为什么这么说。只有真正理解作者的意图,才能给出正确的译法。**

**例2:**
原文:加强法律解释工作,及时明确法律规定含义和适用法律依据。
译文:We need to improve our work regarding the interpretation of laws by promptly clarifying their meaning <u>and why they are applicable</u>.
建议:<u>... or specifying applicable laws</u>.
说明:这一部分讲的是立法部门要加强对法律的解释工作(叫作"立法解释",相对于司法部门对法律的解释即"司法解释"):

> 凡属法律规定需要进一步明确具体含义的或者法律制定后

---

① 《充分发挥人大对立法的主导作用》,引自文汇报网站(http://whb.news365.com.cn/sp_2881/201501/t20150128_1630000.html,读取日期2015-05-05)。

<u>出现新的情况，需要明确适用法律依据的</u>，由全国人大常委会解释，是为立法解释。①

可见，原文的"明确法律规定含义"和（明确）"适用（的）法律依据"说的是两种情况：前者是指法律规定不明确，人大要予以释明；后者是指法律对新出现的情况无规定，人大要告诉法院等请求解释的机构按哪条法律处理新情况。因此建议改为 or specifying applicable laws。原译实际存在逻辑问题：澄清意思和解释为什么适用无逻辑关系。笔者怀疑是外籍审校根据主观猜测修改的。

教训：**理解是正确翻译的基础**。

例3：
原文：党中央向全国人大提出宪法修改建议，依照宪法规定的程序进行宪法修改。

译文：For constitutional revisions, the Central Committee <u>shall</u> make proposals to the NPC, and the <u>NPC shall carry out the revisions</u> in accordance with the procedures stipulated in the constitution.

建议：For constitutional revisions, the Central Committee <u>will</u> make proposals to the NPC, and <u>the amendment will be carried out</u> in accordance with the procedures provided by the constitution.

说明1：这是一份党中央的文件，党中央提修宪建议，是出于自己的意愿（will），不是一种义务（shall）。党中央说自己要做的事情，不能用 shall，而是用 will。

说明2：NPC shall carry out the revisions 意思说人大必须改，这样就不是

---

① 百度百科"立法解释"条（http://baike.baidu.com/view/21188.htm，读取日期 2015-05-05）。

党的建议了,是命令。因此建议改为 the amendment will be carried out。

教训:译者需要理解党和政府之间的关系以及我国权力运作的基本方式。

例 4:
原文:保证<u>公正司法</u>,提高<u>司法公信力</u>。
译文:Ensuring Judicial Impartiality and Improving Judicial Credibility
建议:Fair Administration of Justice to Improve Judicial Credibility
说明 1:judicial impartiality 固然不错,但此处的"司法"是动宾关系,与此相应的英文是 fair administration of justice。*Duhaime's Law Dictionary* 引用一位法官的判决书来定义 administration of justice:

> Administration of justice, with particular reference to the criminal law, is a compendious term that stands for all the complexes of activity that operate to bring the substantive law of crime to bear, or to keep it from coming to bear, on persons who are suspected of having committed crimes. It refers to the rules of law that govern the detection, investigation, apprehension, interviewing and trial of persons suspected of crime and those persons whose responsibility it is to work within these rules. <u>The administration of justice is not confined to the courts; it encompasses officers of the law and other whose duties are necessary to ensure that the courts function effectively.</u> The concern of the administration of justice is the fair, just and impartial upholding of rights, and punishment of wrongs, according to the rule of law.[1]

---

① "Administration of justice",引自 Duhaime's Legal Dictionary 网站( http://www.duhaime.org/LegalDictionary/A/AdministrationofJustice.aspx,读取日期 2015-05-05)。

美国加州曾成立 California Commission on the Fair Administration of Justice（CCFAJ），专门关注冤假错案问题。在"保证公正司法，提高司法公信力"这一标题下，探讨的正是中国刑事司法制度改革，针对的正是冤假错案问题。因此，把"公正司法"译为 fair administration of justice 正好合适。judicial impartiality（司法公正）侧重于法院的行为，administration of justice 涉及所有参与司法活动的公权力。

说明 2："保证公正司法，提高司法公信力"，逗号前后有因果关系，译文处理为并列关系，尽管读者可以从意思上推断，但不如处理为因果关系直截了当：Fair Administration of Justice to Improve Judicial Credibility。**中文里的逗号可以表示各种逻辑关系，不一定是并列关系，译者要根据上下文确定译文判断逻辑关系，必要时在译文中明确这一逻辑关系。**

另外，"司法公信力"在英文中还有更常用的说法：public confidence in the judiciary。通过谷歌检索可发现，judicial impartiality较少使用，public confidence in the judiciary是普遍的用法。

说明 3："保证"一词，已经隐含在 fair administration of justice 当中，不必翻译出来。尽管是重要文件，也不是每个字都需要翻译出来。

教训：**如果一个词表达的意思已经隐含在译文中，就不需要翻译。翻译出来反而累赘，影响意思的有效传达。**

例 5：
原文：对干预司法机关办案的，给予党纪政纪处分；造成冤假错案或者其他严重后果的，依法追究刑事责任。
译文：Those who interfere with the judicial handling of cases must be punished in accordance with Party and government rules of discipline, and

in the event that serious consequences have occurred as a result of such interference, such as false accusations and unjust or erroneous rulings, those accountable must be prosecuted in accordance with the law.

建议：Those who interfere with the judicial process must be punished in accordance with Party and government rules of discipline, and if the interference causes miscarriage of justice or other serious consequences, those accountable must be prosecuted in accordance with the law.

说明1："办案"按字面翻译为 handling of cases 当然没错，但加上 judicial，可能会引起误解：似乎 judicial 之外的干预是允许的。在联合国大会核可的《关于司法机关独立的基本原则》中，有这样的规定：

> 4. There shall not be any inappropriate or unwarranted interference with the judicial process, nor shall judicial decisions by the courts be subject to revision.①

这里的 judicial process 就是指办案的过程，是国际通行的说法，不妨借来使用，便于国际交流。

说明2："冤假错案"，按照字面意思，包括"冤案"，即无罪被定有罪；"假案"，可能是某人出于打击报复等目的，捏造证据，诬蔑陷害；"错案"，可能是出于某些原因导致判决错误。译文为 false accusations and unjust or erroneous rulings 可以说涵盖了"冤""假""错"的各种情形，所以没有错。但"冤假错案"是个

---

① "Basic Principles on the Independence of the Judiciary"，引自 United Nations Human Rights 网站（http://www.ohchr.org/EN/ProfessionalInterest/Pages/IndependenceJudiciary.aspx，读取日期2015-05-05）。

民间说法，学术名词叫作"错案"。《民主与法制》杂志总编刘桂明在其博客中撰文说：

> 其实，冤假错案只是一种社会表达，而不是一个法律表述。以法律的视角观察，对此一般冠以"错案"的学术表达。对于什么是错案，目前好像还没有一个统一的定义，<u>从一般意义的理解来讲，错案是指对无罪或者不应当追究刑事责任的人，而错误地定罪追究刑事责任的案件，以及对构成犯罪应当追究刑事责任而不追究刑事责任的案件。</u>①

可见，在法律上并没有把冤假错案区分为"冤""假""错"三类，而全部称为"错案"。"错案"在英文中是 miscarriage of justice：

> <u>A miscarriage of justice primarily is the conviction and punishment of a person for a crime they did not commit. The term can also apply to errors in the other direction—"errors of impunity", and to civil cases.</u> ..."Miscarriage of justice" is sometimes synonymous with wrongful conviction, referring to a conviction reached in an unfair or disputed trial.②

从定义可见，"错案"与 miscarriage of justice 含义相同，因此可以作为翻译中的对等概念。更为重要的是，miscarriage of justice 简洁上口，便于使用，尤其对于口译来说十分方便。另外，如果

---

① 《冤假错案究竟是什么？》，引自法制博客（http://blog.legaldaily.com.cn/blog/html/81/2441181-49392.html，读取日期 2015-05-05）。

② 维基百科 Miscarriage of justice 条（http://en.wikipedia.org/wiki/Miscarriage_of_justice，读取日期 2015-05-05）。

"冤假错案"单纯指无罪的人被追究，则可直接翻译为 wrongful convictions。

**例6：**
原文：健全行政机关依法出庭应诉、支持法院受理行政案件、尊重并执行法院生效裁判的制度。
译文：We must improve the systems whereby administrative agencies appear and defend themselves in court in accordance with the law, support the court in handling cases filed against them, and respect and carry out effective judgments made by the court.
建议：We must improve the systems whereby administrative agencies will support the court in accepting actions against them, attend court hearings in accordance with the law, and respect and carry out effective judgments of the court.
说明1："出庭应诉"强调的是出庭，针对的问题是行政官员不出庭，请看新华网报道：

### 告官不见官？武汉要求行政机关负责人出庭应诉

> 行政诉讼是"民告官"的制度，而实践中"告官不见官"的问题比较突出。武汉市近日召开市政府常务会，通过《武汉市行政机关负责人出庭应诉暂行规定》，要求对于涉及重大安全责任事故、重大环境保护问题等有重大社会影响的行政诉讼案件，行政机关主要负责人应出庭应诉。①

---

① 《告官不见官？武汉要求行政机关负责人出庭应诉》，引自新华网( http://www.gd.xinhuanet.com/newscenter/2015-04/19/c_1115013940.htm，读取日期2015-05-05）。

出庭后是否辩护，并非焦点。从保护原告利益的角度来讲，政府不辩护才好，那样原告可以轻易胜诉。因此，译文重点也应放在"出庭"上，而不是"应诉"/"辩护"上。所以改为 attend court hearings。

说明 2："受理"是指人民法院对当事人的起诉进行审查后，认为符合法律规定的起诉条件，予以接受并决定立案审理，从而引起诉讼程序开始的一种诉讼活动。这句话针对的问题是行政案件"立案难"的问题。请看环球网的报道：

> 全国人大常委会 1 日表决通过关于修改行政诉讼法的决定，明确规定行政机关及其工作人员不得干预、阻碍人民法院受理行政案件。①

译文是 handling cases，即处理案件，法院的处理，既包括受理，也包括审理、判决。因此，handling cases 意思不准确。改为 accepting 可以准确表达"受理"的意思。

译文产生失误的原因，可能是不懂汉语的国外审校最终修改的结果。因为中国译者一般会把"受理"翻译为 accept。但审校可能觉得本句有逻辑问题：即出庭应诉在先，法院受理在后。因此审校把 accepting 改为 handling，从而梳理了逻辑关系：出庭应诉、支持审理、执行判决。但经过修改之后，改变了原意，因此不可取。问题的根源在于原文。原文的先讲出庭应诉，再讲受理案件。笔者猜测，产生这个逻辑瑕疵的原因，可能是出于汉语节奏的考虑。如果按照逻辑顺序，应该这样说：

---

① 《新行诉法：政府不得干预法院受理 12 种民告官行政案》，引自环球网（http://china.huanqiu.com/article/2014-11/5187515.html，读取日期 2015-05-05）。

健全行政机关<u>支持法院受理行政案件</u>、<u>依法出庭应诉</u>、<u>尊重并执行法院生效裁判</u>的制度。

这样，三个并列成分在长度上有差异，语言节奏显然不如修改之前。但鉴于本句话解决的是"立案难、审理难、执行难"三个具有先后顺序的问题，译文按正确的逻辑进行调整，避免读者的困惑应该是可取的。

汉语文章中因词害义的情况并不少见。往往是为了节奏增加不必要的修饰语或进行语言的压缩；也有为了语言通顺而无视逻辑的情况。鉴于翻译为英语之后，汉语的节奏不复存在，因此，译文应当强调原文意思的传达和逻辑的通畅，为此可对原文词句作适当加工润色。

说明 3：其他两处修订，涉及用词和简洁性问题。"诉讼""案件"不一定一律翻译为 litigation 或 cases；（legal） actions, lawsuit 等也是很好的选择。

教训：关于简洁，**如果去掉一个词不妨碍原文意思的传达，就把这个词删掉，即使原文里可能有这个词。多余的词，就好比庄稼地里的稗草，不仅无益，而且有害。**

例 7：

原文：<u>建立健全司法人员</u>履行法定职责保护机制。

译文：We must establish a <u>sound</u> mechanism to protect <u>those working in the judiciary</u> in the performance of their statutory duties.

建议：We must establish and <u>improve</u> mechanisms to protect <u>judicial officers</u> in the performance of their statutory duties.

说明 1：从全文采取逐字翻译的策略来看，笔者怀疑初稿中"建立健全……机制"翻译为 establish and improve the mechanism；但既存的机制（the mechanism）不可能被建立，因此被母语审校改为 establish a sound mechanism。但这样其实违背了原文的意思。如果原文真的表示"建立"和"健全"两个意思，可以采用 mechanism 的复数形式：establish and improve mechanisms，这样不会产生逻辑问题。

说明2：根据接下来一句的论述（"非因法定事由，非经法定程序，不得将法官、检察官调离、辞退或者作出免职、降级等处分"），本句中的"司法人员"是指法官和检察官。在我国，"司法"一词的狭义解释，包括检察和审判两种职能；而在西方，根据三权分立的制度，"司法"仅仅指审判职能（法院）；检察（公诉）机关属于行政机关。因此建议在译文中第一次出现 judicial / judiciary 时，用注释说明其在中国既包括法院，也包括检察院。如果前文已经通过注释说明 judiciary 包括 prosecutors' office，则把"司法人员"翻译为 those working in the judiciary 就可能被正确理解。但 those working in the judiciary 也不太好。因为在法院、检察院工作的人不一定是法官、检察官。笔者建议使用 judicial officer：

> A **Judicial Officer** is a person with the responsibilities and powers to facilitate, arbitrate, preside over, and make decisions and directions in regard to the application of the law.
>
> Judicial Officers are typically categorized as judges, magistrates, puisne judicial officers such as justices of the peace or officers of courts of limited jurisdiction; and notaries public and commissioners of oaths. The powers of judicial officers vary and are usually limited to a certain jurisdiction.[①]

---

① 维基百科 Judicial officer 条（http://en.wikipedia.org/wiki/Judicial_officer，读取日期 2015-05-05）。

该定义中未包含检察官，但鉴于假定前文已经界定 judiciary 在中国包括 prosecutors' office，读者相应会按中国语境来理解 judicial officer。

因为不存在完全对等的概念，所以，**读翻译过来的文章，一个概念只能放在来源国的语境下来理解，这是读者的责任**。同时，如果同一说法在两个语境下意思有重大不同（如 judiciary），则需要注释说明，这是译者的责任。译者尽量采用便于读者理解和不会导致读者误解的说法。

翻译为 judicial officer 的另一个好处是，以概念译概念，而不是以解释来翻译概念。解释性翻译是不得已而为之。

另外，汉语中还有"司法工作人员"的说法。《刑法》第九十四条规定，"本法所称司法工作人员，是指有侦查、检察、审判、监管职责的工作人员。"可见，"司法"在汉语中还有更广的含义：不仅包括检察和审判人员，还包括公安和监狱管理人员。"司法工作人员"可以翻译为 judicial administrators。这一说法来自前文关于 administration of justice 的定义：

> The administration of justice is not confined to the courts; it encompasses officers of the law and others whose duties are necessary to ensure that the courts function effectively.①

**例 8：**
原文：优化司法职权配置。健全公安机关、<u>检察机关</u>、审判机关、司

---

① "Administration of justice"，引自 Duhaime's Legal Dictionary 网站（http://www.duhaime.org/LegalDictionary/A/AdministrationofJustice.aspx，读取日期 2015-05-05）。

法行政机关各司其职，侦查权、检察权、审判权、执行权相互配合、相互制约的体制机制。

译文：Improving the allocation of judicial functions and powers. We need to improve the systems and mechanisms by which public security organs, procuratorates, and courts as well as administrative agencies for justice each perform their respective functions while investigative, procuratorial, judicial, and enforcement powers complement and constrain each other.

建议：Improving the allocation of judicial functions and powers. We need to improve the systems and mechanisms under which public security organs, procuracies, and courts as well as justice administration authorities each perform their respective functions, with investigative, procuratorial, judicial, and enforcement powers complementing and constraining each other.

说明1：procuratorate（检察院）只有中国在用，一般西方读者不认识。作为这个词来源的苏联，已经用 prosecutors' office 来翻译俄语的"检察院"了。如果中国对 procurator（检察官）这个说法情有独钟，建议把 procuratorate 改为 procuracy（越南已经改了）；这两个词意思相同（后缀 -ate 和 -acy 都可以表示机构），但后者更容易识记。无论用 procuratorate、procuracy 还是 procurator，都应在注释中说明，其基本职能就是 prosecution；procurator 相当于 prosecutor。中国的司法制度在和国际接轨，陈旧的说法，可以考虑修改，否则会影响沟通效果。

说明2："司法行政机关"是指司法部、司法厅、司法局、司法所这个系统。通常译为 justice administration authorities。请注意，我国的司法行政机关（司法部）名为"司法行政"，却并不管司法部门（法院、检察院），不承担和介入司法机关行政组织、人事调动、活动经费等事务（过去曾经有这些职能），只负责司法考试的组织和司法资格的审核、授予工作,以及主管监狱、普法宣传、律师、公证、人民调解、司法协助等职能。

说明3:原文逗号前后不是有对比关系的两件事(while在此处只能作whereas理解)。相反,后半句是对前半句的补充,因为前面的"职"与后面的"权"有一一对应关系:公安负责侦查、检察院负责检察、法院负责审判、司法部负责执行(刑罚)。改为with短语,意思或更清楚。

教训:汉语中逗号可以表示各种逻辑关系,译者要根据意思判断并选择适当翻译方法。

例9:

原文:完善司法体制,推动实行审判权和执行权相分离的体制改革试点。完善刑罚执行制度,统一刑罚执行体制。改革司法机关人财物管理体制,探索实行法院、检察院司法行政事务管理权和审判权、检察权相分离。

译文:We must improve the judicial system, and carry out pilot structural reforms to separate judicial powers from powers of enforcement. We need to improve and unify the systems by which penal decisions are enforced. We need to reform the systems for managing human, financial, and material resources of judicial bodies, and explore ways to separate the judicial and procuratorial powers of courts and procuratorates from their powers to manage judicial administrative affairs.

建议:We must improve the structure of justice administration and push for pilot reforms to separate enforcement from the court. We need to improve the system for enforcement of criminal sanctions and unify the enforcement authorities. We need to reform the systems for managing human, financial, and material resources of judicial authorities, and explore ways to <u>separate the administrative power from adjudicatory and prosecutorial powers in courts and procuracies.</u>

说明 1：以句号隔开的三个句子是并列关系。有时候，一个段落第一句是总括，接下来几句是详述（"总分结构"）；有时候一段就是几个并列的句子。本段为后者。**明白各句子之间的逻辑关系，有助于构建意思连贯的译文。**

同样，一个句号之内、各逗号之间，也可能是总分结构或并列结构。从意思来看，前两句话中的逗号前后应为总分关系，即逗号前是概括，逗号后是详细叙述。比如，"完善司法体制"的具体内容，就是"推动实行审判权和执行权相分离的体制改革试点"。

最后一句话，逗号前后是并列关系：逗号前是指外部司法行政，即由谁来为法院提供人财物；逗号后，是指内部的司法行政，及法院内如何进行"人事管理（如司法官的工作任务分配）、案件分配、司法官的调转和升迁以及司法活动所需装备的管理、办案车辆的调度等"①。

如果译者能够确定逗号前后是总分关系，可以在译文中以某种方式把两部分合并为一个偏正结构，如把第二句话译为："We need to improve the system for enforcement of criminal sanctions <u>by unifying</u> the enforcement authorities." 如果逗号前后是并列关系，则只能用并列的谓语动词或分为几句来翻译。如果译者无法确定前后逻辑关系，则不妨保留中文的并列结构，由读者来判断或交给官方解释。建议译文尊重译文，保留了原文形式上的并列。

**教训：遇到汉语多个逗号连用的情况，需要厘清哪个逗号之前是总**

---

① 张建伟：《司法机关人财物：谁来管，如何管？》，中国党政干部论坛，2015 年第 4 期，第 32—36 页。

括,翻译时需要断在一起。详述部分,可以另外翻译为一句或几句话。

说明2:关于"审执分离",目前是法院内部分离。《人民法院组织法》第四十条规定,地方各级人民法院设执行员,办理民事案件判决和裁定的执行事项,办理刑事案件判决和裁定中关于财产部分的执行事项。将来的改革可能把执行分出去:

> 多位受访的学者告诉财新记者,审判权和执行权相分离,可能将执行权从法院剥离出去,交由其他部门来主管;或者是单独设立专门的执行机关。①

译文依照中文的表述,把"审判权和执行权相分离"译为 separate judicial powers from powers of enforcement,意思成为把审判权从执行权中分出去(光剩下执行权),弄错了剥离的对象。根据上面的调查结果,"相分离"的意思把法院的执行权剥离出去,光剩下审判权。据此,需要改为 separate enforcement from the court。审判权(adjudicatory power)由法院行使,直接翻译为"法院"更明确。实际上,翻译为 judicial power 并不准确,因为中国语境下的 judicial 还包括检察院。如果仅仅指审判权(不包括检察权),不如直接译为"法院"。

"法院、检察院司法行政事务管理权和审判权、检察权相分离"的译法也有同样问题:剥离对象错误。因此改为 separate the administrative power from adjudicatory and prosecutorial powers in courts

---

① 《四中全会解读(一)审执分离改革:学者建议执行权剥离法院》,引自财新网(http://china.caixin.com/2014-10-24/100743044.html,读取日期 2015-05-05)。

and procuracies. 没有严格按照字面翻译。

说明 3：关于"完善刑罚执行制度，统一刑罚执行体制"，有关资料这样论述：

> 《中华人民共和国刑事诉讼法》第一章"基本原则"中配置了公检法三机关在刑事诉讼中的权限，对刑事案件的侦查、拘留、执行逮捕、预审、由公安机关负责。检察、批准逮捕、检察机关直接受理的案件的侦查、提起公诉，由人民检察院负责。审判由人民法院负责。但是，在执行程序中又设定死刑、罚金、没收财产的判决由人民法院执行；拘役、剥夺政治权利公安机关执行；剩余刑期在三个月以下的由看守所代为执行。死刑缓期二年执行、无期徒刑、有期徒刑由监狱（属于司法部管理）或者其他机关执行。①

理解了这句话针对的问题，可以知道这句话和上句话是并列关系，不是进一步提供信息。因为上句话是讲的民事/刑事案件中涉及财产的执行，本句讲的是刑事处罚的执行。同时，也可以选用更为具体的词来翻译"体制"："We need to improve the system for enforcement of criminal sanctions and unify the enforcement authorities."。

说明 4："完善司法体制"中的"司法"，是广义的"司法"，因此建议翻译为 justice administration。从下文来看，"体制"译为 structure 是合适的，可坚持使用。

---

① 《统一刑罚执行体制保障刑罚执行公正》，引自法制网（http://epaper.legaldaily.com.cn/fzrb/content/20141203/Articel10003GN.htm，读取日期 2015-05-05）。

例 10：

原文：最高人民法院设立巡回法庭，审理跨行政区域重大行政和民商事案件。探索设立跨行政区划的人民法院和人民检察院，办理跨地区案件。完善行政诉讼体制机制，合理调整行政诉讼案件管辖制度，切实解决行政诉讼立案难、审理难、执行难等突出问题。

译文：Circuit courts need to be established under the Supreme People's Court to judge major administrative, civil, and commercial cases that extend beyond administrative divisions. We need to explore the establishment of people's courts and people's procuratorates whose jurisdiction extends beyond administrative divisions to handle trans-regional cases. We need to improve the systems and mechanisms for dealing with administrative litigation, make reasonable adjustments to the system of determining jurisdiction for administrative litigation cases, and effectively solve the major difficulties in the filing and trial of administrative litigation and in the enforcement of court rulings.

建议：Circuit courts need to be established under the Supreme People's Court to judge major administrative, civil, and commercial cases that extend beyond an administrative division. We need to explore the establishment of people's courts and people's procuratorates whose jurisdiction extends beyond administrative divisions to handle trans-regional cases. We need to improve the administrative litigation system by adjusting the jurisdiction allocation methods to solve the major difficulties in the filing and hearing of such cases and in the enforcement of judgments.

说明 1：把 beyond administrative divisions 改为单数。复数可能导致歧义，成为"超越多个行政区划的案件"；其实只需要超越一个。**法律起草的规则之一就是尽量是用单数。**

说明 2：画双线的两个逗号，第一个逗号之后的短句，是逗号前短句的手段；第二个逗号后的短句，是逗号前短句的结果。译文可以体现出这层逻辑关系。

说明 3："行政案件"（administrative cases）在中国和美国是两个不同的概念。大陆法系（包括中国）的行政案件，在行政法院（或普通法院的行政庭）进行；美国的行政案件，是指隶属于行政部门的行政法庭（administrative tribunals）处理的案件，对行政法庭裁决不服的，可以上诉到普通法院，作为民事案件处理。美国法院不划分刑事、民事、行政审等判庭。在中国，对行政决定不服的，可以申请行政机关内部的行政复议（administrative reconsideration），对复议结果不服的，可以向法院提起行政诉讼。尽管知道这些区别，译员也没办法作过多解释，只能寄希望于读者了解中国情况，按中国的语境来理解。

说明 4："调整行政诉讼案件管辖制度"，是指哪里发生的行政案件，不让哪里的法院去审，而是让别的法院来审，防止地方政府干预。make reasonable adjustments to the system of determining jurisdiction for administrative litigation cases 意思正确，稍嫌啰唆。建议改为 adjusting the jurisdiction allocation system。

说明 5："合理调整"当中的合理可以不译，因为英文中的 adjust 已经隐含合理性。

例 11：

原文：再审重在解决依法纠错、维护裁判权威。

译文：<u>Retrials</u> should concentrate on correcting <u>erroneous rulings</u> and maintaining the authority of rulings.

建议：<u>Extraordinary legal remedy</u> should concentrate on correcting errors according to law and maintaining the authority of rulings and judgments.

说明:"再审"是为纠正已经发生法律效力(两审终审之后)的错误判决、裁定,依照审判监督程序,对案件重新进行的审理。"重审"是指一审之后,当事人提起了上诉,二审法院发现一审的事实认定有问题,或者程序有违法之处,就把案件发回一审重新审理;还是按照一审的程序处理,判决结果仍然可以上诉。这两个概念有严格区分。翻译为retrial,把"再审"变成了"重审":

> A new trial or <u>retrial</u> is a recurrence of a court case. Depending on the rules of the jurisdiction, a new trial may occur if a jury is unable to reach a verdict; a trial court grants a party's motion for a new trial, usually on the grounds of a legal defect in the original trial; or an appellate court reverses a judgment under circumstances requiring that the case be tried again.[①]

"再审"的说法是 extraordinary legal remedy:

> <u>An extraordinary legal remedy</u> differs from an appeal. The difference relates to whether or not the judgment that the appeals court is reviewing is final or not. An appeal ... involves the appeals court examining a judgment that is not yet final ... <u>An extraordinary legal remedy, on the other hand, involves the reopening of final proceedings, whether those proceedings became final after trial (where no appeal was filed by the parties) or after appeal.</u> As is apparent from the name of this remedy—an extraordinary legal remedy—this sort of <u>reopening of a</u>

---

① 维基百科 New trial 条(http://en.wikipedia.org/wiki/New_trial,读取日期 2015-05-05)。

final judgment occurs only rarely. Even more rare is the reopening of the final judgment by a person other than the accused ...①

根据这段解释，必要时也可以用 reopen（a case）表示"再审"。

## 结　　语

本文通过具体例子，说明在翻译党政文件时应注意的问题。在理解方面，译者首先应该理解文件所针对的弊端，才能理解文字背后的含义。理解不能靠主观猜测，要做广泛的调查研究。同时，译者要关注句子内部及句子之间的逻辑关系，特别注意以逗号隔开的短句，到底是并列关系，还是递进关系，从而选择合适的翻译方法。在表达方面，译者应在理解的基础上，以读者熟悉和专业的说法准确传达出原意，必要时辅之以注释，特别注意检查译文是否有歧义；同一个词（如"司法"），在不同的语境下，有不同含义，需要区别对待，不一定译为同一个词。在取舍方面，译文语言应尽量简洁，视情况决定是否删除冗余表达；对于原文表述不当之处，译者可以适当润色。最后，无论是理解、表达还是取舍，都需要译者要具备一定的专业知识；如不熟悉专业，则需要做大量调查研究或请专家审校译文。

---

① "Appeals and Extraordinary Legal Remedy"，引自 United States Institute of Peace 网站（http://www.usip.org/sites/default/files/MC2/MC2-19-Ch12.pdf，读取日期 2015-05-05）。

# 第七讲

## 陪审团制度及相关术语的翻译

司法审判中需要作出两项决定，一是被主张的事实是否发生（"定罪"）；二是如果发生，按法律应该怎么办（"量刑"）。在不同的司法制度下，作出决定的主体不同。在大陆法系，两项决定通常都由法官作出。在英美法系，事实问题（question of fact）通常交给陪审团认定，法律问题（question of law）则交给法官来决定。因此，陪审团又被称为事实认定者（trier/finder of fact），法官则被称为法律认定者（trier/finder of law）。在英美法系，也有一些案件仅由法官来审理（称为 bench trial），这时，法官既是事实认定者，又是法律认定者。除了量刑之外，审理过程中的法律问题也由法官把控，包括维持法庭秩序、排除非法证据（illegally obtained evidence）、发现（find）和告知（instruct）陪审团相关法律规定。注意：陪审团并非只管发现事实，还包括确定事实后，判断该事实是否属于法律规定的情形，进而作出有罪无罪决定；相关法律规定则由法官告知陪审团。

### Trial by Ordeal 考验式审判

在陪审团审判和其他现代审判方法出现之前，世界各地普遍采用"神明裁判"（*judicium Dei*/judgment of God/divine judgment，或译"神判""圣决"），决定争议双方的胜负。具体方法包括火审

（ordeals by fire or hot iron）①、水审（ordeals by water）②、十字架审（trials by the cross）③、圣餐审（trials by Eucharist）④、吞噬审（trials by corsned）⑤和决斗审（trials by battle/combat）⑥等，统称 trial by ordeal。其理论基础是上帝会站在无辜者一方，并通过干预裁决过程表现出来。trial by ordeal 一般翻译为"神判"或"神明裁判"，与 *judicium Dei* 的译法相同。虽然这两个说法内涵一致，但既然英文是不同的表达方式，侧重点不同，汉语也应该给出不同的译法，否则一些语境下不容易翻译。比如："In such a world, the divine judgment of the trial by ordeal seems reasonable and desirable."，因此，笔者建议译为"考验式审判"。尽管"考验"不能完全反映 ordeal（严酷考验）的意思，但可作为权宜之计，通过解释来说明不是一般的"考验"

---

① 被告人手持烧红的烙铁或赤脚在烧红的犁铧上走几步，如果没有烧伤，即为无罪；或者是，烧伤后包扎起来，过 3 天由专人检查，如果出现愈合迹象，即为无罪；如果开始溃烂，即为有罪（维基百科 Trial by ordeal 条，https://en.wikipedia.org/wiki/Trial_by_ordeal，读取日期 2015-07-01；Columbia Encyclopedia, 6th ed. (New York: Columbia University Press, 2001.)）。

② 被告人被要求从开水中取出一块石头。烫伤的手经过包扎，3 天后如果开始愈合，则无罪。或者是，将被告人摁到水缸里 3 次，如果每次都浮起来，就是无罪；如果沉下去，就是有罪（用于审偷猎者）（同上）。还有一种方法，是把被告人捆起来投入水中，如果水不接受她（即如果浮起来），就是有罪；否则就是无罪（用于审判女巫）（同注①）。

③ 即指控者和被告人分别站在竖立的十字架两边，平举双手，谁先放下，谁认输（同上）。

④ 被告人被要求宣誓自己是无辜的，然后吃下圣餐；如果被告人撒谎，一年内会死掉；如果没有死，就是无罪（同上）。

⑤ 指教士在一块面包或奶酪上念下咒语，让被告人吃下，被告人如果顺利吃完，则他被宣布无罪；如果面包哽在咽喉里，则被认为这是他有罪的证明。念下咒语的面包有时也被称为"corsned"（薛波：《元照英美法词典》，北京大学出版社，2013 年，第 752 页）。

⑥ 双方进行决斗，胜出者的主张得到支持（同上）。

（译为"严酷考验式审判"有些长）。trial by ordeal 以前没有翻译出来，原因恐怕也是 ordeal 无法很简洁地翻译出来。

## Jury Selection 挑选陪审员

挑选陪审员的过程，也叫 striking a jury。在美国，如果一个案件需要由陪审团来审理，法院首先从登记选民名单（registered voters）、驾驶执照名单（driver's license list）或水电气用户名单（utility subscribers）等政府掌握的名单中随机抽取若干人（美国无身份证制度，所以无法通过身份证号码摇号），向每人发放问卷，询问诸如公民资格、有无残疾、能否听懂英语、参加审判有无困难等基本问题。通过初步筛查的人，被集体称作 a jury pool（候选陪审团/候选库/备选库）或 a venire。venire 是拉丁语，简化自 venire facias，字面意思是（you should cause）to come，是法官给法警的令状（writ），命令法警把候选人传唤到庭，转义为被传唤到庭的一群人。其中的每个人，被称为"候选陪审员"（a venireman, prospective/potential juror, candidate）。

法院把候选陪审员传唤（summons）到法院后，进一步筛选，剔除（exclude）不合格候选人。法官和控辩双方律师会通过询问，剔除可能产生偏见的人。比如，询问潜在陪审员是否与被告人有亲属关系、代理律师是否为你或近亲代理过案子、你或你的家人是否遭受过犯罪侵害、是否参与过犯罪等等。如果回答是肯定的，则不得作为本案陪审员。这个过程叫 voir dire，字面意思是 speak the truth（说真话），即要求潜在陪审员实事求是地告诉法庭实际情况，可以译为"资格审查"。提问时，可以面向全体，要求以举手方式回答，也可以逐一询问，要求口头回答。

如果是逐一询问排除，公诉人先问，如果公诉人觉得可以留下，辩护人再问，辩护人也觉得可以留下，就会产生一个双方公认的陪审员。一般情况下，公诉人通过提问剔除可能对被告人产生同情的人；辩护律师通过提问剔除与被害人职业和背景相似的人，因为他们可能同情被害人，这对被告人不利。这种说出原因的排除，叫有因排除（challenge for cause / strike for cause / removal for cause）。双方还有几个"无因排除"（peremptory challenge）名额。无因排除，是指控辩双方律师不说任何理由，从陪审员候选名单中剔除某一潜在陪审员。无因排除可能有几种原因，包括预感这个陪审员可能不利于自己，但不能基于种族或性别因素。涉及死刑的案件，陪审员不得是废除死刑的倡导者或认为凡是可判死刑的故意杀人案件（capital murder）都必须判处死刑的人。排除这两种人的陪审团，叫作 death-qualified jury（符合死刑案资格的陪审团）。

这样，经过筛选，最后剩下大约 15 人，就是双方公认中立的陪审员，其中 12 个是正式陪审员，3 个是备用陪审员。这些人全部自始至终参加审判，如果正式陪审员中有人临时来不了，候补者马上填补。候补陪审员不参加讨论和投票。组成陪审员的过程，叫作 empanel a jury。筛选过程的细节，在联邦法院和各州法院不尽相同[1][2]。

陪审团成员的挑选过程，保证了陪审团的公正性和控辩双方对陪审团的信心，从而使陪审员的裁决为控辩双方和社会所接受。中国一些地方也在试验采用陪审团，以提高法院裁判的公信力（public

---

[1] "Jury Service — Frequently Asked Questions"，引自 Southern Distinct of Illinois United States Distinct Court 网站（http://www.ilsd.uscourts.gov/JuryFAQ.aspx，读取日期 2015-07-01）。

[2] G. Bermant: *Jury Selection Procedures in United States District Courts*. (Washington: Federal Judicial Center, 1982).

confidence），减轻法院面临的压力。

## Jury Instructions 给陪审团的指示

法官在开庭之前、开庭过程中以及开庭结束后，都会向陪审团作出指示。指示的内容基本是标准化的。加利福尼亚州最高法院编写的《刑事案件标准化陪审团指示》长达 600 多页[①]，包括审理各种犯罪的指示。此外，控辩双方可以根据案件具体情况，向法官建议指示的内容。法官的指示发生在庭审的不同阶段，包括开庭审理之前、之中和举证结束之后，主要指示内容包括：庭审的程序；法官和陪审团的职责；法庭中哪些发言属于证据，哪些不属于证据（而是意见）；陪审团只能依据法庭上获得的证据作出判断，不能自行调查，不能以其他任何消息来源作为判断依据；陪审团审查证据时要结合自己的生活常识；陪审团不要受法官可能发表的倾向性言论的影响；如何判断证人的可信度（credibility）；如何对待没有出庭作证的证人的宣誓证言（affidavit）；被告人被指控的罪名；被指控罪名的犯罪要件（elements of the crime）；证明必须达到的标准（standard of proof）；如何对待犯罪前科（criminal record）；做笔记时需要注意的问题；何时可以证言的逐字记录（transcript of testimony）；帮助评议（deliberation）；评议时要选举陪审团团长（foreman）；最后要作出一致裁决并填写裁决书（verdict forms），等等。总之，法官的指示非常详细，语言浅显易懂，只要具备普通的理解能力，完全可以通过法官的讲解，学会本案所需的法律知识。下面以被告人被控"醉酒扰乱公共秩序罪"（disorderly intoxication）为例，说明法官就该罪名向

---

[①] "Florida Standard Jury Instructions in Criminal Cases"，引自 Florida Supreme Court 网站（http://www.floridasupremecourt.org/jury_instructions/instructions-ch1.shtml，读取日期 2015-07-01）。

陪审团作的解释:

To prove the crime of Disorderly Intoxication, the State must prove the following two elements beyond a reasonable doubt:
*Give a or b as applicable.*
a. [1. (Defendant) was intoxicated, and 2. [He] [She] endangered the safety of another [person] [property].]
b. [1. (Defendant) was intoxicated or drank any alcoholic beverage in a [public place] [in or upon a public conveyance] and 2. [He] [She] caused a public disturbance.]

*Definition*

"Intoxication" means more than merely being under the influence of an alcoholic beverage. Intoxication means that the defendant must have been so affected from the drinking of an alcoholic beverage as to have lost or been deprived of the normal control of either [his] [her] body or [his] [her] mental faculties, or both. Intoxication is synonymous with "drunk."

*Optional Definition*

A "public place" is a place where the public has a right to be and to go. The defendant's admission that [he] [she] drank an alcoholic beverage is not sufficient by itself to prove beyond a reasonable doubt that [he] [she] was under the influence of an alcoholic beverage but this admission may be taken into consideration along with other evidence.[①]

---

① G. Bermant: *Jury Selection Procedures in United States District Courts.* (Washington: Federal Judicial Center, 1982).

我相信，即使没有法律知识，陪审团也可以理解这样的解释，并依法作出被告人有罪无罪的判断。不少人认为陪审团对法律一无所知，实际上是一种误解。法官在办案过程中，已经对陪审团进行了普法教育。这也是陪审团制度的一个优点。

## Verdict 陪审团裁决

陪审团经过评议，得出一致的结论后，需要在一张裁决表上打钩。根据被告人数多少，指控罪行数量，填写不同的表格。有多个被告人的，每个被告人需要填写一张表格。下面是两个例子[①]。

用于单一被告人被控单一罪行的裁决表：

　　We, the jury, find as follows, as to the defendant in this case: (check only one)

　　　　___a. The defendant is guilty of (crime charged).

　　　　___b. The defendant is guilty of (a lesser included offense).

　　　　___c. The defendant is not guilty.

用于单一被告人被控多项罪行的裁决表：

　　We, the jury, find as follows, as to Count I of the charge: (check only one as to this count)

　　　　___a. The defendant is guilty of (crime charged).

　　　　___b. The defendant is guilty of (a lesser included offense).

　　　　___c. The defendant is not guilty.

　　We, the jury, find as follows, as to Count II of the charge: (check only one as to this count)

---

[①]　G. Bermant: *Jury Selection Procedures in United States District Courts*. (Washington: Federal Judicial Center, 1982).

    ___ a. The defendant is guilty of (crime charged).
    ___ b. The defendant is guilty of (a lesser included offense).
    ___ c. The defendant is not guilty.

A lesser included offense（内含较轻犯罪）是指包含在被指控犯罪中的较轻犯罪。比如 assault 包含在 robbery 中，battery 包含在 murder 中，false imprisonment 包含在 kidnapping 中。这里的意思是，如果不够资格定一个较重的罪，可以定重罪中包含的轻罪。

陪审团填好表格之后，一般会装在信封里密封，然后交给法官。法官会在法庭之上，当着陪审团的面打开信封，当庭宣布裁决结果。这个信封叫 sealed verdict。所谓 return a verdict，就是填好表交回来，也即作出裁决的意思。

## Mistrial 无效审判／审判失败／失审

如果审判过程出现了根本性错误或失误，可能对当事人造成无法弥补的损害，法官会宣布审判无效或失败（mistrial）。通常导致审判失败的原因有：法院缺乏管辖权（jurisdiction）、不该让陪审团看到的证据陪审团看到了、由于当事人或陪审员作为导致违反正当程序（due process）原则、陪审团组成后发现某成员的资格有问题（disqualification）也无候补陪审员替代等。这是 mistrial 的本义。日常生活中，人们也把陪审团经反复磋商，仍无法取得一致的情形，叫 mistrial，其实更准确的叫法是 hung jury（未决陪审团）。审判无效（失败）等于审判没有发生，这时公诉人可以选择撤诉或由法庭重新挑选陪审员，再次举行审判（retrial，重审）。注意：retrial（也叫 new trial, trial de novo），相当于中国的"重审"（两审终审之内重新审理），而不是"再审"（两审终审之外重新审理）。再审可以译为

reopen a case，或者 extraordinary legal remedy[①]。

## Directed Verdict 指令裁决

如果负有举证责任的一方（公诉人）在法庭上提供的证据显然不能成立（no *prima facie* evidence），任何讲理的陪审团（reasonable jury）都不会认可，则法官无须等陪审团评议，就可以直接指示陪审团作出特定裁决，叫"指令裁决"。在刑事审判中，指令裁决的结果就是无罪释放被告人（acquittal）。这个概念近年来逐步被 judgment as a matter of law（JMOL）取代。JMOL 的意思是"事实已经很清楚了，无须再认定，按法律规定裁判即可"，可以译为"作为法律问题裁判"。也有译为"依法裁判"的，但这个译法要按照英文语境来理解，不等于汉语中的"依法裁判"（作出有法律依据的裁判）。JMOL 需要一方当事人提出申请（motion，也译为"动议"，动词是 move）[②]。

## Summary Procedure 简易程序

民事案件中的 JMOL 也叫 summary judgment，是指未经完整审判程序作出的判决，可以译为"简易程序判决"。如果当事人对案件中的主要事实（material facts）不存在真正的争议（genuine issue），或者案件仅涉及法律问题，法院可以不经开庭审理尽快解决案件。根据美国《联邦民事诉讼规则》，在诉讼开始 20 天后，如通过诉答程序（pleadings）、证据开示（discovery）、宣誓证明（affidavit），一方

---

① 维基百科 Mistrials 条（https://en.wikipedia.org/wiki/Trial#Mistrials，读取日期 2015-07-01）。

② 维基百科 Directed verdict 条（https://en.wikipedia.org/wiki/Directed_verdict，读取日期 2015-07-01）。

当事人认为双方对案件的主要事实不存在真正争议，觉得自己在法律上应当胜诉，则可随时申请法院作出简易程序判决。简易程序判决可就全部案件，也可就案件中的部分事实作出①。

词典通常将 summary judgment 译为"简易判决""即决裁判"，不易理解，没有反映这个概念的实质，"简易程序判决"意思更为清楚明了。summary 一词，在其他搭配中的意思也是"简易程序"的意思。比如 summary trial，是指独任法官主持的审判，相对于陪审团审判。这是爱尔兰某网站的资料：

> There are two types of trial:
> - A summary trial — a trial conducted by a judge sitting alone
> - Trial by jury — a trial conducted by a judge sitting with a jury②

因此，可以把 summary trial 翻译为"简易程序审判"或"独任法官审判"。trial by jury 当然是陪审团审判。这两类审判分别对应于两类犯罪：

> - Summary offences, that is, offences that are tried by a judge sitting alone
> - Indictable offences, that is, offences that can be tried by a judge and jury
>
> Certain indictable offences may be tried summarily.③

---

① 薛波：《元照英美法词典》，北京大学出版社，2014 年，第 1309 页。
② "Criminal Trials: Summary Trial"，引自 Citizens Information 网站（http://www.citizensinformation.ie/en/justice/criminal_law/criminal_trial/criminal_trial.html#laf341，读取日期 2015-07-01）。
③ 同上。

summary offences 可以翻译为"简易程序犯罪",indictable offences 可以译为"普通程序犯罪"(所谓"普通",要放在英美法语境下来理解,即有陪审团参与之义)。法律词典上把 indictable 译为"可被控告的""可被提起公诉的",放在此处行不通:难道简易程序犯罪不需要起诉吗?实际上,indictable 的意思是"可被大陪审团起诉的",因为大陪审团批准的起诉书叫作 indictment。公诉机关直接提起的起诉(不采用大陪审团制度)叫作 information、accusation或 complaint。因此,indictable offences 字面意思是"可被大陪审团起诉的犯罪",作为"简易程序犯罪"的对立面,翻译为"普通程序犯罪"更为清楚明了。

加拿大也是按程序把犯罪分为 summary offences 和 indictable offences,分别相当于美国的 misdemeanor(轻罪)和 felony(重罪)。因此,summary offences 和 indictable offences 也可以直接翻译为"轻罪"和"重罪"[①]。

在美国,可能判 6 个月以下徒刑的轻罪不适用陪审团审判。美国宪法第六修正案规定所有刑事案件都要由陪审团审判,但由于陪审团审判费时费力,所以并没有完全执行。一些人还在争取执行。中国的"普通程序",可以翻译为 regular procedure;"简易程序",可以译为 summary procedure。另外还有"普通程序简易审"的说法,不同于简易程序,可以译为 simplified regular procedure。

summary execution 通常翻译为"即决处决",是指战争中或动乱中不经正常审判程序随意处决被指控人的行为,译为"未经正当程序处决"更为准确。与此意思相近的一个概念是 extrajudicial killing,意思是未经司法程序处决被指控人。有的地方译为"法外处决",意思

---

① 维基百科 Indictment 条(https://en.wikipedia.org/wiki/Indictment,读取日期 2015-07-01)。

似乎不太清楚，也许可以译为"司法外处决"，或"未经司法程序处决"。

## Sentencing 量刑

通过庭审活动（trial），法官或陪审团决定被告人是否有罪。如果被告人被认定有罪，接下来（至少两天之后）就要举行量刑听证（sentence hearing）。

法官在量刑上享有很大的自由裁量权。法官不仅考虑犯罪情节的轻重，还考虑被告人的品质和社会状况。法官会请政府矫正部门（corrections department）提交一份量刑前的调查报告（pre-sentence report）。矫正部门就会对被告人、他的亲朋好友、工作单位进行调查，摸清他的教育情况、就业情况、家庭情况、身体和精神健康状况以及与社区的联系（community connections）。报告中还会包括报告人的前科（criminal records, prior convictions），以及被告人、警察和其他证人对案件事实的认识。这份报告会事先交给控辩双方。在量刑听证上，双方都会利用证据和证人向法官建议自己认为合适的刑期。但即使双方在认罪协商（plea bargaining）中已经就刑期达成一致，法官也可以不予理会。遇到这种情况，被告人可以收回认罪（withdraw a guilty plea），重新走完整的审判程序（full trial，即用陪审团审判）。但先前的认罪不会对庭审产生消极影响。在个别州，陪审团可以提出量刑建议，法官可以根据情况酌减，但不能增加。

控辩双方对量刑不服的，都可以上诉。对量刑的上诉仅限于法官适用法律错误，以及违反了正当程序和平等保护的原则。

联邦量刑委员会制定了《联邦量刑指南》（The Federal Sentencing

Guidelines），以减少各法院在量刑方面的不一致[①]。

中国采用"审"（conviction）"判"（sentencing）合一的模式，没有专门的量刑听证，但近年来也在探讨"审""判"分离改革。中国的控方也可以对定罪量刑进行上诉，但称为"抗诉"，理论基础是检察机关是法律监督机关，地位高于法院，不能用"上"字。译为英文，如用 protest 一词，需要解释。必要时，可以直接翻译为 appeal。

## Grand Jury 大陪审团

大陪审团设在法院，但独立于法官运行。通常由 12—23 人组成，在刑事案件中决定是否有足够证据（sufficient evidence）可对被告人起诉。大陪审团不同于小陪审团（petit jury，即平时所称"陪审团"）。小陪审团决定被告人是否有罪（guilt），大陪审团只需决定检察官是否提供了足够证据，可对被告人正式起诉（indict a defendant）。大陪审团只要认为控方有"合理根据"（probable cause），就可以批准起诉；小陪审团认定有罪的证明标准则是"排除合理怀疑"（beyond reasonable doubt）。大陪审团通常都同意检察官的请求，对被告人起诉。如前所述，经大陪审团批准的起诉书叫作 indictment，否则叫作 information 等。大陪审团在批准起诉时，会在公诉人提交的 bill of indictment 背面写上 A true bill；如不批准则写上 Not a true bill[②]。

---

[①] 维基百科 United States Federal Sentencing Guidelines 条（https://en.wikipedia.org/wiki/United_States_Federal_Sentencing_Guidelines，读取日期 2015-07-01）。

[②] 维基百科 Grand jury 条（https://en.wikipedia.org/wiki/Grand_jury，读取日期 2015-07-01）。

中国没有大陪审团制度。大陪审团的职能，包括在我们的审查起诉活动之中。

## 人民陪审员 Lay Judges

我国有人民陪审员制度，是指国家审判机关审判案件时吸收非职业法官作为陪审员，与职业法官或职业审判员一起审判案件的一种司法制度。人民陪审员在法院执行职务期间，与法官享有同等的权利。人民陪审员在词典上通常翻译为"people's assessor""people's juror"，但国际上通常的说法是 lay judges，有时称为 assessors：

> A **lay judge** is a person assisting a judge in a trial, and as such are sometimes called lay assessors. Lay judges are used in some civil law jurisdictions. Japan began implementing a new lay judge system in 2009. Lay judges are appointed volunteers, and often require some legal instruction. However, they are not permanent officers, attending proceedings about once a month, and often receive only nominal or "costs covered" pay. Lay judges are usually used when the country does not have juries. Unlike jurymen, lay judges are usually politically appointed, not randomly selected, and may not be rejected by the prosecution, defense or the permanent judges. Lay judges are similar to magistrates of England and Wales, although magistrates sit about twice more often.[①]

实际上，lay 的意思就是"普通百姓""人民"。日本的"人民陪审员"叫作"裁判员"，相对于"裁判官"（法官），法务省

---

① 维基百科 Lay judge 条（https://en.wikipedia.org/wiki/Lay_judge，读取日期 2015-07-01）。

等专门规定,正式翻译用音译(saiban-in),说明时用 citizen judge system、lay judge system,因为大陆法系通常使用 lay judges:

> **裁判員制度**(さいばんいんせいど)とは、特定の刑事裁判において、有権者(市民)から事件ごとに選ばれた裁判員が裁判官とともに審理に参加する日本の司法・裁判制度をいう。
> 「裁判員」の英訳については、法務省や最高裁判所などは公式には **saiban-in** を用いるが、説明的に **citizen judge system**(「市民裁判官」)や **lay judge system**(「民間裁判官」)といった訳語が用いられることもある。日本と同じローマ法体系に属するヨーロッパの国々でも裁判員制度が存在し、これらの国々の裁判員は普通は lay judge と英訳されている①。

在传统的大陆法系国家,也有引进英美法系陪审团制度的,如俄罗斯帝国时代,1864 年亚历山大二世实行司法改革,引入陪审团制度,1917 年十月革命后废除,1993 年俄罗斯联邦再次引入陪审团审判②。亚历山大二世引入陪审团时,不像现代陪审团那样仅仅作出有罪或无罪判决,还有第三个选项:有罪但不处罚。因为亚历山大二世认为不讲道义的公正是不公正③。德国历史上也引进过陪审团,但后来被废除。中国一些地方,也在进行司法民主化改革,方式之一就是

---

① 维基百科"裁判員制度"条(https://ja.wikipedia.org/wiki/ 裁判員制度,读取日期 2015-07-01)。

② 维基百科 Jury trial: Russia 条(https://en.wikipedia.org/wiki/Jury_trial#Russia,读取日期 2015-07-01)。

③ 维基百科 Judicial reform of Alexander 条(https://en.wikipedia.org/wiki/Judicial_reform_of_Alexander_II,读取日期 2015-07-01)。

采用类似陪审团的制度。比如河南的一些法院引入"人民观审团",让观审团成员参加法院庭审并独立发表意见,作为人民法院裁判的参考。笔者将其译为 observing jury[①]。

---

① 《安阳中院试水人民观审团机制》,引自和讯网(http://news.hexun.com/2013-09-18/158114768.html,读取日期 2015-07-01)。

# 第八讲

## 美国刑事案件庭审过程及相关术语的翻译

美国刑事案件的庭审程序（trial procedure）一般包括以下阶段：筛选陪审员（choosing a jury）、开场陈述（opening statements）、证人作证〔witness testimony，包括直接询问（direct examination）和交叉询问（cross-examination）〕、最后辩论（closing arguments）、指示陪审团（jury instruction）、陪审团评议和裁决（jury deliberation and verdict）。与陪审团有关的一些内容之前已经作过介绍，本文介绍其他相关内容。

### Opening Statements 开场陈述

Opening statements 的意思是开场白。庭审开始之后，法官会先请公诉人、然后请辩护人向法庭简单介绍案件，说明自己"对案件的主张"（见下一部分），以及将通过什么证人证明自己的主张。辩护人可以选择不作开场陈述，因为辩护人没有证明责任（burden of proof）。

美国的法官或/和陪审团在庭审开始之前，对案情一无所知（中国法官看过案卷），他们对案件的了解，完全依赖审判过程中控辩双方的介绍和出具的证据。开场白的目的，就是为法官和陪审团理解案件提供一个"路线图"（road map）或"路标"（sign post）。

开场陈述好比是议论文的开头部分。作者需要向读者交代清楚自己的观点和论证逻辑，以及将要使用的证据和证据要证明的问题

（只说明要点）。凡是许诺提供的证据，将来举证（presentation of evidence）的时候一定提供。不能作空头许诺，否则会对自己的主张造成重大伤害。

在开场陈述中只作客观"陈述"（statement），不作"论证"（argument）。否则对方会提出"反对"（objection），要求法官制止。"论证"要等到最后论证（closing argument, summation）阶段再做。

法官会告诉陪审团，开场陈述和最后论证都不是证据，而是控辩双方的见解。陪审团要根据双方证人实际作证的情况，判断哪一方的主张更可信。①

## Theory of the Case 对案件的主张

公诉人和辩护人在开庭之前，都会从各自的立场出发，形成一个得到自己证据（事实）支撑的观点。比如，公诉人认为，这是一起故意伤害案，并利用相关事实/证据加以论证；辩护人认为这是一起正当防卫的案件，并利用相关事实加以论证。这样的两个观点及支撑两个观点的事实，就叫案件主张。案件主张可以说是双方分别从自己的角度讲述一个"故事"（story）。

主张可以分为法律主张和事实主张。还有人提出包括情感主张②。法律主张（legal theory of the case）就是"法律站在我的一边"；事实主张（factual theory of the case）就是实际发生了什么事；

---

① *West's Encyclopedia of American Law* 第 2 版，转引自 The Free Dictionary 网站（http://legal-dictionary.thefreedictionary.com/opening+statement，读取日期 2015-08-31）。

② J. G. Douglass: *Trial Advocacy Fundamentals: A (Very Short) Primer on the Basics of Trial Advocacy*, (Richmond: University of Richmond School of Law, 2002).

情感主张（persuasive/thematic theory of the case）就是"判我当事人胜诉是公平的"，即要用情感打动陪审团。法律主张和事实主张要相互契合。

同一个案件，双方可能会基于同一组事实，通过强调事实的不同方面，提出截然相反的主张。公诉人和辩护人在法庭上的对抗（contest），实质上是两个主张的对抗。双方在法庭上的举证、质证和辩论活动，都要围绕自己的主张。公诉人对案件的主张，可以简称公诉主张；辩护人对案件的主张，可以简称辩护主张、辩护思路等。

个别情况下，可能准备几套主张，以应对庭审中出现的各种情况，例如：

> My client didn't take the pig. But if he took the pig, it was actually a gift from the farmer. But if it wasn't a gift, he was so crazy he didn't know what he was doing.[1]

Theory of the case 当中的 theory，意思是"见解""意见""主张"，不是"理论"。直译为"案件理论"会令人费解。

## Witness Testimony and Examination
## 证人作证和询问证人

### 1. Present one's case 举证

在一审（trial）程序中，控辩双方在分别作完开场陈述之后，法官会问："Is the prosecution ready to present its case?"，这句话的字面意思是：控方准备好展示自己的事实了吗？由于美国法庭审判以证人当庭作证为核心，公诉人展示事实的方式就是传唤证人到庭作证，

---

[1] 韦迈乐：《牛津高阶英语词典》，第 7 版，商务印书馆，2007 年。

所以，这句话的实际意思是：公诉人准备好传唤证人了吗？在公诉人举证完毕之后（after the prosecution rests its case），法官会问："Is the defense ready to present its case?"（辩方准备好举证了吗？）。这里的 case 是指诉讼中支持一方的一系列事实或论点（a set of facts or arguments supporting one side in a legal action）①。

注意，美国控辩双方向法庭提交物证（physical evidence；不是 material evidence/实质性证据）、书证（documentary evidence）等，需要首先经过证人确认，而不是直接交给法庭。比如，公诉人有一件凶器，需要提交给法庭，就需要拿起这把凶器，问作证的警察（testifying police）："你认得这把刀吗？"警察："认得。"公诉人："这把刀是从哪里得到的？"警察："在嫌疑人家里起获的。"公诉人："你怎么确定这把凶器就是杀人凶器？"警察："经 DNA 鉴定，上面的血迹是死者的。"如此等等。最后，公诉人会问法官："尊敬的法官，法院能否接受这件证据为本案的证据？"法官会询问辩护人是否有异议。如果没有，法官会宣布将这份证据接受为"证物"（exhibit），并编号。"举证"是法庭审理最重要的阶段。

中国的法院，审判过程中证人很少出庭作证（警察作证更是罕见），所以，控辩双方直接向法庭提交各种证据，包括证人证言（witness statements）；这在奉行口头审理原则（orality principle）的美国是不可想象的。在美国，证人的书面证言，甚至被认为是"传闻证据"。②

## 2. Live testimony 当庭作证

当庭作证的证人，可以称为 live witness（现场证人）。美国法

---

① 韦迈乐：《牛津高阶英语词典》，第 7 版，商务印书馆，2007 年。

② D. J. Capra: "Prior Statements of Testifying Witness: Drafting Choices to Eliminate or Loosen the Strictures of the Hearsay Rule", *Fordham Law Review*, 84 (2016), 1429-53.

院强调证人当庭作证（基于口头审理原则），证人在庭外书写的书面证言，不能在证人不出庭的情况下，被控方或辩方拿到法庭作为证据使用（这在中国是常规，因为证人不愿出庭）。书面证言在法庭只能用来质疑当庭作证的真实性。例如，控方（或辩方）如果发现对方的证人在直接询问时的证言与以前的书面证言（如向警察提供的证言或预审时的证言——这些都可以在开庭前通过证据开示获得）不符，可以通过交叉询问来固定（perpetuate）相关证言（即让证人分别再次确认当庭证言和以前的证言），然后在最后辩论时，向陪审团指出这一矛盾，证明该证人证言不可信。

鉴于美国的认罪协商（plea bargaining，也译为"辩诉交易"）制度，绝大多数案件不经法庭审理，直接进入量刑程序（sentencing），这就意味着在大多数案件中，证人是不用出庭作证的。在强化中国证人出庭制度时，这也是应当注意的事实。因为要求所有情况下证人出庭作证需要大量的司法资源。对于经核实为自愿认罪的轻罪案件，便没有必要要求证人出庭。

## 3. Witness preparation 准备证人

准备证人不是在法庭完成的，但对完成举证工作至关重要。控辩双方要求证人出庭作证之前，必须评估证人在自己完成证明任务中的作用，通过交叉询问发现可能对自己带来的伤害，设法消除证人的疑虑。对证人的准备，不是操纵证言（那是犯罪，叫作 tampering witness 或者 tampering with the evidence），而是与证人沟通好，以可信的方式向陪审团呈现自己的所见所闻。[①]

---

① S. G. Litvin: "Case Preparation & Trial Outline"，引自 American Bar 网站（http://apps.americanbar.org/labor/annualconference/2007/materials/data/papers/005.pdf，读取日期 2015-08-31）。

## 4. Examination and cross-examination 询问和交叉询问

公诉人（或辩护人）逐一传唤自己的证人到庭后，首先通过自己的提问，让证人把自己感知到（看到或听到）的（有利于本方的）事情经过说一遍。这个过程叫"询问"（examination）；询问本方证人时，叫作 direct examination（直接询问）或者 examination-in-chief（主询问）。直接询问只能用开放性问题（open-ended questions），即以 W 和 H 开头的问题；不允许用诱导性问题（leading questions）（见下条）。但如果询问过程中发现自己的证人不配合，可以要求法官确认该证人为 hostile witness（敌对证人），从而准予使用诱导性问题。[①]

交叉询问（cross-examination）是控方或辩方对对方传来证人的询问。因为询问指向对方证人，彼此交叉，故名。交叉询问通常使用诱导性问题。因为对方的证人被默认为"敌对证人"，不会与询问者配合。交叉询问的问题应该简短，只涉及一个需要确认的事实。比如："当时天很黑，是吧？"而不是问："当时天很黑，还下着大雨，你距离事故现场还有 100 米，是吧？"

有些国家允许交叉询问时问及直接询问中没有提及的问题；有些国家只允许在交叉询问中针对直接询问提及的信息提问。

无论是直接询问还是交叉询问，都应围绕自己的主张进行，通过这些问题的回答，一步步证明自己的主张。

交叉询问最后，不要问"画蛇添足的问题"（one question too many），例如：

——所以，你不可能看得见，证人先生，是吧？

---

① 维基百科 Direct examination 条（https://en.wikipedia.org/wiki/Direct_examination，读取日期 2015-08-31）。

这样会招致证人的解释：

——实际上我看得很清楚。我当时带着望远镜呢，正朝那个方向看呢！

律师要等到证人最后论证阶段、证人不在场的时候再面向陪审团作出这样的推断。

经过第一轮直接和交叉询问后，还可以针对交叉询问中出现的问题，进行第二轮直接询问，叫作 redirect (examination)，以及第二轮交叉询问，叫作 recross (examination)。

中国传统的庭审方式没有直接询问和交叉询问，由法官主导查明事实，对被告人/证人的询问由法官来做，而不像英美法系那样由法官维持秩序，让控辩双方提问。现在虽然在向对抗制靠拢，但法律事务工作者并不熟悉直接询问和交叉询问的技巧，甚至对于什么是交叉询问存在误解。据说（顾永忠，口头交流），一些人把法官询问之外的控辩双方问话，都笼统称为"交叉询问"。另外，据笔者的有限观察，中国的律师询问之前往往不会设计问题，不围绕自己的主张（论点）提问，结果问了半天获得的是无用信息。看来中国引入对抗制的道路还任重道远。对于译者来说，当我们听到有人谈"交叉询问"时，一定要明白是不是真的"交叉询问"，否则直译出来，听众可能会产生困惑。

另外，中国法庭在各方出具证据之后，有"质证"的环节，即对对方提出的证据（书证、物证、书面证言等）提出质疑。有人把"质证"译为 cross-examination，是不恰当的。因为 examine 的对象是人，不是物。"质证"可以译为 challenge the evidence。当然，如果质证针对的是人，就是 cross-examination。

## 5. Leading questions 诱导性问题

控辩双方提问的一种方式。诱导性问题隐含了问话人希望听到的答案，一般是"封闭性"问题（close-ended questions），即答案有限的问题，如："事发时现场的光线很暗，是吧？"就是一个诱导性问题。在美国，诱导性问题通常只能在交叉询问时使用；询问自己的证人（直接询问）时用开放性问题，如：事发时现场的光线怎么样？

诱导性问题通常用 Yes 或 No 来回答，用以从证人口中套出（elicit）对自己有利的事实，也用于让证人确认某些事实，如："事发时并没有路灯，是吧？"以便在论证阶段用于攻击证人的可信度（impeach the credibility of the testifying witness），如：向陪审团指出，直接询问时证人说没有路灯，但先前对警察的证言里面说有路灯。

注意：千万不能当面揭穿证人证言矛盾之处，那样就会给证人辩解的机会。一定要等证人退席之后面向陪审团指出。

中国的法庭不准使用诱导性问题，因为涉嫌"诱供"（eliciting a confession）。原因是，中国法庭证人通常不出庭作证，作证的通常只有被告人一个，讯问对象是被告人，所以会出现"诱供"的说法；在美国，被告人有沉默权，通常不作证，询问对象是其他证人，不担心"诱供"。即使存在诱导，陪审团也是听到了两个版本的叙述，可以自行判断哪个版本可信。

## Objections 反对 / 异议

在庭审中，如果控辩双方律师感到对方律师向证人提出的问题、提问的方式或证人回答的方式不妥，可以大声向法庭提出"Objection!"（反对！）。如果法官觉得反对提得有道理，会同意反对的意见，说："Objection sustained!"（反对有效！），然后责令律师撤回问题或换一种方式提问，或指示陪审团不要受刚才提问的影响。如果法官觉得反对意见没有道理，会说："Objection overruled!"（反对无效！），然后请检察官/律师继续提问。

历史上，如果律师（检察官）对法官的现场裁决有异议，打算就此提出上诉，需要明确说出"Exception!"（不是"Objection!"）。不过，现在美国大多数州都没有这样的要求。因为既然已经提出反对，法官作出对自己不利的裁决，律师肯定不赞成法官的意见。[①]

## Side-bar Conference 栏边会议

side-bar 指法官席旁边的位置，律师可在此与法官交谈而不会让陪审团听到。该词也可以指法官与律师在此场所进行的交谈（side-bar conference），又称"法庭会议"（bench conference）。庭审过程中，如果遇到复杂的问题或者在证据上有重要争议，控辩双方当着陪审团的面辩论会对陪审团的判断产生负面影响。这时，一方律师就会向法官提出正式请求（"May I approach the bench?"或"May I approach?"）。法官许可后，双方就可以走近法官席，商讨问题，避免陪审团听见。

## Closing Argument 最后辩论 / 论证

也叫 summation 或 summing up，是法庭活动的最后阶段。控辩双方举证完毕之后，要分别利用举证阶段向法庭呈交的证据和证言，围绕公诉或辩护主张，向陪审团或法官做最后的论证，努力使法官或陪审团相信自己的主张。最后辩论可以进行多轮，但每轮只能就上轮出现的新观点进行辩驳，不能引入新的证据。对最后论证的反驳，叫作 rebuttal。注意，最后辩论和开场陈述不同。开场陈述仅仅是对事实和

---

[①] 维基百科 Objection (law) 条( https://en.wikipedia.org/wiki/Objection_(law)，读取日期 2015-08-31 ）。

证据的介绍；最后辩论是利用已经向法庭展示的证据，论证自己的观点①。closing argument 经常被翻译为"最后辩论"，但笔者认为"最后论证"也许更符合其本意。

## Jury Instructions 指示陪审团

双方辩论结束后，法官会指示陪审团如何进行评议（叫作 judge's charge to the jury；charge 有"指示"的意思），包括告知陪审团争议焦点（issues，争点）、相关法律规定、证明标准〔刑事案件是"排除合理怀疑"（beyond reasonable doubt），民事案件是"优势证据"（preponderance of the evidence）〕，并提醒他们只能依据法庭上看到的证据作出判断，开场陈述和最后论证不是证据，等等。法院对如何指示陪审团有详细规定。比如，《佛罗里达州刑事案件陪审团标准指示》中，关于如何指导陪审团审查判断证据（weighing the evidence，评价证据）有如下规定：

#### WEIGHING THE EVIDENCE②

It is up to you to decide what evidence is reliable. You should use your common sense in deciding which is the best evidence, and which evidence should not be relied upon in considering your verdict. You may find some of the evidence not reliable, or less reliable than other evidence.

You should consider how the witnesses acted, as well as what they

---

① 维基百科 Closing argument 条（https://en.wikipedia.org/wiki/Closing_argument，读取日期 2015-08-31）。

② "Florida Standard Jury Instructions in Criminal Cases",引自 Florida Courts 网站（http://www.flcourts18.org/PDF/criminal.pdf，读取日期 2015-08-31）。

said. Some things you should consider are:

1. Did the witness seem to have an opportunity to see and know the things about which the witness testified?

2. Did the witness seem to have an accurate memory?

3. Was the witness honest and straightforward in answering the attorneys' questions?

4. Did the witness have some interest in how the case should be decided?

5. Does the witness's testimony agree with the other testimony and other evidence in the case?

6. Was the testimony of the witness reasonable when considered in the light of all the evidence in the case and in the light of your own experience and common sense? (*Give the following paragraphs only as required by the evidence*)

7. Has the witness been offered or received any money, preferred treatment, or other benefit in order to get the witness to testify?

8. Had any pressure or threat been used against the witness that affected the truth of the witness's testimony?

9. Did the witness at some other time make a statement that is inconsistent with the testimony [he] [she] gave in court?

10. Was it proved that the witness had been convicted of a felony or a crime involving dishonesty or false statement?

11. Was it proved that the general reputation of the witness for telling the truth and being honest was bad?

You may rely upon your own conclusion about the witness. A juror may believe or disbelieve all or any part of the evidence or the testimony of any witness.

由此可见,陪审团是基于生活常识对证人的可信度作出判断,进而判断证言所支持的法律主张是否可信。陪审团认定的是事实问题,不是法律问题,所以这项工作是普通人可以胜任的,可以打消一些人"陪审员不懂法如何判案"的疑虑。

### The Chinese Trial Procedure 中国法庭的审判程序

根据刑事诉讼法规定,法庭的审判程序分为开庭(opening the session)、法庭调查(court enquiry)、法庭辩论(debates / argumentation)、被告人最后陈述(final statement by the defendant)、评议(deliberation)和宣判(sentencing)几个阶段。

开庭是法庭审理的开始,其任务是为完成实体审理做好程序上的准备。法庭调查是法庭审判的核心阶段。在这一阶段,合议庭要在公诉人、当事人、辩护人、代理人等的参加下,通过展示证据(present the evidence)和质证(challenge the evidence),当庭调查证据,全面查明案件事实,为法庭作出正确的裁判提供事实根据。这个阶段相当于美国法庭的举证阶段。

法庭辩论是指控辩双方在审判长的主持下,依据法庭调查中已经调查的证据和有关法律规定,对证据有何种证明力(probative value / weight)和被告人是否有罪、所犯何罪、罪责轻重、应否处罚和如何处罚等问题,提出自己的意见和理由,在法庭上当面进行论证和反驳(refutation)的诉讼活动。相当于美国的closing argument。

被告人最后陈述是指被告人在法庭审理结束之际,就自己被指控的罪行进行最后辩护和最后陈述的活动。这个环节在美国法庭不存在。美国的被告人享有沉默权,整个开庭过程中可以一句话不说。

被告人最后陈述后，审判长应当宣布休庭，由合议庭（judicial panel）进行评议（deliberation）。合议庭评议，就是合议庭全体成员共同对案件事实的认定（determination of facts）和法律的适用（application of law）进行全面的讨论，评定并作出处理决定的诉讼活动。美国一审采用法官独任审判（bench trial / single-judge trial）或陪审团审判，所以由法官一人或陪审团作出决定。①

## Trial Advocacy 律师执业技能

律师/公诉人从筛选陪审团成员开始到审判结束需要使用一整套技能，所以美国法学院十分重视技能培养。不仅法学院教授相关技能，甚至中小学都有相关课程②。中国的法学院则偏重于理论传授，缺乏职业技能（advocacy skills / lawyering skills）培训。

trial advocacy 字面意思是"庭审辩护"。advocacy 的意思是The act of pleading or arguing in favor of something, such as a cause, idea, or policy; active support③。为了更清楚传达这个概念的意思，可以视情况译为"律师执业技能"。就好比美国法学院的课程 Legal Research，是指如何查到适用的法律，而不是"法律研究"，所以可译为"法律检索"。

---

① 《刑事诉讼庭审阶段中每个阶段的意义是什么？》，引自南宁律师网（http://www.nn148.com.cn/Html/xszh/2008-3/4/08342038264977235.html，读取日期 2015-08-31）。

② 维基百科 Trial_advocacy 条（https://en.wikipedia.org/wiki/Trial_advocacy，读取日期 2015-08-31）。

③ *American Heritage Dictionary*, (Boston: Houghton Mifflin Co., 2000).

# 第九讲

## 劳动法中的几个概念及其翻译

### Labor Law vs. Employment Law 劳动法和雇佣法

在美国，谈到 labor law（劳动法），人们想到的是关于工会（trade unions）、集体谈判（collective bargaining）及其他与工会有关的法律。谈到 employment law（雇佣法），人们想到的是关于雇主和雇员关系方面的各种法律，比如工资（wage）、工时（working hours）、劳动标准（labor standards）和就业歧视（employment discrimination）等。（据某次劳动法会议的资料）在中国，关于工会的内容主要在工会法（trade union law）中规定；关于雇佣的内容，在劳动法（labor law，包括《劳动法》和《劳动合同法》及相关法规）中规定。同一概念在不同的国家称呼不同，不一定要把中国的劳动法译为 employment law，或者把美国的 labor law 翻译为中文的"工会法"。按字面翻译，让读者通过具体内容了解两国称呼的不同也是一种交流，但译者本人要做到心中有数。况且，在世界范围内，labor law 和 employment law 也经常作为同义词使用，比如，维基百科对 labor law 的解释如下：

> Labour law (also labor law or employment law, see spelling differences) mediates the relationship between workers (employees), employers, trade unions and the government. Collective labour law relates to the tripartite relationship between employee, employer and

union. Individual labour law concerns employees' rights at work and through the contract for work.[①]

其中的 collective labour law（集体劳动法）相当于中国的工会法，individual labour law（个人劳动法）相当于中国的劳动法。

## Contract of Service vs. Contract for Services
## 劳动合同和劳务合同

这两个词经常被译为同一个术语——"服务合同"——但这是错误的翻译。两个短语的含义完全不同。简单地说，如果你是一个单位的正式员工，你和用人单位签订的是 contract of service（劳动合同；service 多用单数）；如果你在业余时间兼职做些私活（比如翻译），你与用户签订的合同是 contract for services（劳务合同，即劳动服务合同；service 多用复数）。

中国法律对劳动合同和劳务合同是这样界定的："劳务合同"是经济合同（economic contracts），是劳务方以自己的"劳务"（服务）成果为义务，并得到相应劳务报酬的合同；而"劳动合同"是以劳动关系（labour/employment relationship）为基础的合同，劳动者根据用工单位的安排和规定从事劳动，并按月领取报酬。"劳务合同"是《合同法》和《民法通则》的调整规范；"劳动合同"是《劳动法》（Labour Law）和《劳动合同法》（Labour Contract Law，后者是对前者的细化）的调整规范，两者适用的法律规范是不同的。

如与雇主签订的是"劳动合同"，雇主要遵守最低工资标准和缴纳"三金"（医疗保险金、失业保险金、养老保险金）；如果与雇

---

① 维基百科 Labour law, employment terms 条（https://en.wikipedia.org/wiki/Labour_law#Employment_terms，读取日期 2015-11-04）。

主签订的是"劳务合同",就是干完规定的工作,拿钱走人,雇主什么也不管。所以,有些企业的用人行为,明明是劳动关系,却欺骗员工签订劳务合同,规避法定义务。这也是为什么在签订劳务合同的时候,会特别强调合同双方不存在劳动(国外称"雇佣")关系。例如:

> The Individual contractor shall have the legal status of an independent contractor vis-à-vis the United Nations Development Programme (UNDP), and shall not be regarded, for any purposes, as being either a "staff member" of the UNDP, under the UN Staff Regulations and Rules, or an "official" of UNDP, for purposes of the Convention on the Privileges and Immunities of the United Nations, adopted by the General Assembly of the United Nations on 13 February 1946. Accordingly, nothing within or relating to the Agreement shall establish the relationship of employer and employee, or of principal and agent, between UNDP and the Individual contractor.(引自UNDP与独立承包人签订的一份合同)

好在出现争议时,法院并不看所签订合同的名称,而是看工作的性质到底是提供劳务,还是作为用工单位的员工。同时,即使没有签订任何合同,法院也会根据相关证据确认是否存在劳动关系。

关于劳动合同和劳务合同的区别,国内外相同。我们看看英文解释:

> Employment relationships can be divided into two forms—the employee and the independent contractor. The employee is hired under a <u>contract of service</u> and he is an independent contractor under a <u>contract</u>

for services. The distinction between the two is not always obvious and it falls to the courts to decide on the issue of the nature of the employment relationship.

The distinction is important because it determines the statutory protection that applies. The rights and remedies provided for under the Unfair Dismissals Acts only apply to employees under a <u>contract of service</u>. Likewise of importance is that fact that employers are only vicariously liable for torts committed by employees who are under a contract of service. Independent contractors under a <u>contract for services</u> are responsible for their own torts.

Another reason why it is important to distinguish between a <u>contract of services</u> and a <u>contract for services</u> is that the system of taxation applied to each category is quite different. In a contract of services, the employer is responsible under the PAYE system, whereas in a contract for services, the independent contractor is subject to the self-assessment system.[①]

如果不具备一点劳动法知识，译者可能忽略 of 和 for 的区别，从而无法理解或翻译这两个术语（总不能都翻译为"服务合同"）。

反过来，中文的"劳动合同"可以翻译为 contract of service；"劳务合同"可以翻译为 contract for services。为了保留中国特色，也可以分别翻译为 labour contract 和 labour services contract，但为了避免混淆，最好使用 contract of employment（劳动合同）和 contract for

---

① "Contract for Services v. Contract of Services"，引自 CPA Ireland 网站（http://www.cpaireland.ie/docs/default-source/Students/Study-Support/P1-Corporate-Laws-Governance/contract-for-services-v-contract-of-services.pdf?sfvrsn=0，读取日期 2015-11-04）。

services（劳务合同）。

另外，工作得到长期保障的就业有不同称谓，比如 regular employment（常规就业/用工）、typical forms of employment（典型用工）。而没有长期保障的就业可以称为 non-regular employment（非常规就业）、atypical forms of employment（非典型就业）、alternative employment（替代性就业）、informal employment（非正式就业）等。后者包括 dispatched workers（劳务派遣工人）、independent contractors（独立承揽者）、directly-employed part-time workers（直接雇用的减时/非全时工人），以及 fixed-term workers（签订固定期限合同的工人）等。他们做的可能是"计件工作"（piecework），拿的是"计件工资"（piece rate）；或者是做"计时工作"（hourly work），拿"计时工资"（hourly rate）。

## Fixed Term Contract vs. Indefinite-term Contract
## 固定期限合同和无固定期限合同

固定期限劳动合同（fixed / definite-term / period employment contract），是指用人单位（employer/user）与劳动者（employee）约定合同终止时间的劳动合同。劳动合同期限届满（expire），劳动关系即告终止。如果双方协商一致，还可以续订（renew / extend）劳动合同，延长期限。固定期限的劳动合同可以是较短时间的，如半年、1年、2年，也可以是较长时间的，如5年、10年，甚至更长时间。不管时间长短，劳动合同的起始和终止日期都是固定的。①

无固定期限劳动合同（contract of indefinite duration / period / term,

---

① 百度百科"固定期限劳动合同"条（http://baike.baidu.com/view/1149478.htm，读取日期2015-11-04）。

open-ended employment contract），是指用人单位与劳动者约定无确定终止时间的劳动合同。这里所说的无确定终止时间，是指劳动合同没有一个确切的终止时间，劳动合同的期限长短不能确定，但并不是没有终止时间。只要没有出现法律规定的条件（statutory conditions）或者双方约定的条件，双方当事人就要继续履行劳动合同规定的义务。一旦出现了法律规定的情形，无固定期限劳动合同也同样能够解除。①

持有这两种合同的人，可以分别称为临时雇员（temporary employee）和永久雇员（permanent / regular employees），或者短期雇员（short-term employees）和长期雇员（long-term employees），等等。

两种合同都是劳动合同（合同双方是隶属关系），不是劳务合同（双方之间为平等主体）。

国外劳动法中也有类似区别：

> The distinction between fixed-term employment contracts and contracts of indefinite duration is an important one due to the great difference in the potential damage awards that are available to the employee in the event of possible litigation.
>
> In contracts of an indefinite duration, employment is one of continuous service and intended to last for an indefinite period of time, with no specified or foreseeable end to the relationship. This type of contract is accompanied by a number of rights and obligations, most notably the right to reasonable notice upon termination (解雇通知时

---

① 百度百科"无固定期限劳动合同"条（http://baike.baidu.com/view/1253414.htm，读取日期 2015-11-04）。

间,笔者注).

In fixed-term contracts, the employment relationship is intended to last for only a specific and definite length of time or until a specific project is completed. Once the term or project is finished, the fixed-term employment relationship ends. Such employees are often referred to as being in a "contract" position.①

但如同"劳动合同"和"劳务合同"一样,"长期(劳动)合同"和"短期(劳动)合同"的名称并不重要。如果出现争议,法院要看合同的实质,来决定合同性质:

The type of contract that the employment relationship falls under is not determined solely by the terminology used in the contract itself. The overall character of the employment is the determining factor for whether a contract is considered fixed-term or one of indefinite duration.

For example, a person may be subject to a series of fixed-term contract over several years, but the overall character of the employment suggests that the person is actually an employee of indefinite duration. In such cases, courts may set aside the fixed-term contract and view it instead as one of indefinite duration, which is accompanied by associated entitlements and obligations, such as reasonable notice of termination.②

---

① "Types of Employment Contracts – Fixed Term vs. Indefinite Duration",引自 Minken Employment Lawyers 网站(http://www.minkenemploymentlawyers.com/employment-law-issues/types-of-employment-contracts-fixed-term-vs-indefinite-duration/#sthash.CIRlQxO8.dpuf,读取日期 2015-11-04)。

② 同上。

# Full-time vs. Part-time vs. Casual Employment
# 满时、减时和不定时就业

一个概念的含义常被相对的概念所界定,因此要理解某一概念的实质,必须先理解其相对的概念。full-time employment 是指:

> ... employment in which a person works a minimum number of hours defined as such by his/her employer. ... Full-time status varies between company and is often based on the shift the employee must work during each work week. The "standard" work week consists of five eight-hour days, commonly served between 9:00 AM to 5:00 PM totaling 40 hours.①

与此相对的概念是 part-time:

> A **part-time contract** is a form of employment that carries fewer hours per week than a full-time job.②

据此,full-time employment 可以翻译为"全时就业"(或者更确切一点:"满时就业",隐含意思是"满工作负荷",而不是"全时"所隐含的"全部时间"),full-time employee 可以翻译为"全时雇员"或"满时雇员"。part-time employment 的翻译比较困难:如果译为"部分时间就业",意思准确,但比较冗长,"部分时间雇员"也不够简洁;翻译为"半时就业"虽然简洁,但不够确切,因为"部

---

① 维基百科 Full-time 条(https://en.wikipedia.org/wiki/Full-time,读取日期 2015-11-04)。

② 维基百科 Part-time contract 条(https://en.wikipedia.org/wiki/Part-time_contract,读取日期 2015-11-04)。

分时间"不一定是"满时"的一半。一些词典和机构（包括联合国）将其翻译为"非全时就业"，通常情况下说得过去，因为 full-time 相对于 part-time 而言。但这个说法也并非无懈可击：如果对就业的种类采用"三分法"，就会出现逻辑困难。例如：

> An employee, including a shiftworker (倒班工人，笔者注), can be hired as:
> - full-time
> - part-time or
> - casual.[1]

这里的 casual，显然也属于汉语中的"非全时"：

> A casual employee:
> - has no guaranteed hours of work
> - usually works irregular hours
> - doesn't get paid sick or annual leave
> - can end employment without notice, unless notice is required by a registered agreement, award or employment contract.[2]

因此，这三个概念作为相互对立的概念，必须统筹兼顾，才能找到相互协调的翻译方法。full-time 译为"全时""满时"，与英文

---

[1] "Casual employees"，引自 Fair Work Ombudsman 网站（https://www.fairwork.gov.au/employee-entitlements/types-of-employees/casual-part-time-and-full-time/casual-employees，读取日期 2015-11-04）。

[2] "Casual, part-time & full-time"，引自 Fair Work Ombudsman 网站（https://www.fairwork.gov.au/employee-entitlements/types-of-employees/casual-part-time-and-full-time，读取日期 2015-11-04）。

字面和意思完全对应；part-time 不妨换个角度，译为"减时"，这样 part-time employment 就是"减时就业"，part-time employee 就是"减时雇员"（新概念，新译法）；casual employment 看起来像中文的"打零工"，但中文打零工显然不是雇佣关系，而英文的 casual employment 在法律上还是雇佣关系，只不过福利少一些，因此不妨按照内涵译为"无定时就业"。

词典中一般把 full-time 翻译为"全职"（"在本职之外不担任其他职务"），把 part-time 翻译为"兼职"（"在本职之外担任其他职务"），这是两个概念的日常含义，在一定的语境下是正确的。例如：

> There was a time when moonlighting — taking on work in addition to your full-time employment — was for underemployed workers and the severely cash-strapped.
>
> Today, even working professionals can be strapped for cash, and people in all fields and income groups are supplementing their main income by moonlighting. For some, the second job isn't just for the bucks but also for the skills and the sense of being a free agent. And although extra, part-time jobs used to be verboten, many supervisors are flexible about a team member who picks up a gig on the side.[①]

上文中，moonlighting、the second job、part-time jobs 为同义词，都是"兼职"的意思，与 full-time job（"全职"）相对。另外，在日

---

① L. Buhl: "Moonlighting: Pros and Cons of a Second Job"，引自 Career-Advice 网站（http://career-advice.monster.com/job-search/getting-started/moonlighting-pros-and-cons-of-a-second-job-hot-jobs/article.aspx，读取日期 2015-11-18）。

常语境下，casual jobs（零工）和 odd jobs（零活）恐怕也不意味着雇佣关系。

## Equal Pay for Equal Work vs. Equal Pay for Work of Equal Value 同工同酬和同值同酬

"同工同酬"的概念大家可能比较熟悉，意思是同样的工作，应当得到同样的报酬。这一概念的提出，是为了解决男女同工不同酬问题，即男女做同样的工作，女性的报酬却偏低。目前在国有和正规单位，男女已基本实现同工同酬，民营或私营单位可能还存在问题。但是，同工不同酬的现象在中国有另外一种表现形式，即正式工（签订无固定期限合同的员工）和临时工（包括农民工、劳务派遣工）之间的差异。所以，在中国实现同工同酬的任务远未完成。

"同值同酬"是后来提出的概念，原因是男女职业隔离（occupational segregation，即男女从事不同工作）现象严重，女性职业的报酬普遍低于男性（即使工作所需技能和教育相似），沿用同"工"同酬的概念无法解决对妇女的歧视问题（因为不同"工"）。这一概念要求如果两种工作所需技能、努力、责任相同，即两种工作的价值相同，就需要给予同等报酬。这样，即使男女分属不同工作，在价值相同的基础上，应当给予同等待遇。

可能是由于不理解这两个概念的区别，有些联合国文件中把国际劳工组织第 100 号公约 Convention Concerning Equal Remuneration for Men and Women Workers for Work of Equal Value（简称 Equal Remuneration Convention）翻译为《关于男女工人同工同酬的公约》（有些文件中翻译正确，译为《对男女工人同等价值的工作付予同等报酬公约》）。

# Affirmative Action vs. Temporary Special Measures
# 平权行动和暂行特别措施

affirmative action 和 temporary special measures 意思相同。在劳动法范畴，是指国家为了纠正历史上对女性（或其他少数者群体）的就业歧视，而临时采取的照顾措施，比如降低录用标准、同等条件下优先录用、分配就业指标，等等。前者的翻译五花八门，主要有：平权行动、积极行动、扶持行动；后者在联合国文献中翻译为"暂行特别措施"，但笔者认为"临时特别措施"可能更上口。关于 affirmative action 等概念，负责监督缔约国落实《消除对妇女一切形式歧视公约》情况的条约机构（treaty body）"消除对妇女歧视委员会"（CEDAW）在其关于《消除对妇女一切形式歧视公约》（简称也是 CEDAW）第四条第一款的一般性建议中有一段话（第 17 段），解释了这几个概念之间的关系：

> The travaux préparatoires (准备材料[①]) of the Convention use different terms to describe the "temporary special measures" included in article 4, paragraph 1. The Committee itself, in its previous general recommendations, used various terms. States parties often equate "special measures" in its corrective, compensatory and promotional sense with the terms "affirmative action" (平权行动), "positive action" (积极行动), "positive measures" (积极措施), "reverse discrimination" (反向歧视), and "positive discrimination" (积极的区别对待). These terms emerge from the discussions and varied practices found in different national contexts. In the present general recommendation, and in accordance

---

① 本段引用中，笔者所注的对应中文表述均来自该文件中译本。

with its practice in the consideration of reports of States parties, the Committee uses solely the term "temporary special measures", as called for in article 4, paragraph 1.①

## On-call vs. Standby 电话待命和现场待命

on-call 和 standby 在多数情况下意思相同，都是指雇主要求雇员待命，接到电话或通知随时到岗。比如在捷克共和国：

> On-call or "standby" duty is defined by the new Labour Code, valid from 1 January 2007, as a period during which an employee is in a state of readiness to perform work, as set out in his or her employment contract. It relates to work that must be done in addition to the employee's normal work schedule in the event of urgent need. The employee must be on standby at a location agreed with that employee, which must not be the employer's workplace. On-call duty is considered as working time.②

但在一些国家，这两个概念有区别。on-call 是指工人待在家里（或自己选择的地方），随时等待电话通知，如有工作，随时到岗。standby（"站在旁边"），是指工人在工作场所或指定场所等待，随

---

① "General recommendation No. 25"，引自联合国网站（http://www.un.org/womenwatch/daw/cedaw/recommendations/General%20recommendation%2025%20(English).pdf，读取日期 2015-11-04）。

② "Definition and Regulation of On-call Work or Duty"，引自 CESifo Group 网站（https://www.cesifo-group.de/ifoHome/facts/DICE/Labour-Market-and-Migration/Labour-Market/Working-Time/def-reg-on-call_work/fileBinary/def-reg-on-call_work.pdf，读取日期 2015-11-04）。

时待命。在德国：

> No statutory definition of <u>on-call duty</u> (Rufbereitschaft) exists, but the Federal Labour Court (Bundesarbeitsgericht) has defined it as a "background service", whereby employees have to be available <u>by telephone contact to be called on to work</u> at a place of their choice, which they must indicate to the employer. This is in contrast to <u>standby duty</u> (Bereitschaftsdienst), whereby employees have to be available at a place designated by the employer.[①]

对于翻译而言，如果 on-call 和 standby 无区别，则都翻译为"待命"即可。如果有区别，不妨把前者翻译为"电话待命"，后者译为"现场待命"。

关于待命时间是否算 working time / hours worked（工作时间）或者加班（overtime），通常要看这段时间是否在雇主控制之下。如果在雇主控制之下，就算作工作时间；即使不工作，也支付工资，但比较低。

另外，在荷兰有 on-call contract（待命合同）的概念，包括两种。第一种属于"劳动合同"，规定雇员平时不工作，仅在电话通知时工作。如果双方在合同中商定了最多和最少的工作时数，就叫"min / max" contract（"最多/最少工时"合同）；不保证工时，则叫作"zero hours" contract（"零工时"合同）。第二种待命合同叫作 framework agreement（框架合同），只规定工作条件（working

---

① "Definition and Regulation of On-call Work or Duty"，引自 CESifo Group 网站（https://www.cesifo-group.de/ifoHome/facts/DICE/Labour-Market-and-Migration/Labour-Market/Working-Time/def-reg-on-call_work/fileBinary/def-reg-on-call_work.pdf，读取日期 2015-11-04）。

conditions），不规定工时（working hours）。每次雇主有工作时打电话，再签订一个固定期限合同（fixed term employment contract）。①

## Labor Dispatch 劳务派遣

劳务派遣又称人力派遣（manpower / worker dispatch）、人才租赁（human resource leasing）、劳动派遣（labor dispatching）、劳动力租赁（labor leasing）、雇员租赁（employee / staff leasing），是指由劳务派遣机构（labor dispatch agency / dispatched work agency）与被派遣劳工（dispatched workers / laborers）订立劳动合同（employment contract），并支付报酬（remuneration），把劳动者派向其他用工单位（user enterprise），再由其他用工单位向派遣机构支付一笔服务费用的一种用工形式。劳动力给付（delivery of service）的事实发生于被派遣劳工与要派企业（实际用工单位）（host enterprise, user enterprise）之间，由要派企业向劳务派遣机构支付服务费，劳务派遣机构再向劳动者支付劳动报酬。实际用工单位和劳务派遣公司之间签订的协议叫"劳务派遣协议"（labor dispatch agreement / business service agreement），工人与实际用工单位之间没有劳动合同。特定情形下，也可以把劳务派遣公司和实际用工单位分别称为 nominal employer（名义用工单位）和 actual employer（实际用工单位）。按法律规定，劳务派遣用工只能用于"三性"（"临时性、辅助性或者替代性"）工作岗位（used to fulfill temporary, auxiliary or replaceable/ substitute positions）。但一些企事业单位不同程度存在着滥用劳务派

---

① "Definition and Regulation of On-call Work or Duty"，引自 CESifo Group 网站（https://www.cesifo-group.de/ifoHome/facts/DICE/Labour-Market-and-Migration/Labour-Market/Working-Time/def-reg-on-call_work/fileBinary/def-reg-on-call_work.pdf，读取日期 2015-11-04）。

遣制度的现象，致使派遣工占比过大，且在长期性、关键性岗位工作。①②

## Employment at Will Doctrine 雇用自由原则

也可译为"任意雇用原则"，这是美国雇佣法的基本原则。如果有雇员受到集体劳动协议保护，或者在一些公共部门工作，雇主要解雇雇员需要有"正当理由"（just cause）；如果雇员没有集体劳动协议，雇主可以以"好的理由"（for a good reason，如经常旷工）、"坏的理由"（for a bad reason，如把头发染成绿色），或者是"不说明任何理由"（for no reason at all），随时解除雇员（雇员也可以以同样理由随时离开，所以叫"雇用自由"），除非有法律明文禁止（如法律明确禁止基于种族、肤色、信仰、性别、族裔等的歧视）。at-will workers / employees，即按任意雇用原则雇用的工人/雇员。在美国，绝大多数雇员都是此类雇员。在几乎每个州，法律都推定劳资关系是"任意雇用"关系，除非雇员能提出相反证据。这叫作"at will" presumption（"任意"推定）。

## 其他常见概念

back pay 补发工资：如果雇主非法解雇员工，或该晋升的时候不予晋升，雇员通过劳动仲裁或诉讼得到的应得工资。

collective bargaining 集体谈判：雇主和工会之间的谈判；通过谈

---

① 百度百科"劳务派遣"条（http://baike.baidu.com/view/15253.htm，读取日期 2015-11-04）。

② 维基百科 Dispatched labor 条（https://en.wikipedia.org/wiki/Dispatched_labor，读取日期 2015-11-04）。

判签订集体劳动协议,确定工资、工作时间和其他劳动条件。

constructive dismissal 推定解雇:本来是自己主动离职,但原因在于雇主,此时推定为被解雇,享受相关待遇。

hostile working environment 敌对工作环境:让雇员感到不舒服的工作环境,以至于影响到雇员有效工作,比如经常遭受性骚扰(sexual harassment)。

leaves 休假。各国关于休假的规定不同,以下是德国允许的休假:adoptive leave 收养假,母亲可休,单身养父也可休。annual leave 带薪年假,不必加 paid 一词。carer's leave 护理假,有家人患病等情况需护理时准予的休假。force majeure leave 不可抗力假,即由于家人突然生病或受伤等紧急原因而准予的休假。maternity leave 孕产假,因怀孕或生产而准予的休假。注意 maternity 一词意思为"母性",当然包括孕产两方面,所以"孕产保护"之类的汉语说法,只需要翻译为 maternity protection 等即可,不必分别翻译"孕"和"产"。parental leave 育儿假,8 岁以下儿童(残疾儿童为 16 岁)父母的休假。paternity leave 陪产假,妻子产后父亲可休的假(非法定)。

noncompetition agreement 禁止竞争协议:雇员通过协议承诺离职后在一定时间内不为竞争对手工作或开办与雇主直接竞争的企业。

pension 通常是指养老金(old-age pension)。该词的词源意思是 payment(给付),所以也用来指养老金之外的给付。联合国有些文件统一把 pension 翻译为"养恤金",old-age pension 译为"老年养恤金",disability pension 译为"残疾养恤金",以此类推。

severance package 遣散协议：规定雇员离职后应得到的报酬和福利。severance pay 遣散费，联合国有文件翻译为"解职费""离职金""解雇金"。改革开放初期，有"买断工龄"（非法）的提法，可以译为 severance pay。

# 第十讲

## "职务犯罪"等罪名译法探讨

### 职务犯罪 Crimes Committed in Violation of Public Duties

"在我国当前,狭义的职务犯罪,即国家工作人员职务犯罪。是指国家工作人员利用职务上的便利,进行非法活动,或者滥用职权,或者对工作严重不负责任,不履行或不正确履行职责,破坏国家对职务行为的管理活动,致使国家和人民利益遭受重大损失,依照刑法应受到刑罚处罚的犯罪行为的总称。"[①]

关于职务犯罪,网上和出版物中见到的译法五花八门,比如 crime by taking advantage of duty、duty crime、official crime、job-related crime、duty-related crimes。第一个译法语法不通,第二个搭配不存在,第三个("官方的犯罪")无意义,第四个、第五个意思不明确。顾名思义,职务犯罪是违反公共职责的犯罪。因此可以翻译为 crimes committed in violation of public duties。联合国毒品与犯罪办公室(UNODC)提供的一份文件中有类似的说法:

> Crimes committed in violation of the duties attached to a public office or a public service, such as disclosure of state secrets (Article 204

---

[①] "什么是职务犯罪",引自最高人民检察院举报中心网站(http://www.12309.gov.cn/delict/business/Nicbussinessfile104.html,读取日期 2016-04-28)

PC) and disclosure of official secrets (Article 253) ...①

职务犯罪也可以翻译为 crimes committed by public officers/officials。经济合作与发展组织（OECD）提供的《菲律宾刑法》（经修订）第七章（Revised Penal Code Title VII）题目就叫 Crimes Committed by Public Officers②。鉴于在当前语境下，职务犯罪主要是贪污腐败犯罪，日常交流中可以直接说 corruption(-related) crimes/offenses。"职务犯罪案件"可直接翻译为 corruption cases。（注意：职务犯罪不是一个单一的罪名，而是多种犯罪行为的统称，所以 crime 要用复数形式。）

## 贪污贿赂罪 Crimes of Embezzlement and Bribery

我国《刑法》从反腐败角度出发，将贪污贿赂罪归为一类，所以日常交流中可以把"贪污贿赂罪"（职务犯罪的主要形式）简单翻译为 corruption crimes。如果更具体地进行翻译，则是 crimes of embezzlement and bribery。

根据《刑法分则》第八章规定，贪污贿赂罪共有 12 个具体罪名。这 12 种犯罪可分为两类：一类是贪污犯罪（embezzlement），包括贪污罪（embezzlement）、挪用公款罪（misappropriation of public funds）、巨额财产来源不明罪（possessing huge amounts of assets of

---

① "Sentencing Policy and Guidelines for Judges"，引自 UN Office on Drugs and Crime 网站（https://www.unodc.org/documents/easternafrica/Criminal%20Justice%20Compendium%20in%20Somaliland/UNODC_ROEA_-_Sentencing_Policy_and_Guidelines_for_Judges_WEB_LR.pdf，读取日期 2016-04-28）。

② "Revised Penal Code Title VII: Crimes Committed by Public Officers"，引自 OECD 网站 https://www.oecd.org/site/adboecdanti-corruptioninitiative/46816917.pdf，读取日期 2016-04-28）。

unknown origin / unaccounted assets）、隐瞒境外存款罪（concealing overseas deposits）、私分国有资产罪（privately dividing up state-owned assets）和私分罚没财产罪（privately dividing up confiscated assets）。（注意：本节中"贪污"既是一个上位概念，也是一个下位概念。）

另一类是贿赂犯罪（bribery），包括受贿罪（accepting bribes）、单位受贿罪（accepting of bribes by an institution）、行贿罪（giving bribes）、对单位行贿罪（bribing an institution）、介绍贿赂罪（intermediating bribery）、单位行贿罪（giving of bribes by an institution）。

贪污和挪用公款罪都属于贪污贿赂罪，但两者的手段、目的都不相同。贪污罪是指国家工作人员利用职务之便非法占有公共财物。挪用公款罪是指国家工作人员利用职务之便挪用公款归为个人使用，进行非法活动。虽然两者都是以非法占有为目的的，但贪污是永久地占有，挪用公款是暂时性地占有；贪污是通过侵吞、窃取、骗取等手段达到目的，而挪用公款一般都为擅自私用公款，没有也不必要采用贪污所实施的手段。

英文中 embezzlement 与 misappropriation 的区别与上述两个概念的区别相似：

> As nouns the difference between embezzlement and misappropriation is that embezzlement is (legal/business) the fraudulent conversion of property from a property owner while misappropriation is the wrongful, fraudulent or corrupt use of other's funds in one's care.[1]

---

[1] "Embezzlement vs. Misappropriation"，引自 The Difference Between 网站（http://the-difference-between.com/misappropriation/embezzlement，读取日期 2016-04-28）。

与贪污罪类似的还有职务侵占罪。职务侵占罪，是指公司、企业或者其他单位的人员，利用职务上的便利，将本单位财物非法占为己有，且数额较大的行为。贪污和职务侵占的区别之一，是贪污罪的犯罪主体是国家工作人员，职务侵占罪的犯罪主体是企业工作人员（其他区别可上网查找）。还有一个适用于一般主体的（官员或企业领导之外的其他人）的"侵占罪"。该罪是指以非法占有为目的，将他人的遗忘物、埋藏物或者交给自己保管的财物非法占为己有，数额较大，拒不交还的行为。英文中如有必要区分这三个概念，可以分别译为：embezzlement by a public official、embezzlement by a business officer 和 embezzlement。如上下文明确，则都可以用 embezzlement。

## 诽谤 Defamation

《刑法》第二百四十六条规定了诽谤罪："以暴力或者其他方法公然侮辱他人或者捏造事实诽谤他人，情节严重的，处三年以下有期徒刑、拘役、管制或者剥夺政治权利。""诽谤"在《刑法》有的译本中译为 defame：

> Whoever, by violence or other methods, publicly humiliates another person or invent stories to <u>defame</u> him, if the circumstances are serious, shall be sentenced to fixed-term imprisonment of not more than three years, criminal detention, public surveillance or deprivation of political rights.[1]

在有的译本中译为 slander：

---

[1] 《〈刑法〉英译本》，引自中国人大网（http://www.npc.gov.cn/englishnpc/Law/2007-12/13/content_1384075.htm，读取日期 2016-04-28）。

Those openly insulting others using force or other methods or those fabricating stories to slander others, if the case is serious, are to be sentenced to three years or fewer in prison, put under criminal detention or surveillance, or deprived of their political rights.①

汉英词典中通常也是罗列几个近义词，如 defame、slander、libel，不区分不同含义。实际上，在英语中，defamation（诽谤）是一个上义词，其中包含 slander（口头诽谤）和 libel（书面诽谤）：

Defamation: Any intentional false communication, either written or spoken, that harms a person's reputation; decreases the respect, regard, or confidence in which a person is held; or induces disparaging, hostile, or disagreeable opinions or feelings against a person.

Defamation may be a criminal or civil charge. It encompasses both written statements, known as libel, and spoken statements, called slander.②

《刑法》当中的"诽谤"，既包括口头诽谤，也包括书面诽谤，因此译为英文应选用 defamation 一词。顺便提及：libel 来自拉丁语 *liber*（book），可以通过 library（图书馆）来记住 libel 和 slander 的区别。

在很多西方国家，defamation 仅仅是民事侵权行为，不是刑事犯罪。因此，为了区分，作为犯罪的 defamation 叫作 criminal

---

① 《〈刑法〉英译本》，引自中国外交部网站（http://www.fmprc.gov.cn/ce/cgvienna/eng/dbtyw/jdwt/crimelaw/t209043.htm，读取日期 2016-04-28）。

② *West's Encyclopedia of American Law* 第 2 版，转引自 The Free Dictionary 网站（http://legal-dictionary.thefreedictionary.com/defamation，读取日期 2016-04-28）。

defamation；作为民事侵权行为（tort）的 defamation 叫作 civil defamation。

中国民事法律中规定了"名誉权"（right to reputation）。《民法通则》第一百〇一条规定："公民、法人享有名誉权，公民的人格尊严受法律保护，禁止用侮辱、诽谤等方式损害公民、法人的名誉。""名誉侵权"可以直译为 reputation infringement，也可以直接用（civil）defamation。

最后，defamation、slander、libel 并非在所有国家都区分得很清楚。Article 19[①] 在其编写的 *Defining Defamation: Principles on Freedom of Expression and Protection of Reputation*[②] 注释 4 中写道：

> For the purposes of these Principles, laws which purport, at least at a *prima facie* level, to strike this balance will be referred to as "defamation laws", <u>recognising that in different countries these laws go by a variety of other names, including insult, libel, slander and *desacato*</u>.[③]

因此，在英译汉时，是否把 libel 翻译为"书面诽谤"、把 slander 翻译为"口头诽谤"，要看情况。说不定作者是指所有"诽谤"。必须区分时，再作区分。

## 抢夺罪 Snatch Theft

抢夺罪（《刑法》第二百六十七条），是指以非法占有为目

---

① 机构名称。

② "Defining Deformation"，引自 ARTICLE 19 网站（https://www.article19.org/data/files/pdfs/standards/definingdefamation.pdf，读取日期 2016-04-28）。

③ 同上。

的，乘人不备公开夺取数额较大的公私财物的行为。是中国《刑法》第五章侵犯财产罪中的一项罪名，是介于盗窃罪（theft）与抢劫罪（robbery）之间的一种犯罪形态。

一些中国《刑法》译本将其译为 snatch 或 forcibly seize①。snatch 有"抢夺"的意思：

> If something **is snatched** from you, it is stolen, usually using force. If a person **is snatched**, they are taken away by force.②

但这属于第二个义项。第一个义项并无"抢劫"之意：

> If you **snatch** something or **snatch at** something, you take it or pull it away quickly. ③

法律语言讲求确定性，所以简单使用 snatch 似乎不能准确传达"抢夺"的法律含义。而 seize 本身就包含"用力"之义，再用 seize forcibly 显得重复：

> If you **seize** something, you take hold of it quickly, firmly, and forcefully.④

---

① 《〈刑法〉英译本》，引自中国外交部网站（http://www.fmprc.gov.cn/ce/cgvienna/eng/dbtyw/jdwt/crimelaw/t209043.htm，读取日期 2016-04-28）。

② "Snatch"，引自 Collins Dictionary 网站（http://www.collinsdictionary.com/dictionary/english-cobuild-learners/snatch，读取日期 2016-04-28）

③ 同上。

④ 同上。

经查找，更为通行的说法是 snatch theft。这是维基百科对 snatch theft 的定义：

> In Malaysia and Southeast Asia in general, snatch theft is a criminal act of forcefully stealing from a pedestrian's person while employing rob-and-run tactics. It is typical for two thieves to work together and ride a moped to make theft and escape easier. A person steers the vehicle while another does the act of theft itself. However, some snatch thieves work alone or do not use a motorcycle to rob.①

既然抢夺介于 theft 和 robbery 之间，也可以 robbery 为基础来定义。美国佛罗里达州的法律中就使用"robbery by sudden snatching"：

> "Robbery by sudden snatching" means the taking of money or other property from the victim's person, with intent to permanently or temporarily deprive the victim or the owner of the money or other property, when, in the course of the taking, the victim was or became aware of the taking.②

"抢夺"作为动词使用，当然可以说 rob by sudden snatching。也可以考虑使用合成动词 snatch-rob 或 snatch-steal。笔者检索网络资料时发现，使用 snatch-rob 和 snatch-steal 的例子不多，但确有人在用，

---

① 维基百科 Snatch theft 条（https://en.wikipedia.org/wiki/Snatch_theft，读取日期 2016-04-28）。

② "2015 Florida Statutes: Robbery by sudden snatching"，引自 Florida Legislature 网站（http://www.leg.state.fl.us/Statutes/index.cfm?App_mode=Display_Statute&URL=0800-0899/0812/Sections/0812.131.html，读取日期 2016-04-28）

例如：

> In theory, if safety is a major factor of your trip, choose Nha Trang over SHV. However, I have never been robbed in SHV but was <u>snatch-robbed</u> twice in Vietnam (Vung Tao and Chao Doc). Either will be a billion times safer than Philippines, so I'd say it is a toss-up.①

上下文明确时，也可以直接用 snatch 来翻译"抢夺罪"。

## 强奸 Rape

本罪名是指强迫（forcibly）或是在暴力威胁下（under threat of injury）进行的违背受害者意愿的（against the will of the victim）非法性活动（unlawful sexual activity），通常指性交（sexual intercourse）。传统意义上限于男性对女性的侵犯（attacks on women by men），近年来强奸的定义扩大到同性之间的性侵犯（same-sex attacks）、对配偶的性侵犯（婚内强奸/marital rape）、对不能有效表达意愿（incapable of valid consent）的受害人，如精神疾病（mental illness）患者、（因吸毒或酗酒而）迷醉（intoxication）者等实施的性侵犯。我国法律规定的强奸罪中不包括强奸男性、同性强奸或婚内强奸。这些行为造成伤害的，以其他罪名处罚。②

法定强奸（statutory rape）是指与未成年人（minors）的性交（各国对何谓未成年有不同规定）。在大多数司法辖区，无论未成年人是否同意（consent），与未成年人性交都是严重犯罪（a serious

---

① "Untitled Reply"，引自 Thai Visa Forum 网站（http://www.thaivisa.com/forum/topic/763785-nha-trang-vs-sihanoukville/，读取日期 2016-04-28）。

② "Rape"，引自 Find Law 网站（http://dictionary.findlaw.com/definition/rape.html，读取日期 2016-04-28）。

crime）。在中国，法定强奸叫作"奸淫幼女罪"，是指行为人与不满 14 周岁的幼女发生性关系的行为。"奸淫幼女罪"可以译为 the crime of having sex with an underaged girl。注意：此处没有用 rape，而是用 having sex，因为 rape（强奸）隐含"强迫"，而"奸淫"既包括强迫，也包括"自愿"。在平时的交流中，"奸淫幼女罪"可以直接借用 statutory rape 的概念。这是新加坡对"法定强奸"的定义：

>　　What constitutes statutory rape? A girl under 14 years of age is deemed not to be able to consent to sex. Thus, the sexual penetration of a person under 14 years old is deemed to be rape or unlawful sexual penetration, liable to imprisonment for a term up to 20 years plus fine or caning.①

中国在 1997 年《刑法》修订时，规定了"嫖宿幼女罪"（the crime of prostituting an underaged girl），与原来刑法中的强奸幼女罪相区别。但这一罪名争议很大，被认为不利于未成年人保护，2015 年全国人大将其废除，再次将此类行为纳入强奸罪。②

顺便提及一个法律用词严谨性问题。《刑法》第二百三十六条第二款规定："奸淫不满 14 周岁幼女的，以强奸论，从重处罚"。笔者第一次听到"不满 14 周岁幼女"的说法时，以为还有"14 岁以上的幼女"。调查发现后者并不存在。其实更严谨的说法应该是"不满 14 周岁的女性"。"幼女"即为"不满 14 周岁的女性"。全国人大

---

　　①　"Underage Sex & Statutory Rape"，引自 AWARE 网站（http://www.aware.org.sg/underage-sex-and-statutory-rape/，读取日期 2016-04-28）。

　　②　《刑法取消嫖宿幼女罪 11 月 1 日起施行》，引自中国经济网（http://www.ce.cn/xwzx/gnsz/gdxw/201508/29/t20150829_6355957.shtml，读取日期 2016-04-28）。

代表、全国妇联副主席赵东花建议将奸淫幼女罪改为"奸淫儿童罪"（the crime of having sex with a child）①，这既将男童性侵害案件囊括在内，也使得法律用语更加严谨。

## Assault 企图伤害罪

我们在翻译法律文件时，常把 assault 翻译为"袭击""袭击罪"，但这只是 assault 在日常生活中的含义（见义项1）。在法律中，该词的意思是"企图伤害"（见义项2）：

*1 a:* a violent physical or verbal attack *b:* a military attack usually involving direct combat with enemy forces *c:* a concerted effort (as to reach a goal or defeat an adversary)

*2 a:* a threat or attempt to inflict offensive physical contact or bodily harm on a person (as by lifting a fist in a threatening manner) that puts the person in immediate danger of or in apprehension of such harm or contact — compare <u>battery</u> 1b *b :* <u>rape</u> 2 ②

已经发生的"袭击"，不叫 assault，而叫作 battery，词典上通常翻译为"殴击"，可以接受。《元照英美法词典》的解释很清楚：

> battery n.（1）殴击罪　普通法上和制定法上的轻罪。指对他人非法使用暴力的行为。构成此罪有3个基本构成要件：1 被

---

① 《对人大议案奸淫幼女罪改为奸淫儿童罪的浅论》，引自找法网（http://china.findlaw.cn/lawyers/article/d323056.html，读取日期2016-04-28）。

② "Assault"，引自 Merriam-Webster Dictionary 网站（http://www.merriam-webster.com/dictionary/assault，读取日期2016-04-28）。

告实施了犯罪行为。包括作为和不作为；2 被告的心理状态，可能是故意，也可能是轻率；3 对被害人的伤害结果，可能是身体伤害，也可能是侵犯接触。有时，殴击可能是合法的，在某些情形下，受害人的同意可构成抗辩的理由。assault 指企图实施武力伤害他人，battery 指对这种威胁的实施，它包含 assault，即企图伤害在内，所以，"assault and battery"经常在一起使用，指殴打、人身攻击等。①

中国刑法规定了"故意伤害罪"，是指故意非法伤害他人身体并达到一定的严重程度、应受刑法处罚的犯罪行为。这项犯罪与 battery 有相似之处，日常交流中可用 battery 翻译"故意伤害"。但在翻译法律文本时，为慎重起见，还是按字面翻译为好。建议译为：the crime of intentionally causing injury。这个罪名在国外也有，如澳大利亚：

1. The offence of <u>intentionally causing injury</u> is created by Crimes Act 1958 s18.
2. The offence has the following four elements:
   a. The complainant suffered an "injury";
   b. The accused caused the complainant's injury;
   c. The accused intended to cause injury; and
   d. The accused acted without lawful justification or excuse.②

"故意伤害罪"建议不翻译为 intentional injuries，因为该词与

---

① 薛波：《元照英美法词典》，北京大学出版社，2013 年，第 139 页。

② "Bench Notes: Intentionally Causing Injury"，引自 Victorian Criminal Charge Book 网站（http://www.judicialcollege.vic.edu.au/eManuals/CCB/index.htm#4924.htm，读取日期 2016-04-28）。

unintentional injuries 是用于讨论健康与人身安全的。①

## Homicide 杀人罪

英文中常用三个词表示"杀人"：homicide、murder、manslaughter。murder 通常在词典中翻译为"谋杀"，homicide 和 manslaughter 通常都笼统翻译为"杀人"。实际上，这三个词在英文中有明确区分。

Homicide (Latin *homicidium, homo*, human being and *caedere*, to cut, kill) refers to the act of killing another human being. Although homicide does not necessarily define a criminal act, some jurisdictions use the word to indicate the unlawful killing of a person. Generally, however, homicide includes murder (intentional killing) and manslaughter, as well as non-criminal killings, or "justifiable homicides". There are a number of justifications, including self-defense, execution of capital punishment, and killing enemy combatants during war, that may make homicide legally justifiable. More complex defenses include euthanasia ("mercy killing" or "assisted suicide" at another's request) and abortion (legal termination of the life of an unborn fetus). ②

可见，homicide 是一个中性词，既包括合法杀人（处决罪犯、正

---

① "Unintentional Injuries vs. Intentional Injuries: Definitions & Differences"，引自 Study.com 网站（http://study.com/academy/lesson/unintentional-injuries-vs-intentional-injuries-definitions-differences.html，读取日期 2016-04-28）。

② "Homicide"，引自 New World Encyclopedia 网站（http://www.new-worldencyclopedia.org/entry/Homicide，读取日期 2016-04-28）。

当防卫、战场杀敌），也包括非法杀人（murder、manslaughter）。《元照英美法词典》对 homicide 的解释为：

> n. 杀人　指一人导致或促使他人死亡的一般用语。该词是中性词，只描述客观行为，而对其道德或法律性质并没有作出判断。杀人并不必然构成犯罪，在依法执行死刑、自卫以及作为追捕逃犯的唯一可能手段时，杀人则是合法的。但如果一人蓄意、明知、轻率或疏忽致使他人死亡的，该人则犯有杀人罪。英美普通法和制定法都把杀人罪分为谋杀（murder）和非预谋杀人（manslaughter）。在苏格兰，杀人分为有罪杀人（culpable homicide）、正当杀人（justifiable homicide）以及意外、疏忽或可宽恕杀人（accidental, negligent, or excusable homicide）。①

这一解释与上段的解释一致。同时也可知，杀人在不同国家的划分和称呼有所不同。词条中把 murder 翻译为"谋杀"，manslaughter 翻译为"非预谋杀人"，两相对比，形成一组概念。那么，是否可以比照中国的说法，把 murder 和 manslaughter 分别翻译为"故意杀人"和"过失致人死亡"呢？故意杀人，是指故意非法剥夺他人生命的行为②，包括"故意""非法""剥夺生命"三个关键词。过失致人死亡罪（俗称"过失杀人"），是指行为人因疏忽大意没有预见到或者已经预见到而轻信能够避免造成的他人死亡，剥夺他人生命权的行为③。这个定义中不强调故意。而英文对 murder 的定义是：

---

① 薛波：《元照英美法词典》，北京大学出版社，2013年，第645页。
② 王作富《刑法》，第4版，中国人民大学出版社，1999年，第403页。
③ 同上，第406页。

Murder is the killing of another human being without justification or valid excuse, and it is especially the unlawful killing of another human being with malice aforethought.①

我们发现，malice aforethought 的意思是："A predetermination to commit an act without legal justification or excuse."。② 看来 murder 的定义强调"非法""预谋""剥夺生命"。murder 与"故意杀人"似乎能够对应。但调查发现，manslaughter 的定义中也包含"故意"（intentional）：

Manslaughter: The unjustifiable, inexcusable, and intentional killing of a human being without deliberation, premeditation, and malice. The unlawful killing of a human being without any deliberation, which may be involuntary, in the commission of a lawful act without due caution and circumspection.

Manslaughter is a distinct crime and is not considered a lesser degree of murder. The essential distinction between the two offenses is that malice aforethought must be present for murder, whereas it must be absent for manslaughter. Manslaughter is not as serious a crime as murder. On the other hand, it is not a justifiable or excusable killing for which little or no punishment is imposed.③

---

① 维基百科 Murder 条（https://en.wikipedia.org/wiki/Murder，读取日期 2016-04-28）。

② *West's Encyclopedia of American Law* 第 2 版，转引自 The Free Dictionary 网站（http://legal-dictionary.thefreedictionary.com/malice+aforethought，读取日期 2016-04-28）。

③ *West's Encyclopedia of American Law* 第 2 版，转引自 The Free Dictionary 网站（http://legal-dictionary.thefreedictionary.com/manslaughter，读取日期 2016-04-28）。

可见 murder 和 manslaughter 的最主要区别是"预谋";在"故意"方面无区别。看来两者译为"故意杀人"和"过失杀人"并不妥当,译为"预谋杀人"("谋杀")和"非预谋杀人"是经过认真考虑的。另外,manslaughter 分为 voluntary 和 involuntary:

> Voluntary manslaughter is commonly defined as an intentional killing in which the offender had no prior intent to kill, such as a killing that occurs in the "heat of passion". The circumstances leading to the killing must be the kind that would cause a reasonable person to become emotionally or mentally disturbed; otherwise, the killing may be charged as a first-degree or second-degree murder.
>
> For example, Dan comes home to find his wife in bed with Victor. In the heat of the moment, Dan picks up a golf club from next to the bed and strikes Victor in the head, killing him instantly.[①]

《元照英美法词典》将 voluntary manslaughter 译为"非预谋故意杀人",意思是正确的:

> 激情杀人是<u>非预谋故意杀人</u>的典型形式,即被告人因受到强烈的刺激,致使其在盛怒心理状态下实施的故意杀人行为。[②]

而与中国的"过失杀人"比较对应的,是英文的 involuntary manslaughter。《元照英美法词典》中这样解释 involuntary manslaughter:

---

① "Voluntary Manslaughter Overview",引自 Find Law 网站(http://criminal.findlaw.com/criminal-charges/voluntary-manslaughter-overview.html#sthash.euw-NPjNt.dpuf,2016-04-28)。

② 薛波:《元照英美法词典》,北京大学出版社,2013年,第1408页。

过失杀人罪是非预谋杀人罪（manslaughter）的一种类型，与非预谋故意杀人罪（voluntary manslaughter）相对。指<u>没有杀人或重伤</u>的<u>故意</u>但出于犯罪性疏忽（criminal negligence）或在实行不包括在重罪-谋杀规则（felony-murder rule）之内的重罪的过程中造成他人死亡的行为。①

如果觉得中文不好懂，这里是相关英文解释：

Involuntary manslaughter, on the other hand, occurs when someone dies as a result of the defendant's non-felonious illegal act or as a consequence of the defendan's irresponsibility or recklessness.②

《元照英美法词典》在翻译 voluntary 和 involuntary manslaughter 时，对 manslaughter 的处理不一致。前者处理为"故意杀人"，后者处理为"杀人"；显然，译者看到了后者如果处理为"故意杀人"与定义中非故意性的矛盾。原因在于，manslaughter 本身并无故意的含义。它的字面意思就是"杀人"。"故意"是我们根据前者的语境添加的，而这一添加不适用于后者。所以，为了保持翻译的一致性，同时为了避免回译麻烦，不妨把 voluntary manslaughter 翻译为"自主杀人"，把 involuntary manslaughter 译为"非自主杀人"。"自主"隐含了"故意"，"非自主"隐含无故意（过失）。与英文定义完美对应。同时 manslaughter 作为与 murder 相对的概念，仍可翻译为"非预

---

① 薛波：《元照英美法词典》，北京大学出版社，2013年，第730页。

② "Voluntary Manslaughter Overview"，引自 Find Law 网站（http://criminal.findlaw.com/criminal-charges/voluntary-manslaughter-overview.html#sthash.euw-NPjNt.dpuf，2016-04-28）。

谋杀人"。

有词典中把 voluntary manslaughter 翻译为"故意杀人",未尝不可,但可能与"谋杀"混淆;翻译为"志愿杀人",词不达意。反过来,中国法律中的"故意杀人",可以直译为 intentional homicide;"过失致人死亡"("过失杀人")可以翻译为 negligently causing death(negligent homicide)。

# 第十一讲

## 与税收相关的几个概念及其翻译

### 分税制

新中国成立以来最重大的税制改革,是1994年的分税制改革:

中国1994年分税制改革,简称分税制改革,是中国政府在1992年着手设计、1993年准备并颁布、1994年实施的一项财税体制改革,它对中央和地方政府之间的**税收分配制度**①及税收结构进行了一次较大规模的调整,标志着中国的财政体制由计划经济向市场经济的改革迈出了实质性的一步。分税制改革的主要目的是缓解自1980年代末以来中央财政入不敷出的情况,在改革取得显著成效的同时,也产生了诸如增加地方政府财政负担等问题,催生了严重的土地财政进而推高了土地、住房价格。因此,分税制改革被认为是解开"中国土地财政增长之谜"的关键。②

"分税制"从一开始就被译为tax sharing system,沿用至今:

The tax sharing system introduced in 1994 stabilized central

---

① 着重号为笔者所加。下同。

② 维基百科"中国1994年分税制改革"条(https://zh.wikipedia.org/wiki/中国1994年分税制改革,读取日期2016-07-11)。

government's revenue growth. The central government got greater fiscal power as it had more revenue. This made local government more dependent on central government for transfer payments.①

《中国日报》的 language tips 给出的译文也是 tax sharing system②。

也有用其他译法的，如 tax assignment system：

> The 1994 reform was an attempt to replace the old discretion-based system of revenue-sharing with a new rule-based system of revenue-sharing. The new system was called the <u>tax assignment system</u>③ (*fenshuizhi*).④

两种译法哪个正确？

要准确翻译，首先必须准确理解。作为分税制主要推手的朱镕基总理在 1993 年 7 月 23 日的全国财政、税收工作会议上这样说：

> 分税制是什么意思呢？就是在财政体制上不再搞什么包干、什么分成，而是按税种划分中央和地方的财政收入，中央收哪几

---

① "China: fiscal and tax reform since the third plenum"，引自 GOV.UK 网站（https://www.gov.uk/government/publications/china-economy-fiscal-and-tax-reform-since-the-third-plenum/china-economy-fiscal-and-tax-reform-since-the-third-plenum，读取日期 2016-07-11）。

② "Language Tips. tax sharing system"，引自中国日报网站（http://language.chinadaily.com.cn/60th/economy.html，读取日期 2016-07-11）。

③ 下画线为笔者所加。下同。

④ S. Wang: "China's 1994 Fiscal Reform: An Initial Assessment"，(Department of Political Science Yale University, 1997).

种税，地方收哪几种税。实行市场经济的国家都是这样的。要尽量减少共享税，当然共享税一点没有也不行，但原则是尽量分税。分别征收是什么意思呢？就是组建两套税务征收机构，一个叫中央税务局，完全是垂直的，收中央税；一个叫地方税务局，收地方税。共享税由中央税务局负责征收，统一政策，统一征管，收完以后，把地方应该分得的共享税收入退给地方税务局，分钱不分权。①

由此可见，这里所说的"分"，相对于过去的"合"。过去不分地税局、国税局，只有一个税务局。各地税务局（代表中央政府）把各种名目的税收上来后，通过不同安排（统收统支、分成、包干）与中央共享。这里所说的"税"，是指"税种"，不是"税收"。

理解后，再说翻译。看到"税"字，我们往往不假思索翻译为 tax。但"税"既可以指"税种"，也可以指"税收"。前者翻译为 tax，后者翻译为 revenue，不能随意使用。tax 是指对产品、收入、活动所征收的费用：

> A fee charged ("levied") by a government on a product, income, or activity. If tax is levied directly on personal or corporate income, then it is a direct tax. If tax is levied on the price of a good or service, then it is called an indirect tax. The purpose of taxation is to finance government expenditure. One of the most important uses of taxes is to finance public goods and services, such as street lighting and street cleaning.②

---

① 《十四大以来文献选编：整顿财税秩序，严肃财经纪律，强化税收征管，加强财税》，引自中国共产党新闻网（http://cpc.people.com.cn/GB/64184/64186/66685/4494229.html，读取日期 2016-07-11）。

② "Tax"，引自 Investor Words 网站（http://www.investorwords.com/4879/tax.html#ixzz4Dlo2COEF，读取日期 2016-07-11）。

revenue 是指政府通过征税等活动获得的收入：

> Revenue, the income of a government from taxation, excise duties, customs, or other sources, appropriated to the payment of the public expenses.①

因此有 tax revenue 一说：

> Tax revenue is the income that is gained by governments through taxation.②

可见，tax 是手段，revenue 是结果。"分税制"改革是对税种进行分配。有的税种让中央征收，有的税种让地方征收，有的税种（"共享税"）由中央征收，但收入与地方分成。因此，分税制当中的"税"，译为 tax 是正确的。tax assignment system（对税种进行分配的制度）的说法是成立的。

tax sharing system 的译法，虽然用对了 tax，但 sharing 值得商榷。因为在过去的税制中，全部税种（taxes）都是共享的；现在的税制中，只有少量共享税（shared taxes）。引入分税制，就是要改革过去的共享税制（"尽量减少共享税"）。用 tax sharing 命名，等于用旧制度命名新制度。

另外，"分税制"把税分为中央税（central taxes）、地方税（local taxes）和共享税（*shared taxes*），如果该税制以 tax sharing 命

---

① *Random House Unabridged Dictionary*，转引自 Dictionary.com 网站（http://www.dictionary.com/browse/revenue，读取日期 2016b-07-11）。

② 维基百科 Tax revenue 条，（https://en.wikipedia.org/wiki/Tax_revenue，读取日期 2016-07-11）。

名,也导致概念体系混乱,因为大概念和子概念名称相同。

那么,能否基于"分税制"改革的实质,把新税制命名为 revenue sharing system(收入分享制度)呢?revenue sharing 在英文中是个术语,定义如下:

> A transfer of tax revenue from one unit of government, such as the federal government, to other units, such as state governments. ①

鉴于旧税制本来就是单一机构征收、然后分享的制度,即"收入分享制"(revenue sharing system),因此,新税制不能命名为 revenue sharing system。但讲到税制改革时,可以说 revenue sharing (system) reform,因为改革的实质,就是重新分配课税收入。

对于 1994 年的税制改革,也有些地方采用更简单的说法,即 the 1994 fiscal reform,这是完全正确的:

> China's 1994 Fiscal Reform: An Initial Assessment Asian Survey (September, 1997) ②

有人认为"分税制"就是中国的财政联邦制(fiscal federalism)③或税收联邦制(tax federalism)。tax federalism 的意思是:

> The separation of taxation power between the Centre and the

---

① The New Dictionary of Cultural Literacy,转引自 Dictionary.com 网站( https://www.dictionary.com/browse/revenue-sharing?s=t,读取日期 2016-07-11)。

② S.Wang: "China's 1994 Fiscal Reform: An Initial Assessment Asian Survey", (Department of Political Science Yale University, 1997).

③ 冯兴元:《大国之道:中国私人与公共选择的宪则分析》,福建教育出版社,2013 年。

Regions in a unitary country and between the Centre, Federal Regions, and Regions in a federal state.[①]

受此定义启发，也可以把"分税制"译为 separated taxation system。因为 1994 年税制改革的一项重要举措，就是设立中央和地方两套征管机构。实际上，朱镕基讲话显示，"分税制"当中的"分"有两个意思，一个是"划分"（税种），一个是"分别"（征收）。tax assignment 的译法取的是前一个意思，separated taxation 取的是后一个意思。实际上，separated taxation 可能隐含 tax assignment，反过来却不一定；可惜这一译法很少有人用。

另外，分税制当中的"共享税"应当译为 shared taxes（复数）。这里的"税"，是指"税种"，不是 revenue。中国的共享税包括增值税、企业所得税、个人所得税、印花税等。

尽管做了以上分析，但 tax sharing system 的译法已经用了 20 多年，单凭一篇文章的声音，恐怕已经无力回天。但我们心里要明白，这个译法并非最优。

当年笔者在北外读书时，正值"分税制"改革热火朝天之时，各种相关会议铺天盖地。当时在会议上听到 tax sharing system 的说法，觉得难以理解，但由于缺乏网络工具，无法进行详细调查，便人云亦云。这个例子说明，概念的首次翻译非常重要，特别是译者在有影响的部门工作时。所以确定译名要慎之又慎，否则会以讹传讹，贻害无穷。

---

[①] V. Papava: "Necroeconomics — the theory of post-Communist transformation of an economy", *International Journal of Social Economics*, 10 (2002), pp.796-805.

## 财权和事权

财权是指在法律允许下,各级政府负责筹集和支配收入的权力,主要包括税权、收费权及发债权①。所谓事权,简单说是指一级政府在公共事务和服务中应承担的任务和职责②。看来"事权"不是"权力",而是"职责",分税制改革即中央和地方财权的重新划分。财权划分的基础是事权划分。

"财权"如何翻译?吴光华主编的《汉英大词典》③以及网上资料给出了两种解释和译文:

1.(财产所有权)property ownership; right of property; ownership of movable property
2.(经济大权)economic rights; power over financial affairs

这显然不是财政领域的含义。

同一词典对"事权"的翻译是:powers or authority of office④。这显然也不是财税改革中讨论的概念。

网上有资料将两者分别译为 administrative and financial powers。但"事权"和"行政权"(administrative powers)似乎不是同一概念。

这些看似具有中国特色的概念,其实是各国都在讨论的问题;即使是在中国发生的事情,国际上也有广泛关注。因此,最好的翻译不是闭门造车,而是看看其他人在谈到这些问题时,是怎么说的。

---

① 曾庆敏:《法学大辞典》,第 6 版,上海辞书出版社,1998 年,第 732 页。
② 谭建立,杨晓宇:《关于事权概念的几点理论认识》,《山东经济》2008 年第 6 期,第 80 页。
③ 吴光华:《汉英大词典》,上海交通大学出版社,1993 年,第 206 页。
④ 同上,第 2314 页。

伦敦政治经济学院亚洲研究中心的 Ehtisham Ahmad 在 "Should China Revisit the 1994 Fiscal Reforms?"①一文中写道：

> The 1993/4 reforms were partial in that the focus was on the tax system and revenue sharing arrangements, and the budget system reforms and <u>spending assignments</u> were not addressed at that time.

这里的 spending assignments 即"事权划分"。其中还写道：

> The absence of own-source tax handles for local governments, combined with the increasing <u>devolution of spending responsibilities</u>, and inability to rationalize spending that should normally be the responsibility of higher levels——especially involving the pooling of risks, such as for pensions or unemployment benefits has led the local governments to greater reliance on operations involving land.

这里的 devolution of spending responsibilities 是指事权的下放。"事权"是 spending responsibilities。后面还有：

> International experience suggests that clarity in <u>spending responsibilities</u>, together with appropriate own-source revenues, are critical in engendering incentives for improved governance at the subnational level.

这里再次用 spending responsibilities 表示"事权"。

---

① E. Ahmad: "Should China Revisit the 1994 Fiscal Reforms?"，引自 LSE Asia Research Centre 网站（http://www.lse.ac.uk/asiaResearchCentre/_files/ARCWP52-Ahmad.pdf，读取日期 2016-07-11）。

由此可见，"事权"可以说 spending responsibilities。

McLure 等有一篇文章，标题就叫 The Assignment of Revenues and Expenditures in Intergovernmental Fiscal Relations[①]。其中的 assignment of revenues 即"财权的划分"，assignment of expenditures 即"事权划分"。

同样的说法在该文中多处出现：

> Designing the other important pieces of a system of decentralized finances, revenue assignments and transfers, in the absence of a clear expenditure assignment is to put the car before the horse.

该文中还说：

> The first fundamental step in the design of a system of intergovernmental fiscal relations should be a clear assignment of functional responsibilities among different levels of government.

其中的 functional responsibilities 也是指"事权"。

白素珊（Susan H. Whiting）在 Central-Local Fiscal Relations in China[②] 一文中说：

---

[①] C. E. McLure & J. Martinez-Vazquez: "The Assignment of Revenues and Expenditures in Intergovernmental Fiscal Relations"，引自 The World Bank 网站（http://www.worldbank.org/publicsector/pe/PEAMMarch2005/AssignmentRevenues.pdf，读取日期 2016-07-11）。

[②] S. H. Whiting: "Central-Local Fiscal Relations in China"，引自 National Committee on US China Relations 网站（https://www.ncuscr.org/sites/default/files/page_attachments/Central-Local-Fiscal-Relations.pdf，读取日期 2016-07-11）。

Central-local fiscal relations have undergone a series of fundamental changes during the course of China's transition from a planned to a market economy. Current challenges grow out of a number of features of the Chinese political economy, the most important of which is the mismatch between the <u>allocation of revenues</u> and the <u>assignment of expenditure responsibilities</u> across levels of government.

此处的 allocation of revenues 即财权的划分；assignment of expenditure responsibilities 即事权的划分。在另一处说：

The <u>mismatch between revenues and expenditure responsibilities</u> also leads to unusually heavy reliance on intergovernmental fiscal transfers that, nonetheless, have not yet effectively redressed the high levels of inequality that have emerged in the context of economic reform.

此处的 revenues 可以理解为"财权"。

下面一段的 the misalignment of revenues and expenditures 即"财权和事权不匹配"：

The second section lays out the rationale for the conference and an overview of the proceedings organized around the five major themes: 1) <u>the misalignment of revenues and expenditures</u>, 2) the problem of revenue inadequacy at the local level, 3) the quest for additional local revenue through off-budget finance and debt, 4) the state of intergovernmental fiscal transfers and inequality, and 5) the political aspects of fiscal problems.

从以上例子可以看出，国外文献在讨论中文财税制度时，对财权和事权概念的表述是相对一致的。简单的说法即 revenue 和 expenditure，必要时用 spending/functional responsibilities。事权和财权的划分/分配，用 assignment 或 allocation。

尽管国外多数文献把"事权"称为一种责任（responsibilities），但也可以看到把"事权"称为 power（权力）的说法。某网站这样定义 spending power：

> Authority granted by a legislature to an administration (government) to spend public funds in accordance with an approved budget.①

这个说法与中文"事权"比较对应。McLure 的文章中也有同样用法：

> Decentralization of <u>taxing and spending power</u> allows subnational governments to tailor schemes that match the demand of their constituency which will increase efficiency ultimately because local governments have better information about their residents' needs than the central government.

对于中央向地方下放事权，却不下放财权，英文中有 unfunded mandates 的说法：

> An unfunded mandate is a statute or regulation that requires a state or local government to perform certain actions, with no money provided

---

① "Spending Power"，引自 Business Dictionary 网站（http://www.businessdictionary.com/definition/spending-power.html#ixzz4DtyDljQL，读取日期 2016-07-11）。

for fulfilling the requirements. Public individuals or organizations can also be required to fulfill public mandates. ①

据此，必要时也可以用 mandates 来翻译"事权"。

## Tax Deduction 和 Tax Credit

英语中有一系列与税收优惠有关的说法，如 tax exemption、tax credit、tax deduction、tax break、tax relief、tax holiday 等。这些说法有的意思相同，有的差别很大，译者有必要了解。

tax exemption 是"税收减免"，既包括"减"，也包括"免"；因为 exemption 包括部分免除，即"减"。减免的方式可以是完全免税、降低税率或减少应纳税项目。维基百科的定义是：

> Tax exemption refers to a monetary exemption which reduces taxable income. Tax exempt status can provide complete relief from taxes, reduced rates, or tax on only a portion of items. ②

MBA 智库百科对"税收减免"的定义是："税收减免是指对纳税人应纳税款给予部分减少或全部免除。税收优惠的重要形式之一。"③

tax credit 是指直接减少应纳税额。可以译为"税额抵免"，或"纳税抵免额"。比如，收入 1 万元，税率 10%，应纳税额是 1000

---

① 维基百科 Unfunded mandate 条（https://en.wikipedia.org/wiki/Unfunded_mandate，读取日期 2016-07-11）。

② 维基百科 Tax exemption 条（https://en.wikipedia.org/wiki/Tax_exemption，读取日期 2016-07-11）。

③ MBA 智库百科"税收减免"词条（http://wiki.mbalib.com/wiki/税收减免，读取日期 2016-07-11）。

元。但如果你有 300 元的 tax credit（抵税额），则只需要缴纳 700 元的税。

大多数 tax credit 是 non-refundable（不可退换）的，即如果你有 300 元的纳税抵免额，但你依法无须交税，则这 300 元不会退给你。也有 refundable tax credit（可退税抵免额），意思是，即使你不交税，这 300 元钱也会退给你。

tax deduction 是"税前列支"或"税前扣除"，是指纳税前在毛收入中扣除费用，仅就剩余部分纳税。比如，毛收入是 1 万元，可扣除的费用（tax deductible expenses）是 3000 元，剩余 7000 元，税率是 10%，则应纳税额（tax payable）是 700 元。有的词典将其译为"应税收益额扣减"。

tax deduction 的英文解释及其与 tax exemption 和 tax credit 的区别：

> Tax deduction is a reduction of income that is able to be taxed, and is commonly a result of expenses, particularly those incurred to produce additional income. The difference between deductions, exemptions and credit is that deductions and exemptions both reduce taxable income, while credits reduce tax.[1]

上述三种减免税的方法可以统称 tax break（税收优惠）：

> Tax break is a term referring to any item which avoids taxes, including any tax exemption, tax deduction, or tax credit.[2]

---

① 维基百科 Tax basis 条（https://en.wikipedia.org/wiki/Tax_basis，读取日期 2016-07-11）。

② 维基百科 Tax break 条（https://en.wikipedia.org/wiki/Tax_break，读取日期 2016-07-11）。

从翻译的角度看，tax break、tax relief、tax holiday 恐怕都可以译为"税收减免""税收优惠"等，但这些词的实际用法还是有所不同的。这也是翻译感到无奈的时候。如需要，tax relief 也许可以直译为"收税照顾""收税救济"，因为它往往针对特定事件：

> Tax relief is any program or incentive that reduces the amount of tax owed by an individual or business entity. Examples of tax relief include the allowable deduction for pension contributions, and temporary incentives such as tax credits for the purchase of new high-efficiency heating and cooling equipment.
>
> Tax relief is intended to reduce the tax liability of an individual or business entity. Often, the tax relief is targeted at providing aid for a certain event or cause. For example, hurricane victims may be allotted some form of tax relief when a hard-hit area is declared a disaster area. Tax relief is also available periodically to support environmental causes, as seen with tax credits for the purchase of energy-efficient appliances or the installation of energy-efficient windows. ①

tax holiday 可以直译为"税收假日"，往往用于作为招商引资的手段：

> A tax holiday is a temporary reduction or elimination of a tax. It is synonymous with tax abatement, tax subsidy or tax reduction. Governments usually create tax holidays as incentives for business investment. ②

---

① "Tax Relief"，引自 Investopedia 网站（http://www.investopedia.com/terms/t/tax-relief.asp#ixzz4E0Hcil00，读取日期 2016-07-11）。

② 维基百科 Tax holiday 条（https://en.wikipedia.org/wiki/Tax_holiday，读取日期 2016-07-11）。

## Tax Refund 和 Tax Return

　　tax refund 也叫 tax rebate，可译为"退税"，顾名思义，把已经征缴的税退回。比如，工薪税通常采用源头扣缴的办法征收（叫预扣税，withholding tax）。一年到头，（美国）纳税人要填写一份纳税申报表（tax return），说明自己本年度收入、费用、减免额、应税收益额和应纳税额等内容。如果平时扣多了，多出的部分税务局会退还。

　　注意：tax return 的意思是"纳税申报（表）""报税单"，不是"退税"的意思。这里的 return 是 report 的意思。类似的用法还有 election returns（选举结果报告）。这个说法容易和 tax refund 混淆。美国人也不例外。

## Tax Base 和 Tax Basis

tax base 的定义是：

　　Tax base is defined as the income or asset balance used to calculate a tax liability, and the tax liability formula is tax base multiplied by tax rate. The rate of tax imposed varies depending on the type of tax and the tax base total. Income tax, gift tax and estate tax are each calculated using a different tax rate schedule. [1]

这一概念相当于汉语的"计税依据"：

　　　　计税依据又称税基，是计算应纳或应征税款所依据的标准，是根据税法所确定的，用以计算应纳税额的基数。应纳税款是依

---

　　[1]　"Tax Base"，引自 Investopeida 网站（http://www.investopedia.com/terms/t/taxbase.asp#ixzz4EOv8vUjG，读取日期 2016-07-11）。

照计税依据乘以适用的税率计算得出的。没有计税依据，则无法计算应纳税款，就无法确定纳税义务的内容。①

比如，个人所得的计税依据，就是毛收入减去税前扣减和各种费用，也即 taxable income。tax base 还有另一个意思：

> The value of all assets that a government may tax. The tax base may increase for a number of reasons, particularly with the creation of wealth or when persons with high income move to an area. The tax base is particularly important to local governments because persons with large amounts of assets can move in and out with relative ease. The tax base is also the reason that government revenues tend to increase during economic growth and shrink during recessions.②

这一定义相当于汉语的"课税基础"：

> 课税基础又称税基，指建立某种税或一种税制的经济基础或依据。例如，流转税的课税基础是流转额，所得税的课税基础为所得额，房产税的课税基础为房产等等。选择税基是税制建设上的一个重要问题。选择的课税基础宽，税源比较丰富，这种税的课征意义就大，否则，税源不多，课征意义小。③

---

① 《税收法制通论第三章第五节"计税依据"》，引自北京市地方税务局网站（http://shiju.tax861.gov.cn/ssxc/sszt/fztl/index.asp，读取日期 2016-07-11）。

② *Farlex Financial Dictionary*，转引自 The Free Dictionary 网站（http://financial-dictionary.thefreedictionary.com/tax+base，读取日期 2016-07-11）。

③ 百度百科"课税基础"词条（http://baike.baidu.com/view/634790.htm，读取日期 2016-07-11）。

所以，tax base 可以译为"税基"（两个意思），或视情况分别译为"纳税依据"或"课税基础"。

容易与 tax base 混淆的是一个会计上的概念，叫作 tax basis，也叫 cost basis。举例说明：

> Where an asset is purchased, tax basis generally includes cash paid plus liabilities assumed. For example, if Joe acquires a building for $10,000 cash and assumes a mortgage for $80,000 (which is his liability assumed), Joe's basis in the building is $90,000. [①]

这个概念中文叫作"计税基础"，是 2006 年发布的《企业新会计准则》中提出的概念。它分为资产的计税基础、负债的计税基础两类内容。具体含义可在网上查询。

## Tax Burden 和 Tax Incidence

tax burden（税负）是指实际计缴的税款占相对应的应税销售收入的比例。tax incidence（"税负归宿""税收归宿""赋税归宿""课税归宿"）是指税负最终由谁负担。

纳税人交了税，但这笔税款最终不一定由他负担。比如，税法规定卖一盒烟收税一元。如果对烟的需求没有弹性，即无论多贵烟民都要买，这一元钱可以加入售价，由消费者负担（叫作税负转嫁，tax shifting）。这时候，税的法定归宿（statutory incidence）或名义归宿（nominal incidence）是销售者，但经济归宿（economic incidence）落

---

① 维基百科 Tax basis 条（https://en.wikipedia.org/wiki/Tax_basis，读取日期 2016-07-11）。

在消费者身上。

incidence 的来源：

From Middle French *incidence*, from Medieval Latin *incidentia* ("a falling upon"), from Latin *incidens*, present participle of *incidere* ("to fall upon"), from in ("on") + *cadere* ("to fall").[1]

因此有"落在何处"之义。译为"归宿"恰如其分。

---

[1] "incidence"，引自 Your Dictionary 网站（http://www.yourdictionary.com/incidence，读取日期 2016-07-11）。

# 第十二讲

## 刑法学中的几个概念及其翻译

刑法学教科书将刑法学内容分为刑法总论和刑法分则。总论部分探讨刑法的基本原则、刑法的效力范围、犯罪的概念和构成、犯罪客体、犯罪客观方面、犯罪主体、犯罪主观方面、正当行为、故意犯罪的停止形态、共同犯罪、罪数形态、刑事责任、刑罚概说、刑罚的体系和种类、刑罚裁量、刑罚裁量制度、刑罚执行制度、刑罚的消灭。分则部分包括概述、危害国家安全罪、危害公共安全罪、破坏社会主义市场经济秩序罪、侵犯公民人身权利民主权利罪、侵犯财产罪、妨害社会管理秩序罪、危害国防利益罪、贪污贿赂罪、渎职罪、军人违反职责罪。本文探讨其中的若干概念及其翻译。

### Elements of a Crime 犯罪要件

《Lexis Nexis 英汉法律词典》对犯罪（crime）的定义是：

> An illegal act punishable by the state. Normally, a crime is seen as comprising the act of committing an offence (*actus reus*) and a culpable mental state (*mens rea*). However, it is possible for the legislature to introduce offences not requiring any *mens rea* — "strict liability offences". In order to secure a conviction, the prosecution is expected to prove beyond reasonable doubt each and every element of the crime charged.

从定义里面可以看到，犯罪要件（elements of crime）有两个，一是 *actus reus*（犯罪行为），二是 *mens rea*（犯罪意图）。公诉人只有排除合理怀疑后，证明嫌疑人同时具备犯罪行为和犯罪意图，被告人才能被定罪。当然，有些情况下即使没有犯罪意图，也要受到刑事追究，这叫作严格责任（strict liability）。*actus reus* 和 *mens rea* 是拉丁语，字面意思分别是 guilty act 和 guilty mind。*actus* 的意思是 act，*mens* 的意思是 mind，后者可结合 mental 来记；*rea*（*reus*）的意思是 guilty。这两个概念也可以用 criminal act 和 criminal intent 来表示。

以上是英美法系的犯罪要件。新中国的犯罪构成理论源自苏联，采用"四要件说"（The Four Elements Doctrine），即犯罪的主体（subject）、犯罪的客体（object）、犯罪的主观方面（the subjective side of a crime）、犯罪的客观方面（the objective side of a crime）。定罪必须满足这四个要件[1][2]。

犯罪主体，是指实施犯罪并且承担刑事责任的人。按照我国《刑法》的一般规定，只有达到一定年龄并具有责任能力的自然人，才能成为犯罪主体。比如，张某杀了人，张某 18 岁，是完全行为能力人，所以符合犯罪主体的要求。犯罪的主观方面是犯罪嫌疑人对犯罪结果的主观认识或追求的心理状态（state of mind），如犯罪目的（purpose）、动机（motivation），分为故意（intentional）和过失（negligent）两大类。张某具有故意剥夺他人生命的主观目的动机，所以符合主观方面的要求。犯罪的客体是犯罪所破坏或侵犯的由法律所保护的社会关系。张某非法剥夺了李某的生命权，而生命权受到法

---

[1]　关于四要件的英文表达，笔者长期以来不敢确定，直到听到俄罗斯专家的介绍，并在相关文献中得到验证。

[2]　F. J. Ferdin, et al.: *Encyclopedia of Soviet Law*, 2nd Revised Edition (Boston: Martinus Nijhoff Publishers, 1985), p. 217.

律保护，所以符合第三个要件的要求。犯罪的客观方面是犯罪实际所表现出来的外在事实特征，多指犯罪行为或犯罪结果，即本案中张某刺死李某的行为。本案也符合第四个要件的要求。

在四要件之外，还规定了"排除犯罪的行为"（circumstances removing the criminality of an act; justifications and excuses，即不认为是犯罪的行为），例如正当防卫（self-defense）、紧急避险（necessity）、法令（order of law）行为（如执行枪决）、正当业务行为（抓捕逃犯）等。

前些年我国刑法理论界引入了大陆法系犯罪的"三阶（层）论"（Three-Level Concept of Crime、Three-Pronged Concept of Crime）理论，与"四要件说"竞争。三阶层递进式的犯罪构成体系包括"构成要件该当性"（来自日语）、"违法性"和"有责性"。"构成要件该当性"也称"构成要件符合性"（即"符合构成要件"之义；"该当性"为日语表达，不易理解），来自德语 *Tatbestandsmäßigkeit*。据网络资料，该词的前半部分是 *Tatbestand*，译为 the statutorily defined constituent elements of a crime（犯罪的法定构成要件）。也有学者将 *Tatbestand* 译为英文的 paradigm，整个词翻译为 realization of the paradigm（构成要件的实现，即所发生的事实与刑法条文所规定的构成要件相一致，此所谓"该当""符合"）。

三阶层理论里面的"法定构成要件"（*Tatbestand*）包括：1."主体"，即实施犯罪的行为主体；2."行为"，即危害行为，行为人在人的意识支配下实施的侵犯法益（interests protected by law）的身体活动；3."行为对象"即犯罪对象、行为客体，包括物与人；4."危害结果"和"因果关系"（causation）。

犯罪行为不仅要符合法定符合构成要件（具备"该当性"），而且实质上必须具有违法性（wrongfulness or unlawfulness，德语：

Rechtswidrigkeit）。判断是否违法，要看是否存在"违法阻却事由"（为日语表达；"违法阻却"即"排除违法""不视为违法"之义；英文：grounds of justification and excuse）。违法阻却事由包括正当防卫（self-defense）、紧急避险（necessity）等。

有责性（culpability or blameworthiness，德语：*Schuld*）是指只有当行为人存在主观的责任时，其行为才构成犯罪。所谓主观责任，是指行为人具有责任能力（penal capacity）与故意（intent）或过失（negligence）、违法性意识（consciousness of wrongdoing）以及可被合理期待实施合法行为（Zumutbarkeit，即 fair expectability of lawful conduct）。有责性中包括对刑事责任能力（capacity for criminal responsibility）、刑事责任年龄（age of criminal responsibility）、故意、过失的判断。

同一个张某杀人案，用三阶层理论分析就是：第一步，张某的行为是否符合故意杀人罪的构成要件，即一个人故意剥夺他人的生命？看来符合。第二步，张某的行为是否具有违法性？经查，张某没有正当防卫、紧急避险、执行职务等违法性阻却事由，因此具有违法性。第三步，张某是否具有有责性？经查，张某精神正常，年满 18 周岁，因此，应当负责，具有有责性。三个条件同时具备，张某的行为构成犯罪。

以上讨论和英文说法基于相关研讨会资料和网络资料。另请参照《犯罪构成理论比较研究》[1]。

从上面的比较中，我们可以看出，无论是大陆法系的三阶层理论还是我国的四要件构成理论，本质都是一样的，即行为人客观上违反了刑法的规定，实施了违法行为，但不一定要被定罪，只有行为人应

---

[1] 蔡飞，曹礼坤：《犯罪构成理论比较研究》，引自中国法院网（http://old.chinacourt.org/html/article/200906/12/360826.shtml，读取日期 2016-09-09）。

该承担责任时该行为才是犯罪。

大陆法系的犯罪构成理论将排除违法性的行为包含在理论体系内，在第二步"违法性"中进行判断。四要件构成理论则将排除犯罪的行为放在理论体系外，单独命名为"排除犯罪的行为"。这使得三阶层体系从体系上看起来更圆满。

## 共同犯罪 Complicity in an Offence

共同犯罪，是指二人以上共同故意犯罪。"共同犯罪"作为一个抽象名词，应当翻译为 complicity (in a crime/offence)；作为一个具体名词，可以翻译为 multidefendant crimes。许多地方翻译为 joint crime，但这种说法在其他国家的刑法中看不到，讲给外国专家听，他们也不理解。

"共犯"意思为"共同犯罪的人"时，翻译为 an accomplice，与该词搭配的介词是 in 或 to，例如："She became his unwitting accomplice in the robbery. /an accomplice to murder."。[1]

中国的《刑法》规定，对组织、领导犯罪集团的**首要分子**（ringleader，mastermind），按照该集团所犯的全部罪行处罚。**主犯**（principal）的刑事责任应当按照其所参与或者组织、指挥的全部犯罪处罚（"共同主犯"译为 joint principal）。对于**从犯**（accessories 或 secondary participants in crime），应当从轻、减轻处罚或者免除处罚。对于被胁迫参加犯罪的**胁从犯**（forced accomplice，coerced accomplice，或 unwilling accomplice），应当按照他的犯罪情节减轻处罚或者免除处罚（be exempted from punishment）。教唆

---

[1] "Accomplice"，引自 OZDIC 网站（https://www.ozdic.com/collocation-dictionary/accomplice，读取日期 2016-09-09）。

他人犯罪（instigate the commission of crime by another person）的**教唆犯**（instigator 或 abettor），应当按照他在共同犯罪中所起的作用处罚。教唆不满 18 周岁的人犯罪的，应当从重处罚（to aggravate punishment）。如果被教唆的人没有犯被教唆的罪，对于教唆犯，可以从轻或者减轻处罚。

## Inchoate Crimes 初始罪

此罪也译为"未完成罪"，有两个意义。1. 英美法系将导致其他犯罪的一种刚开始的犯罪称为 inchoate crime，例如故意伤害罪（assault）就是殴击罪（battery）的初始罪。初始罪也可以作为独立的犯罪存在。2. 美国的《模范刑法典》将未遂（attempt）、教唆（solicitation）和共谋（conspiracy）三种情况统一称为 inchoate crime。①

相关英文解释为：

Inchoate crimes, which are also referred to as incomplete crimes, are acts involving the tendency to commit, or to indirectly participate in a criminal offense. In the past, several inchoate crimes used to be regarded as minor offenses. However, in recent times, several inchoate offenses are considered serious crimes, and have shifted from the grade of misdemeanors to felony offenses. Inchoate crimes include attempt to commit the crime, conspiracy to commit the crime, and solicitation to commit the crime. Being an accessory or an accomplice to a crime is also

---

① *Model Penal Code*, (Philadelphia: The American Law Institute, 1985), pp. 74-77.

an inchoate crime.[①]

犯罪按终止时的状态分为：犯罪预备（preparation）、犯罪未遂（attempt）、犯罪中止（voluntary abandonment）、犯罪既遂（completed crime）。其中，犯罪既遂属于犯罪完成形态，其他情形属于犯罪未完成形态（uncompleted crime，或 incomplete crime）。在未完成形态中，犯罪未遂和犯罪中止较为常见，也容易引起理论和实践上争议与分歧。

## Indictable Offence vs. Summary Offence
## 适用普通程序的犯罪 vs. 适用简易程序的犯罪

indictable offences 在有些词典上被翻译为"可诉罪""公诉罪"；与之相对的 summary offence 被翻译为"简易罪"。这两种翻译方法都不达意。

在美国，犯罪分为两类：felony（重罪）和 misdemeanor（轻罪）。现在，许多普通法系国家不再使用 felony、misdemeanor 的划分方法，而是以程序来划分，把犯罪分为 indictable offences 和 summary offences，用以强调这两种犯罪的处理程序不同。凡是重罪，必须采用 indictment（经过大陪审团或相当程序批准签发的起诉书）来提起公诉，由小陪审团审理；凡是轻罪，采用简易程序审理，不需要经过大陪审团或相当程序的批准，庭审也不用小陪审团。（两个程序还有其他方面一些区别。）所以，本质上，indictable offence 就是"重罪"，summary offence 就是"轻罪"；必要时也可以这样翻译。如果要翻译出程序上的区分，可以比照中国的刑事诉讼程序，把 indictable

---

① "Inchoate Crimes"，引自 US Legal 网站（http://criminallaw.uslegal.com/incohate-crimes/，读取日期 2016-09-09）。

offence 翻译为"适用普通程序的犯罪",把 summary offence 翻译为"适用简易程序的犯罪"。summary 在英文中的意思就是"适用简易程序的":"(of legal proceedings, jurisdiction, etc.) conducted without, or exempt from, the various steps and delays of a formal trial."。在加拿大,summary offences 被称为 summary conviction offences[①]。

如果一个犯罪行为既可以适用普通程序,又可以适用简易程序,则叫作 an either way offence(可适用任一程序的犯罪)、hybrid offence(可适用不同程序的犯罪)、dual offence(可适用两种程序的犯罪)、Crown option offence(公诉人可选程序的犯罪)、dual procedure offence(可适用两种程序的犯罪),或者 wobbler(可选程序犯罪)[②]。

在中国,刑事案件有三种审理程序:普通程序(regular procedure)、简易程序(summary procedure)和普通程序简易化审理〔简称:普通程序简化审或普通程序简易审,simplified (regular) procedure〕。

简易程序审理适用的条件是:事实清楚、证据充分(the facts of the case are clear, the evidence is complete);被告人及辩护人对所指控的基本犯罪事实没有异议(the defendant and defence attorney do not contest the alleged facts);依法可能判处 3 年以下有期徒刑(imprisonment)、拘役(*juyi* or criminal detention)、管制(*guanzhi* or public surveillance)或者单处罚金(fines only)。

---

① "What is the Difference between a Summary and Indictable Offence?",引自 Find Law 网站(http://www.findlaw.com.au/faqs/1188/what-is-the-difference-between-a-summary-and-indic.aspx,读取日期 2016-09-09)。

② 维基百科 Hybrid Offence 条(https://en.wikipedia.org/wiki/Hybrid_offence,读取日期 2016-09-09)。

普通程序简易审与简易程序的要求大同小异，不同之处是该案涉及的刑罚须超过 3 年。而且普通程序简易审需要更多的程序步骤，例如，庭审时检察院必须有人到庭，但检察官只需要"概述"一下事实。与简易程序一样，无须询问被告和其他证人，庭审仅仅是用来讨论适当的刑罚。

其他案件适用普通程序。实行简繁分流，主要是为了减轻法院办案的负担。

顺便说明，summary execution 是指未经正常司法程序（summary）执行处决，联合国文件中翻译为"即决处决"。在游击战争、恐怖活动和平叛活动中经常使用。国际法认为，许多情况下的 summary execution 是非法的，因为它违反了一个人接受独立和中立的法庭公平和公开审判的权利。

## Aggravating Circumstance 加重罪行的情节

这个概念以前涉及过，本文再作深入探讨。英美法中的 aggravating circumstance 是指导致罪行更加严重的犯罪情景，可以译为"加重罪行的情节"。具有加重情节的罪行（aggravated offence）要受到更重的处罚（a greater penalty）。加重情节包括犯罪时持有武器（possession of a weapon）、违反信托关系（breach of trust）或犯罪时怀有特定意图。受害人的某些特征也可造成罪行加重，如受害人是儿童或游客。有组织犯罪（organized crime）也是加重情节。相关术语：aggravated assault（有加重情节的袭击罪）、aggravated burglary（有加重情节的入室盗窃罪）、aggravated manslaughter（有加重情节的非预谋杀人）。mitigating/extenuating circumstance/factors 是指相反的情况，即减轻罪行的情节。

中国法律规定了从轻/从重处罚的情节以及减轻/加重处罚的情

节。**从轻**处罚是指在法定处罚种类（types of punishment）和幅度（latitude）内对行为人适用较轻种类或者较小幅度的处罚。如罪行按法律应判有期徒刑（处罚种类）2 至 10 年（处罚幅度），法官酌情判2年，但不能再减轻为"拘役"，因为"拘役"已经不属于"有期徒刑"这个种类。**减轻**处罚是指在法定的最轻处罚种类和最小处罚幅度以下给予处罚。例如，本该有期徒刑，改为拘役；本该判 2 至 10 年，判 1 年。从重和加重处罚的规定与之相反。

刑事犯罪法定减轻、从轻的情节有：特殊主体犯罪（如未成年人）、犯罪预备、中止或未遂、自首、立功（cooperation）[①]、从犯/胁从犯、防卫过当等。

由此可见，英美法从罪行（原因）的角度规定犯罪情节轻重，中国法律从处罚（结果）的角度规定犯罪情节轻重；不过，最终的结果都一样。只是英美法系似乎没有区分"从轻"和"减轻"、"从重"和"加重"。这可能是因为这些国家有详细的量刑指南（sentencing guidelines），有加重情节的犯罪（aggravated offence）和情节一般的犯罪（basic offence）应该量什么刑，都有详细的规定，法官自由裁量的幅度不大，只能"从轻""从重"，不能"减轻""加重"。

这就涉及汉语的"减轻处罚"和"从轻处罚"的翻译问题。由于前者缺乏对等词，可以译为 to reduce punishment，必要时解释为 to reduce punishment (sentence) to a level below the statutory minimum period；后者可以译为 to mitigate a sentence/punishment。也可以把两者都笼统翻译为 mitigation，必要时补充说明 within 或 beyond the

---

[①] "立功"经常被翻译为 render meritorious service。但在与国外专家沟通时，发现对方听不懂。在我国，"立功"包括犯罪分子揭发他人的犯罪行为或提供重要线索，使侦查机关从而得以侦破其他案件的行为。这样的行为在英语国家称为 cooperation（配合警方调查）。

statutory sentencing range。"从轻、减轻处罚",连在一起翻译,就是 to mitigate or reduce a sentence。

## 刑罚的种类 Criminal Sanctions

刑法分为主刑和附加刑。主刑(principal sanction/punishment; primary sanction/punishment)是附加刑的对称,是法院判处刑罚时独立适用的刑罚。中国刑法规定的主刑有(从轻到重):管制(*guanzhi*, or surveillance, or police supervision in the community, from three months to two years)、拘役(*juyi*, criminal detention, from one month to six months),有期徒刑(fixed-term imprisonment)、无期徒刑〔non-fixed term imprisonment, life imprisonment (with parole)〕、死刑(death penalty)。

附加刑(accessory sanction/punishment; secondary sanction/punishment):除主刑之外的刑罚,包括罚金(fines)、剥夺政治权利(deprivation of political rights)、没收财产(forfeiture of property)、驱逐出境(deportation)。

# 第十三讲

## 法律援助中的几个概念及其翻译

### 法律援助 Legal Aid

法律援助是对无钱聘请律师的人的法律帮助，不收费或少收费，包括代理他们到法庭诉讼。有的国家也叫 legal assistance。

在中国，法律援助由法律援助中心（Legal Aid Center）提供。法律援助中心办不完的案子，指派社会律师办理。在刑事案件中，符合以下条件的案件可享受法律援助：

1. 被告人是盲（blind）、聋（deaf）、哑（mute）或者未成年人（children / minors）而没有委托辩护人的（retain a lawyer）；

2. 被告人可能被判处死刑（punishable by death）而没有委托辩护人的或者人民法院一审判处死刑的被告人没有委托辩护人的；

3. 公诉人出庭公诉的案件，被告人因经济困难或者其他原因没有委托辩护人，人民法院决定为其提供指定辩护的。（《中华人民共和国刑事诉讼法（2012年修正版）》

除了刑事案件外，一些民事案件和行政案件也可以获得法律援助，例如：追索（claim for）赡养费（parental support）、抚养费（child support）[①]、扶养费（spousal support）、劳动报酬（remuneration）的

---

① 赡养费（晚辈给长辈）、抚养费（长辈给晚辈）、扶养费（同辈之间）在中国法律中有区别，统称为"扶养费"（广义，包括三者）。英文统称为 family provision / provision for the family 或者 aliment。维基百科对 aliment 的解

案件；追索抚恤金（disability and death pension）、最低生活保障金（minimum income payment）、社会保险金（social insurance payment）的案件；交通事故（traffic accident）、医疗事故（medical accident）、工伤事故（industrial accident）或者其他人身伤害（personal injury）事故的受害人追索医疗费用（medical costs）和赔偿（compensation）的法律事项；请求国家赔偿的行政复议（administrative reconsideration）和诉讼案。

在美国，获得法律援助是刑事被告享有的宪法权利。200多年前通过的《宪法》第六修正案规定了被告人获得律师帮助的权利：

> In all criminal prosecutions, the accused shall enjoy the right to a speedy and public trial, by an impartial jury of the State and district where in the crime shall have been committed, which district shall have been previously ascertained by law, and to be informed of the nature and cause of the accusation; to be confronted with the witnesses against him; to have compulsory process for obtaining witnesses in his favor, <u>and to have the Assistance of Counsel for his defence.</u> ①②

---

释是："Aliment, in Scots law and in other civil systems, is the sum paid or allowance given in respect of the reciprocal obligation of parents and children, husband and wife, grandparents and grandchildren, to contribute to each other's maintenance."（在苏格兰法和其他大陆法系国家，aliment 是父母与子女之间、夫妻之间、祖孙之间为尽相互扶养义务而给予的费用或津贴）。（维基百科 Aliment 条，https://en.wikipedia.org/wiki/Aliment，读取日期 2016-11-11）。不过，在美国法律里面，aliment 仅仅指离婚之后一方给与另一方的扶养费，也叫 maintenance 或 spousal support。

① 中译：在所有刑事案件中，被告人享有以下权利：由罪案发生地之州或区的公正的陪审团予以迅速及公开之审判的权利，罪案应属何区应由法律事先确定；获悉被控罪名和理由的权利；与控方证人对质的权利；要求法院强制对自己有利的证人出庭作证的权利；<u>由律师协助辩护的权利</u>。另外，文中画线和加着重号均为笔者添加，下不赘述。

② "U. S. Constitution: Six Amendment"，引自 Cornell Law School Legal Information Institute 网站（http://www.Law.cornell.edu/constitution/sixth-amandment，读取日期 2016-11-11）。

虽然宪法这么规定，但美国最高法院最初对该条的解释是：获得律师辩护的权利仅仅适用于联邦法院。各州没有义务为贫困被告人提供免费律师。直到 1961 年，最高法院才通过一个判例，确立了州法院必须为贫困被告提供律师的义务，但仅限于死刑案件；1963 年，通过另一个判例（Gideon v. Wainwright），确立了所有重罪案件（felony cases），如果被告人无钱聘请律师，法院都要免费提供辩护人；1979 年，最高法院进一步作出裁决，认定所有可能导致被告人被剥夺自由的案件，如果被告人无力聘请律师，法院要免费提供。①

在美国，法律援助的提供，主要有三种方式。第一种方式是通过政府设立的公设辩护人办公室（Public Defenders Office）提供，这里的律师是专职工作人员（staff attorney 或 dedicated defenders），从政府那里拿工资；第二种方式是政府出资，通过非营利机构，如 Defender Service、Defender Office 或 Legal Aid Society 等提供法律援助服务；第三种方式是政府在需要的时候，聘请私人律师（private attorneys），按小时付费，为贫困当事人提供法律服务，这种模式叫作 Judicare Model。

## 法律援助中心 Legal Aid Center

中国的法律援助机构，设在国家的司法行政系统，包括司法部（Ministry of Justice）、各省的司法厅（Department of Justice）、市区县的司法局（Bureau of Justice）。虽然乡（township）、镇（town）、

---

① 法院的司法解释同样具有法律效力，这就是所谓的"判例法"（case law），或者"法官创造的法律"（judge-made law）。每个法院的判例对下级法院都有约束力，但自己可以推翻。最高法院每作一次新的解释，就意味着推翻以前的判例法。从这个例子可以看出，同一条宪法规定，法官可以随着社会进步，作出不同解释，这也是美国宪法历经 200 多年没有多少修订，却仍然能够适应社会需要的原因。

街道办事处（sub-district office）设有司法所（Office of Justice），但司法所没有法律援助中心，其下属的"基层法律服务所"提供的是有偿法律服务。原则上，司法部和省级的法律援助中心主要负责法律援助政策制定和管理，市区县的法律援助中心负责承办或指派律所承办具体案件，但实际上，中央和省级法律援助中心也承担相应审级（主要是上诉案件）的法律援助。

## 民事法律援助 vs. 刑事法律援助
## Civil Legal Aid vs. Criminal Legal Aid

顾名思义，民事法律援助是指为民事案件中的贫困当事人（indigent defendant）提供法律援助；刑事法律援助是指为刑事案件中的特定被告人提供法律援助。

在中国，政府提供的法律援助既涵盖民事案件当事人，也涵盖刑事案件当事人。在美国，只有可判监禁的刑事案件中的贫困被告，才有权获得政府提供的法律援助。民事案件的当事人没有获得政府法律援助的权利。但也有大量的民间组织自发为贫困的民事被告提供法律援助，包括社区或法学院的"法律诊所"（legal clinics）。

我国的《法律援助条例》规定："法律援助是政府的责任"，援助内容既包括民事案件，也包括刑事案件。如前所述，在美国，联邦政府提供法律援助的责任是由 1963 年最高法院的判决确立的。该判决认为"《宪法》第六修正案所称律师帮助权，要求政府在刑事案件中为贫困被告提供律师"。因为这句话当中没有涉及民事案件，所以，民事法律援助不是美国政府的责任。

## 公设辩护人 Public Defender

公设辩护人是政府为贫困被告人指派的律师，国家承担费用。

美国有 public defenders' office，相当于中国法律援助中心，但他们仅为符合一定资格要求的（eligible）刑事被告提供法律援助。美国的法律援助机构还可称为 legal clinic、legal aid、legal service office、legal assistance office 等。

### 指派律师 Ex Officio Lawyers

笔者在翻译联合国禁止酷刑委员会的文件中，遇到这样一段话：

> The Committee is also concerned at reports about the low quality of the work of *ex officio* lawyers, who often meet their clients only in court, and about the fact that persons summoned and interrogated by the police as witnesses, but later charged as defendants, have a right to counsel only from the moment they are charged.①

其中的 *ex officio* lawyer 如果按照字面翻译，就是"依职权律师"，联合国的术语库翻译为"依职指定律师"。但无论怎么称呼，这究竟是一种什么律师？请看下面一段资料（下画线为笔者所加）：

> Legal aid in Hungary is characterised by a lack of unified management. In criminal matters, if a person cannot afford a lawyer, they will be given an <u>*ex officio* appointment of a private lawyer as defence counsel</u>. These lawyers are appointed by whoever conducts that particular phase of the proceedings; the police, prosecutor or court. Lawyers are selected from a list compiled by the regional bar associations, but the appointing

---

① Committee Against Torture. Fifty-fourth session, 20 April — 15 May 2015, Consideration of Reports Submitted by States Parties under Article 19 of the Convention.

authorities are completely free in making their choice. Appointed lawyers are not required to have experience or training in criminal defence.[①]

由此可见，*ex officio* lawyers 是在诉讼的不同阶段（侦查、审查起诉、庭审），由公、检、法依职权指派的为刑事被告提供法律服务的私人（社会）律师。因此联合国的译法可以接受。国内将这些律师称为"指派律师"，所以也可以这样翻译。中国各市县的法律援助中心有自己的专职律师，但如果人手不够，可以指派社会律师承办法律援助案件。中国所谓的"社会律师"就是私人执业律师（private lawyers 或 private practice lawyers）。

## 公益法律服务 *Pro Bono (Publico)* Legal Services

*pro bono publico* 是拉丁语，字面意思是 for the public good。*pro bono (publico)* legal services 一词专门指社会律师出于公益目的，为穷人、宗教团体、慈善机构和其他非营利机构提供的免费法律服务（下画线为笔者所加）：

> As members of a profession, lawyers are bound by their ethical rules to charge reasonable rates for their services and <u>to serve the public interest by providing free legal service to indigent persons or to religious, charitable, or other non-profit groups. A lawyer's free legal service to these types of clients is designated as *pro bono* service.</u>[②]

---

① "Hungary: Outline of the Legal System"，引自 Open Society Foundation 网站（https://www.opensocietyfoundations.org/sites/default/files/eu-legal-aid-hungary-20150427.pdf，读取日期 2016-11-11）。

② *West's Encyclopedia of American Law* 第 2 版，转引自 The Free Dictionary 网站（http://legal-dictionary.thefreedictionary.com/Pro+bono+publico，读取日期 2016-11-11）。

看来 *pro bono* services 也是一种法律援助，但不是官方提供的，是个人出于自愿，自掏腰包（或律师事务所赔钱），免费为客户提供的。美国律师协会（American Bar Association）的执业行为规范中有一条规定：

> A lawyer should aspire to render at least fifty (50) hours of *pro bono publico* legal services per year.①

我国的《律师法》第四十二条也规定了律师的法律援助义务："律师必须按照国家规定承担法律援助义务，尽职尽责，为受援人提供法律服务"。这里的义务，也是指为一定数量的案件免费提供法律服务（*pro bono* services）。为个案提供免费法律服务的私人执业律师（社会律师），可以称为 *pro bono* lawyers（按字面意思翻译是"公益律师"）。但在中国，"公益律师"有特定含义，他们不是社会律师，而是受雇于特定机构、服务于公益的机构律师：

> 公益律师是指受雇于政府法律援助机构、公益机构、非政府机构、非营利机构，免费为某类人群提供法律服务的律师。例如工会的维权律师，人权机构的维权律师。②

虽然公益律师提供的也是免费服务，但那是职业行为，律师仍然拿工资。这不同于社会律师在个案中免费提供法律援助。

---

① "Pro Bono Guide: An Introduction to Pro Bono Opportunities in Law Firm Setting"，引自 Harvard Law School 网站（http://hls.harvard.edu/content/uploads/2008/07/guide-pro-bono.pdf，读取日期 2016-11-11）。

② 张旭:《关注社会民生,实现律师价值——谈我国转型时期的公益律师》，《黑龙江史志》，2009 年第 5 期，第 3—4 页。

英文中也有 public interest lawyers，但与汉语的"公益律师"不完全对等。前者含义更广，除了中国所称的"公益律师"外，还包括政府的律师：

> Another distinction among lawyers is between those who work in private firms and/or for companies, and those who work for government or in non-profit work. The first type is generally referred to as "private practice" while the second is called "public interest" (or, occasionally, "public service"). Attorneys in private practice working in a law firm are generally paid (directly or indirectly) by their clients on either an hourly or flat rate basis. ... Attorneys working for companies ("in-house counsel") and those working in government or non-profits are usually on salary — their clients are generally not paying for the legal representation at all. Rather the firm pays the attorneys a set rate based on their experience and expertise. ...
>
> Attorneys in private practice represent individuals or companies. Those in public service (government) represent or advise federal, state or local government agencies and officials. Public interest attorneys work on behalf of organizations and/or causes, or on behalf of individuals who cannot afford private attorneys (usually in "legal aid" or "legal services" organizations). Some public interest attorneys are employed by the government to represent indigent criminal defendants — "public defenders."①

---

① "Private Practice vs. Public Service/Public Interest"，引自 UMass Pre-law Advising Office 网站（http://prelaw.umass.edu/topics/private_vs_public，读取日期 2016-11-11）。

从以上资料可以看出，pro bono lawyers 与 public interest lawyers 意思不同。前者是指在个案中为当事人免费提供法律服务的社会律师，后者是服务于公益的机构律师，提供免费服务，靠工资生活，范围大于中国的"公益律师"。在汉译英时，遇到"公益律师"或"公益法律服务"，要注意先区分不同情况，再决定用 pro bono 还是 public interest。

## 基层法律工作者与律师助理 Paralegals

我国法律援助的实施主体包括律师（private lawyers / practitioners）、高校学生志愿者（law student volunteers）、民间法律援助组织（civil society organizations）、基层法律服务工作者。其中的"基层法律服务工作者"不具有律师身份，不能翻译为 grassroots lawyers，可以直译为 grassroots legal service workers，或借用美国的概念 paralegals。

"基层法律服务工作者"与律师的区别包括："律师"的执业机构叫"律师事务所"（law firm），对外执业统称"律师"，执业持《律师执业证》（Lawyer's Certificate of Practice）。基层法律服务工作者的执业机构叫"法律服务所"（legal service office），对外执业统称"法律服务工作者"，执业持《法律服务工作者执业证》。律师可以从事刑事诉讼业务（criminal defense），法律服务工作者不得从事刑事业务，不能跨省办案。现在一些大城市已经不允许法律工作者出庭参加诉讼活动。律师要求具备本科以上学历，必须通过全国统一司法考试（与法官、检察官一样），通过率很低。基层法律服务工作者只需要具有高中文化程度、掌握基本法律知识，通过地方司法机关组织的考试或考核，事实上基本都能通过。

英语中的 paralegal 和 legal assistant 意思相同，都可以译为"律师助理"。美国的 National Association of Legal Assistants（简称 NALA）对 paralegal 的定义是：

> Legal assistants <u>(also known as paralegals)</u> are a distinguishable group of persons who assist attorneys in the delivery of legal services. Through formal education, training and experience, legal assistants have knowledge and expertise regarding the legal system and substantive and procedural law which qualify them to do work of a legal nature under the supervision of an attorney.①

由此可知，美国的 paralegals 不能独立办案，只能作为律师的助理，而中国的基层法律工作者可以独立开展广泛的业务。所以，严格来说，"基层法律服务工作者"也不同于英语中的 paralegal。但由于两者均指较低层次的法律服务人员，所以，国外学者在谈到中国的"基层法律服务工作者"时，也用 paralegals 或者 paralegal workers 来表达。当然，即使使用 paralegals，这个词也要按照中国的定义来理解。

## 值班律师 Duty Counsel

值班律师制度，是指由法律援助机构指派（assign）执业律师（licensed lawyer）在拘留场所（detention center）或法院等部门轮流值班，免费为已被采取强制措施②（compulsory measures）但尚未获得辩护人帮助的犯罪嫌疑人、被告人即时提供法律咨询（legal

---

① "Code of Ethics and Professional Responsibility"，引自 National Association of Legal Assistants 网站 https://www.nala.org/certification/nala-code-ethics-and-professional-responsibility，读取日期 2016-11-11）。

② 强制措施有五种：拘传（subpoena）、取保候审（bail）、监视居住〔supervised residence (residential surveillance)〕、拘留〔custody (pre-charge detention)〕、逮捕〔remand (pre-trial detention)〕。

advice）、指导（guidance）或作为代理人帮助其办理申请法律援助等法律服务的制度。中外皆有这种制度。在加拿大，如果值班律师和当事人短暂接触之后，在后续诉讼中继续代理该案，则叫作 expanded duty lawyer（职能扩充型值班律师）。

## 指派 Assign

指派是指法律援助机构把法律援助案件分配给（allocate）法律援助中心之外的律师或机构。有的法律援助中心是指派给具体律师，有的是分配给律师事务所并由其安排。

## Eligibility 和 Qualification

如果当事人符合法律援助的条件，可以说 she/he is eligible for legal aid。判断当事人是否符合条件，英文叫作 eligibility test（资格审查）。主要看当事人的收入水平，即所谓 means test（收入审查/测试、资产审查/测试）。means 在英文中的意思是 the amount of money or the property, income etc that someone has[1]。

由于 eligibility 和 qualification 都可以译为"资格"，所以汉译英时容易混淆。两者的区别如下：

> As adjectives the difference between eligible and qualified is that eligible is suitable; meeting the conditions; worthy of being chosen; allowed to do something while qualified is meeting the standards, requirements, and training for a position.[2]

---

[1] "Means"，引自 Macmillan Dictionary 网站（http://www.macmillandictionary.com/dictionary/british/means，读取日期 2016-11-11）。

[2] "Eligible vs. Qualified"，引自 WikiDiff 网站（http://wikidiff.com/qualified/eligible，读取日期 2016-11-11）。

eligible 和 elect 同源，所以，基本意思是"可入选的"。qualified 来源于 quality（素质），基本意思是达到一定的素质要求。因此，如果说当事人符合法律援助的条件，就用 eligible；如果说某人达到了从事法律援助工作的资质要求，则说 a person is qualified to provide legal aid。

## 获得司法救济的机会 Access to Justice

国家之所以承担法律援助的责任，是为了实现"法律面前人人平等"（equality before the law）这个基本法律原则。该原则也可以表述为 equal access to justice（平等获得司法保护）或 equal access to legal protection（平等获得法律保护）。

access to justice 的意思是能够利用司法途径维权，具体译法需要根据上下文确定。可以译为"获得司法救济（的机会）""扫除司法障碍"等。笔者甚至看到有学者将其直译为"接近司法"（笔者认为还不如说"接近正义"），这个译法在汉语中意思不通，只能转化为英语概念才能理解。这样翻译，恐怕也是无奈之举。

## 获得律师帮助权 Right to Counsel

right to counsel 是指个人在法律程序中获得律师帮助的权利。既然是个人的权利，就意味着有人来承担义务。义务的主体就是国家。如果个人无钱聘请律师，国家就要为其指派一名律师或者支付被告人聘请律师的费用。这项权利来源于公平审判权（right to a fair trial）。在刑事或民事诉讼中，如果双方的经济力量悬殊，有一方无法聘请律师辩护，审判结果很难公平。为了确保法律面前人人平等，就要求政府为贫困被告人（indigent defendant）指派律师。服务于贫困被告的辩护服务，叫作 indigent defense service。

## 法律援助 vs. 司法协助
## Legal Aid vs. Judicial Assistance

legal aid 和 judicial assistance 在中英文中是完全不同的概念。前者译为"法律援助",后者译为"司法协助"。US Legal 对"司法协助"的定义是:

> Judicial assistance means the assistance given by a court of one jurisdiction to a court of another jurisdiction by admitting and enforcing the judicial order of the former court. Such assistance is carried out on the basis of the treaty made by the governments of the two jurisdictions between them.[①]

这里的定义仅包括国外法院判决的承认(recognition)和执行(enforcement),显然是狭义的司法协助(又称"一般司法协助")。广义的"司法协助"还包括代为送达诉讼文书;代为调查证据,询问证人;根据委托向对方提供有关法律资料和文件;承认和执行外国仲裁机构生效裁决[②]。

可见,"法律援助"和"司法协助"是两个完全不同的概念。judicial(司法)一词在英语中专门指法院,所以 judicial assistance 是指各国法院之间的协助;legal aid 是对贫困当事人提供的免费法律服务,所以用 legal 一词。

---

① "Judicial Assistance",引自 US Legal 网站(http://definitions.uslegal.com/j/judicial-assistance/,读取日期 2016-11-11)。

② 曾庆敏:《法学大辞典》,第 6 版,上海辞书出版社,1998 年,第 373 页。

# 第十四讲

## 国际人权法中的几个概念及其翻译

### Temporary Special Measures 暂行特别措施

"暂行特别措施"是指为了加速实现事实上的男女平等（*de facto* equality，相对于 *de jure* equality，法律上的平等）而在短期内对女性采取的照顾措施。Temporary Special Measures 是联合国的说法，其他机构可能用 affirmative action、positive action、positive measures、reverse discrimination、positive discrimination 等说法。

Temporary Special Measures 在《消除对妇女一切形式歧视公约》以及绝大多数联合国文件中都翻译为"暂行特别措施"，有少数文件翻译为"临时特别措施"。

根据《现代汉语词典》，"暂行"的意思是"短时间之内"[①]。"临时"的意思有两个：一是"临到事情发生的时候"；二是"暂时的""短期的"[②]。看来用两种说法意思都正确。但既然联合国文件约定使用的是"暂行"，译者不妨就沿用"暂行"。况且，"临时"的本义是义项一，义项二是引申义。从意思的确定性来看，"暂行"略胜一筹。

affirmative action 有多种译法。联合国文件中译为"扶持行动"或"平权行动"，有的地方译为"积极行动""肯定行动"等。但"积

---

[①] 中国社会科学院语言研究所词典编辑室：《现代汉语词典（第6版）》，商务印书馆，2012年，第1621页。

[②] 同上，第821页。

极行动"在汉语中的意思宽泛,"肯定行动"按字面解释没有意义:不知道肯定什么。国内妇女团体常用的说法是"平权行动"。维基百科中文版将其翻译为"平权法案",意思不正确。action 的意思是"行动",它包括但不限于立法:

> "Affirmative action" means positive steps taken to increase the representation of women and minorities in areas of employment, education, and culture from which they have been historically excluded. When those steps involve preferential selection—selection on the basis of race, gender, or ethnicity—affirmative action generates intense controversy.[①]

笔者译文:

> "平权行动"是指采取积极措施,提高女性和少数者群体在就业、教育、文化等领域的代表比例,因为历史上他们在这些领域受到排斥。如果这些措施中包含优先选择,即基于种族、性别或族裔的选择,平权行动就会产生强烈争议。

positive action、positive measures,通常按字面意思翻译为"积极行动""积极措施"。reverse discrimination、positive discrimination 可以翻译为"反向歧视"和"积极歧视"(或"积极的区别对待")。作为外来概念,必要时可以加引号,以告诫读者不要按字面理解。

affirmative action 也适用于其他处境不利的群体(disadvantaged groups),如少数民族。很多国家对少数民族就实施优惠政策(pre-

---

[①] "Affirmative Action",引自 Stanford Encyclopedia of Philosophy 网站(https://plato.stanford.edu/entries/affirmative-action/,读取日期 2016-12-31)。

ferential policies），只有马来西亚对多数民族（马来人）实行 affirmative action，因为传统上，作为少数民族的华人在经济上处于优势地位。

## 几个公约的简称

　　Convention on the Elimination of All Forms of Discrimination against Women（英文简称 CEDAW），联合国中文处译为《消除对妇女一切形式歧视公约》，汉语简称为《消除对妇女歧视公约》。但该简称不够简洁，所以国内妇女团体经常称之为《消歧公约》。这个称呼足够简洁，但不够准确。因为联合国还有一个《消除一切形式种族歧视国际公约》（International Convention on the Elimination of All Forms of Racial Discrimination，ICERD），汉语简称为《消除种族歧视公约》。如果脱离上下文，《消歧公约》无法区分这两个公约。

　　联合国还有一些公约没有汉语简称，或者简称不简，如：《残疾人权利公约》（Convention on the Rights of Persons with Disabilities，CRPD；汉语无正式简称）、《儿童权利公约》（Convention on the Rights of the Child；汉语无正式简称）、《禁止酷刑和其他残忍、不人道或有辱人格的待遇或处罚公约》（Convention against Torture and Other Cruel, Inhuman or Degrading Treatment or Punishment, CAT；汉语简称《禁止酷刑公约》）、《经济、社会及文化权利国际公约》（International Covenant on Economic, Social and Cultural Rights, ICESCR；汉语无正式简称，国内俗称《经社文公约》）、《公民权利和政治权利国际公约》（International Covenant on Civil and Political Rights, ICCPR；汉语无简称）。

　　缺乏汉语简称，或简称不简，行文和口头叙述都会显得比较啰唆。鉴于这几个公约在英文中除了首字母缩写外，还有其他非正式称呼，如 CEDAW 还可称为 the Women's Convention；ICERD 还可称为 the Race Convention；CPRD 还可称为 the Disability Convention，不妨在汉语中也使用类似的简称，把 CEDAW 翻译为《妇女公约》，把 ICERD 翻译为《种族公约》，把 CRPD 翻译为《残疾公约》或《残疾人公约》。联合国把 CAT 译为《禁止酷刑公约》，还可以简化为《酷刑公约》。国内把 ICESCR 简称为《三权公约》，我们不妨类推，把 ICCPR 称为《两权公约》。

顺便提及，《公民权利和政治权利国际公约》（"公约"有时也作"盟约"）这一译法为现在通用的译法（包括在联合国文件中），但这个译法并非联合国当初通过的作准文本。作准文本的译法是《公民及政治权利国际盟约》。关于这两个译本，请参见孙世彦《〈公民及政治权利国际公约〉的两份中文本：问题、比较与出路》[1]。

同样，《三权公约》的作准文本译为《经济、社会、文化权利国际盟约》，与今天通行的译法（《经济、社会及文化权利国际公约》）也有不同。

## Commission on Human Rights 和 Human Rights Committee

Commission on Human Rights 有时也简称 Human Rights Commission，与 Human Rights Committee 几乎相同。如果不熟悉情况，很可能以为这是同一个机构，都译为"人权委员会"。但实际上，两者是完全不同的机构。在联合国领域 commission 为职司部门（functional body），committee 为专家组成的机构。为作区分，联合国中文处把

---

[1] 孙世彦：《〈公民及政治权利国际公约〉的两份中文本：问题、比较与出路》，环球法律评论，2007 年第 6 期。

前者译为"人权委员会",把后者译为"人权事务委员会"。这也是不得已而为之。2006年,联合国人权理事会(Human Rights Council)成立,取代原来的"人权委员会"(Human Rights Commission),才结束中文译者的梦魇。但作为历史名词,仍需要区分人权委员会和人权事务委员会。

关于两个委员会的区别,简单地说,人权事务委员会(Human Rights Committee)是依据《公民权利和政治权利国际公约》成立的机构,负责监督该公约的落实。这样的机构叫作条约机构(treaty bodies)或者条约监测机构(treaty-monitoring bodies)。机构成员是来自不同国家的人权专家(不是政府官员),独立开展工作,不代表本国政府。这样的条约机构,联合国还有8个,分别是:监督《经济社会文化权利国际公约》执行的经济、社会和文化权利委员会,监督《消除一切形式种族歧视国际公约》执行的消除种族歧视委员会,监督《消除对妇女一切形式歧视公约》执行的消除对妇女歧视委员会,监督《禁止酷刑和其他残忍、不人道或有辱人格的待遇或处罚公约》执行的禁止酷刑委员会和防范酷刑小组委员会,监督《儿童权利公约》执行的儿童权利委员会,监督《保护所有移徙工人及其家庭成员权利国际公约》执行的移徙工人问题委员会,监督《残疾人权利公约》执行的残疾人权利委员会,监督《保护所有人免遭强迫失踪国际公约》执行的强迫失踪问题委员会。[①]

条约机构的主要工作包括审议(consider)缔约国定期提交的履约报告(periodic reports),提出结论性意见(concluding observations);发表对公约条款内容的一般性评论(general comments)。人权事务委员会,经济、社会和文化权利委员会,消除种族歧视委员

---

① "联合国人权机构",引自外交部网站(http://www.mfa.gov.cn/chn//pds/gjhdq/gjhdqzz/lhg/jbqk/t358601.htm,读取日期2016-12-31)。

会，消除对妇女歧视委员会，禁止酷刑委员会，移徙工人委员会，残疾人权利委员会等还有权受理个人申诉（individual complaints）。

可以看到，除了人权事务委员会外，其余委员会的名字都使用了条约名称中的关键词，很容易与相关条约联系起来。但 Human Rights Committee 因为名字选用不当，困扰了译者几十年。

另一方面，人权理事会（Human Right Council）的级别更高。人权理事会依据联合国宪章（而非某个条约）成立，是联合国大会（General Assembly）下属机构，总部设在日内瓦。理事会不是专家组，而是一个政治论坛（political forum），容许成员国就所有国际上的人权议题进行讨论。理事会的一项重要工作是开展国别人权审查（称为 Universal Periodic Review / 普遍定期审议），对所有联合国会员国的人权状况进行评估。

原来的人权委员会（Commission on Human Rights）归联合国经济和社会理事会（ECOSOC）管辖，改为人权理事会后地位提升了。两者在成员的地域分配、产生方法、任期、会期、职能上也有所不同。

## Gender Mainstreaming 性别视角主流化

gender mainstreaming 是一种性别视角，即政府在制定任何政策、通过任何法律的时候，都先戴上性别平等的眼镜，审查这些政策法律是否对男女两性造成不同影响。以下是维基百科的解释：

> Gender mainstreaming is the public policy concept of assessing the different implications for women and men of any planned policy action, including legislation and programmes, in all areas and levels. [1]

---

[1] 维基百科 Gender mainstreaming 条（https://en.wikipedia.org/wiki/Gender_mainstreaming，读取日期 2016-12-31）。

笔者的译文：

性别视角主流化是一个公共政策概念，目的是评估在所有领域和层面计划制定的任何政策行动（包括立法和方案）对男女带来的不同影响。

这个概念联合国文件中译为"性别平等主流化"。但也许翻译为"性别视角主流化"更加达意，因为 mainstream 的对象是 gender perspective：

Mainstreaming gender perspective is the process of assessing the implications for women and men of any planned action, including legislation, policies or programs, in all areas and at all levels.[①]

笔者译文：

性别视角主流化是评估所有领域和层面任何的规划行动（包括立法、政策或方案）对男女带来的影响的过程。

无论采取何种译法，"主流化"都不易理解。因此，并非所有情况下遇到 mainstream 就机械地翻译为"主流化"。如果有可能，可采用更达意的译法。例如：

Gender is mainstreamed throughout the Institute's programmes.

---

① "Definition of gender mainstreaming"，引自 Social Research Center 网站（http://www.aucegypt.edu/src/engendering/definitions.html，读取日期 2016-12-31）。

笔者译为:"该学会的所有方案都纳入了性别视角"。如果译为"性别平等在学会的所有方案中都成为主流"则不易理解。

不仅性别可以"主流化",任何传统上被边缘化(marginalized)的议题都可以"主流化":

> The focus for the last two years has been to mainstream HIV/AIDS education in curriculum and textbooks for non-formal education. The Bureau of Non-formal Education has been in the lead for this initiative. As planned, HIV/AIDS has been mainstreamed, and textbooks and other materials already prepared are being tested and will be used in training of teachers/instructors of NFE. (184 EX/4-Draft 36C/3)

笔者译文:

> 过去两年的重点是把艾滋病毒/艾滋病教育纳入非正规教育课程与教科书。非正规教育局一直在领导这个倡议。按照规划,艾滋病毒/艾滋病教育已经主流化,目前已编制完成的教科书与其他材料正在接受检验,并将用于非正规教育的师资培训。

此处译者根据情况对 mainstream 作了不同处理,译为"纳入"。再如:

> Media literacy should be mainstreamed in curricula to better prepare future citizens to take an active part in the public life of their societies. (184 EX/4-Draft 36C/3)

笔者译文：

应将媒体扫盲纳入学校课程，让未来的公民做好准备，积极参与社会的公共生活。

## Communications Procedure 来文和调查程序

如前所述，联合国的人权公约设置了个人投诉程序（individual complaints procedure）。如果个人认为自己的权利受到国家的侵害，可以向相关条约机构提出申诉（complaints），条约机构进行调查，然后向当事国提出建议（recommendations）。申诉的材料叫作 communications，联合国将其翻译为"来文"。

"来文"一词，显然是站在条约机构角度看问题，而英文的 communications 其实并没有方向性。鉴于此，汉语译文可能出现逻辑问题。比如，残疾人权利委员会通过的一份文件名为：

Revised guidelines for submission of communications to the Committee on the Rights of Persons with Disabilities under the Optional Protocol to the Convention adopted by the Committee on the Rights of Persons with Disabilities. [1]

该文件的中文名称为：残疾人权利委员会通过的关于根据《残疾人权利公约任择议定书》<u>提交残疾人权利委员会来文</u>的订正准则[2]。

英文的意思很清楚：communications to the Committee on the

---

[1] "Individual Communications"，引自 United Nations Human Rights 网站（http://www.ohchr.org/EN/HRBodies/TBPetitions/Pages/IndividualCommunications.aspx，读取日期 2016-12-31）。

[2] 同上。

Rights of Persons with Disabilities（向残疾人权利委员会提交 communications），但中文"提交残疾人权利委员会来文"会引起误解：读者可能认为文件来自残疾人权利委员会，但需要提交给别人。即使改为"向残疾人权利委员会提交来文"，逻辑上也有不通：因为提交者无法提交"来文"，只能"发文"，委员会收到的才是"来文"。

然而，要找一个更好的译法并不容易。如果容易，联合国中文处那么多专业译员，也早就想到了。既然已经约定俗成，我们不妨遵照翻译，同时认识到"来文"不过是一个代表 communications 的符号。如果真的还有修改机会，也许可以改为"申述（状）"，因为这个说法与"申诉"和"投诉"同义，就如同在英文中，communications 与 complaint 和 petition 为同义关系：

> COMPLAINT: In legal terms, the initial document that begins an action; a complaint sets forth a brief summary of what happened and argues why relief should be granted. In a human rights case, the complaint (or PETITION, or COMMUNICATION) alleges that government, or individual or institution that must answer to human rights standards (such as a surrogate of the government) has violated the HUMAN RIGHTS of specific individuals or groups of individuals.[1]

笔者译文：

> COMPLAINT：在法律术语中，complaints（起诉状）是启动诉讼初始文件。起诉状中简要总结案情，说明为何应当给予救济。在人权案件中，申诉人在 complaint（申诉状，或者叫 peti-

---

[1] "Complaint"，引自 Glossary of Human Rights Terms 网站（http://fs2.american.edu/mertus/www/hr%20glossary.htm，读取日期 2016-12-31）。

tion 或 communication）中指控政府或对人权标准负责的个人或机构（如政府的代理人）侵犯了申诉人个体或群体的权利。

顺便提及，并非所有条约机构的投诉机制都已生效。上述 9 个条约机构中，移徙工人委员会（现已应中国代表团要求，将译名改为"移民工人委员会"）和儿童权利委员会的个人投诉机制尚未生效。另外，中国也没有加入个人来文制度，所以，中国公民到联合国"上访"是行不通的。

## Violence against Women 暴力侵害妇女行为

这个概念最初翻译为"对妇女的暴力行为"，但在一些行文中，这样翻译十分拗口，例如："世界妇女大会通过的《行动纲领》中第一次明确对对妇女的暴力行为作出界定"。后来的联合国文件中，改用"暴力侵害妇女行为"。

联合国消除对妇女的暴力行为宣言对"暴力侵害妇女行为"的界定是：

Any act of gender-based violence that results in, or is likely to result in, physical, sexual or psychological harm or suffering to women, including threats of such acts, coercion or arbitrary deprivation of liberty, whether occurring in public or in private life. (A/RES/48/104)

官方译文：

"对妇女的暴力行为"一词系指对妇女造成或可能造成身心方面或性方面的伤害或痛苦的任何基于性别的暴力行为，包括威

胁进行这类行为、强迫或任意剥夺自由，而不论其发生在公共生活还是私人生活中。（联大第 48/104 号决议）

宣言进一步指出，暴力侵害妇女行为包括但不限于：

a) Physical, sexual and psychological violence occurring in the family, including battering, sexual abuse of female children in the household, dowry-related violence, marital rape, female genital mutilation and other traditional practices harmful to women, non-spousal violence related to exploitation; b) Physical, sexual and psychological violence occurring within the general community, including rape, sexual abuse, sexual harassment and intimidation at work, in educational institutions and elsewhere, trafficking in women and forced prostitution; c) Physical, sexual and psychological violence perpetrated or condoned by the State, wherever it occurs.

官方译文：

（a）在家庭内发生的身心方面和性方面的暴力行为，包括殴打、家庭中对女童的性凌虐、因嫁妆引起的暴力行为、配偶强奸、阴蒂割除和其他有害于妇女的传统习俗、非配偶的暴力行为和与剥削有关的暴力行为；（b）在社会上发生的身心方面和性方面的暴力行为，包括强奸、性凌虐、在工作场所、教育机构和其他场所的性骚扰和恫吓、贩卖妇女和强迫卖淫；（c）国家所做或纵容发生的身心方面和性方面的暴力行为，无论其在何处发生。

其中所述 dowry-related violence 多发生在南亚国家，female genital mutilation 多发生在一些非洲国家；marital rape（国内叫"婚内强奸"）世界各地都有发生，但法律上不一定承认；psychological violence 也叫 psychological abuse、emotional abuse 或 mental abuse，包括谩骂、阻止女性与外界交往等行为。国内常说的"冷暴力"（冷淡、轻视、放任、疏远和漠不关心），常被直译为"cold violence"，也是精神暴力的一种表现形式。

## Sexual Harassment 性骚扰

性骚扰是近年来经常听到的概念。欧洲性别平等研究院（the European Institute for Gender Equality, EIGE）给"性骚扰"下的定义是：

Any form of undesired verbal, non-verbal or physical action or behaviour of a sexual nature with the effect or intent of adversely affecting the dignity of a person, especially where this involves the creation of an intimidating, hateful, degrading, shaming or insulting environment.[1]

笔者译文：

任何形式与性有关的不受欢迎的言语、非言语或身体行为，其后果或目的是负面影响一个人的尊严，尤其是该行为涉及制造恐吓性、仇恨性、贬低性、羞辱性或侮辱性的环境。

---

[1] "Slovenia-Sexual Harassment-Legal Definition"，引自 The European Institute for Gender Equality 网站（http://eige.europa.eu/gender-based-violence/regulatory-and-legal-framework/legal-definitions-in-the-eu/slovenia-sexual-harassment，读取日期 2016-12-31）。

性骚扰可以分为两类：*quid pro quo* sexual harassment 和 hostile environment sexual harassment。*quid pro quo* 是拉丁语，字面意思是 this for that，可以译为"交换"。*quid pro quo* sexual harassment 就是"交换型性骚扰"，指的是雇主或上司以雇员给予性好处（sexual favors）为条件，为雇员提供就业、晋级、加薪、倒班、考评方面的照顾；如果被拒绝，就会在以上各方面报复雇员。hostile environment sexual harassment 可以译为"敌意环境型性骚扰"，意思是故意制造一种环境，让异性感到恐惧、反感、不舒服。

In United States labor law, a hostile work environment exists when one's behavior within a workplace creates an environment that is difficult for another person to work in. Common complaints in sexual harassment lawsuits include fondling, suggestive remarks, sexually-suggestive photos displayed in the workplace, use of sexual language or off-color jokes.[①]

笔者译文：

根据美国的劳动法，所谓敌意工作环境，是指一个人在工作场所的行为致使另一个人难以工作。在性骚扰诉讼中常见的投诉包括调戏、暗示性语言、在工作场所张贴有性暗示意味的照片、使用色情语言或讲荤笑话。

有些文件把这个概念翻译为"由于不利环境造成的性骚扰问题"或"敌意环境中的性骚扰"，意思都不准确。因为此处的 hostile environment 本身就构成性骚扰。

---

① 维基百科 Hostile work environment 词条（https://en.wikipedia.org/wiki/Hostile_work_environment，读取日期 2016-12-31）。

# 第十五讲

## 青少年司法中的几个术语及其翻译

### Minors 未成年人

在我国，未成年人是指未满十八周岁的公民；而在其他国家，可能被定义为不同的年龄。例如，在日本，未成年人是指未满二十周岁的公民；在美国，未成年指未满十六周岁的公民。法律中，"未成年人"经常被翻译为 minors，那么"成年人"（adult）是否可以翻译为 majors 呢？从法律词典的定义来看，是可以的。例如，《布莱克法律词典》（*Black's Law Dictionary*）对 major 的定义第一项即是："Roman law. An older person, esp. one older than 25 and hence of full capacity"①。

但事实上，无论是在法律中还是日常生活中，将"成年人"译为 major 的情况都很少，笔者似乎从未见过。美国的儿童福利信息门户网站（Child Welfare Information Gateway）中，有 minor 作为"未成年人"的情况，例如 unaccompanied refugee minors（URMs，无人陪伴的难民儿童）②，但没有发现 major 作为"成年人"解释的用例。抽象名词 majority（成年）较为常用，比如，"达到成年"可以说 attain

---

① B. A. Garner: *Black's Law Dictionary*, 9th ed. (Saint Paul: Thompson West, 2009), p. 1040.

② "Grounds for Involuntary Termination of Parental Rights"，引自 Child Welfare Information Gateway 网站（https://www.childwelfare.gov/pubPDFs/groundtermin.pdf，读取日期 2017-03-19）。

(the age of) majority。

我国的《中华人民共和国未成年人保护法》通常翻译为 Law of the People's Republic of China on the Protection of Minors，但国外的儿童保护立法，通常都用 children，较少使用 minor 一词。因此，在汉译英中，不一定见到"未成年人"就翻译为 minors。例如，全国律协的"未成年人保护专业委员会"，就可以译为 Child Protection Committee，而不说 Minors Protection Committee。另外，"未成年人"在英文中还有一个说法，叫作 infant。《布莱克法律词典》对 infant 的定义为："1. A newborn baby. 2. MINOR"[①]。可见，在法律中，infant 可以指婴儿，也可以指包括婴儿在内的未成年人，译者要注意区分。

## Status Offence/Crime 身份违法/犯罪

由于一个人的身份，致使某种行为构成违法或犯罪，即身份违法或身份犯罪。如青少年的酗酒、逃学（truancy）、不服管教（ungovernability）、离家出走行为等。成年人实施这些行为不构成违法，但（在美国）青少年实施这些行为就构成违法。再如，美国法律规定，严重犯罪刑满释放人员（felons）不得持有枪支，如果这类人持有枪支，就是身份犯罪。历史上，有些国家（如南非、德国）规定不同种族之间不得通婚，违反者即为身份犯罪。

中国也使用身份犯罪这个概念，但不限于青少年，是指只有特定犯罪主体才能实施的犯罪。比如，贪污贿赂犯罪、渎职犯罪、军人违反职责罪等。这些罪行，只有特定身份的人才会犯，一般老百姓不会犯。在美国，虽然身份犯罪的主体主要是青少年，但青少年实施

---

① B. A. Garner: *Black's Law Dictionary*, 9th ed. (Saint Paul: Thompson West, 2009), p. 847.

的犯罪，不一定都是身份犯罪，如盗窃（theft）、暴力犯罪（violent crimes）就是普通的犯罪。青少年的身份犯罪和其他犯罪，统称青少年犯罪/违法（juvenile delinquency/offending）。

新近还出现一个概念，叫作 identity crimes 或者 identity-related crimes，也翻译为"身份犯罪"或"与身份相关的犯罪"，是指身份盗窃（identity theft）或身份诈骗（identity fraud），比如信用卡诈骗、医保诈骗、贷款诈骗。这与 status crime 毫无关系，是因为汉语找不到合适的译法才出现的问题。

## Child Abuse 虐待儿童

中国没有独立的"虐待儿童罪"。如果家庭里长期虐待儿童，可以按照"虐待罪"（maltreatment）处理；如果是一次性虐待，造成"轻伤"（light injury）以上结果，可以以"故意伤害罪"（intentionally causing injury）处理。但对于学校幼儿园等儿童照管机构的工作人员，不能适用虐待罪，因为他们不是家庭成员。

在国外，虐待儿童（child abuse，也叫 child maltreatment）无论发生在何处，都是犯罪行为。对虐待儿童的处罚包括剥夺亲权（parental right）、社会考察（probation）、监禁（imprisonment），甚至终身监禁（lifetime imprisonment）等。如果是猥亵儿童（child sexual abuse/molestation），政府会将犯罪者登记为"儿童性犯罪者"（child sexual offenders），并告诉邻里周围生活着这样一个人。[1]

在中国，虐待多被理解为身体虐待（physical abuse）。在国外，child abuse 包括多种形式，身体虐待仅仅是一种。其他形式

---

[1] "Child Abuse Penalties and Sentencing"，引自 Find Law 网站（http://criminal.findlaw.com/criminal-charges/child-abuse-penalties-and-sentencing.html，读取日期 2017-03-05）。

包括性虐待（sexual abuse/maltreatment）、心理虐待（psychological mistreatment）、疏于照管/忽视（neglect of a child）。前三者属于"作为行为"（acts of commission），最后一种形式（neglect）属于"不作为行为"（acts of omission）。世界卫生组织对 child abuse 的定义为：

> all forms of physical and/or emotional ill-treatment, sexual abuse, neglect or negligent treatment or commercial or other exploitation, resulting in actual or potential harm to the child's health, survival, development or dignity in the context of a relationship of responsibility, trust or power[①]

child abuse 和 child maltreatment 经常互换使用，但也有人把 child maltreatment 当作一个上义词，下面涵盖疏于照管（neglect）、剥削儿童（exploitation）、拐卖儿童（trafficking）[②]。child neglect 是指家长疏于满足孩子的基本需求：

> Child neglect is a form of child abuse, and is a deficit in meeting a child's basic needs, including the failure to provide adequate health care, supervision, clothing, nutrition, housing as well as their physical, emotional, social, educational and safety needs.[③]

---

① "Child Abuse and Neglect by Parents and Other Caregivers"，引自 WHO 网站（http://www.who.int/violence_injury_prevention/violence/global_campaign/en/chap3.pdf，读取日期 2017-03-03）。

② 维基百科 Child Abuse 条（https://en.wikipedia.org/wiki/Child_abuse，读取日期 2017-03-05）。

③ 维基百科 Child Neglect 条（https://en.wikipedia.org/wiki/Child_neglect，读取日期 2017-03-05）。

中文文献中，通常把 neglect 翻译为"忽视"，优点是既可以作为动词，也可以作为名词使用——唯一缺憾是不像法律术语。建议把名词翻译为"疏于照管"，动词可用"忽视"，但缺点是一个词的译法不统一。

sexual abuse 并非汉语固有概念，虽然可以翻译为"性虐待"，但令人费解。根据维基百科的解释，其意思其实就是猥亵（molestation）：

> Sexual abuse, also referred to as <u>molestation</u>①, is usually undesired sexual behavior by one person upon another. When force is immediate, of short duration, or infrequent, it is called <u>sexual assault</u>. The offender is referred to as a sexual abuser or (often pejoratively) molester. The term also covers any behavior by an adult or older adolescent towards a child to stimulate any of the involved sexually.②

按上述解释，儿童性虐待（child sexual abuse）就是猥亵儿童（child molestation）。中国法律的解释如下：

> 猥亵儿童罪，是指以刺激或满足实施者性欲为目的，用性交以外的方法对儿童（包括男童和女童）实施的淫秽行为。③

但是，维基百科又把 child sexual abuse 等同于法定强奸（statutory

---

① 本文下画线均为作者所加。

② 维基百科 Sexual abuse 条（https://en.wikipedia.org/wiki/Sexual_abuse，读取日期 2017-03-05）。

③ 百度百科"猥亵儿童罪"条（http://baike.baidu.com/item/猥亵儿童罪，读取日期 2017-03-05）。

rape）：

> The use of a child, or other individuals younger than the age of consent, for sexual stimulation is referred to as child sexual abuse or <u>statutory rape</u>.①

而强奸（rape）的概念，在中文里和"猥亵"是完全不同的。看来这些说法之间的关系很复杂，恐怕只能通过各自法律体系的定义来理解，即使翻译出来，也不能完全按照译入语语境理解。法定强奸（statutory rape）是指强奸未成年人。未成年人即使同意，也不是被告人的抗辩理由，因为按法律规定，未成年人还没有达到能够表示同意的年龄（age of consent）。statutory rape 经常用来指强奸已到青春期的未成年人；强奸不到青春期的儿童，称为 child sexual abuse 或 molestation，罪责更大。"法定强奸"是个统称，具体法律规定通常用别的词。以下说法都表示法定强奸：sexual assault（性侵犯）、rape of a child（强奸儿童）、corruption of a minor（玷污未成年人，corrupt 的本义是 ruin、destroy）、unlawful sex with a minor（与未成年人非法发生性关系）、carnal knowledge of a minor（字面意思是"在肉体上认识未成年人"，含义是"与未成年人发生性关系"）、unlawful carnal knowledge（"非法肉体知识"，简称 carnal knowledge），以及 sexual battery（性暴力）②。以 knowledge 作为"性交"的委婉语，源自《圣经》中的用法。在《创世记》（4:1）中，谈到亚当和夏娃生育第一个孩子的时候这样说："And Adam <u>knew</u> Eve his wife; and

---

① 维基百科 Sexual abuse 条（https://en.wikipedia.org/wiki/Sexual_abuse，读取日期 2017-03-05）。

② 维基百科 Statutory rape 条（https://en.wikipedia.org/wiki/Statutory_rape，读取日期 2017-03-05）。

she conceived, and bore Cain, and said, I have gotten a man with [the help of] Jehovah." ①

## Child Abduction 儿童拐骗

我们通常把 child abduction 理解为犯罪分子出于某种目的（例如敲诈勒索）而"绑架儿童"，即 child kidnapping。但在法律领域，这仅仅是其含义之一。另一个含义是，父母离婚或分居，本来孩子依法由一方照管，但另一方未经对方许可把孩子偷走（theft），这叫作"父母拐骗儿童"（parental child abduction）。为了解决跨国婚姻导致的父母拐骗儿童，甚至还出台了一项国际公约，叫 The Hague Convention on the Civil Aspects of International Child Abduction，联合国将其翻译为《国际儿童拐骗事件的民事问题海牙公约》，香港特区政府翻译为《国际掳拐儿童民事方面公约》，澳门特区政府翻译为《国际诱拐儿童民事方面公约》。这也反映了 abduction 一词准确翻译出来并不容易。维基百科的定义如下：

> Child abduction or child theft is the unauthorized removal of a minor (a child under the age of legal adulthood) from the custody of the child's natural parents or legally appointed guardians. ②

可见，abduction 的含义中并不包括"引诱"或"欺骗"这样的手段，汉语中之所以加入这样的手段，是因为汉语需要一个双音节词。从

---

① "Genesis 4"，引自 Bible Hub 网站（http://biblehub.com/kjv/genesis/4.htm，读取日期 2017-03-19）。

② 维基百科 Child abduction 条（https://en.wikipedia.org/wiki/Child_abduction，读取日期 2017-03-05）。

这个意义上说,香港的译法("掳拐")可能更贴近原文。但细抠起来,"拐"字本身就包含"欺骗"的意思①,因此,也不完全对等。"掳"字的意思是"把人抢走"②,可能比较达意,因为 abduct 的意思正是"to seize and take away (as a person) by force"③。但汉语要求双音节,必须再配一个字,也许可以如下例说"掳掠":

> 据广东省档案馆藏国民党政府档案记载,华南日军仅在广东一地就掳掠了上千名儿童,经广西南宁一路前往越南谅山,后因德国投降奉令返回广西、湖南、湖北等地。④

但既然这三种译法都已经成为不同地区的官方译本,修改起来也并不容易。再说,"掳掠"的手段,恐怕主要也是"引诱""欺骗",采用"绑架"方式的,恐怕还是少数。所以,现有的说法也没有太大不妥。

与此相反的例子是,联合国把 trafficking in persons 翻译为"人口贩运",恐怕就是严格遵循 traffic 的本义。如果按照中文的习惯说法,可能是"拐卖"人口(如"拐卖妇女儿童")。但汉语"拐卖"(妇女儿童)译为英语,却没有严格遵循翻译本义的原则,而是照顾英语的习惯,变成了 trafficking (in women and children)。所以,翻译没

---

① 商务印书馆辞书研究中心:《新华词典(第4版)》,商务印书馆,2013年,第349页。

② 中国社会科学院语言研究所词典编辑室:《现代汉语词典(第6版)》,商务印书馆,2012年,第843页。

③ "Abduct",引自 Merriam-Webster Dictionary 网站(https://www.merriam-webster.com/dictionary/abduct,读取日期 2017-03-22)。

④ 《揭秘:日军曾为"补充兵源"掳掠上千广东儿童》,引自人民网(http://history.people.com.cn/n/2014/0415/c372327-24899681.html,读取日期 2017-03-05)。

有绝对原则，无论如何翻译，都不影响制度的实际运行，因为对一个概念的理解，不是只看字面意思，而是看各自语境中的界定。换言之，即使把 trafficking 翻译为"拐卖"，也必须按照联合国文件的界定理解，文字只是一个符号——当然，如果这个符号的本义和定义一致，读者会少一些困惑。这是译者努力的方向。

## Adjudication 违法宣告

为了避免给青少年违法贴上罪犯的标签，美国的青少年司法制度所用的术语与普通刑事司法制度有所不同。比如，普通法院的定罪（认定有罪），叫作 conviction；少年法庭宣告少年实施了违法行为叫作 adjudication（认定违法、宣告违法），全称是 adjudication as a juvenile delinquent（少年违法认定）。下一页有基于儿童服务通讯网站[①]编制的术语区别表（见表1）。

当然，有些涉及青少年司法的文献，并没有严格区分。不过，了解两套体制的目的和用语区别，可以更好地理解英文，确定适当的译法。比如，commitment of juveniles 意思是"少年违法者的监禁"，不是"青少年的承诺"；institution 是指矫正机构或监禁场所，不是任何一个机构。

## Juvenile Disposition 青少年处置

青少年违法案件的审理结束后，如果法官认定被告人违法，随后会举行处置听证（disposition hearing），决定处置方式。处置方式分两类：一是监禁措施（incarceration）；二是非监禁措施（non-

---

① "Juvenile Justice Terms"，引自 Practice Notes 网站（http://www.practicenotes.org/vol12_no4/terms.htm，读取日期 2017-03-05）。

## 表1　美国不同司法制度的术语区别表

| 青少年司法 | 刑事司法 |
| --- | --- |
| adjudication hearing 裁判听证。通过听证，确定是否有充分的证据支持控方对青少年的指控。 | trial 审理，庭审 |
| aftercare 后续关怀。是指少年违法者离开矫正机构（institution）后得到的持续监督。 | parole 假释。在监狱中服刑者被有条件释放，接受相关部门监督。 |
| commitment 投送矫正机构。指少年法庭法官决定把青少年交付（commit to）矫正机构改造。 | sentence to prison 被判监禁 |
| delinquent act 违法行为 | crime 犯罪 |
| delinquent 违法 | criminal / guilty 有罪 |
| detention center 拘留中心。用于听证前羁押违法嫌疑人，目的不是惩罚，而是为了给予照顾和防止继续危害社会，也叫juvenile detention center、juvenile hall，简称juvy。 | jail 看守所，审前羁押场所。 |
| disposition 处置。对被认定违法少年的制裁。 | sentence 量刑 |
| disposition hearing 处置听证。青少年被认定违法后，决定如何制裁的听证。 | sentence hearing 量刑听证。成年人被定罪后，法院决定如何量刑的听证。 |
| institution（矫正）机构。被认定违法后的长期羁押场所（confinement centers）。 | prison 监狱，定罪后的羁押场所。 |
| petition 请求书。有两种：一是 delinquency petitions（违法认定请求书），控方在上面列举青少年违法行为、请求法院作出违法认定；二是waiver petitions（弃权请求书），控方请求法院放弃对该案本应享有的管辖权，将案件移交（transfer）刑事法院审判。如获批准，案件改由刑事法院审判。 | indictment 公诉书 |
| taken into custody 被拘留 | arrest 拘捕 |

incarceration）。

监禁类处置不是简单送往监狱，而是采用多种方式。美国的处置方式包括：家庭监禁／软禁（home confinement / house arrest），即除了上学、上班、接受辅导外，必须待在家里；安置在父母或监护人（guardian）之外的家庭，包括亲属照管（kinship care）、寄养照管（foster care）、小组之家（group home）；在拘留中心（叫作 juvenile hall 或 juvenile detention facility）短期羁押；拘留后社会考察（probation after juvenile hall）；在设防的青少年设施（secured juvenile facilities，也叫 camps）长期羁押；到成人监狱（adult jail）服刑；先到青少年矫正机构服刑，成年后再转到成人监狱（叫作混合量刑／blended sentence）。

非监禁措施包括：口头警告（verbal warning）、罚金（fine）、心理辅导（counseling）、社区服务（community service）、电子监控（electronic monitoring）、社会考察（probation）[1]。

## Appropriate Adult 合适成年人

为保障未成年犯罪嫌疑人的合法权益，中国 2013 年 1 月 1 日实施的《刑事诉讼法》第二百七十条规定了"合适成年人"制度：

> 对于未成年人刑事案件，在讯问和审判的时候，应当通知未成年犯罪嫌疑人、被告人的<u>法定代理人</u>到场。无法通知、法定代理人不能到场或者法定代理人是共犯的，也可以通知未成年犯罪嫌疑人、被告人的<u>其他成年亲属</u>，<u>所在学校</u>、<u>单位</u>、<u>居住地基</u>

---

[1] K. Michon: "Juvenile Court Sentencing Options"，引自 Nolo Law for All 网站（http://www.nolo.com/legalencyclopedia/juvenile-court-sentencing-options-32225.html, 读取日期，2017-03-06）。

<u>层组织或者未成年人保护组织的代表</u>到场,并将有关情况记录在案。

规定中所称"法定代理人""其他成年亲属"和其他成年人"代表",被业界人士统称为"合适成年人",英语为 appropriate adult。这个概念来源于英国法律:

> In English law, an appropriate adult is a parent, guardian or social worker; or if no person matching this is available, any responsible person over 18. The term was introduced as part of the policing reforms in the Police and Criminal Evidence Act 1984 and applies in England and Wales.
>
> In England and Wales, an appropriate adult must be called by police whenever they detain or interview a child (under the age of 18) or vulnerable adult. They must be present for a range of police processes, including interviews, intimate searches and identification procedures, as detailed in the Police and Criminal Evidence Act 1984 (PACE) Codes of Practice, primarily Code C.[①]

父母亲属之外,专门提供"合适成年人"服务的,叫作"专业合适成年人"(professional appropriate adults):

> Professional appropriate adults are defined as those coming from an organised appropriate adult service who have been trained and CRB checked, whether they are paid staff or volunteers. They can be supplied

---

① 维基百科 Appropriate Adult 条(https://en.wikipedia.org/wiki/Appropriate_adult,读取日期 2017-03-05)。

directly by youth offending teams or local authorities or by voluntary or private sector organisations.①

广义的"合适成年人"包括父母、亲属和专业的合适成年人；狭义的"合适成年人"专指"专业合适成年人"。

## Expungement 犯罪记录（前科）消灭

2012年3月14日第十一届全国人民代表大会第五次会议表决通过的《刑事诉讼法修正案》第二百七十五条规定："犯罪的时候不满十八周岁，被判处五年有期徒刑以下刑罚的，应当对相关犯罪记录予以封存。"未成年人犯罪记录封存的目的，是为了便于失足青少年回归社会重新做人，不影响儿童将来的就学、就业、婚姻。犯罪记录封存的制度来自国外，英文是 sealing of criminal record，简称 record sealing。"未成年人犯罪记录封存"可以说 sealing of juvenile criminal records。犯罪记录封存制度有别于犯罪记录消灭制度，后者叫作 expungement of record：

> Many would confuse an expungement, which is a physical destruction, namely a complete erasure of one's criminal records, and therefore usually carries a higher standard[s], with a record sealing, which is only to restrict the public's access to records, so that only certain law enforcement agencies or courts, under special circumstances, will

---

① "Appropriate Adult Provision in England and Wales"，引自 National Appropriate Adult Network 网站（https://www.gov.uk/government/uploads/system/uploads/attachment_data/file/117683/appropriate-adult-report.pdf，读取日期 2017-03-05）。

have access to them.①

在中国，目前只规定了犯罪记录封存制度，还没有规定犯罪记录（前科）消灭制度。而且犯罪记录封存仅限于青少年的某些犯罪。在美国，既有封存制度也有消灭制度，而且不仅适用于青少年违法，成年人犯罪也可以申请封存或消灭犯罪记录，只是申请消灭需要满足的条件更高一些。有些案件不能申请封存或消灭，比如蓄谋杀人、侵害青少年的严重犯罪、性犯罪等。在中国，青少年的犯罪记录按法律规定自动封存，在美国一般需要青少年18岁之后申请封存，但有的州规定自动封存。申请封存或消灭，属于一次民事诉讼，虽然要求封存的是刑事犯罪记录。

封存或消灭后公众无法查询，但以后当事人再次犯罪时，执法人员仍然可以查询。大多数情况下当事人不需要向雇主或房东披露犯罪记录，个别情况下仍需要。所以，封存或消灭只是减少了犯罪记录对将来工作或生活的影响，但并没有完全消除，请看这里的解释：

> <u>An expunged arrest or conviction is not necessarily completely erased, in the literal sense of the word.</u> An expungement will ordinarily be an accessible part of a person's criminal record, viewable by certain government agencies, including law enforcement and the criminal courts. This limited accessibility is sometimes referred to as a criminal record being "under seal". In some legal proceedings, such as during sentencing for any crimes committed after an expungement, or in immigration / deportation proceedings, an expunged conviction that is

---

① 维基百科 Record Sealing 条（https://en.wikipedia.org/wiki/Record_sealing，读取日期 2017-03-05）。

"under seal" may still be considered as proof of a prior conviction.①

另外，尽管 expungement 的本义是"擦除""涂掉"，与 seal 的意思有清楚区分，但在实际运用中，expungement 往往被当作 seal 的同义词：

> Expungement (also called "expunction") is a court-ordered process in which the legal record of an arrest or a criminal conviction is <u>"sealed", or erased</u> in the eyes of the law. When a conviction is expunged, the process may also be referred to as "setting aside a criminal conviction".②

可以认为，狭义的 expungement 是"消灭"，广义是"封存"。因为"封存"在法律上可视同"消灭"（erased in the eyes of the law）。另外，setting aside a criminal conviction 意思是"封存犯罪记录"，但 set aside a judgment 意思是推翻原来的判决。

在英国、爱尔兰、澳大利亚等国，犯罪记录封存叫作 spent conviction，字面意思是"有罪认定的用尽"（有的词典翻译为"失效的判决"，为表达不当）。如果一个人的有罪认定被"用尽"，他就可以声称自己没有犯过罪，雇主就不能因为他未披露犯罪前科而解雇他。别人恶意披露用尽情况也属于诽谤。③

---

① "Expungement Basics"，引自 Find Law 网站（http://criminal.findlaw.com/expungement/expungement-basics.html，读取日期 2017-03-05）。

② 同上。

③ E. A. Martin: *Oxford Dictionary of Law* (London: Oxford University Press, 2003), p. 473.

# Social Investigation Report 社会调查报告

在美国等西方国家，被告人如果被定有罪，缓刑部门（probation officer）会调查此人的社会背景和犯罪背景，供法院、检察官和公设辩护人（public defenders）在讨论量刑时参考，这份报告通常叫作 pre-sentencing report。与此类似，对青少年犯罪案件进行"处置"（disposition）之前，缓刑部门也要出具一份报告。这份报告的名字在各地有不同称呼，包括 predisposition report（处置前报告）、social investigation report（社会调查报告）、social study report（社会研究报告）、social background report（社会背景报告）、social inquiry report（社会调查报告）、social history report（社会历史报告）、probation report（考察报告）等。

我国也引入了类似制度。最高人民法院《关于审理未成年人刑事案件的若干规定》第 21 条规定：

> 开庭审理前，控辩双方可以分别就未成年被告人性格特点、家庭情况、社会交往、成长经历以及实施被指控的犯罪前后的表现等情况进行调查，并制作书面材料提交合议庭。必要时人民法院也可以委托有关社会团体组织就上述情况进行调查或者自行进行调查。①

实践中，法院常委托社会团体进行调查，包括委托共青团组织、未成年保护委员会（Child Protection Committee）、司法行政机构（judicial administrative authorities）、社会工作者（social workers）、社会志愿者（volunteers）进行调查。

---

① 《关于审理未成年人刑事案件的若干规定》，引自最高人民法院网站（http://www.hflib.gov.cn/law/law/fal0vfagui2/XF/FLFG/ZL/1001.htm，读取日期 2017-03-05）。

# 第十六讲

## Court of Cassation 等相关概念及其翻译

### Court of Cassation 再审法院

很多大陆法系国家设有 court of cassation（法语 Cour de Cassation），一直不知道怎么翻译。写本文时发现百度百科有个词条"法国翻案法院（Cour de Cassation）"，词条语言半通不通，显然是翻译过来的文章。这样的文章提供的译文，自然也不令人信服。网上其他汉语资料也不多，但有一些翻译例句。这些例句将 court of cassation 翻译为"最高法院""上诉法院""最高上诉法院"等。

通过联合国内部的机辅翻译界面，可以查到联合国文件中的译法。这些译法除了上述三个外，还包括"翻案法院"，即百度百科提供的译法。举例如下：

原文：Appeals on points of law can be filed with the Court of Cassation in metropolitan France.
译文：对法律观点的上诉可提交法国本土的最高法院。

原文：Cour de Cassation [French Supreme Court] Chambre Criminelle
译文：上诉法院[法国最高法院]，刑事厅

原文：Court: a special court with levels of first instance, and appeal. Cassation will be through the regular Cassation court.
译文：法院：设有一审和上诉两级机构的特别法院，而撤销原判则将通过常设的最高上诉法院进行。

原文：In that sense, the appeals chamber could be said to combine the functions of appeal and cassation in French law.
译文：从这种意义上讲，可以说上诉法庭将法国法律中的"上诉"和"翻案"两种职能结合了起来。

翻译一个术语，既可以从功能入手，也可以从字面意思入手，最好是字面翻译符合功能定义。根据维基百科的解释：

> A court of cassation is a high instance court that exists in some judicial systems. Courts of cassation do not re-examine the facts of a case, they only interpret the relevant law. In this they are appellate courts of the highest instance. In this way they differ from systems which have a supreme court which can rule on both the facts of a case and the relevant law.[1]

笔者译文：

> court of cassation 是一些司法体系中的高审级法院。这些法院不重新审查案件事实，而是仅解释相关法律，在这个意义上，它们是最高审级的上诉法院。这样，这些法院就不同于既裁判事实争议又裁判法律争议的最高法院。

这段话原是英文，作者站在英美法系的角度看待 court of cassation。在英美法系，上诉法院仅审查法律问题，不审查事实问题；

---

[1] 维基百科 Court of cassation 条（https://en.wikipedia.org/wiki/Court_of_cassation，读取日期 2017-05-08）。

中国的上诉法院（包括最高法院），对法律问题和事实问题一并审查。

从这个定义可以看出（或推断），court of cassation：

1. 是高审级法院（最高审级的上诉法院）；

2. 仅审查上诉案件中提出的法律问题，不审查事实问题；

3. 与（其他国家）既审查事实问题又审查法律问题的"最高法院"重合部分功能（都进行法律审查）。

从这三个特征来判断，翻译为"上诉法院""最高上诉法院""最高法院"都有道理。但如果把抽象的概念放在一国的法律体制中来观察，会发现有些译法可能不合适：

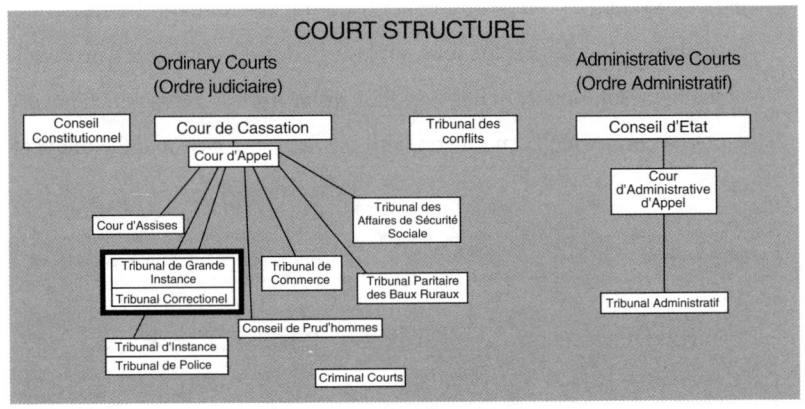

**图 1 法国的法院体系**[①]

上图 1 是法国的法院体系。结合维基百科词条 Court of Cassation，法国最高层级的法院（"最高法院"）有 3 个：普通法院系统（ordinary courts/ordre judiciaire）是 Cour de Cassation，行政法院系统

---

[①] "Court structure"，引自 Cornell University 网站（https://courses2.cit.cornell.edu/frenchlaw/images/FrcourtsLg.gif，读取日期 2017-05-08）。

是 Conseil d'Etat（国务院），宪法系统是 Conseil Constitutionnel（宪法法院）。普通法院系统还有一个 Cour d'Appel（上诉法院）低于 Cour de Cassation。管辖权裁判系统只有一个 Tribunal des conflits（管辖权争议法庭），一审即终审，无高低之分。

据此，在法国的语境下，Cour de Cassation 翻译为"最高法院"可能以偏概全，因为还有2个名称不是最高法院的最高法院。作为补救，译为"普通法院系统的最高法院"，则意思周全。

如果翻译为"上诉法院"，则与 Cour d'Appel 冲突。翻译为"普通法院系统的最高上诉法院"，则意思周全。其他大陆法系国家情况相似，如意大利（仅显示普通法院系统）：

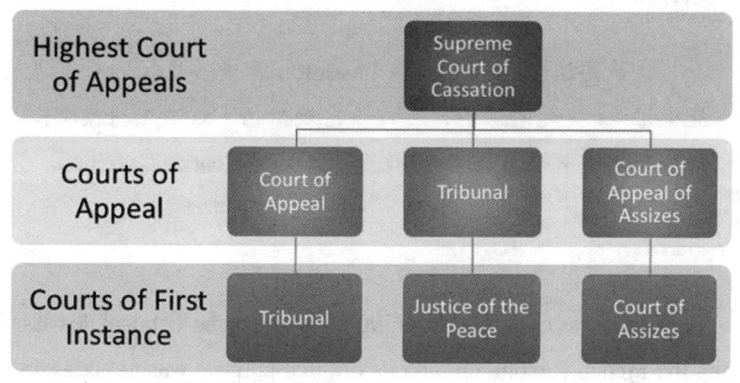

图2　意大利的普通法院体系①

在意大利语境下，只有一个 Supreme Court of Cassation（没有 court of cassation），翻译为最高上诉法院，通常情况下没问题。但假如翻译上图2，就会出现困难：如果翻译为"最高上诉法院"，就占用了作

---

①　"Italy court structure"，引自 Word Press 网站（https://lawandcourtsblog.files.wordpress.com/2016/02/italy-court-structure.jpg?w=863，读取日期 2017-05-08）。

为解释的 highest court of appeals 的译法。

所以，按照功能翻译，似乎有局限性，至少不够简洁。能否找到一个字面译法，既反映功能，又简洁易懂？这就要首先弄清 cassation 的含义。维基百科这样解释 court of cassation 的由来：

> The Supreme Court reviews the appeal on the record and may affirm or set aside lower court rulings; if set aside, the ruling is said to be *cases* (French for "quashed"), hence the French name of *Cour de Cassation*, or "Quashing Court".①

笔者译文：

> 该最高法院[指 Cour de Cassation]审查当事人针对下级法院庭审记录②提起的上诉，可以维持或撤销下级法院的裁决；"撤销"在法语中叫作 casser，故有法语名称 Cour de Cassation。

维基百科进一步解释道：

> The Court was established in 1790 under the name Tribunal de cassation during the French Revolution, and its original purpose was to act as a court of error with revisory jurisdiction over lower provincial prerogative courts (Parlements).③

---

① 维基百科 Court of Cassation (France) 条（https://en.wikipedia.org/wiki/Court_of_Cassation_(France)，读取日期 2017-05-08）。

② "针对下级法院庭审记录提起的上诉"，意思是二审不再听取证人证言，不再认定事实，仅就一审记录反映出来的法律问题进行书面审查。

③ 同注 ①。

笔者译文：

该法院成立于法国大革命期间的 1790 年，当时的名字叫 Tribunal de cassation，最初目的是作为纠错法院，对下级各省的特权法院（Parlements）行使修正管辖权。

再查什么叫 Parlements，法语版维基百科这样解释：

Un parlement est, sous l'Ancien Régime dans le royaume de France, une cour de justice de dernier ressort, dite aussi cour souveraine, puis cour supérieure à partir de 1661, qui rend la justice au nom du roi, dans un territoire délimité.①

笔者译文（大意）：

Parlement 是古代法国的终审法院，也叫 sovereign court（主权法院）；1661 年以后，改为 superior court（高级法院），负责在一定区域内以国王的名义进行司法审判。

综合以上英法文资料的解释，这个法院当初的目的，就是为了纠正终审判决的错误。而对终审判决进行纠错的机制，在中国叫作"再审程序"：

再审程序一般指申诉和审判监督程序，学理上称之为审判监督程序，是法院对经过生效裁判的案件复核审理的法律程序。人民法院、人民检察院对于已经发生法律效力的判决和裁定，如果

---

① 维基百科 Parlement 条（https://fr.wikipedia.org/wiki/Parlement_(Royaume_de_France)，读取日期 2017-05-08）。

发现在认定事实或适用法律上确有错误，依法提出并进行重新审理。民事再审程序，是我国民事诉讼中的一项重要制度，该程序强调无论在事实认定或法律适用上，只要有错误即应通过再审制度加以纠正，贯彻了我们国家有错必纠、有错必改、实事求是、司法公正的司法理念。①

据此，不妨根据 court of cassation 设置的最初目的，将其翻译为"再审法院"。或者按照字面意思翻译为"修正法院""纠错法院"（"撤销法院"有歧义）；这两个说法，也足以让中国的法律工作者想到"再审"。百度百科翻译为"翻案法院"意思也正确，但"翻案"听起来不像"法言法语"。"再审""修正""纠错"可能略胜一筹。一些国家功能类似的法院，就叫 Court of Revision（修正法院）。

当然，尽管 court of cassation 翻译为"再审法院"，但"再审"和 cassation 两个概念（至少在今天）还是有所不同。前文提到，court of cassation 仅仅审查下级法院适用法律是否正确，不再重新认定事实（即不再重新听取证人证言），而中国的"再审"既要纠正事实认定错误，又要纠正法律适用错误。尽管如此，两者已经有足够的相似性（即都是为了纠正生效判决），所以可以用来互译。必要时，可通过解释来说明两国具体内涵的差异。

翻译为"再审法院""修正法院""纠错法院"不仅简洁易懂，还可以解决翻译中的一系列问题。比如，前文列举的几个联合国文件译例，可以再作修改：

原文：Appeals on points of law can be filed with the Court of Cassation

---

① 互动百科"再审程序"条（http://www.baike.com/wiki/再审程序，读取日期 2017-05-08）。

in metropolitan France.

原译：对法律观点的上诉可提交法国本土的最高法院。

改译：对法律问题的上诉，可提交法国本土的再审法院（或"修正法院""纠错法院"）。

原文：Cour de Cassation [French Supreme Court] Chambre Criminelle

原译：上诉法院[法国最高法院]，刑事厅

改译：再审法院[法国最高法院]刑事庭

原文：Court: a special court with levels of first instance, and appeal. Cassation will be through the regular Cassation court.

原译：法院：设有一审和上诉两级机构的特别法院，而撤销原判则将通过常设的最高上诉法院进行。

改译：设有一审和上诉两个审级的特别法院。纠错（或"再审"）则通过普通的再审法院进行。

原文：In that sense, the appeals chamber could be said to combine the functions of appel and cassation in French law.

原译：从这种意义上讲，可以说上诉法庭将法国法律中的"上诉"和"翻案"两种职能结合了起来。

改译：从这种意义上讲，可以说上诉庭将法国法律中的"上诉"和"纠错"[或"再审"]两种职能结合了起来。

其他例子：

原文：On 27 February 2009, the author filed an appeal in Cassation with the Tribunal Supremo (Supreme Court), which denied the appeal on

15 October 2010.

原译：2009年2月27日，提交人向最高法院提出撤销原判的申诉；2010年10月15日，申诉被驳回。

改译：2009年2月27日，提交人向最高法院提出再审申请；2010年10月15日，再审申请被驳回。

原文：Her appeal in Cassation was dismissed by the Cassation Chamber of the Qostanay Regional Court on 9 November.

原译：她的撤销原判上诉于11月9日被库斯塔奈地区法院撤销原判委员会驳回。

改译：她的再审申请于11月9日被库斯塔奈地区法院再审庭会驳回。

原文：Appeal and Cassation procedures have been introduced;

原译：案件现在可以上诉复审和提交最高法院；

改译：（法律）规定了上诉和再审程序；

原文：Cases can now be reviewed on appeal and by way of Cassation;

原译：案件现在可以上诉复审和提交最高法院；

改译：案件现在可以通过上诉或再审程序得到复查；

注意：最后两个例句原文不同，但意思相同，所以原译相同。改译照顾原文措辞，改用不同说法。

顺便提及，"上诉""重审""再审"三个概念完全不同。"上诉"（appeal）是指当事人对法院所作的尚未发生法律效力的一审判决在法定期限内提请上一级法院重新审判的活动。"重审"（retrial，在台湾地区叫作"更审"）是指上诉案件被第二审法院发回原审法院重新进行审理，即当事人不服第一审裁判提起上诉后，第二审法院经过审理认为原审裁判确实有错误，且不宜直接改判，于是裁定撤销原裁判，发回原审法院，由原审法院对案件重新进行审理。"再审"（revision）是指法院对裁判已经发生法律效力的案件再一次进行审理并重新作出裁判的诉讼活动。

## Supreme Court 最高法院

美国的最高法院不分普通法院、行政法院、宪法法院，而是只有一个 Supreme Court（最高法院）。最高法院是最高的司法部门，是联邦法院系统和州法院系统的共同上诉法院，也是终审法院（court of final instance / court of final appeals）。美国最高法院并不是受理所有上诉到那里的案件，而是仅仅受理涉及重大宪法问题的案件。[①] 它每年收到 7000 多份要求复查的上诉状，但一般只能受理 80 起左右。[②]

美国最高法院共有 9 个大法官（justice），其中一个是 Chief Justice（首席大法官），8 个是 Associate Justice（普通法官。注意，此处的 associate 是"同事"之义，即作为首席大法官同事的法官。也可根据上下文，直接翻译为"法官"）。目前的首席大法官是约翰·罗伯茨（John Roberts）。法官由总统提名，参议院批准，只要不糊涂，可以终身任职。工资直接来自国会预算，而不受制于行政部门。要弹劾（impeach）法官，需要先获得众议院（Congress）简单多数（simply majority）通过，然后交给参议院（Senate）审判，不由政党

---

[①] 这叫作 discretionary jurisdiction 裁量管辖权，即法院自由裁量决定是否管辖。如果一个法院必须受理一个上诉过来的案件，则叫作"强制管辖权"（mandatory jurisdiction）。

[②] "supreme"，引自 The Leadership Conference on Civil and Human Rights 网站（http://www.civilrights.org/judiciary/courts/supreme.html，读取日期 2017-05-08）。

或行政部门控制。参议院定罪，需要三分之二多数。美国历史上，只有一个最高法院大法官塞缪尔·蔡斯（Samuel Chase，《独立宣言》签署者之一）受到过众议院指控，说他的判决受到了他联邦主义的政治倾向（federalist political leanings）影响，但参议院认定所有罪名不成立，并确认法官的独立性，不受任何干扰。他一直担任法官职务，直至去世。美国法官的待遇和职位保障，使美国法官更容易独立作出判决，不受外界干扰。

最高法院法官分为两个主要的思想派别，一派叫 judicial activists（司法能动派），一派叫 strict constructionists（严格解释派）。前者认为，宪法是一份活的文件，法官应当与时俱进，在不同的时期，对宪法作出不同的解释，适应时代变化的需要。比如，通过这一派法官对宪法的重新解释，使妇女获得了堕胎的权利。后者认为，应当从狭义上解释宪法，遵从宪法的字面规定，而不是遵从宪法的精神。①

首席大法官对法院的走向影响很大。第一任首席大法官约翰·马歇尔（John Marshal）在位时，最高法院通过"马伯里诉麦迪逊"（Marbury v. Madison）一案，确立了司法审查（judicial review）的原则，即最高法院可以对国会通过的立法进行审查，并宣布违反宪法的立法无效；又通过"吉本斯诉奥格登"（Gibbons v. Ogden）一案，确立了各州不得通过立法、干扰美国国会监管跨州贸易的权力。

首席大法官沃伦（Earl Warren）在公民权利方面采取司法能动主义的立场，通过审理一系列的案件，促使国会通过许多民权立法。比如，他在任职期间，最高法院作出了"布朗诉托皮卡教育局"（Brown v. Board of Education of Topeka）一案的判决（1954年），推翻了 1896 年最高法院在"普莱西诉弗格森"（Plessy v. Ferguson）

---

① "Government: Judiciary"，引自 USA Online 网站（http://www.theusaonline.com/government/judiciary.htm，读取日期 2017-05-08）。

一案中作出的、维护种族隔离政策的判决,宣布让黑人和白人在不同的学校接受教育违反宪法。当时,"普莱西诉弗格森"一案作出的裁决并非全体一致。在9名大法官中,有一名大法官约翰·马歇尔·哈伦(John Marshall Harlan)持反对意见。他认为宪法是不分种族的(color-blind)。他的意见尽管占少数,但推动了种族平等的观念。他的意见在后来的案件中成为最高法院的多数意见。他任职期间审理的另一起著名的案件是"米兰达诉亚利桑那州"案(Miranda v. Arizona,1966年)。通过本案,最高法院确定,警察拘捕任何人,都应当向其宣读其法律权利,即:

> You have the right to remain silent. Anything you say can and will be used against you in a court of law. You have the right to speak to an attorney, and to have an attorney present during any questioning. If you cannot afford a lawyer, one will be provided for you at government expense.[①]

笔者的译文:

> 你有权保持沉默。但你如果选择开口,你所说的话就有可能甚至一定会在法院中用作对你不利的证据。你有权跟律师沟通,也有权在接受讯问时请律师到场。如果你没有钱请律师,政府会花钱给你请一个。

19世纪中叶,首席大法官是罗杰·布鲁克·塔尼(Roger Brooke Taney),思想十分保守。提到他,人们就会想起他在"德雷德·斯

---

① "Introduction",引自 Miranda Rights 网站(http://www.mirandarights.org/,读取日期 2017-05-08)。

科特诉桑福德"(Dred Scott v. Sandford)一案中代表多数法官撰写的判决意见。他说,在起草宪法时,美国黑人被认为"低人一等,根本不适合与白人相提并论"(an inferior order and altogether unfit to associate with the white race),因此不能被看作美国公民[①]。当然,这个判例最后被推翻了。1921—1930 年,威廉·塔夫托(William Taft)是首席大法官,他后来成为美国总统。他领导下的最高法院以优柔寡断著称。他任职的十年间,最高法院只作出了一件对国家有影响的判决。

其他著名的判例(landmark cases)包括 1973 年的"罗诉韦德"(Roe v. Wade)一案,通过该案,最高法院认定堕胎合法,确立了妇女通过堕胎终止妊娠的权利;2000 年的"布什诉戈尔"(Bush v. Gore)一案,最高法院阻止了正在佛罗里达州进行的重新计票活动,允许佛罗里达州务卿出具证明,证明布什(George W. Bush)在佛罗里达州的选举中获胜,从而使布什成为美国总统。

## Judicial Review 司法审查

上文提到的 appeal、cassation 都是上级法院对下级法院的审查,目的是纠正下级法院可能发生的事实认定或法律适用错误。如果法院对行政部门的决定或立法进行审查,则叫 judicial review(司法审查)。

judicial review 在香港特区译作"司法复核",是司法机关(狭义,专指法院)对行政机关、立法机关以及公共机构行为合法性(legality)、合宪性(constitutionality)的审查。通常情况下,英美法

---

[①] "Dred Scott Decision",引自 Digital History 网站(http://www.digitalhistory.uh.edu/disp_textbook.cfm?smtID=3&psid=293,读取日期 2017-05-08)。

系国家以普通法院（court of general jurisdiction）行使司法审查权，而大陆法系国家多设立行政法院（administrative court）进行司法审查。中国作为大陆法系国家，是在普通法院设行政法庭（administrative division），进行有限的司法审查。

在香港特区，司法复核与违宪审查虽然都翻译为英语的 judicial review，但违宪审查包括针对违反基本法（Basic Law）的行为与立法，两者不宜混淆①。为了区分两者，笔者建议把违宪审查译为 constitutional review，因为违宪审查是司法审查的一种情形。

司法审查制度的理论依据是：宪法是国家的根本大法（美国人称之为 supreme law of the land），具有最高法律效力，是（议会、政府）立法和执法的基础和根据。宪法至上（constitutional supremacy），法律法规从形式到内容都不得同宪法条文相抵触；司法机关（主要是最高法院或宪法法院）是保障宪法的机关，对宪法有最后的解释权。议会、政府的法律法规如果违反宪法，司法机关可以裁决其违宪（unconstitutional）而无效。②

## Administrative Litigation 行政诉讼

"行政诉讼"（administrative litigation）是中国的司法审查，俗称"民告官"。如果当事人认为行政机关的决定侵犯了自身权利（如土地所有权），可以提起行政诉讼。

提起行政诉讼前，有些情况下（如农民对征地决定不服）需要先经过行政复议（administrative reconsideration/review），该复议程序叫

---

① 维基百科"司法复核"条（https://zh.wikipedia.org/wiki/司法复核，读取日期 2017-05-08）。

② 叶细金：《浅议美国司法审查制度》，引自正义网（http://www.jcrb.com/jcpd/jcll/201010/t20101026_458761.html，读取日期 2017-05-08）。

作"前置程序"（pre-procedure）。对复议结果不服，再起诉政府。如果经过了复议程序再起诉，"复议机关决定维持原具体行政行为的，作出原具体行政行为的行政机关是被告；复议机关改变原具体行政行为的，复议机关是被告"（《行政诉讼法》第二十六条）。有些类型的权利，可以选择进行行政复议或直接起诉；如果选择复议，就不能再起诉。

一般情况下，申请复议的对象只能是具体行政行为（specific act），不能是抽象行政行为（abstract act）。具体行政行为就是行政机关作出的决定，包括行政处罚（administrative sanctions）（如行政拘留7天）、行政检查（administrative inspection）、行政许可（administrative licensing）、行政强制执行（administrative enforcement）。抽象行政行为是据以作出决定的依据，包括行政法规、规章和其他规范性文件三类。对"行政法规、规章"的规定不服的，不能申请行政复议（因为法律规定由人大负责审查）；认为"其他规范性文件"不合法的，在对具体行政行为申请行政复议时，可以一并向行政复议机关提出对该规定的审查申请。[①]

中国的行政诉讼，类似于西方的司法审查。但西方的司法审查一般允许法院对政府的具体行政行为、抽象行政行为以及国会的立法进行审查，看其是否违反上级法律或宪法。[②] 在美国，司法审查一般指法院对法律是否符合宪法（constitutionality）进行的审查，叫合宪性审查（constitutional review 或者 constitutionality review）。司法审查制

---

[①] "行政复议决定"，引自中国人大网（http://www.npc.gov.cn/npc/flsyywd/susong/2000-11/25/content_8274.htm，读取日期2017-05-08）。

[②] 英美法系的"民告官"（政诉讼）属于普通民事案件，由普通法院审理，法院不设专门的行政庭，也没有专门的行政法院。美国的 administrative tribunals（行政法庭），实际上属于行政部门的行政复议机构，不属于司法部门。

度是一种权力制衡的方式，法院通过对行政和立法行为的审查，制衡行政和立法机关。中国的行政诉讼是一定程度的司法审查。今后改革的方向是扩大司法审查的范围，使之包括所有抽象行政行为（法律法规）。

中国主要的行政法立法（administrative law legislation）包括：《行政诉讼法》（Administrative Litigation Law）、《行政监察法》（Administrative Supervision Law）、《行政复议法》（Administrative Reconsideration Law）、《国家公务员暂行条例》（Provisional Regulations on State Civil Servants）、《国家赔偿法》（State Compensation Law）、《行政处罚法》（Administrative Penalties Law）。其中的《行政诉讼法》兼有程序法和实体法的内容，而且后者是重点，因此不翻译为 Administrative Procedure Law。民事和刑事诉讼法都是真正的程序法，所以都译为 procedure law；刑事和民事方面的实体法（substantive law）是《刑法》和《民法通则》以及各领域的民事立法。另外，中国多年来一直想制订《行政程序法》，所以，Administrative Procedure Law 的说法，就留给这部法律。

# 第十七讲

## 几个拉丁语法律术语及其翻译

法律英语中存在大量拉丁语短语,为法律学习者和译者带来挑战,本文选择了若干常见的拉丁语法律术语,分析其字面意思,揭示其使用场景,必要时结合译例,分析译法和用法。

### *ab initio* 自始

*ab initio* 的字面意思是:from the beginning[①];ab 的意思是 since、from,*initio* 与 initial(开始)同源,意思是 beginning。*ab initio* 可以翻译为"自始""从一开始"。与 *ab initio* 常见的搭配是 void *ab initio*(自始无效),指一项合同或行为从一开始就无效,视同当事双方从来没有签署过合同或一项行为从来没有发生过,与之相对的是 voidable(可撤销的),如 voidable contract or action。例如:A voidable contract is a formal agreement between two parties that may be rendered unenforceable for a number of legal reasons(可撤销合同是指一份双方签署但可能基于一些法律原因被认定不可执行的合同)[②]。

再如:

---

① 维基百科 List of Latin legal terms 条(https://en.wikipedia.org/wiki/List_of_Latin_legal_terms,读取日期 2017-07-04)。

② "Voidable Contract",引自 Investopedia 网站 http://www.investopedia.com/terms/v/voidable-contract.asp?lgl=rira-baseline-vertical,读取日期 2017-07-04)。

原文：International law establishes that acts related to medical treatment are immune from criminal prosecution ***ab initio***. Dr. Polo Rivera has been convicted and is currently imprisoned for acts that do not constitute a crime.[①]

原译：国际法规定，涉及医疗服务的行为从来都是免于刑事起诉的。Polo Rivera 医生因为并不构成犯罪的行为而被定罪和坐牢。

改译：国际法确立了医疗服务相关行为**自始**不受刑事起诉的原则，而 Polo Rivera 医生却因不构成犯罪的行为而被定罪，目前正在坐牢。

说明：从文件（联合国人权理事会任意拘留工作组的一份意见）内容可知，Polo Rivera 因为给恐怖分子治病，被政府追究责任。在审判过程中，程序又出现严重瑕疵。于是有人告到联合国，称政府的做法属于"任意拘留"，根据之一是，按照国际人道主义法原则，医疗人员无论给谁看病，都不能追究责任。言外之意是，自始就不应该提起刑事起诉，更不用说程序上存在这么多瑕疵。这就是 immune from criminal prosecution *ab initio* 的含义。原译"从来都是"描述一种现实状况，不是规定或原则。

## *condominium* 共有权，共有物业

*dominium* 的词源是 *domin(us)*（lord, master）+ *-ium*（-ium），意思是：complete power to use, to enjoy, and to dispose of property at will，即"绝对支配权"或"绝对所有权"。*condominium* 的词源

---

[①] 本文所用例句，除注明出处的例句外，其余都来自双语语料库 cn.linguee.com，其中收集的双语例句原文及原译，多数来自联合国官方文件系统网站（documents-dds-ny.un.org）。改译由笔者在原译基础上修改而成。

是 *con-* (together) + *dominium*，字面意思就是"共同所有权"或"共有财产"。在国际法上，*condominium* 是指：joint sovereignty over a territory by several states（几个国家对一块领土的共同主权）或者 the territory itself（主权被分享的领土）。[①] 该词已经成为英语日常词汇。

在美国和加拿大，condominium（简称 condo）一般用来指一种不动产的共同所有形式，即：部分财产共同所有，部分财产分别所有，相当于我国的单元房小区（既包括商业性住宅小区，也包括商用物业）。在小区内，房屋单元〔units，既包括高层建筑的一个单元，也包括 townhouse（联体别墅），甚至 detached house（独立式住宅）〕为业主分别拥有，附属设施为业主共有。

网上多把 condominium 翻译为"共管式公寓"或"共管公寓"，这个译法不够准确。首先，从本义来看，该词的重点在于"共有"，而不是"共同管理"。第二，condominium 的形式不仅仅是"公寓"。比如，在加拿大安大略省，condominium 有五种基本形式：1. standard condominiums；2. common element condominiums；3. leasehold condominiums；4. phased condominiums；5. vacant land condominiums[②]。standard condominiums 是指包含单元房和公共部分（common elements）的物业；common element condominiums 是指只有公共部分，没有单元房的物业，为居住在周围的永久性业主（freehold homes）共同拥有；leasehold condominium 是指在租用的土地上建设的物业（与我国的商业小区最为接近）；phased condominium 是指分期开发建设

---

[①] *Random House Unabridged Dictionary*，转引自 Dictionary.com 网站 http://www.dictionary.com/browse/condominium，读取日期 2017-07-04）。

[②] "2001-1 Condominium Act, 1998"，引自 Ontario 网站（https://www.ontario.ca/land-registration/2001-1-condominium-act-1998，读取日期 2017-07-04）。

的物业；vacant land condominiums 是指只有公共部分，单元房需要自己建造的物业。如果把 condo 翻译为"公寓"（通常理解为能容许多人家居住的房屋），无法兼容这五种形式，比如，common element condominiums 就不包括单元房（公寓）。因此，建议按照 condo 的本义，视情况将其译为"共同所有权"（抽象名词）或"共有物业"（具体名词）。这样，在法律语言中，上述五种类型的 condo 就可以分别译为：标准型共有物业、共有元素型共有物业、租用土地型共有物业、分期开发型共有物业、空置土地型共有物业；Condominium Property Act 就可以翻译为"共有物业法"。

condo 还可以指共有物业的一个单元。中国《物权法》当中的"建筑物区分所有权"[①]即为 condominium 的概念。但由于使用"建筑物"这个用词，似乎只包括建筑部分，不包括道路、绿地等非建筑共有部分。加拿大魁北克省民法典中的类似概念 divided co-ownership of immovables（不动产的区分共有权），使用了 immovables（"不动产"）一词，就可以包括不动产中的非建筑共有部分，用词更为严谨。

加拿大和美国的 condo 作为公司（corporation）注册，业主（owners）相当于公司的股东。公司成立董事会（board of directors），董事会成员由业主协会（homeowners association）选举产生。董事会聘任物业管理公司（property management company）进行日常管理，支付物业公司管理费用。物业费（assessments）交给董事会。物业公司除此项收入外，无其他收入。物业公司在小区不搞经营性活动。董事会还控制着维修基金（加拿大叫 reserve funds，即

---

① 建筑物区分所有权，英文为 divided ownership of building，即业主对建筑物内的住宅、经营性用房等专有部分享有所有权，对专有部分以外的共有部分享有共有和共同管理的权利。

"储备金"），并聘请专业人员投资。董事会是重大事项的决策机构，物业管理公司执行董事会的决策。董事会和物业公司是雇佣关系。

在加拿大安大略省，与物业管理相关的法律是 1998 年的《共有物业法》（Condominium Act, 1998）。各共有物业公司（condominium corporation）根据该法律制定公司章程（declaration）、公司条例（by-laws）和公司规定（rule）等。业主购买房产之前，就要保证遵守这些文件中的规定。如不遵守，其他业主可通过法院把违规业主驱逐出去。

## *ex parte* 单方面

*ex parte* 字面意思是：from (by or for) [the/a] party[①]，可以译为"单方面"或"对方不在场的情况下"等。通常，法院作出任何决定，都必须听取当事双方的意见。但有时候一方提出救济申请时，情况紧急，如果听取对方意见后再作决定，可能造成不可挽回的损失。这时，法院就会作出临时决定，将来再安排时间，听取对方意见，然后作出最终决定。这种根据单方面意见作出的决定，就叫作 *ex parte* decision（依单方面申请作出的决定）。比如，A、B 两家地界上有棵千年古树，不仅美化环境，还可以供大家乘凉。但 A 家偶然听说 B 家过两天要把树砍掉，于是要求法院阻止这一行为。但如果等到法院排期举办双方都参加的听证会，古树可能已经不复存在。这时，A 家就可以申请法院临时发布 *ex parte* order（单方面申请的命令），暂时阻止 B 家伐树，直到有机会听取双方的辩论，作出最终决定。

---

① 维基百科 Ex Parte 条（https://en.wikipedia.org/wiki/Ex_parte，读取日期 2017-07-04）。

*ex parte* 还可以用于另一情景，即 *ex parte* communication（单方面沟通，另一方不在场的沟通）。按照律师的职业伦理，与法官的任何接触，都必须有对方律师在场，以避免律师与法官之间的不正当交易。如果一方不通知另一方，私自与法官见面，就叫作 *ex parte* communication。在中国，法官和一方当事人存在广泛的单方面接触，但在西方国家，这样的接触是严格禁止的。

## *non bis in idem* 一事不再理

*non bis in idem*（也叫 *ne bis in idem*），字面意思是："not twice in the same"[①]。*bis* 的意思是 twice，可以结合前缀 *bi-*（二）来记。*idem* 意思是 the same，与 identical（the same）同源。英文解释为：prohibition against double jeopardy. A legal action cannot be brought twice for the same act or offense[②]。中文翻译为"一事不再理"，即同一事项，不得被追究两次。在英美法系国家，该原则被称为"（禁止）双重危险"（prohibition against double jeopardy）原则。国际刑法中有时译为"一罪不二审""一案不二理"等。

结合具体例子，这个短语的意思是，如果一个人被起诉一项罪行，但最终（即经过了所有上诉程序）被无罪开释（acquitted），则公诉机关不能因为不高兴，就同一犯罪事实再次提起公诉（发现新罪重新起诉者不在此限）。但这个原则也不是绝对的。如果后来就同一罪行发现了有力的新证据（new and compelling evidence），可以重新起诉。另外，在美国，如果州法院和联邦法院对同一罪行均有管辖

---

① 维基百科 Non bis in idem 条（https://en.wikipedia.org/wiki/Non_bis_in_idem，读取日期 2017-07-04）。

② 维基百科 List of Latin legal terms 条（https://en.wikipedia.org/wiki/List_of_Latin_legal_terms，读取日期 2017-07-04）。

权,州法院作出无罪判决,联邦检察官可以就同一案件再次向联邦法院起诉。

顺便提及,在法律条文中,也经常遇到 bis 一词,如 article 10 bis (第十条之二)。这种编号方法用在法律修订中。如果在第十条之后,又增加了一条,但不想重新编号,便可以把新增的这条称为"第十条之二"。一条之后可以无限增加,如 ter(之三;可参照 tiertiary 记忆)、quarter(之四;参照 quarter)、quinquies(之五;参照法语 cinq [c 和 q 均可读作 k]、英语 quintet [五重奏]等)、sexies(之六;参照 six;注意拼写确实如此)、septies(之七;参照法语sept [七]、September [本义是 7 月])、octies(之八;参照 October [本义是8 月],与 eight 同源 [o 与 ei 对应,c 与 g 对应])、novies(之九;参照法语 neuf [九])、November [本义是 9 月])、decies(之十;参照 decade、December [本义是 10 月])①。原来的第十条,自然成为 semel(之一),但通常不作标记。

## nolo contendere 不争辩

nolo 的意思是 to be unwilling,contendere 的意思是 contend、dispute、contest。nolo contendere 的字面意思是 I do not wish to dispute,英语经常译为 no contest。② 汉语可以译为"不争辩"。美国的刑事诉讼程序中有一个辩诉交易制度(plea bargain),如果被告人承认有罪

---

① 古罗马一年 10 个月,从 March 开始,所以,September 是 7 月,October 是 8 月,以此类推。后来在一年的开头增加了两个月(January 和 February),但 September 等月份的名称没有变,所以现在 September 是 9 月,October 是 10 月,以此类推。(维基百科 September 条,https://en.wikipedia.org/wiki/September,读取日期 2017-07-04。)

② 维基百科 List of Latin legal terms 条(https://en.wikipedia.org/wiki/List_of_Latin_legal_terms,读取日期 2017-07-04)。

（plead guilty，作有罪答辩），检察官可以减轻起诉的罪名、减少起诉的罪状、向法官建议较轻的量刑。但有的嫌疑人既不承认指控，也不否认指控，这样的答辩（plea）就叫作"不争辩"（no contest）答辩。[①]"不争辩"答辩即默认有罪，视同有罪答辩（guilty plea），但后续效果与有罪答辩不同，比如，如果被告人以后再犯罪，以前的"不争辩"答辩会被视为加重处罚的情节（aggravating factor），大概是对"不老实交代"的惩罚。

中国最近两年在推广"认罪认罚从宽制度"，与辩诉交易制度有相似之处。笔者咨询了懂中文的美国专家，专家建议把"认罪认罚从宽"制度翻译为 plea leniency system。笔者问 plea for leniency 是否更符合逻辑，专家回答前者听起来更像一个专有名词。我们姑且认为他们正确。

## *nulla poena sine lege* 罪刑法定

*nulla poena sine lege* 的字面意思是 no penalty without a law，即 one cannot be prosecuted for doing something that is not prohibited by law。该格言的全称是 *nullum crimen, nulla poena sine praevia lege poenali*，英语译为 no crime, no punishment without a previous penal law，也可以译为 no law, no crime, no law, no punishment。汉语译为"罪刑法定"，十分简洁。由于拉丁文和英文表述过长，该格言经常被简化为 *nullum crimen sine lege*（no crime without law），或者 *nulla poena sine lege*（no

---

[①] 美国联邦系统，被告人在 *nolo contender* plea 之前需要事先得到法院许可。因为在美国刑事诉讼中，被告人都有律师代理进行答辩和辩护（极少数人要求自行辩护，但亦有之），不需要被告人开口说话，而在州系统何种情况下可作此答辩由州法规定。

punishment without law）。①

为便于记忆，可以把这些拉丁词和相关英语单词联系起来：*nullum* = no，*crimen* = crime，*poena* = penalty，*sine* = without（法语 sans），*praevia* = previous，*lege* = legislation，*poenali* = penal。

这条原则的意思是，要想认定一个人有罪，法律必须在事发当时规定该行为属于犯罪并应受特定处罚。在大陆法系国家，该原则意味着不能制定溯及以往的法律（retroactive legislation）或者"事后条款"（*ex post facto* clauses），不能依据普通法（common law，即判例法或习惯法，相对于成文法）定罪，不能依据含糊不清的法律定罪，不能依靠类推（analogy）定罪。我国1979年《刑法》第七十九条明确规定了类推制度："本法分则没有明文规定的犯罪，可以比照本法分则最相类似的条文定罪判刑，但应当报请最高人民法院核准"。我国1997年《刑法》明确废除了类推制度，取而代之的是罪刑法定原则，即：法律明文规定为犯罪行为的，依照法律定罪处刑；法律没有明文规定为犯罪行为的，不得定罪处刑。

在英美法国家，有些犯罪（比如谋杀）并没有成文法明确规定；在国际司法中，对海盗的起诉，也是依据习惯国际法（customary international law）②。

在英美法国家，"罪刑法定"的原则称为"合法性原则"（legality principle），比大陆法系的表述简洁许多。这一说法在汉英同传中用以翻译"罪刑法定"十分方便。拉丁语或英语直译的任何说法，都过于冗长，同传中难以有效表达。

---

① 维基百科 List of Latin legal terms 条（https://en.wikipedia.org/wiki/List_of_Latin_legal_terms，读取日期2017-07-04）。

② 维基百科 Nulla poena sine lege 条（https://en.wikipedia.org/wiki/Nulla_poena_sine_lege，读取日期2017-07-04）。

## *prima facie*（看上去）显然成立的、初步的

这个短语的字面意思是 at first face 或 at first appearance。*prima* 即 first，*facie* 即 face[①]。

*prima facie* 用来说明一方提出的证据看起来显然成立，另一方要想反驳，必须提出相反的证据。

> The term *prima facie* is used in modern legal English (including both civil law and criminal law) to signify that upon initial examination, sufficient corroborating evidence appears to exist to support a case. In common law jurisdictions, *prima facie* denotes evidence that, unless rebutted, would be sufficient to prove a particular proposition or fact.[②]

上文的意思是：现代法律英语中使用的术语 *prima facie*（包括在民法和刑法中）是指经初步审查，发现一项主张似乎存在足够的证据支撑。在普通法系国家，*prima facie* 意指除非被反驳，否则足以证明一项主张或事实的证据。

在英汉词典和翻译实践中，经常把 *prima facie* 翻译为"表面的""表面证据确凿的"，但这样翻译让人想到"表面如此，但事实上并非如此"。例如：

原文：In cases where a ***prima facie*** **case** of retaliation or threat of retaliation has been found by the organization's ethics office and the

---

① 维基百科 List of Latin legal terms 条（https://en.wikipedia.org/wiki/List_of_Latin_legal_terms，读取日期 2017-07-04）。

② 维基百科 Prima facie 条（https://en.wikipedia.org/wiki/Prima_facie，读取日期 2017-07-04）。

internal oversight office declines to undertake the investigation, the executive head, or the head of the ethics office, should refer the matter to the Joint Inspection Unit for investigation.

原译：如果组织的道德操守办公室发现**表面证据确凿**的报复或威胁报复**案情**，但内部监督办公室拒绝进行调查，行政首长或道德操守办公室主任应将此事提交联合检查组进行调查。

改译：如果组织的道德操守办公室发现报复或威胁报复的**证据显然成立**，但内部监督办公室拒绝调查，行政首长或道德操守办公室主任应将此事提交联合检查组进行调查。

说明："表面证据确凿"，隐含意思是实际不确凿。"表面"一词，含有消极否定的意思。另外，case 并非"案件""案情"的意思，而是"证据"的意思："the evidence offered in court to support a claim"①。

再举二例：

原文：In connection with *prima facie* cases of torture and ill-treatment, implicated officers should as a rule be subject to suspension or reassignment during the process of investigation, especially if there is a risk that he or she might interfere with or impede the investigation.

原译：对于**明显的**酷刑和虐待案件，在调查过程中，嫌疑人应当停职或调职，以免嫌疑人干涉或阻碍调查。

说明：*prima facie* 译为"明显的"可以接受。也可以改为"证据显然

---

① "Case"，引自 Collins Dictionary 网站（https://www.collinsdictionary.com/dictionary/english/case，读取日期 2017-07-04）。

成立的"。

原文：The Committee recommends that, as part of its harmonization of federal antidiscrimination laws, the Racial Discrimination Act be amended, as far as civil proceedings are concerned, to require the complainant to **prove *prima facie* discrimination**, at which point the burden shifts to the respondent to prove no discrimination existed.

原译：委员会建议就民事诉讼程序而言，修改《种族歧视法》，以此作为使联邦反歧视法统一协调程序的一部分，该条要求申诉者证明能从**初步的事实便可看出的歧视**，在这一点上，举证责任应转向被告，应由后者证明不存在歧视。

改译：委员会建议缔约国在协调联邦反歧视立法的过程中，修订《种族歧视法》，规定在民事程序中，原告首先**提供本人遭受歧视的初步证据**（或：原告须提供本人显然遭受歧视的证据），然后举证责任转向被告，由被告证明不存在歧视。

说明：原译对 *prima facie* 的处理本身不错（但可改进），但由于译者不懂"初步证据"意味着什么（意味着对方需要提供反证），导致整句话理解不到位。另外，原文并不涉及具体条款的修改，只是整体修改建议，因此原译"该条"没有依据。at which point 的意思是"在这时""在这个时间点"，不是"在这一点上"。

与 *prima facie* 相关的一个说法是 *res ipsa loquitur*，字面意思为 the thing speaks for itself（事情本身就说明了问题）。*ipsa* 的意思是"自己"；*loquitur* 的意思是 he (she) speaks（参照 interlocutor / 对话

者）。① 例如：

> There is a *prima facie* case that the defendant is liable. They controlled the pump. The pump was left on and flooded the plaintiff's house. The plaintiff was away and had left the house in the control of the defendant. **Res ipsa loquitur**.②

这个例句可以译为：有初步证据（或"显然成立的证据"）证明被告承担责任。被告控制着水泵，开着水泵离开了现场，水淹了原告的房屋。原告不在家，请被告代管房屋。**事实本身就是很好的证明**。

## *res judicata* 既判事项，"事已决"原则

*res judicata* 的字面意思是 a matter judged③。*res*（*rem*）的意思是 thing（event/affair/business; fact; cause; property），如 *in rem* jurisdiction（对物管辖权）、republic（来自*re(s)+public*，本义是"公共事务"）。

*res judicata* 在法律中有两个含义。一是"既判事项""已决事项"，即案件已经过终审判决，不可以再上诉。例如：

原文：One is presumed innocent and treated as such until **a *res judicata* conviction** has been delivered.

---

① 维基百科 Res ipsa loquitur 条（https://en.wikipedia.org/wiki/Res_ipsa_loquitur，读取日期 2017-07-04）。

② 同注 ①。

③ 维基百科 List of Latin legal terms 条（https://en.wikipedia.org/wiki/List_of_Latin_legal_terms，读取日期 2017-07-04）。

原译：在某一案件判决之前，嫌犯是被推定无罪的，此推定维持**至基于一事不再理原则的判决**做出为止。

原译文中，"基于一事不再理原则的判决"难以理解。实际上，根据 res judicata 在此处的意思（"经终审判决"），可以改为"被告人在被最终认定有罪之前，被推定为无罪并享有无罪待遇。"另外，作为一项原则，res judicata 指如果当时双方已经就某一事项在一个法院起诉，法院也作出了判决，当事双方便不能就同一事项再次向另一法院起诉（目的是维持法院判决的稳定性、节约司法资源）。如果出现这种情况，法院会以 res judicata（"事已决"）为由，驳回起诉。这个原则既适用于民事案件，也适用于刑事案件。

res judicata 也叫作 ne bis in idem（一事不再理）、autrefois acquit（曾经开释）、autrefois convict（曾经定罪）。autrefois acquit（法语，formerly acquitted，autrefois = other time）和 autrefois convict（formerly convicted），显然只能用于刑事案件，是被告人的两种抗辩（defense）方式。具体来说，如果有人被起诉，他可以跟法院说："以前我曾经因同一犯罪事实和同一罪名被起诉过，法院已经把我放了（或定过一次罪），所以你们不能再起诉我。"当然他不必说这么多话，而只须说：autrefois acquit 或者 autrefois convict。

ne bis in idem 的字面意思是"一事不再理"，显然可以用于民事案件，但从用法实例来看，更多用于讨论刑事案件，作为 prohibition against double jeopardy（禁止双重危险原则）的同义词使用。

既然 res judicata 与 ne bis in idem 意思相同，那么也可以译为"一事不再理"。但如果有必要区分，则可以把 res judicata 译为"事已决"原则。"事已决"是笔者建议的译法。《元照英美法词典》[①]等

---

① 薛波：《元照英美法词典》，北京大学出版社，2013年，第1189页。

词典将其翻译为：既决事项；既判力；一事不再理。这些都可以在适当的时候使用。例如：

原文：Even though the regional human rights courts may in a broader sense be considered monitoring bodies, they are included in the second category because their decisions **constitute *res judicata*.**

原译：尽管区域人权法院可能在更广泛的意义上被视为监督机构，却被列入第二类，因为这些机构的决定**构成既判力**。

说明："构成既判力"搭配不当，可以改为"具有既判力"或者"构成既判事项""构成既决事项"。

原文：The complainant refers to domestic jurisprudence which indicates that, once an order for the dismissal of proceedings has become final, it has **the force of *res judicata*.**

原译：申诉人提及的国内判例表明，一旦驳回诉讼的命令成为最终裁决，即具有**既决案件的效力**。

说明："既决案件的效力"可以改为"既判力"（也可以不改）。

原文：The Federal Court rejected the application on 22 January 2007 pursuant to **the principle of *res judicata*.**

原译：2007年1月22日联邦法院根据**定案原则**驳回了这一请求。

改译：2007年1月22日联邦法院根据**"事已决"**（或者**"一事不再理"**）原则驳回了这一请求。

说明："定案"原则显然不是我们平时理解的意思，但具体指什么，汉语中并不清楚。

在民事案件中，*res judicata* 可以区分为 claim preclusion（请求排除）和 issue preclusion（争点排除）。"请求排除"是指，如果原告败诉，便不能基于同样的案由（诉讼理由，cause of action）起诉被告，期待下次碰到"好"法官转败为胜。"请求排除"还指，胜诉的原告不得基于同样事由，再次起诉被告，以便得到更多赔偿。"争点排除"是指，如果双方在一起诉讼中有多个争议问题，其中一个是问题 E，法院就此作出了认定，但后来双方基于不同事由再次诉讼，又遇到了问题 E，这时双方不能请求法院就问题 E 再次作出认定。①

## *status quo* 现状

这个短语的直译是 the state in which②，通常中文翻译为"现状"。例如：

原文：No executions had taken place over the past decade, and any change in the ***status quo*** would have to be carried out with the involvement and acceptance of the people.

译文：已经有十年内没有执行过死刑，改变**现状**必须有人民参与并得到人民接受。

英译汉时，通常不会出错。汉译英时，中国译者经常把"历史、现状和未来"当中的"现状"翻译为 *status quo*，属于用法错误。只

---

① "Res Judicata"，引自 Cornell Law School Legal Information Institute 网站（https://www.law.cornell.edu/wex/res_judicata，读取日期 2017-07-04）。

② 维基百科 List of Latin legal terms 条（https://en.wikipedia.org/wiki/List_of_Latin_legal_terms，读取日期 2017-07-04）。

有在"现状"与"维持""恢复"等词搭配时,才可以翻译为 *status quo*。请看该词的英文搭配①:

**status quo** - noun

VERB + STATUS QUO

**defend, keep, maintain, preserve**
- There are many people who wish to maintain the status quo.

| **threaten, upset | change | restore**
-

PHRASES

**a return to the status quo**
- They wanted a return to the status quo before the war.

"历史、现状和未来"可以译为 the history, present state and future,或者说 the past, the present and the future。其他语境下的"现状",也需要视情况翻译,比如,译为 the realities、the present situation、the current state、the present status、the present、where something stands。译者可以从英译汉语料库(如 linguee.com)中找到灵感。

与 *status quo* 相似,*status quo ante* 是指 the way things were before(先前状态),比如:

原文:We have repeatedly stressed that there cannot be a return to the *status quo ante*.

译文:我们已反复强调,绝不能恢复原状。

---

① "Status",引自 OZDIC 网站(http://www.ozdic.com/collocation-dictionary/status,读取日期 2017-07-04)。

原文：In the same resolution, the Council noted that Djibouti had withdrawn its forces to the ***status quo ante***.

译文：安理会在同一项决议中注意到吉布提已将其部队撤回到事件发生之前的位置。

## *stare decisis* 遵循先例

*stare decisis* 的字面意思是 to stand by things decided（坚持已经作出的决定）[①]。*stare* 的意思不是"凝视"，而是 stand firm。作为一项法律原则，这个短语经常被翻译为"遵循先例"，用英语表达即 the doctrine of binding precedent（先例约束原则）。

在英美法系国家，如果法律没有明确规定，较高级别的法院就某一事项作出判决后，该法院或同级法院和下级法院在遇到同类案件时，也比照判决，即遵循先例。比如，一位妇女长期遭受家庭暴力，也无处可逃。一天晚上丈夫喝酒回来又把她毒打一顿，她终于忍无可忍，趁丈夫熟睡，将丈夫杀死。这样的情形，法律可能没有具体规定——法律可能只是抽象规定了什么是故意杀人，什么是正当防卫。上述案件是否正当防卫？不同的法官可能有不同理解，导致相似的案件在不同法院有不同判决。如果上级法院有活生生的案例，其他法院就可以依葫芦画瓢。但遵循先例原则不是绝对的。随着时代进步，法院也会推翻自己的判例，确立新的判例。

"先例约束原则"并非是指先例（判例）的全部内容都有约束力。只有判例中的 *ratio decidendi* 部分，才有约束力。该短语的字面

---

① 维基百科 List of Latin legal terms 条（https://en.wikipedia.org/wiki/List_of_Latin_legal_terms，读取日期 2017-07-04）。

意思是 reason for the decision（注意 *ratio* = rationale）[1]，可以译为"判决理由"。判决书中顺带提及的其他事项，叫作 *obiter dicta*（可简称为 *obiter* 或者 *dicta*），不具备约束力。比如，法院因管辖权问题驳回了一项起诉，但还是顺带就案件的实体问题（merits of the case）发表了看法，这些看法就是 *obiter dicta*，对后面类似的案件不具备约束力。

*obiter dicta* 译为"附言""随附意见"，字面意思是"a thing said in passing"[2]。*obiter* = by the way, in passing；*dicta* = things said；*dicta* 与 dictation 同源。

判决书的中的不同意见（dissenting opinion），也没有约束力，但有一定的说服力，今后还可能演变为"多数意见"（majority opinion），从而具备约束力。

---

[1] 维基百科 List of Latin legal terms 条（https://en.wikipedia.org/wiki/List_of_Latin_legal_terms，读取日期 2017-07-04）。

[2] 同上。

# 第十八讲

## Merits of a Case 等法律概念的翻译

### Merits of the Case 案件的实体（实质）问题

在联合国文献中有多种译法，比如"案件的是非曲直""案情""案情实质""案件实质"等。比如，在联合国内部使用的机辅翻译系统 eLuna 中，可以看到以下句对：

The State party reserved the right to make observations on <u>the merits of the case</u> at a later date, if relevant.
缔约国保留日后对<u>案件的是非曲直</u>提出意见的权利。

It nevertheless provides an overview of its legislative and institutional framework for protecting and supporting victims of domestic violence and makes comprehensive observations on <u>the merits of the case</u>.
尽管如此，它概述了其保护和支助家庭暴力受害人的法律和制度框架，并就<u>本案案情</u>提出了综合性意见。

Therefore, the author deems the State party's submission as misleading, given that she has to pursue further processes after the accused has been acquitted on <u>the merits of the case</u>.
因此，来文人认为，缔约国的呈文有误导作用，因为在宣告被告人对<u>案情实质</u>无罪之后，来文人就无权采取进一步的程序。

As a matter of fact, the formulation of paragraph 56 of the advisory Opinion makes it clear that the Court did not actually pronounce itself on <u>the merits of the case</u>.

事实上，咨询意见第 56 段的措辞明确指出，法院并没有就<u>案件实质</u>表明立场。

笔者建议将 merits of the case 翻译为"案件的实体问题"或"案件的实质问题"，相对于程序性或技术性问题。请看以下资料对 on the merits 的解释：

资料 1：

"On the merits" is a term that has its roots in the law: a judge, having reviewed the materials relevant to a lawsuit, may render a verdict based not on <u>issues of procedure or other technicalities, but strictly on the facts introduced into evidence and the law as it applies to those facts</u>. A judge who decides a case on the merits considers that any technical or procedural issues that have been raised are either dealt with or irrelevant. The purpose of deciding cases in this way is to ensure that justice is done, rather than reward or punish one of the parties unfairly because of adherence to, or failure to follow, procedural requirements.[①]

笔者译文：

"on the merits"的说法来自法律：法官在审查案件相关材料之后，不是根据程序性问题或其他技术性问题作出裁判，而是严格

---

① "What Does 'on the Merits' Mean?"，引自 wiseGEEK 网站（http://www.wisegeek.com/what-does-on-the-merits-mean.htm，读取日期 2017-11-02）。

按照作为证据采纳的事实以及适用于这些事实的法律作出裁判。法官如果 decides a case on the merits，就会认为案件中提出的任何技术性或程序性问题已作处理或无关紧要。此种裁判方式是为了保证实现公正，而不是因为一方遵守或没有遵守程序性规定而对其作出不公平的奖赏或惩罚。

**资料2：**

**on the merits:**

adj. referring to a judgment, decision or ruling of a court based upon the facts presented in evidence and the law applied to that evidence. <u>A judge decides a case "on the merits" when he/she bases the decision on the fundamental issues and considers technical and procedural defenses as either inconsequential or overcome.</u> Example: An attorney is two days late in filing a set of legal points and authorities in opposition to a motion to dismiss. Rather than dismiss the case based on this technical procedural deficiency, the judge considers the case "on the merits" as if this mistake had not occurred. [①]

笔者译文：

"on the merits"是指法院的判决或裁定基于证据中呈现的事实以及适用于该证据的法律。<u>法官 decides a case "on the merits"，意思是法官基于根本性问题作出裁判，认为技术性或程序性抗辩不重要或被否定</u>。例如：律师需要针对对方提出的驳回起诉动议，

---

① "On the Merits"，引自 The Free Dictionary 网站（http://legal-dictionary.thefreedictionary.com/on+the+merits，读取日期 2017-11-02）。

提交一套辩护意见和法律依据，但晚交了两天。这时，法院并没有因为这一技术和程序瑕疵而驳回案件，而是假定律师没有犯这个错误，进而 considers the case "on the merits"。

从以上定义来看，decision on the merits of the case 是指法官不考虑程序瑕疵，"就事实而论"作出的裁判。这种裁判与程序性裁判相对，中文称为"就实体问题作出的裁判"，简称"实体裁判"：

## 二、实体裁判和程序裁判

根据刑事裁判针对对象的不同，刑事裁判在学理上还可划分为实体裁判和程序裁判。对于这一分类，日本刑事诉讼法中称之为实体裁判和形式裁判。在日本刑事诉讼中，广义而言的实体裁判是判断诉讼事实是否存在的裁判，形式裁判是判断诉讼程序是否合法的裁判。狭义而言的实体裁判是指对案件作出的有罪或无罪判决，形式裁判则包括管辖错误判决、驳回公诉的决定、免诉判决等。"[①]

merits of the case，就等于 substantive issues（实体问题）。见 WordReference 的英语定义（以及西班牙语翻译）[②]：

| WordReference | WR Reverse (1) |
|---|---|
| WordReference English-Spanish Dictionary © 2017: | |
| **Principal Translations** | |
| Inglés | Español |
| merits of the case *npl* (law: substantive issues) | fondo del asunto *loc nom m* <br> fondo del caso *loc nom m* |

---

① 胡之芳：《刑事裁判根据研究》，中国法制出版社，2006 年，第 21 页。

② "Merits of the Case"，引自 Word Reference 网站（http://www.wordreference.com/es/translation.asp?tranword=merits+of+the+case，读取日期 2017-11-02）。

"实体问题"即"实质问题",后者是更通俗的说法,就好比 relief 在法律中翻译为"救济",但通俗的说法是"补救"。在谷歌中同时搜索"程序问题"和"实体问题",结果为 23.9 万个;同时搜索"程序问题"和"实质问题",结果为 26.7 万个。看来,两者被并列讨论的频率差不多。

但浏览具体内容,可以发现"实体问题"多为中国学者讨论国内法时使用;"实质问题"多为讨论联合国事务或国际法时使用。两者的意思相同。产生这一差异的原因,可能是涉及国际法的用词来自于翻译,译者使用了通俗的说法;而涉及国内法的概念是土生土长(也可能是来自日本)的法律概念。无论如何,既然"实质问题"的说法在国际法中已经得到广泛应用,为保持连续性,当然可以继续运用。

merits of the case 译为"案件的是非曲直"意思正确,但与"程序问题"不能构成显著的对比;译为"案件实质",意思比较抽象;译为"案情",意思不到位,因为"案情"是与案件有关的人、事、物、时空等一切相关情况。译为"案情实质"搭配不当。因此建议译为"案件的实体问题"或"案件的实质问题"。基于上述分析,前面的4个例子可以改译为:

> 缔约国保留日后对<u>案件实体问题</u>提出意见的权利。
> 尽管如此,缔约国概述了其保护和支持家庭暴力受害者的法律和制度框架,并就<u>案件的实体问题</u>提出了全面看法。
> 因此,来文人认为,鉴于她必须在法院基于<u>实体问题</u>判决被告人无罪后进一步采取司法程序,缔约国的呈文有误导作用。
> 事实上,咨询意见第 56 段的措辞明确指出,法院实际上并没有就<u>案件实体问题</u>表明立场。

尽管如此，也不是"一刀切"地把 merits of the case 译为"实体问题"或"实质问题"，必须根据情况灵活处理。以下为 eLuna 机辅翻译系统中提供的更多句对和笔者的改译：

The Committee is of the opinion that the arguments before it raise substantive issues which should be dealt with <u>on the merits</u> and not on admissibility considerations alone.
原译：委员会认为，所提出的论点涉及实质性问题，应该根据<u>案情</u>加以审议，而不是仅仅按照可否受理的问题加以审理。
改译：委员会认为，申诉人的观点提出了实质性问题，应该根据<u>事实</u>处理，不应仅仅考虑案件受理标准。

Upon receipt of a request for assistance, counsel from the Office first <u>assesses the merits of the case, both substantive and procedural.</u> Should the counsel determine that the case has <u>legal merit</u> and will be receivable by the Tribunals, he or she provides legal advice to the staff member...
原译：在接到协助请求后，该办公室一名法律顾问将首先从<u>实质和程序角度评估案件的是非曲直</u>。如果法律顾问确定案件在法律上站得住脚而且法庭会受理，那么该法律顾问将向工作人员提供法律咨询意见……
改译：在接到法律援助请求后，该办公室一名法律顾问首先从<u>实体和程序两方面评估案件的优势</u>。如果法律顾问认定案件<u>有法律依据</u>而且法庭可能受理，该法律顾问就会向工作人员提供法律咨询意见……

Some judges take the view that they could discuss case management issues, issues of timing, use of cross-border agreements and identifying which court might resolve which issue, but <u>not substantive issues that touch upon the merits of the case.</u>

原译：一些法官认为，他们可讨论案件管理问题、时间安排问题、跨国界协议的使用问题，以及由哪个法院解决哪个问题，但不能讨论涉及案情的实质性问题。

改译：一些法官认为，他们可讨论案件管理问题、时间安排问题、跨国界协议的使用问题，以及由哪个法院解决哪个问题，但不能讨论涉及<u>案件事实</u>（或"<u>是非曲直</u>"）的<u>实质性问题</u>。

## Legal Representation 法律代理

记得第一次到联合国做翻译时，我把 legal representation 译为"法律代理"，被一位审校改为"法律代表"，我心里不服气。今天在联合国的术语库 UNTERM portal 中，该词已经译为"法律代理"，我感觉到了联合国翻译的进步：

| — *legal* consultation and representation | — 法律咨询和代理 | UNOG UNHCR Humanitarian issues Migrations, refugees and displaced persons |
|---|---|---|
| — Office for the *Legal Representation* of Rights of Victims | — 受害人权利法律代理办公室 | UNOG National/Subnational institutions |

但在历史文献中，legal representation 译为"法律代表"的情况仍无法改变。比如，在 eLuna 提供的句对中可以看到：

right of access to <u>legal representation</u>
获得<u>法律代表</u>的权利

The organization provides a hotline for women who are discriminated on the basis of gender at their workplace, and provides pro bono <u>legal representation</u> for women who have been fired from their employment.

该组织为因性别而在工作场所受到歧视的妇女提供一条热线,并为被解雇的妇女无偿担任<u>法律代表</u>。

It also facilitated visits by family members and access to <u>legal representation</u> and interpretation.

它还提供方便,让家人探监,让有关人士获得<u>法律代表</u>和解释。

而有的文献中则正确地翻译为"法律代理":

In their opinion, legal assistance to staff should cover procedural issues, the assessment of the merits of a case, as well as <u>legal representation</u>.

他们认为,向工作人员提供的法律协助应涵盖程序问题、对案件实质的评估以及<u>法律代理</u>。

access per se, i.e., the possibility to gain access to the justice system with adequate <u>legal representation,</u> which is fundamental for converting a problem into a judicial claim

诉诸本身即指有可能通过相关的<u>法律代理</u>诉诸司法系统,这是把问题转化为司法诉求的根本

legal representation 的定义是:The legal work that a licensed attorney performs on behalf of a client.① 据此,似乎可以翻译为"律师代理"。但翻译为"律师代理"有时会影响译文的逻辑。比如:

> The issues presently before the court in this divorce action arise out of plaintiff's efforts to discharge her counsel and <u>to substitute a non-lawyer, Theodore Kamasinski, as her "attorney-in fact."</u>...... There the court cited approvingly cases from other jurisdictions which had held that statutes similar to RSA 311:1 were intended to <u>allow "only... isolated instances of legal representation"</u> by non-lawyers.②

笔者译文:

> 该离婚案向法院提出的问题源于原告试图解聘原来的律师,<u>让一个非律师 Theodore Kamasinski 作为自己的"事实代理"</u>。……法院以赞同的口吻援引了其他司法辖区的判例,这些判例认为,与 RSA 311:1 类似的法律意在<u>允许非律师"仅在……个别情况下做法律代理"</u>。

在本例中,如果译为"非律师做律师代理",则会自相矛盾,而译为"法律代理",则不会出现语言逻辑问题。实际上,我国也没有实行律师强制代理制度,所以经人民法院许可的其他公民也可以代理民事诉讼(但不能代理刑事诉讼),legal representation 按字面翻译为

---

① *West's Encyclopedia of American Law* 第 2 版,转引自 The Free Dictionary 网站(https://legal-dictionary.thefreedictionary.com/Legal+Representation,读取日期 2017-11-02)。

② "Lisa A. Holmes v. Ralph F. Holmes Opinion and Order",引自 New Hampshire Bar Association 网站(http://www.nhbar.org/pdfs/Holmes.pdf,读取日期 2017-11-02)。

"法律代理",也可以将我国的实际情况包括进去。

legal representation 译为"法律代表",从字面上也解释得通,但容易和汉语中的"法定代表人"混同。法定代表人是指依法代表法人行使民事权利、履行民事义务的主要负责人(如工厂的厂长、公司的董事长等),英文为 statutory representative:

> The statutory representative represents a company to third parties and is responsible for the company's management. The statutory representative is obliged to exercise his/her function with due professional care and in keeping with the company's interests.[①]

笔者译文:

> 法定代表相对于第三方代表一个公司,负责公司的管理工作。法定代表有义务以应有的专业审慎履行职责,维护公司的利益。

在普遍使用机辅翻译的情况下,译员如果看到联合国语料库中出现两种译法,可能不假思索地任选一种,认为既然都是联合国文件中的译法,必然都可以使用。但实际上联合国文件也在不断改进,译者还是要具备研究和鉴别能力,才能作出正确的选择判断。

## Attribution 归属、归责

在翻译有关国际组织的责任(responsibility of international organi-

---

① Ingrid Jalčová: "Statutory Representatives Have Complicated Tax Position in Slovakia",引自 The Slovak Spectator 网站(https://spectator.sme.sk/c/20016329/statutory-representatives-have-complicated-tax-position-in-slovakia.html,读取日期 2017-11-02)。

zations）的相关文件时，可以看到反复出现 attribution of conduct to an international organization 的说法，先前的文件都翻译为"将行为归于一国际组织"。我最初觉得"行为的归属"归根结底是为了确定"责任的归属"，因此决定将这个短语的译法改为"将行为<u>归责</u>于国际组织"。具体依据是《国际组织的责任条款草案》某版本第三条：

### Article 3 General Principles

1. Every internationally wrongful act of an international organization entails the international responsibility of the international organization.

2. There is an internationally wrongful act of an international organization when conduct consisting of an action or omission:

(a) is attributable to the international organization under international law; and

(b) constitutes a breach of an international obligation of that international organization.

（A/66/10）

官方译文：

### 第3条
### 一般原则

1. 一国际组织的每一国际不法行为均引起该国际组织的国际责任。

2. 在下述情况下，一国际组织有国际不法行为：

（a）依国际法，由作为或不作为构成的行为可归于该国际组织；并且

(b)该行为构成该国际组织义务的违反

(A/66/10)

该条第二款规定何时产生不法行为（行为的归属），第一款规定责任的归属；行为的归属和责任的归属是统一的。而且《条款草案》的主题就是"国际组织的责任"。所以，把 attribution 翻译为"归责"，而不是按字面翻译为"归属"，使意思更为具体，应该是更优的选择。这样翻译，也便于今后单独使用"归责"一词，或者含有该词的词组。因为"归属"的意思比较宽泛，一旦脱离上下文，不容易理解。比如，后文出现的 dual attribution（双重归责，即将一项不法行为同时归责于成员国和国际组织）和 attribution rule（归责规则），如果翻译为"双重归属"和"归属规则"，就需要提供更多的上下文，才能理解。

但看了另外一份相关报告后，我以上的观点出现动摇。该报告中有这样一段话：

(3) Like articles 4 to 11 on the responsibility of States for internationally wrongful acts, articles 6 to 9 of the present articles deal with attribution of conduct, not with attribution of responsibility. Practice often focuses on attribution of responsibility rather than on attribution of conduct. This is also true of several legal instruments. For instance, Annex IX of the United Nations Convention on the Law of the Sea, after requiring that international organizations and their member States declare their respective competences with regard to matters covered by the Convention, considers in article 6 the question of attribution of responsibility in the following terms:
"Parties which have competence under article 5 of this Annex shall

have responsibility for failure to comply with obligations or for any other violation of this Convention."

Attribution of conduct to the responsible party is not necessarily implied.①

这句话的中心意思是：如同（2007版的）第四至十一条一样，2011版的第六至九条也是讲的 attribution of conduct（行为归属），而不是 attribution of responsibility（责任归属）。但实践中经常被关注的是后者。比如《海洋法公约》里有一条，就是探讨责任归属的问题。责任归于谁，并不一定隐含着行为也归于谁。言外之意是：有时一个国际组织没有做错什么事，但却要承担责任。这个意思在上一段说得很明确：

> (2) The responsibility of an international organization may in certain cases arise also when conduct is not attributable to that international organization. In these cases conduct would be attributed to a State or to another international organization. In the latter case, rules on attribution of conduct to an international organization are also relevant.②

由此看来，把 attribution of conduct to an international organization 翻译为"将行为归责于国际组织"，并没有准确反映原文的意思。原来的译文"将行为归于一国际组织"，意思更为准确。至于 attribution 单独使用或与其他词结合使用时如何翻译，还需要酌情译为"归

---

① "Report of the International Law Commission"，引自 International Law Commission 网站（http://legal.un.org/docs/?symbol=A/66/10，读取日期2017-11-02）。

② 同上。

属""行为的归属""责任的归属""归责"等。

这说明在法律翻译中对词语的选择,要十分慎重,不能想当然。

## Coordination vs. Harmonization
## 协调 vs. 调和

在翻译一份国际法委员会的报告中,我看到这样一句话:

> The principle of mutual supportiveness was not expressly cited in that report, but the notions of complementarity, <u>coordination and harmonization</u> were clearly implied.

后文又出现:

> The postulate on which it was based appeared to be that, in specialized fields, there were significant gaps and overlaps in international treaties because little or nothing had been done to <u>coordinate or harmonize</u> them.

harmonization 是这份文件的关键词,在文件中出现 25 次。在相关文献的翻译中,该词基本都翻译为"协调"。现在突然跳出一个真的"协调"(coordinate),不知如何是好。

实际上,harmonization 翻译为"协调"意思是正确的,因为它与 coordination 同义:

> Unification focuses upon substituting or combining two or more legal systems and replacing them with a single system. Harmonisation on the other hand seeks to coordinate different legal systems by "eliminating major differences and creating minimum

requirements or standards".

Harmonisation can be seen as a step towards unification and, in a way, harmonisaiton aims or strives towards unification.①

笔者译文：

（法律的）"统一"旨在把两个以上的法律制度合并为同一个法律制度或用一个法律制度替代两个以上的法律制度。harmonization 却旨在通过"消除主要差异、创设最低要求或标准"，协调不同的法律制度。

可以把 harmonisation 看作走向统一的第一步，而且在某种意义上，harmonisation 的目标就是实现或努力实现统一。

但这两个词同时出现时，便出现翻译困难。鉴于 coordination of law 除了"法律的协调"之外，很难想到其他译法，所以只能从 harmonization 入手。经调查，我发现有些文件中将其翻译为"统一"，根据上面一段话，这显然不符合 harmonization 的本义。有人用"调和化"，但该词只能作为名词使用，不能作为及物动词用。有日本学者将其翻译为"调和"，笔者认为是不错的选择。这个词的优点是，既可以作为及物动词使用（"调和各国法律"），也可以作为名词使用（法律的调和）。这样，principle of harmonization 可以译为"调和原则"，harmonious interpretation 可以译为"调和性解释"。

译为"调和"的唯一不便之处，是与之前众多的文件不一致。所以，现在面临一个困难抉择：是在此处作技术性处理，得过且过，

---

① K. L. Bhatia: *Textbook on Legal Language and Legal Writing* (New Delhi: Universal Law Publishing Co. Pvt. Ltd., 2010), p. 23.

还是借此机会修改 harmonization 已经形成惯例的译法？笔者为此请教了日内瓦联合国办事处中文处资深审校赵兴民先生。经赵先生同意（2017年09月24），将其答复抄录如下：

> principle of harmonization 在今年的国际法委员会报告里译为"协调原则"。说来话长，这个词在国际法不成体系专题（fragmentation of international law）的文件里多次出现（专题的全部文件见 http://legal.un.org/ilc/guide/1_9.shtml）。
>
> 最早出现 harmonize（harmonization）一词是在这个专题的大纲里（委员会报告 A/55/10 的附件），当时的中文本里的译法为"协调"。后来在不成体系研究组的报告里，这个词多次出现，译法也不统一，先后有过"协调""统一""一致性"等。principle of harmonization 出现得较晚，有过"统一原则""一致的原则""一致性的原则"等译法。
>
> A/CN.4/L.682 和 Add.1 是研究组的最后报告草稿，很有意思：harmonize 与 coordinate 当成同义词使用，多译为"协调"，偶尔也译为"调和"。当两个词并用时，harmonize 则译为"统一"。
>
> 在委员会 2006 年报告所收的研究组报告的结论 4 中，principle of harmonization 采用了"一致的原则"这个译法。现在看来，其缺点是，"一致"不能用作动词，所以无法表达 harmonize 作为动词的含义（见 ILC Report A/61/10, 2006, chap. XII，第237—251段）。
>
> "协调"一词容易反映 harmonize、harmonized、harmonization 这三种形式的意思，也是用得比较多的译法。故今年委员会的报告里采用了"协调原则"。
>
> 我注意到，对 harmonious interpretation，有台湾学者用过

"调和性解释",大陆学者对 the principle of harmonious interpretation 则用过"协调性解释原则"。另外,国内国际法学者在谈论国际法不成体系时也大量使用"协调"的说法(有时也用"协调一致")。

在联合国词汇里(UNTERM网站),对于 harmonize、harmonized、harmonization,用"协调""统一"的译法最多。

"协调原则"肯定有其局限性,但这一说法呼应了先前文件里大量使用过的"协调"译法,从连续性上看比较可取。我们暂时使用这一译法如何?

"调和原则"和"调和性解释"很有启发性,但由于以前用得不多,容我征求一下纽约和日内瓦两地有关同事的意见,看他们有何反馈。另外,关于保护大气层的指南草案 9 明确提到这个 principle of harmonization,在指南草案最后二读时,我也会征求国际法委员和外交部条法司的意见,他们也会对译法提出反馈。我们到时候会作最后修订。

如果按照笔者的意见,前文两个句子可以译为:

原文:

The principle of mutual supportiveness was not expressly cited in that report, but the notions of complementarity, <u>coordination and harmonization</u> were clearly implied.

笔者译文:

该报告中没有明确引用相辅相成的概念,但明显暗含了互补、<u>协调和调和</u>的概念。

原文：

The postulate on which it was based appeared to be that, in specialized fields, there were significant gaps and overlaps in international treaties because little or nothing had been done to <u>coordinate or harmonize</u> them.

笔者译文：

相互关系所依据的假设似乎是，在专门领域，由于很少或从未进行过<u>协调或调和</u>，导致国际公约存在明显的缺陷和重叠现象。

其中将 harmonize 处理为"调和"。但为了保持与历史文件的一致，在全篇的翻译中不再坚持把 harmonize 统一处理为"调和"，而是继续按照先例将其译为"协调"。毕竟 harmonize 和 coordinate 是可以相互解释的词语，即使本文内处理前后不一，也不会造成实质伤害。当然，如果下决心将 harmonize 改译为"调和"，就会一劳永逸地解决 coordinate 和 harmonize 的译法问题。

# 第十九讲

## Summary Execution 等联合国术语的翻译

### Special Rapporteur on Extrajudicial, Summary or Arbitrary Executions
### 司法程序外、直接或任意处决问题特别报告员

Special Rapporteur on Extrajudicial, Summary or Arbitrary Executions 在联合国的文件中有两个译法:"法外处决、即审即决或任意处决问题特别报告员"和"法外处决、即决处决或任意处决问题特别报告员"。前者是联合国日内瓦办事处(United Nations Office at Geneva, UNOG)中文处的译法,后者是联合国总部(UNHQ)中文处的译法。两者的区别在于:summary execution 分别被译为"即审即决"和"即决处决"。造成不一致的原因,是过去通讯不便,各地译员之间缺乏沟通。随着联合国系统共用数据库的建立,有必要检审现有译法,择优选用,或者借统一之际,寻找更好的译法。

维基百科(Wikipedia)对 summary execution 的解释是:

> A **summary execution** is an execution in which a person is accused of a crime and immediately killed without benefit of a full and fair trial. Executions as the result of summary justice (such as a drumhead court martial) are sometimes included, but the term generally refers to capture, accusation, and execution all conducted simultaneously or within a very short period of time, and without any trial at all. Under international

law, refusal to accept lawful surrender in combat and instead killing the person surrendering (no quarter) is also categorized as a summary execution (as well as murder).①

笔者译文

summary execution 是指不经充分和公正审判、立即处决被控犯罪的人。虽然有时这个概念也包括临时军事法庭等通过简易审判处决犯人，但通常是指不经任何审判，即刻或在极短的时间内指控和处决被抓获的人。根据国际法，拒绝接受合法投降、将投降者处死的做法（"不纳降"），也被归为 summary execution。

上述定义中的 summary，是指快速且不经正常程序。请看几本词典的定义：

*Longman Dictionary of Contemporary English*:
done immediately, and not following the normal process ②

*Merriam Webster Learners Dictionary*:
done quickly in a way that does not follow the normal process ③

*Collins Dictionary*:
**Summary** actions are done without delay, often when something else

---

① 维基百科 Summary execution 条（https://en.wikipedia.org/wiki/Summary_execution，读取日期 2017-12-31）。

② "Summary"，引自 Longman Dictionary of Contemporary English Online 网站（https://www.ldoceonline.com/dictionary/summary，读取日期 2017-12-31）。

③ "Summary"，引自 Merriam-Webster Learner's Dictionary 网站（http://learnersdictionary.com/definition/summary，读取日期 2017-12-31）。

should have been done first or done instead.①

*Merriam Webster*:
a: done without delay or formality: quickly executed
b: of, relating to, or using a summary proceeding②

从这些词典及其他网络资料提供的例句看，summary 有两个相似的意思，一是作为贬义词，表示是"不经正常程序"；二是作为中性词，表示"简易程序"。比如：③

第一个意思：

a **summary** court proceeding 简易法庭程序
a **summary** trial 简易程序审判（比如省略举证程序）
a **summary** judgment 简易程序判决（通过简易程序作出的判决）
This is classed as gross misconduct, justifying **summary** dismissal, i.e. without notice. 这属于严重行为失当，可以直接开除，无须事先通知。（直接开除，即不用事先通知的开除）
Section 24 provides for a power of **summary** arrest in respect of arrestable offences as defined in that section. 第 24 条规定了针对该条所称可拘捕犯罪的无证拘捕权。（即无须事先获得司法院的拘捕证即可实施拘捕。）

---

① "Summary"，引自 Collins Dictionary 网站（https://www.collinsdictionary.com/zh/dictionary/english/summary，读取日期 2017-12-31）。
② "Summary"，引自 Merriam-Webster 网站（https://www.merriam-webster.com/dictionary/summary，读取日期 2017-12-31）。
③ 此处例句的译文和解释为笔者所提供。

summary offense（加拿大等国）适用简易程序的犯罪（美国叫作"轻罪"）；与 indictable offense 即适用普通程序的犯罪（美国叫作"重罪"）相对

第二个意思：

The four men were killed after a **summary** trial. 经过简单审判，这四人被处决。

13 people were **summarily** executed (= killed without any trial or legal process) by the guerrillas. 有13人未经审判，被游击队直接处决。

a **summary** execution 直接处决（不经正常司法程序处决）

It says torture and **summary** execution are common. [报告]称酷刑和直接处决的状况司空见惯。

Were students satisfied with this **summary** justice? 学生们对这种不讲程序（缺乏正当程序）的正义满意吗？

There is no doubt that some considered that a beating was no more than **summary** justice. 毫无疑问，有人会认为"痛打一顿"不过是不讲程序的正义。

笔者之所以将 summary execution 译为"直接处决"或"不经正常司法程序处决"，是因为若译为"即审即决"，给人的印象是审理之后当场宣判，但实际上 summary execution 可能根本就没有审判，比如就地处决战俘；若译为"即决处决"，给人的印象是"当即决定（的）处决"，相对于推迟决定，没有隐含程序不当的意思。（顺便提及，调查发现 summary 在日本也译为"即决"，不知道哪国首先使用。）译为"直接处决"虽然不是完美的译法，但通过解释，可以使之与"经过正常司法程序的处决"相对。翻译为"直接"，还受到

summarily 英文解释的启发：

1. in a prompt or direct manner; immediately; straightaway.
2. without notice; precipitately: to be dismissed summarily from one's job.①

在联合国的多语种术语库（unterm.un.org）中，extra-legal execution 被定义为："Killings committed—e.g., by vigilante groups or secret government agents—outside judicial or legal process—that is, in contravention of, or simply without, due process of law."。该词条同时列出了同义词：extra-legal killing、extrajudicial killing (execution)。在 extrajudicial execution 词条下，也将 extra-legal execution 列为变体（variant）。但在 extrajudicial execution 词条下，又指出相关词条并不存在公认的定义："There is no single accepted meaning for this and for other, related terms. (e.g. summary execution, extrajudicial killing, extra-legal killing, arbitrary execution, targeted killing, targeted assassination)"。

尽管如此，上述信息对于翻译这两个词条已经够用：extra-judicial 就是 outside judicial process；extra-legal 就是 outside legal process。因此，可以分别翻译为"司法程序外"和"法律程序外"，与通过司法程序杀人（比如依法判处死刑）或合法杀人（比如警察执法活动中出于自卫杀人）相对。

将 extra-judicial 译为"法外"，可以解释为"司法程序之外"或"法律程序之外"，因此也算正确。但缺点是无法区分 extrajudicial 和 extra-legal。尽管这是一对同义词，但上下文需要形式对等时，可能需要把这两个短语翻译为不同说法。据此，可以把 extrajudicial

---

① *Random House Unabridged Dictionary*，转引自 Dictionary.com 网站（http://www.dictionary.com/browse/summarily?s=t，读取日期 2017-12-31）。

execution/killing 译为"司法**程序**外处决/杀人";如换用 legal,则译为"法律**程序**外处决/杀人"。换句话说,就是"非法杀人",但既然英语用 extra,不妨就译为"外"。

如果不添加"程序"二字,直接译为"司法外"或"法外",意思似乎不够明确。另外,arbitrary executions 在联合国术语库中收录的定义为:"The deprivation of life as a result of the killings of persons carried out by the order of a government or with its complicity, or tolerance or acquiescence without any judicial or legal process."(笔者译文:通过政府命令或与政府合谋或在政府容忍或默许下,不经司法或法律程序剥夺生命的行为)。按照 arbitrary 的本义,翻译为"任意处决"没有问题。

综上,Special Rapporteur on Extrajudicial, Summary or Arbitrary Executions 建议翻译为"司法程序外、直接或任意处决问题特别报告员"。需要指出,这三个短语都是指不经法律程序任意剥夺人的生命。三个概念放在一起使用,不是为了彰显三者的区别,而是为了表达上的周全:无论使用什么说法,都是联合国禁止的行为。联合国文件中没有明确定义或区分这三个概念,就是为了通过模糊的概念,涵盖所有相关行为。

## Sexual and Gender Based Violence
## 性暴力和社会性别暴力

在联合国文件中,这个短语翻译为"性暴力和性别暴力"或者"性暴力和基于性别的暴力",例如:①

---

① 本文引用的双语例句均来自联合国内部使用的机辅翻译系统 eLuna 提供的语料库。

The Security Council strongly condemns the M23 and all its attacks on the civilian population, United Nations peacekeepers and humanitarian actors, as well as its abuses of human rights, including summary executions, sexual and gender based violence and large scale recruitment and use of child soldiers.

语料库中的译法：

安全理事会强烈谴责3月23日运动和该运动对平民、联合国维和人员和人道主义行动者发动的所有袭击，并谴责它的侵犯人权行为，包括即决处决、**性暴力和基于性别的暴力**和大规模招募和使用儿童兵。

如果译文读者问："性暴力"和"基于性别的暴力"有何区别？译者恐怕答不上来。

sex 和 gender 在历史上是同义词，但近年来被逐渐赋予不同含义。sex 用来指一个人的生理性别，gender 被用来指一个人的社会性别。所谓社会性别，就是社会对男性和女性的不同期待。

If sex is a biological concept, then gender is a social concept. It refers to the social and cultural differences a society assigns to people based on their (biological) sex.[①]

---

① "Sex and Gender"，引自 The University of Minnesota Libraries 网站（http://open.lib.umn.edu/sociology/chapter/11-1-understanding-sex-and-gender/，读取日期2017-12-31）。

笔者译文:

如果说 sex 是个生理概念,那么 gender 就是一个社会概念。gender 是指社会赋予(生理)性别不同者的社会和文化差异。

社会对女性(带有偏见)的期待就是要有女人气质(femininity),比如:gentle、sensitive、nurturing、delicate、graceful、cooperative、decorative、dependent、emotional、passive、weak;对男性的期待就是要有男子汉气魄(masculinity),比如:strong、assertive、brave、active、independent、intelligent、competitive、insensitive、unemotional、aggressive。

为了在中文里区分这两个概念,相关领域的专家把 sex(sexual)翻译为"性""性别",把 gender 翻译为"社会性别"。虽然把一个英文单词翻译为四个字,是很少见的做法,但也是不得已而为之。反过来,汉语中的"社会性别",翻译为英语不是 social gender,而是一个词 gender。

在联合国本身的文件中,对于 violence against women、gender-based violence、sexual violence 进行了如下区分解释[①](译文由笔者提供):

For the sake of clarification of some concepts that are interrelated and are sometimes used interchangeably in this assessment, it is important to define some of the basic concepts in the sections below:

在本次评估中,为了澄清几个相互联系甚至可互换使用的概念,有必要在下面几段中界定一些基本概念:

---

① "Country Assessment on Violence against Women Rwanda",引自联合国网站(http://www.un.org/womenwatch/ianwge/taskforces/vaw/VAW_COUNTRY_ASSESSMENT-Rwanda-1.pdf,读取日期 2017-12-31)。

The term **violence against women** refers to any act that results in, or is likely to result in, physical, sexual and psychological harm to women and girls, whether occurring in private or in public. Violence against women is a form of gender-based violence and includes sexual violence.

"对妇女的暴力行为"是指任何导致或可能导致女性身体、性或心理伤害的行为,无论这些行为是在私密或公共场所发生。对妇女的暴力行为是"社会性别暴力"的一种形式,包括性暴力。

**Gender-based violence** is an umbrella term for any harmful act that is perpetuated against a person's will, and that is based on socially ascribed (gender) differences between males and females. Examples include sexual violence, including sexual exploitation/abuse and forced prostitution; domestic violence; trafficking; forced/child marriage; and harmful traditional practices such as female genital mutilation, honor killings, widow inheritance, and others.

"社会性别暴力"是一个统称,指违背个人意愿、基于社会赋予男女两性的差异而实施的任何有害行为,比如性暴力,包括性剥削/性侵害和强迫卖淫;家庭暴力;人口贩运;强迫婚姻/童婚;以及有害传统,如残割女性生殖器、名誉杀人、继承寡妇等。

**Sexual violence**, including exploitation and abuse, refers to any act, attempt or threat of a sexual nature that results, or is likely to result, in physical, psychological and emotional harm. Sexual violence is a form of gender-based violence.

"性暴力",包括性剥削和性侵害,是指导致或可能导致身体、心理或感情伤害的任何性行为、性企图或性威胁。

根据以上区分，建议把 sexual and gender-based violence 翻译为"性暴力和社会性别暴力"（或"性暴力和基于社会性别的暴力"）。如果可以判断在一篇文章中，sexual violence 和 gender-based violence 是互换使用的，或者一篇文章仅使用其中一个概念，则都可以简单翻译为"性暴力"。在不要求特别严谨的情况下，甚至可以将两者合并翻译为"性暴力"。

综上，前文例句的译文可以改为：

安全理事会强烈谴责 3 月 23 日运动和该运动对平民、联合国维和人员和人道主义行动者发动的所有袭击，并谴责它的侵犯人权行为，包括直接处决、**性暴力和基于社会性别的暴力**、大规模招募和使用儿童兵。

## Human Rights-based Approach to Development
## 基于人权的发展观

human rights-based approach to development（简称 human rights approach to development）是联合国机构（如开发计划署）、一些经济合作与发展组织（OECD）国家（如瑞典、挪威、英国、澳大利亚）、非政府组织〔如 Oxfam（乐施会）〕在国际发展合作（也叫"技术援助""国际援助""海外援助""官方发展援助""对外援助"）中将人权与援助挂钩的方法。根据联合国人权高专办（OHCHR）的解释，这种方法包括三个要素：一、在制定发展（注意：国际开发领域的"发展"需要理解为"对外援助"）政策和计划时，以实现国际人权文书中规定的人权为主要目标。二、要确定谁是权利主体、他们享有什么权利；谁是义务主体，他们承担什么义务；加强权利主体主张权利的能力和义务主体履行义务的能力。三、以国际人权条约中规定的原则和标准，指导所有部门的国际发展合作和方案制定，包括在方案制定的所有阶段遵守人权原则和标准[①]。

human rights-based approach 区别于传统的 charity-based approach 和 needs-based approach：后两者把扶贫作为慈善活动，也称为"福利模式"（welfare model）；needs-based approach 旨在满足弱势群体的需求，如食品、住房、土地、服务；human rights-based approach 要求更公平地分享资源、加强弱势群体获得资源的能力。随着国际安全局势的恶化，有人提出把发展援助和国际安全结合起来，称之为 security-based approach。

human rights-based approach 和 rights-based approach 通常可以互换使用，尤其是后者可以作为前者的简称。比如，一份文件标题为 **Rights**-based Approaches to Increasing Access to Water and Sanitation，但目录中的几个小标题都用 **human rights**，具体如下："Understanding the International Framework of **Human Rights** — with Special Reference to the Rights to Water and Sanitation"；"Key Elements/Components in the **Rights** to Water and Sanitation"；"Understanding the **Human Rights**-based Approach"；"Applying **Human Rights**-based Approaches: Water Aid's Experience"；"The Way forward to Embedding a **Human Rights**-based Approach at Water Aid"[②]。毫无疑问，文件标题中的 rights-based approaches 就是指 human-rights based approaches。翻译的时候应考虑统一用词。

---

① "Frequently Asked Questions on a Human Rights-based Approach to Development Cooperation"，引自 United Nations Human Rights 网站（http://www.ohchr.org/Documents/Publications/FAQen.pdf，读取日期 2017-12-31）。

② "Rights-based approaches to increasing access to water and sanitation"，引自 WaterAid 网站（https://washmatters.wateraid.org/publications/rights-based-approaches-to-increasing-access-to-water-and-sanitation，读取日期 2017-12-31）。

不过，也可以把 human-rights based approaches 和 rights-based approaches 当作不同的概念使用，前者指基于国际人权标准的方法，后者是基于国内法定权利的方法。根据同一文件：

> The terms rights-based approach and human rights-based approach have generally been used interchangeably. However, there could be a nuanced distinction drawn between the two. A rights-based approach can refer to an approach that is based on the justiciable rights/entitlements that are already obtainable within a country. A human rights-based approach on the other hand (wherever this distinction is made) can refer to an approach that is based on international human rights standards ... Consequently, this latter approach brings in a moral dimension by introducing international human rights law into the broader policy and development debate within countries, and is directed at promoting and protecting these rights, even if such rights have not been translated into individual country legislation. In this understanding, the rights-based approach is then a subset of the larger universe of the human rights-based approach.

笔者译文：

> rights-based approach 和 human rights-based approach 两个概念通常可以互换使用，但也可以赋予两者微妙的区分。rights-based approach 可以指可通过诉讼获得的国内法定权利/应得权利（entitlements），而 human rights-based approach（如要作区分）可以指基于国际人权标准的方法……鉴于后者把国际人权法纳入更广泛的国内政策和发展辩论中，这种方法便具有一个道德

维度，即，即使这些权利还没有转化为国内立法，也要促进和保护这些权利。按照这种理解，rights-based approach 是更广义的 human rights-based approach 的子集。

在联合国的文件中，human rights-based approach to development 的译法很多，包括"基于人权的发展办法""立足人权的发展方针""注重人权的发展方针""以尊重人权的方式实施发展""以人权为准""人权本位办法""在发展问题上考虑人权"，可谓五花八门。对这样一个反复出现的重要概念，笔者认为有必要适当统一表达方法。

根据前面的分析，human rights-based approach to development 是一种发展观念上的转变。过去是基于慈善目的或基于弱势群体需求的发展观，现在转换为以保障人权为目的的发展观。因此不妨翻译为"基于人权的发展观""以人权为本的发展观"。我们在具体例子中看看这个译法是否可行：

原文：There is a need to integrate **a human-rights-based approach to development** as the Assembly begins its work to prepare the post-2015 development agenda.

原译：在大会开始拟定 2015 年后发展议程的工作之际，需要将**基于人权的做法纳入发展**。

评论：原译此处有个理解问题。integrate 后面的介词是 into / with，不是 to，所以，应当把 a human-rights-based approach to development 视为一个整体，而不是把 integrate ... to development 视为一个整体。建议改为：在大会开始拟定 2015 年后发展议程之际，有必要将**基于人权的发展观**纳入发展议程。

原文：Thus, **a human rights-based approach to development** requires that disability-inclusive policies consider the demands and needs of persons with disabilities.

原译：因此，**基于人权的发展办法**要求包容残疾人的政策考虑残疾人的要求和需要。

评论："办法"比较具体。approach 是一种切入方法、视角、观念。改为"**基于人权的发展观**"意思更清楚。

原文：The insistence on pursuit of **a human rights-based approach to development** had presented obstacles to the realization of the right to development and had deepened divisions that manifested along regional lines in the United Nations human rights system.

原译：主张在发展问题上考虑人权为发展权的实现设置了障碍，并加深了联合国人权系统内各区域立场的分歧。

评论：并非所有国家都赞同这种发展观。这是某发展中国家对此种发展观的批评。中国也认为把援助和人权扯在一起，涉嫌干涉内政。原译仅仅说"考虑"还不够；这个观念要求在发展中贯穿彻底的人权理念。建议改为：坚持奉行**基于人权的发展观**为发展权的实现设置了障碍，并加深了联合国人权系统内各区域立场的分歧。

原文：UN-Habitat continued to support the mainstreaming of **the human rights-based approach to development**, particularly in the context of rapid urbanization.

原译：人居署继续支持把**立足人权的发展方针**纳入主流，特别是在快速城市化的背景之下。

评论：译文没问题。mainstreaming 是指时时处处考虑，也可以说：人居署继续支持全面落实**基于人权的发展观**，特别是在快速城市化的背景之下。

原文：Though the inclusion of Goal 5 as a stand-alone goal augured well for the future, it was important for the implementation of the Sustainable Development Goals to be soundly grounded in **a human-rights based approach to development**.

原译：将目标5列为独立目标是一个好兆头，但还必须使可持续发展目标的落实工作切实植根于**注重人权的发展方针**。

评论：不仅是"注重"人权，而是只考虑人权、以人权为基础。可改为"**基于人权的发展观**"。

除了在发展方面采取 a rights-based approach（"基于人权的观念""人权视角"）之外，在各个领域的工作，都可以采用 a rights-based approach。例如：

原文：Participants, including a number of ministers, considered the major education issues before Africa with regard to progress, challenges and the path to equity and **a rights-based approach** to inclusive quality education.

原译：包括多位部长在内的与会者审议了非洲教育的若干重要问题，包括实现公平和获得包容性优质教育的**权利**的进展、挑战与步骤。

评论：译文没有将重要的概念 right-based approach 翻译出来。但译为"人权观"也行不通。建议改为：包括多位部长在内的与会者审议了非洲教育中的若干重要问题，包括在教育公平、**以人权为视角**实现全纳优质教育方面取得的进步、面临的挑战和前进的道路。

原文：Stress the importance of **a human-rights-based approach** to combating trafficking in persons which emphasizes the rights of victims.

原译：强调应**以人权为准**，打击人口贩运，注重受害者的权利。

评论：这句话强调某种方法的重要性，所以，approach 还是应该体现出来。建议改为：强调应采用注重受害者权利的**人权视角**，打击人口贩运。

原文：It is imperative that legislative and policy responses use **a gender and human rights-based approach** to prevent trafficking, punish perpetrators and provide support to victims and survivors.

原译：针对人贩活动的立法和政策应以**性别和人权本位办法**防止人贩活动、惩治行为人、支持受害人和幸存者。

评论：把"性别和人权本位办法"改为"性别和人权视角"，可能更便于理解，建议改为：针对人贩活动的立法和政策应采用**性别和人权视角**，防止人贩活动、惩治行为人、支持受害人和幸存者。

原文：UNIFEM aims to redress and address the gender inequalities and discrimination of women and girls through **a rights-based approach** to all its work.

原译：妇发基金打算**以基于权利的做法为导向**开展所有工作，以解决和纠正两性不平等现象及对妇女和女孩的歧视。

评论：为简洁起见，建议改为：妇发基金打算在所有工作中采取**人权视角**，解决和纠正两性不平等问题及对妇女和女童的歧视。

# Declaration on the Independence and Impartiality of the Judiciary, Jurors and Assessors and the Independence of Lawyers 关于司法机关、陪审员和参审员的独立性和公正性以及律师独立性的宣言

这份宣言在联合国术语库中的译名是"关于**审判员**、陪审员和**助审员**的独立公正以及律师的独立的宣言"。但在人权理事会后来通过的决议（A/HRC/RES/15/3）中，作为决议名称的 Independence and Impartiality of the Judiciary, Jurors and Assessors and the Independence of Lawyers 却翻译为"**司法机关**、陪审员、**襄审员**的独立性和公正性以及律师的独立性"（A/HRC/RES/23/6）。后者似乎是对前者的修正。

在西方三权分立的语境下，judiciary 是指"司法部门（机关）"，相对独立于行政部门和立法部门。司法部门就是指法院，司法部门独立，就是指法官个人独立。从这个意义上讲，把 judiciary 翻译为"审判员"（理解为"全体法官"）意思也不错。

问题在于，决议本身既用到 judiciary 一词，如 members of the judiciary（司法部门成员），也反复用到 judges 一词，如 frequent attacks on the independence of judges, lawyers, prosecutors and court officials（频繁攻击法官、律师、检察官和法院官员独立性）。如果把 judiciary 翻译为"审判员"，将导致全文 judiciary 译法的不统一。另外，在汉语语境下，"审判员"严格来讲，不能指代全体法官。法官是个统称，"审判员"只是法官队伍中的级别较低的职称。根据《中华人民共和国法官法》，法官包括助理审判员、审判员、副庭长、庭长、审判委员会委员、副院长、院长。因此，把 judiciary 译为"司法机关"是更好的选择。

但 judiciary 译为"司法机关"，并非完美无缺。因为"司法机

关"在中国的语境下还包括检察机关。尽管如此,译为"司法机关"也不至于引起误解。因为熟悉西方政治制度的读者,自然不会以中国定义来理解西方"司法"的概念。

两个版本都把 juror 翻译为陪审员。陪审员是英美法系陪审团（jury）的成员。"陪审团"或"陪审员"的名称是否确切,其实存在争议。汤维建认为 jury 一词翻译为"陪审团"是错误的:

> "陪审员"的称法究竟源于何时何地我不得而知,但是我的确知道无论是在英美法国家还是在大陆法国家,它们所用的概念都很难翻译为"陪审员"。众所周知,在英美,"陪审团"的英文单词是"jury",陪审团成员的用语是"juror"。查"jury",其词根为拉丁语"*jus*",而"*jus*"这个词的含义是"法""法律""法律的原则"等。显而易见,"jury"这个词与法律团体有关。而相联系的概念为"jurist","jurist"则有"法律专家、法官、律师、法理学家、法律著述家"等含义。虽然我不能确当地找出一个适合"juror"原意的概念来,但我可以断言将这个概念翻译成"陪审员"是有问题的,这里面丝毫没有"陪审"的意思。我还可以找出一个例证,就是在英美有所谓大、小陪审团之分。如果说小陪审团（petty jury）的翻译尚可差强人意、勉强说得过去的话,那么,将"grand jury"翻译成"大陪审团",是极有问题的,因为"grand jury"明明不是"陪审"的组织,而是行使控诉权的公诉组织。这可以反向佐证"jury"一词不是"陪审团"之义。①

笔者又查了 jury 的词源,发现该词来源于 swear/oath（宣誓）:

---

① 汤维建:《论民事诉讼中的参审制度》,《河南财经政法大学学报》,2006年第21卷第5期,第41—48页。

"set number of persons, selected according to law and sworn to determine the facts and truth of a case or charge submitted to them and render a verdict," early 14c. (late 12c. in Anglo-Latin), from Anglo-French and Old French *juree* (13c.), from Medieval Latin *iurata* "an oath, a judicial inquest, **sworn body of men**," noun use of fem. past participle of Latin *iurare* "to swear," from *ius* (genitive *iuris*) "**law, an oath**" (see **jurist**). [1]

如果把 jury 理解为"已宣誓团体",则符合 petty jury 和 grand jury 的共同特征。因为两种 jury 都需要宣誓依法履行职责或依据证据作出裁判。

至于 jury 是否与 jurist 同源,同一词典上没有确定答案:

mid-15c., "one who practices law;" 1620s, "a legal writer, one who professes the science of the law," from Middle French *juriste* (14c.), from Medieval Latin iurista "jurist," from Latin ius (genitive iuris) "a right," especially "legal right or authority, law," also "place where justice is administered, court of justice," from Old Latin *ious*, perhaps literally "sacred formula," a word peculiar to Latin (not general Italic) that originated in the religious cults, from PIE root *yewes-* "law" (compare Latin *iurare* "to pronounce a ritual formula," Vedic *yos* "health," Avestan *yaoz-da-* "make ritually pure," Irish *huisse* "just"). [2]

---

[1] "Jurist",引自 Online Etymology Dictionary 网站(https://www.etymonline.com/word/jurist,读取日期 2017-12-31)。

[2] "Jury",引自 Online Etymology Dictionary 网站(https://www.etymonline.com/word/jury,读取日期 2017-12-31)。

这段解释中，并未提及 jurist 来源于 oath。倒查拉丁语–英语词典，发现 oath 的拉丁语（*iūro*）只是与"法律"的拉丁语（*ius* 或 *iuris*）接近而已①：

**iūro** *v. intran. āvi, ātum, 1*

1. active, and **to swear, to take an oath**

2. In general, absolute

3. In particular, to conspire; with infinitive (*jurarunt inter se barbaros necare*)

4. **Called upon or taken to witness in an oath**

5. **Under an oath, bound by an oath**

6. **having sworn, that has sworn** *v. tran.*

**alternate spellings**: jūro

不过，也有词典将 *jus/juris* 同时解释为"法律"和"宣誓"的②：

1. binding decision

2. code

3. court

4. duty

5. justice

6. law

7. legal system

---

① "iūro"，引自 Ultralingua 网站（http://www.ultralingua.com/onlinedictionary/dictionary#src_lang=Latin&dest_lang=English&query =i%C5%ABro，读取日期 2017-12-31）。

② "jus-juris"，引自 Latdict 网站（http://www.latin-dictionary.net/definition/25013/jus-juris，读取日期 2017-12-31）。

8. oath

9. right

考察这些义项，发现它们的共同之处可能是 binding，因此，jury 和 jurist 很可能是同源，至少来源接近。那么能否按字面意思将 jury 翻译为"宣誓团""司法团"？恐怕比较困难。"陪审团""陪审员"的说法已经根深蒂固。除非有国家宣传机器强行纠正，否则很难改变。

关于 assessor，两个版本分别译为"助审员"和"襄审员"。大家知道，英美法系和大陆法系均有公民参与审判的做法。英美法系采用 jury system，其成员叫作 jurors，译为"陪审员"；大陆法系采用 assessors (lay judges) system，我国法律中称之为"人民陪审员制度"。这就为翻译带来了困难：两个法系下的陪审制度，中文说法相同，无法区分。因此，把 assessor 翻译为"助审员"和"襄审员"（"襄"也是"协助"之义），恐怕也是无奈之举。

然而，熟悉陪审制度讨论的人都知道，为区分两个法系的陪审制度，中国和日本学者将英美法系的 jury system 称为"陪审团制度"，将大陆法系的 assessors system 称为"参审制度"，汤维建指出：

在不同的司法制度背景下，陪审制的含义不同，具体地说主要有两种含义：第一种含义指的是英美式的陪审团制度。按照这种制度，在民事诉讼或刑事诉讼过程中，由当事人选择若干普通公民组成一个陪审团，由陪审团负责对案件事实的判定，从而由法官适用法律作出最终裁判的制度。另一种含义就是指大陆法国家的参审制。所谓参审制，是指作为法律外行人的参审员与职业法官一起组成合议庭，共同就法律问题和事实问题行使审判权的制度。①

他进一步认为，中国的"人民陪审员制度"，名为"陪审制"，实为"参审制"，因此，中国的"人民陪审制"应该改为"人民参审制"：

> 我国实行人民陪审员制度。人民陪审制与参审制在基本的构成原理上是一致的，参审员和人民陪审员的功能也大致相同，因而可以将它们归为一类加以认识。
>
> 且不说各国的本国语言，这里仅说其英文名称"assessor"。这个"assessor"是"评估师""评定者"的意思。这里也看不出"陪审"的含义。因此，学理界正确地将大陆法国家使用的"assessor"这个词翻译为"参审员"，而将相关的审判制度翻译为"参审制"。可见，大陆法国家只有"参审制"，而无"陪审制"或"陪审员制度"。
>
> 由此来看，在我国陪审制度改造的系统工程中，有必要将"陪审员"改为"参审员"，将"人民陪审制"改为"人民参审制"。唯其如此，才能词尽其义，名实相符，全面地营造我国正在蓬勃发展的大众参与司法、司法民主化的形象，才能克服由字面含义不可避免地带来的"陪同审判"的消极观念，才能使公众切实地参与司法审判之中，发挥实际的有效作用。②

日本学者同样将大陆法系的 assessors (lay judges) system 称为"参审制"，并综合陪审制（jury system）和参审制，创造了独具特色的

---

① 汤维建：《论民事诉讼中的参审制度》，《河南财经政法大学学报》，2006年第21卷第5期，第41—48页。

② 同上。

"裁判员"制度,但"裁判员"的英文仍基本用参审制的说法,即citizen judge system 或 lay judge system。具体见下表1:

表1　各制度の詳細一覧表[①]

|  | 裁判官関与 | 有罪無罪 | 量刑 | 任期 | 選任 |
|---|---|---|---|---|---|
| 陪審制度 | 陪審員のみ | 判断する | 判断しない | 事件ごと | 無作為 |
| 参審制度 | 裁判官と共同 | 判断する | 判断する | 任期制 | 団体等推薦等 |
| 裁判員制度 | 裁判官と共同 | 判断する | 判断する | 事件ごと | 無作為 |

综上所述,把 assessor 称为"参审员",似乎已经在学界形成共识。因此建议将 assessor 译为"参审员",以区别于英美法系的"陪审员"。原译"助审员"在中国语境下,是"助理审判员"的简称。"襄审员"只有在极个别词典中看到,并未得到广泛使用,况且其含义仍然是协助审理,与实际情况不符。

最后需要指出,尽管笔者建议将 Declaration on the Independence and Impartiality of the Judiciary, Jurors and Assessors and the Independence of Lawyers 译为"关于司法机关、陪审员和参审员的独立性和公正性以及律师独立性的宣言",但在实际工作中如果引用该宣言中文名称,还应该以联合国通过的文本为准。因为联合国文件一旦在联大获得通过,很难修改。即使是错误,也只能留作遗憾。

---

[①] "裁判员制度",引自 Saibanin 网站(http://www.saibanin.courts.go.jp/qa/c8_2.html,读取日期 2017-12-31)。

# 第二十讲

## 法律翻译中的咬文嚼字

最近为联合国某专门机构审校了一本远程学习教程的翻译，教程是介绍如何通过传统的知识产权制度[①]和专门制度（*sui generis* system）保护传统知识（Traditional Knowledge，简称 TK）和传统文化表现形式（Traditional Cultural Expressions，简称 TCEs）的。审校中遇到一些例子，可以说明译者应如何在翻译中咬文嚼字，现摘取若干，在这里与读者分享。本文中"原译"指初译者机辅翻译的版本或自己的草稿，"改译"为笔者修改后的译文。

### Verbal（in words）以言语形式

原文：

Fixed TK can be either **verbal** or non-verbal. According to the *Oxford English Dictionary*, "verbal" means "finding expression in **words** only, without being manifested in action". Verbal TK includes traditional norms and recipes, or TK recorded in a song, a book or film. Non-verbal TK, on the other hand, includes, for example, TK embodied in traditional architecture or rock art.

---

[①] 涉及版权和相关权（copyrights and related rights）、商标（trademarks）、证明和集体商标（certification and collective marks）、地理标志（geographical indications）、工业品外观设计（industrial design）、反不正当竞争（包括假冒）（unfair competition [including passing off]）、专利（patents）等。

原译：

固定传统知识既可以是口头的，也可以是非口头的。根据《牛津英语词典》，"口头"是指"仅用文字而不用行动体现的方式所采用的表达形式"。口头传统知识包括传统规范和传统方法，或用歌曲、书籍或电影形式记录的传统知识。另一方面，非口头传统知识包括传统建筑或岩画中所包含的传统知识。

除个别语言不通顺外，原译有两个明显矛盾："'口头'是指'仅用文字……的表达形式'"，以及"口头传统知识包括……书籍……"。"口头"和"书面"（"文字"）相对，怎么可能用来相互解释？

问题出在 verbal 和 words 的翻译上。verbal 来自于拉丁语的 word：

Late 15th century (describing a person who deals with words rather than things): from French, or from late Latin *verbalis*, from *verbum* "word" (see verb).①

word 既包括口头，也包括书面：

1.2 (usually **words**) Something that someone says or writes; a remark or piece of information.
*"his grandfather's words had been meant kindly"*
*"a word of warning"*②

---

① "Verbal"，引自 Oxford Dictionaries 网站（https://en.oxforddictionaries.com/definition/us/verbal，读取日期 2018-02-08）。

② "Word"，引自 Oxford Dictionaries 网站（https://en.oxforddictionaries.com/definition/us/word，读取日期 2018-02-08）。

但 verbal 的用法却在使用中逐渐演变为"口头的"。《牛津英语词典》中关于 verbal 的用法是这样说的：

> It is sometimes said that the true sense of the adjective verbal is "of or concerned with words," whether spoken or written (as in verbal abuse), and that it should not be used to mean "spoken rather than written" (as in a verbal agreement). For this strictly "spoken" sense, it is said that the adjective oral should be used instead. In practice, however, verbal is well established in this sense and, even in legal contexts, a verbal agreement is understood to mean a contract whose accepted terms have been spoken rather than written.①

笔者译文：

> 有人认为形容词 verbal 的真正意义是"与言语相关的"，无论是口语还是书面语（如 verbal abuse [谩骂、言语虐待]）；不能用以表达"口头"之义（如 verbal agreement [口头协议]）。如果要表达"口头"之义，要用 oral 一词。但在实践中，verbal 用以表达"口头"之义由来已久。即使在法律语境中，谈到 verbal agreement 也被理解为"口头协议"而非"书面协议"。

然而，在本句的翻译中，根据上下文，verbal 则只能理解为该词的本义，即既包括口头表达，也包括书面表达的"言语"。"言语"才能和"行动"（action）相对，"口头"和"文字"都不能与"行

---

① "Verbal"，引自 Oxford Dictionaries 网站（https://en.oxforddictionaries.com/definition/us/verbal，读取日期 2018-02-08）。

动"形成对比。word 则可以翻译为常见的"词语"。"词语"作为"言语"的解释,既包括口头形式,也包括书面形式。

改译:

  **固定传统知识既可以以言语形式存在,也可以以非言语形式存在**。根据牛津英语字典,verbal("言语的")是指"仅以词语形式表达,不体现在行动中"。**言语形式的传统知识**包括传统规范和方法,或以歌曲、书籍或影片记录下来的传统知识。另一方面,**非言语形式的传统知识**包括传统建筑或岩画艺术中所包含的传统知识等。

## Codification 编纂,法典化,整理

在联合国文件中,codify 一直被翻译为"编纂",例如《联合国宪章》第十三条:

  The General Assembly shall initiate studies and make recommendations for the purpose of:
  a. promoting international co-operation in the political field and encouraging the progressive development of international law and its **codification**;[①]

官方译文:

---

① "Chapter IV: The General Assembly",引自联合国网站(http://www.un.org/en/sections/un-charter/chapter-iv/index.html,读取日期 2018-02-08)。

一、大会应发动研究，并作成建议：

（子）以促进政治上之国际合作，并提倡国际法之逐渐发展与编纂。①

国内学者也用"法典化"：

从法律的发展史来看，法律的发展轨迹是由习惯到习惯法再到成文法和法典法。**法的法典化也称为法律编纂**，是指在法的清理和汇编的基础上将现存的同类法或同部门法研究审查，根据统一的原则决定其存废，或者加以修改、补充，最终形成集中、统一、系统的法。②

从 codify 的英文解释看，确实可以译为"编纂"或"法典化"：

Codification is the process through which rules of law are committed to written form. It is usually mentioned in one breath with progressive development. Within the broader topic of the sources of international law, codification holds a peculiar place. The process of codification tends to change the law, because transforming unwritten rules into written rules requires precision, systematization, and definition of the relevant terms and rules. These changes can be minor or substantial.③

---

① 《联合国宪章·第四章：大会》，引自联合国网站（http://www.un.org/zh/sections/un-charter/chapter-iv/index.html，读取日期 2018-02-08）

② 崔西彬：《三次民法法典化浪潮》，引自北京法院网（http://bjgy.chinacourt.org/article/detail/2014/07/id/1333702.shtml，读取日期 2018-02-08）。

③ "Codification"，引自 Oxford Bibliographies 网站（http://www.oxfordbibliographies.com/view/document/obo-9780199796953/obo-9780199796953-0079.xml，读取日期 2018-02-08）。

笔者译文：

法典化（或译"编纂"）是把法律规则转化为书面形式的过程。这个词经常与"逐步发展"（progressive development）相提并论。关于国际法渊源的宏观话题中，法典化占据特殊的位置。法典化的过程往往会导致法律发生变化，因为书面化要求精准、系统化并界定相关术语和规则。这些变化可能是细微的，也可能是重大的。

译为"编纂"的好处是，可以用作及物动词，如"编纂和逐步发展国际法"；翻译为"法典化"的好处是，能够和编纂的最终结果"法典"直接联系起来。基于以上理解和翻译传统，笔者在翻译审校该机构文件时，最初继续将 codify 处理为"编纂"：

TK can be either **codified** or non-codified. **Codified** TK is that which is arranged in some systematic and structured form, in which the knowledge is ordered, organized, classified and categorized in some manner. **Codified** TK may be imbued with some authority or legitimacy.

笔者译文：

传统知识既可以是**经过编纂的**，也可以是未经过编纂的。**已编纂的**传统知识以某种系统化、结构化的形式呈现，即以某种方式对传统知识进行排序、组织、分门别类。**已编纂的**传统知识可能被赋予某种权威性或合法性。

**Codified** TK may include, for example, traditional medicinal, agricultural and environmental knowledge systems which have been **codified** in ancient scriptures and passed on from generation to generation on the basis of those scriptures or through recognized courses of study.

笔者译文：

**已编纂的**传统知识可包括用古文字形式**编纂的**传统医学、农业和环境知识体系等，这些知识体系在古代经典的基础上或通过公认的学习课程世代相传。

迄今为止一切都好，直到翻译接下来的一段：

While **codified** TK will usually be fixed in some material form, **it may also be unfixed or, at least, unwritten.** For example, **codified** TK may include systematized, organized information embedded in languages, cultural practices, skills and experience, such as know-how, **which remains unfixed and resides in a person or community.**

原译：

虽然**已编纂的**传统知识通常以某种物质形式固定下来，**但也可能是不固定的，或至少是非书面的**。例如，**已编纂的**传统知识可包括嵌入语言、文化习俗、技巧和经验之中的系统化有组织信息，例如个人和社群持有的诀窍等仍未固定的信息。

编纂的意思是"编辑（多指资料较多、篇幅较大的著作）：～词典｜～百科全书"①，编纂的结果毫无疑问以书面形式呈现。但译

---

① 中国社会科学院语言研究所词典编辑室：《现代汉语词典（第6版）》，商务印书馆，2012年，第77页。

文说"已编纂的传统知识……也可能是不固定的，或至少是非书面的"，在语言内在逻辑上显然矛盾。

这就迫使我们研究 code/codify 的含义。《牛津英语词典》对 code 的定义是：

**3** A systematic collection of laws or statutes.

"*a revision of the penal code*"

**3.1** A set of conventions or moral principles governing behaviour in a particular sphere.

"*a strict dress code*"

"*a stern code of honour*"①

同一词典对 codify 的定义是：

**1** Arrange (laws or rules) into a systematic code.

"*the statutes have codified certain branches of common law*"

"*in the United Kingdom there is no codified constitution*"

**1.1** Arrange according to a plan or system.

"*this would codify existing intergovernmental cooperation on drugs*"②

从这些定义看，code 是指系统的法律或规则，codify 就是将（分散的）法律规则等系统化。至于这些规则是口头还是书面，并不是

---

① "Code"，引自 Oxford Dictionaries 网站（https://en.oxforddictionaries.com/definition/code，读取日期 2018-02-08）。

② "Codify"，引自 Oxford Dictionaries 网站（https://en.oxforddictionaries.com/definition/codify，读取日期 2018-02-08）。

重点——尽管通常是书面的。所以，英文讲 codified TK may also be unfixed or unwritten 在语言的内在逻辑上是说得通的，但翻译为"已编纂（或译"法典化"）的传统知识也可能是不固定的或非书面的"就说不通了（"法典"的"典"也是书面形式）。

为解决这个问题，可能需要再找一个汉语词，来翻译 codify。搜索我们的汉语词汇储备，也许这里可以用"整理"一词来担当此任。根据《现代汉语词典》，"整理"的意思是："使有条理秩序；收拾①：～行装｜～房间｜～账目｜～文化遗产。"①

据此改译如下：

> 虽然**已整理的**（codified）传统知识通常以某种物质形式固定下来，但也可能是非固定形式的，或至少是非书面的。例如，**已整理的**传统知识可包括嵌入语言、文化习俗、技巧和经验之中的系统化有组织信息，例如**个人和社群持有的诀窍等仍未固定**的信息。

这样翻译就比较容易理解：传统知识既可以以书面形式整理，也可以是口头形式整理。文化习俗中体现的系统知识，即使没有人去记录，也属于 codified TK。换个译法的坏处，是与其他文件中的翻译不一致。解决方案，是在第一次使用"整理"时，加括号注明 codify，甚至还可以说明"也译作'编纂'"。实际上，如果当初将 codification of international law 译为"国际法的整理"，可能比"编纂"更符合本义，但既然"编纂"已经广泛接受，也不必修改。现在

---

① 中国社会科学院语言研究所词典编辑室：《现代汉语词典（第6版）》，商务印书馆，2012年，第1659页。

给 codify 建议一个新的译法，也许在翻译某些文件的时候用得上。

## Documentation 文献编制，文献化，文献，记录，收集

另一个难以翻译的概念是动词 document 和名词 documentation。在一份该机构的术语汇编中，后者被翻译为"文献编制"：

> Documentation
>
> The *Oxford English Dictionary* defines "documentation" as the accumulation, classification and dissemination of information; the material as collected. Documenting traditional knowledge and traditional cultural expressions may include recording them, writing them down, taking pictures of them or filming them—anything that involves recording them in a way that preserves them and could make them available for others. It is different from the traditional ways of preserving and passing on traditional knowledge and traditional cultural expressions within the community.①

官方译文：

> 文献编制
>
> 《牛津英语词典》将"文献编制"（documentation）定义为信息的积累、分类和传播；收集的资料。传统知识和传统文化

---

① "Intergovernmental Committee on Intellectual Property and Genetic Resources, Traditional Knowledge and Folklore"，引自 World Intellectual Property Organization 网站（http://www.wipo.int/meetings/en/details.jsp?meeting_id=42302，读取日期 2018-02-08）。

表现形式的文献编制可能包括对其进行记录、书写、摄影或录像——以任何将其保存下来并能够向公众提供的方式进行记录的行为。它有别于社区内部保存和传播传统知识和传统文化表现形式的传统方法。

从中文的角度看，该译文有部分逻辑不通，因为汉语的"文献编制"（过程）不能涵盖"收集的资料"（结果）。问题的根源在于，documentation 在英语里面是一个概念，在中文里变成两个概念：编制文献的过程（"文献编制"）和编制文献的结果（"文献"）。

一个处理方法是，直接把 documentation 翻译为两个词语："文献编制、文献"。整个词条可以翻译为：

**文献编制，文献**

**《牛津英语词典》将（documentation）定义为信息的积累、分类和传播（"文献编制"）；收集的资料（"文献"）**。传统知识和传统文化表现形式的文献编制可以包括对其进行记录、书写、摄影或录像——以任何将其保存下来并能够向公众提供的方式进行记录的行为。它有别于社区内部保存和传播传统知识和传统文化表现形式的传统方法。

这样，在相关文件中，中文读者看到"文献编制"或"文献"，都会联想到它们来自同一英文概念 documentation。但这种看似周全的处理方法，还是解决不了全部问题。比如下文中的动词 document：

TK can be either **documented** or **non-documented**. According to the *Oxford English Dictionary*, **"to document" is "to record, for purposes of furnishing evidence"**. Documented TK can take many forms, such as text, video, audio, etc., or a combination thereof.

如果根据该段的英文解释翻译为"记录",似乎可以这样翻译:

> 传统知识既可以是**有记录的**,也可以是**无记录的**。根据《牛津英语词典》,"**记录**"(to document)就是"为提供证据而**记录**"。传统知识可以以多种形式记录,如文本、录像、录音,等等,或以上形式的结合。

这样翻译的好处是,读者看到"记录"一词,也可以联想到该词来源于document,从而与"文献""文献制作"建立联系。但这段话也有缺陷:"'**记录**'(to document)就是'为提供证据而**记录**'"有循环定义之嫌。看来最好能够找到一个词直接翻译document,而不是用document的释义(record)来翻译。

检索与传统知识有关的中文文献,可以发现在中文语境下通常使用"收集""整理""研究"3个词。例如以下来源于网络的例句:

> 组成研究组,负责**收集**、**整理**、**研究**散在本地区的单、验、秘方和特效疗法……
> 深入潮汕民间,**收集**、**整理**、**探究**潮汕文化的点点滴滴并编辑成册……
> 把宗教音乐的**收集**、**整理**、**研究**引入了一个新的阶段……
> 在研究宗教和美学的同时,开始**收集**、**整理**、**研究**日本、朝鲜的民艺……

前文探讨过的codification,笔者建议翻译为"整理";documentation是否就是整理之前的"收集"工作呢?英汉词典上从来没有把这两个词对应起来。但我们不妨再回头看看 documentation 的定义。定义中的 accumulation（累积、集聚）意思就是 collect together。定义中把收集的结果称为 material as collected，收集的过程（动词 document）当然就是 collect。再看看 document 所涉及的内容：recording、writing down、taking pictures、filming，这也正是汉语语境中"收集"的内容："通过调查、采访，将各类非遗项目以文字、录音、录像、数字化多媒体的形式记录下来"。①

看来是可以在表示动作的 documentation / document 和"收集"（或"采集"）之间建立联系的。这样，本段就可以改译为：

> 传统知识既可以是**已收集的**（documented），也可以是**未收集的**。根据《牛津英语词典》，"**收集**"（to document）就是"**为提供证据而记录**"。传统知识可以以多种形式收集，如文本、录像、录音，等等，或以上形式的结合。

然而，无论把 document 翻译为"记录"还是"收集"，都会产生一个问题，即英文中名词 documentation 和动词 document 明显为同一概念，汉语却译为多个不同的说法。为了加强文件内部的连贯性以及本文与其他文件之间的联系（不同译者可能采用多种不同译法），不妨在翻译词条 documentation 的时候，把 document 和 documentation 的各种译法都反映在里面，并以括号注明英文 documentation：

> 文献编制，文献化，文献，收集，记录（documentation）
> 《牛津英语词典》将（documentation）定义为信息的积累、分类和传播（译为"文献编制""文献化""[材料的]收

---

① 李长庚：《加强乡村传统文化的保护与传承》，引自学习时报网（http://www.studytimes.cn/zydx/WHJY/2017-11-12/11161.html，读取日期 2018-02-08）。

集""记录");收集的资料(译为"文献""记录")。传统知识和传统文化表现形式的文献编制可以包括对其进行记录、书写、摄影或录像——以任何将其保存下来并能够向公众提供的方式进行记录的行为。它有别于社区内部保存和传播传统知识和传统文化表现形式的传统方法。

此处在 documentation 的诸多译法中,又新增了"文献化"的说法,因为有些语境下这一表述意思可能更加明确。比如:documentation of TK 如果翻译为"传统知识文献制作",可能不明确是"传统知识(已有)文献"的加工,还是"制作关于传统知识的文献"。但翻译为"传统知识文献化"意思就很清楚。documentation 的译法中也没有排除"记录"。因为在不与 record 冲突的情况下,译为"记录"也不会产生语言逻辑问题。

使用"文献""文献化""文献制作"有个缺点,即录音、录像等不出现文字的记录,也被视为"文献"。不过,语言也在发展,"文献"已经成为一种隐喻,"录音文献""录像文献"的说法也时常出现。比如:

> 声像型文献是指利用摄像、录音、复制等技术记录的声音及图像文献,又称视听型文献。分为录音文献及录像文献两类。[①]

## Indigenous Peoples and Local Community
## 土著人民和地方社区

在联合国(包括专门机构)文献中 indigenous peoples 通常被翻译

---

① 《声像型》,引自中国书史网站(https://cn.chiculture.net/0705/html/d10/0705d10.html,读取日期 2018-02-08)。

为"土著人民"（不是"土著民族"），这可能出于多种考虑，我们不去质疑。local 的译法包括"地方""当地""本地"；community 通常译为"社区""社群"。两者相互组合，便出现六种说法：地方社区（社群）、当地社区（社群）、本地社区（社群）。下面分别举例说明（未注明出处的，均来自联合国文件翻译语料库eLuna）。

译为"地方社区"：

...knowledge, innovations and practices of indigenous and **local communities** embodying traditional lifestyles relevant for the conservation and sustainable use of biological diversity...

……土著和**地方社区**体现传统生活方式而与生物多样性的保护和持久使用相关的知识、创新和做法……①

译为"地方社群"：

We further recognize that mountains are often home to communities, including indigenous peoples and **local communities**, who have developed sustainable uses of mountain resources.

我们还认识到，山区通常是包括土著人民和**地方社群**在内的多个社区的家园，他们以可持续方式开发利用山区资源。

翻译为"当地社区"：

Approximately 60 million people, mainly members of indigenous and **local communities**, reside in forests.

大约有 6,000 万人居住在森林里，主要是土著社区和**当地社**

---

① 《生物多样性公约》，引自联合国网站（https://www.cbd.int/doc/legal/cbd-zh.pdf，读取日期 2018-02-08）。

区的成员。

翻译为"当地社群":

Access to new technologies and the sharing of best practices would help women, indigenous peoples, **local communities** and smallholder farmers.

获得新技术并共享最佳做法将为妇女、土著人民、**当地社群**和小农提供帮助。

翻译为"本地社区":

Where appropriate, limited and regulated economic activities, including activities of indigenous and other **local communities**, should be allowed in order to help finance and manage the protected areas; …

应当酌情允许有限和有管制的经济活动,包括土著和其他**本地社区**的活动,以帮助保护区的筹资和管理;……

翻译为"本地社群":

Ultimately, smart infrastructure requires the participation of **local communities** for success.

归根结底,智能基础设施只有在**本地社群**的参与下方能成功。

根据《现代汉语词典》,"当地"的解释是:"人、物所在的或事情发生的那个地方;**本地**:～百姓｜～风俗"[1]。"本地"的解

---

[1] 中国社会科学院语言研究所词典编辑室:《现代汉语词典(第6版)》,商务印书馆,2012年,第259页。

释是："人、物所在的地区；叙事时特指的某个地区：～人｜～口音｜～特产"①。"地方"的解释是：

① 中央下属的各级行政区划的统称（跟"中央"相对）：这项工程由中央投资也有～投资。……③ **本地；当地**：他在农村的时候，常给～上的群众治病。②

虽然词典上三个词有互通之处，但也有差别。根据词典解释和本人观察，如果相对于"中央"或较高的层级，则须要用"地方"；如果相对于"外地"，则用"本地"或"当地"；如果站在"外人"角度，则用"当地"；如果站在"当地人"角度，则用"本地"。如以下来自网络的例句：

早期改良派已初步认识到，要进行资产阶级土地改革，必须得到中央政府的支持，只有从**中央**到**地方**设立机构，统一布置，变革才能奏其成效。

马尼亚规定可以辞退工作人员的条件是：……（3）单位迁往别地，并能在**当地**找到必要的人员；（4）单位迁往**外地**，本人不愿同往；

如善于研究，就会比**外地**的工业更容易占领**本地**农村市场。

关于 local，《牛津英语词典》的解释是：

**1** Relating or restricted to a particular area or one's neighbourhood.

---

① 中国社会科学院语言研究所词典编辑室：《现代汉语词典（第6版）》，商务印书馆，2012年，第61页。

② 同上，第283页。

*"researching local history"*

*"the local post office"* ①

这个解释包含两层意思：（1）涉及或限于特定区域；（2）涉及或限于某人的邻里地区。第一个意思可以概括为"地方性的""局部的"（如"研究地方史"）；第二个意思可以概括为"本地的""当地的"（如"当地邮局"）。所以，local 一个词对应汉语三个词。

把 local 翻译为汉语时，选择哪个说法，取决于 local 相对于什么而言：如果相对于 subnational（国家下一级）、national（国家）、regional（区域）、global（全球），显然应当翻译为"地方"；如果相对于外部，则应翻译为"当地"或"本地"（看讲话人的身份）。

关于"社区"和"社群"，《现代汉语词典》是这样定义的："社区"是指"在一定地域形成的社会生活共同体：旧金山华人～"②；"社群"是指"社会群体：华人～"③。

关于 community，《牛津英语词典》的定义是：

**1** A group of people living in the same place or having a particular characteristic in common.

*"Montreal's Italian community"*

*"the gay community in London"*

*"the scientific community"*

**1.1** A group of people living together and practising common

---

① "Local"，引自 Oxford Dictionaries 网站（https://en.oxforddictionaries.com/definition/local，读取日期 2018-02-08）。

② 中国社会科学院语言研究所词典编辑室：《现代汉语词典（第6版）》，商务印书馆，2012年，第1149页。

③ 同上。

ownership.

"*a community of nuns*"

**1.2** A particular area or place considered together with its inhabitants.

"*a rural community*"

"*local communities*" ①

从总的解释看，community 既可指在同一地方居住的一群人（"社区""聚居区"），如蒙特利尔的意大利人社区（聚居区）；也可以指有共性（但不住在一起）的一群人（"社群""群体"），如伦敦的同性恋群体、科研群体（科学界）。1.1 的解释可以理解为"公社"，1.2 的解释把侧重点放在了地理位置上，如乡村社区、地方社区。

举例中正好有 local communities，看来 community 是指"社区"。尽管维基百科把 local community 的重点放在"人"上："A local community is a group of interacting people sharing an environment" ②，但仍然强调生活在同一区域，所以仍旧可翻译为"社区"。

indigenous peoples and local community 是在生物多样性保护、气候变化、可持续发展的国际对话中出现的概念。过去主要靠政府和科学家的努力，后来发现在丛林、山地、极地等地方世代居住的原始部落，其实积累了非常丰富的生活、生产、医学、文化知识，可对生物多样性保护等国际社会面临的重大议题作出贡献，所以提出了这些人

---

① "Community"，引自 Oxford Dictionaries 网站（https://en.oxforddictionaries.com/definition/community，读取日期 2018-02-08）。

② 维基百科 Local community 条（https://en.wikipedia.org/wiki/Local_community，读取日期 2018-02-08）。

参与国际进程并保护这些人利益的问题。因此，这里的 local 相对于 international，是级别的不同，不是内外的不同。local communities 翻译为"地方社区"可能更便于形成对比关系。比如：

Indigenous peoples and local communities have much to contribute to global discussions concerning sustainability and have a right to participate in matters that may affect them. As proponents and practitioners of both biological and cultural diversity or biocultural diversity, indigenous peoples and local communities have unique insights into possible solutions both locally and globally.[①]

笔者译文：

土著人民和**地方社区**可为全球可持续性讨论作出重要贡献，并有权参与可能影响到他们的事项。土著人民和地方社区作为生物多样性和文化多样性（或称生物-文化多样性）的倡导者和实践者，对于在**全球和地方**层面找到解决方案都可贡献独到见解。

顺便提及，在一些文献中，traditional knowledge（传统知识）、indigenous knowledge（土著知识）和 local knowledge（地方性知识）作为相同的概念使用，并不作具体区分。indigenous peoples 和 local community 两个概念也有密切联系。在某个地方居住的群体

---

① "Inter-Agency Support Group on Indigenous Peoples' Issues. The Knowledge of Indigenous Peoples and Policies for Sustainable Development: Updates and Trends in The Second Decade of the World's Indigenous People"，引自联合国网站（http://www.un.org/en/ga/president/68/pdf/wcip/IASG_Thematic_Paper_Traditional_Knowledge_rev1.pdf，读取日期 2018-02-08）。

（community），就是local community；如果是土生土长的"世居民族"，就是 indigenous peoples。

联合国的多语种术语库（unterm.un.org）把 local communities 翻译为"地方社区"，应当是准确的翻译。

# 附录

## 杨宇冠：《刑事诉讼法》英译本指瑕

李教授是我敬重的老师，对英语和法律，特别是刑事诉讼法有很深的造诣。这本书中有很大部分是关于刑事诉讼概念的辨析。我读后深受启发，但是觉得意犹未尽。希望作者能够多写一些，例如系统研究和阐述我国《刑事诉讼法》英文本若干翻译问题。兹借为李教授大作写"序"的机会谈谈我自己的看法，供李教授和读者参考。我这样做可能会被谴责为"夹带私货"。我确实有这个意思，因为李教授在翻译界很有名气，我可以借此机会表达自己的观点，但更重要的是引起人们对法律翻译的注意。

2012 年 3 月，第十一届全国人民代表大会第五次会议通过了《关于修改〈中华人民共和国刑事诉讼法〉的决定》，新刑事诉讼法于 2013 年生效施行。鉴于英文不是中国的官方语言，也不是我国的任何民族的母语，我国所有法律，包括《刑事诉讼法》译成的英文本并无正式作准文本。但是，由于中国的国际交往日益增加，《刑事诉讼法》等许多中国法律都被译为英文和其他文字，其中英文最为普遍。法律英文本对于世界了解中国的法制发展，了解《刑事诉讼法》等相关法律不可或缺，而且在司法实践中对于外国人在华犯罪之处理也是不可缺少的工具，因为虽然我国刑事诉讼的行为，特别是法庭审理的行为是用中文进行的，但是对于不懂中文的外国人和无国籍人，我国有关部门将为其提供翻译。

我国 1996 年《刑事诉讼法》颁布之后，曾经出现若干英文译本，由于该法中的大多数内容被 2012 年《刑事诉讼法》所吸收，因而新法英文本较少。听说李教授已经将新法全书译为英语，但目前还没有出版。我希望能够早日见到李教授翻译的文本。我主要以 1996 年《刑事诉讼法》英文本中存在的翻译问题进行深入研究和讨论，希望这有助于正确理解我国的刑事司法制度，提高新法英文本的准确性，保障中外刑事诉讼法学界交流的顺利进行，并供李教授和读者参考。

从现有的材料来看，1996 年《刑事诉讼法》的英文版本主要有：全国人大法工委主编的《中华人民共和国刑事诉讼法：中英文对照》[1]，法律出版社法规出版中心编的《中华人民共和国刑事诉讼法（中英对照）》[2]，以及全国人大官方网站中刊登的刑事诉讼法英文版[3]。这些版本基本一致，较为准确地翻译了 1996 年《刑事诉讼法》的全部条文，成为外国人了解我国刑事诉讼的主要资料来源。但是仔细阅读后可以发现，英文本中也存在着一些漏译、误译的情况，有些专业术语在表述上存在着不严谨之处，这些问题可能会影响到外国学者对我国刑事诉讼法和相关制度的理解和认识。

## 一、中英文名词的理解差异

翻译最基本的要求是忠于原文，《刑事诉讼法》是国家的基本

---

[1] 全国人大法工委编：《中华人民共和国刑事诉讼法：中英文对照》，中国检察出版社 1998 年版。

[2] 法规出版中心编：《中华人民共和国刑事诉讼法（中英对照）》，法律出版社 2002 年版。

[3] 全国人民代表大会：《中华人民共和国刑事诉讼法（英文版）》，来源：http://www.npc.gov.cn/huiyi/lfzt/xsssfxg/2011-08/23/content_1666668.htm，发布日期 2011 年 8 月 23 日，访问日期 2016 年 11 月 12 日。

法律，对惩罚犯罪、保障人权乃至整个公民社会的正常运行具有重大意义。对法条中相关概念、内容的漏译可能会导致理解的片面性，应当予以高度关注。下面以全国人大网站发布的《刑事诉讼法》英文本为对象，分析其中存在的问题。

1. 第九条[①]："各民族公民都有用本民族语言文字进行<u>诉讼</u>的权利。"对应的英文表述是："Citizens of all nationalities shall have the right to use their native spoken and written languages in <u>court proceedings</u>."。

此处将"诉讼"译作 court proceedings。该英文词组回译成中文应为"法庭的诉讼"。但是，《刑事诉讼法》第九条所强调的是"用本民族语言、文字进行诉讼"的原则不仅指法庭审理活动。根据我国《刑事诉讼法》，我国的刑事诉讼包含五个阶段，即立案、侦查、审查起诉、审判和执行。如果根据英文本之理解，当事人使用本民族语言文字的权利仅在法庭审理阶段（court proceedings）方可享有，这就从内涵上极大地削减了第九条所保障之权利的行使范围。

中国是一个幅员辽阔、民族众多的国家，许多少数民族都有自己的语言和文字。为了在刑事诉讼中切实保障诉讼参与人，特别是被指控人的诉讼权利，使其能够充分地知悉诉讼情况并表达诉求，法律还规定"在少数民族聚居或者多民族杂居的地区，应当用当地通用的语言进行审讯，用当地通用的文字发布判决书、布告和其他文件。"可见，这种使用本民族语言文字的权利不仅在法庭审判时可以享有，在侦查阶段和审查起诉等阶段同样适用，并贯穿于刑事诉讼始终。因此，本处宜译为"Citizens of all ethnic groups shall have the right to use their native spoken and written languages in criminal procedures."。

2. 第三十一条："本法第二十八条、第二十九条、第三十条的

---

[①] 以下凡法律条款，如无特定说明，皆指 1996 年颁布的《中华人民共和国刑事诉讼法》。

规定也适用于<u>书记员</u>、翻译人员和鉴定人。"英文本的对应翻译是："The provisions of Articles 28, 29 and 30 of this Law shall also apply to <u>court clerks</u>, interpreters and expert witnesses."。

英文本中将"书记员"翻译成为了 court clerks，回译成中文为"法院的书记员"。《刑事诉讼法》中第二十八至三十一条是关于回避制度的规定。回避源自于古老的"自然正义"法则，即"自己不能做自己的法官"，其目的在于保障刑事诉讼的公正性，使得与案件有利害关系的公权力机关之工作人员不得参与相关案件的处理。我国回避制度的突出特点在于其适用范围的广泛性，不仅包括通常认为的法官、检察官、侦查人员等直接处理案件的公安司法人员，还包括书记员、翻译人员等。在我国刑事司法制度中，书记员可以由人民法院聘请，也可以由检察院聘请。同时，人民法院与人民检察院所聘请的书记员，在回避程序上也有所区分，前者的回避决定由院长作出，后者由检察长作出。因此，将"书记员"译为 court clerk 是不全面的，并不能将检察院聘请的书记员涵括在内。

另外，中国法院中的书记员的职责主要担任审判庭的记录工作，并办理有关审判的辅助性事项，如开庭的准备工作、保管证据、整理卷宗、处理文书工作，司法统计工作，接待来访、处理来信工作，协助审判人员进行调查以及对政策、法规的宣传工作等。在英美法系国家的法院中，clerk 通常指由法学院校学生充当的法官助手，此类人负责的是法官的秘书工作，而不是法庭的记录工作。我国《刑事诉讼法》中规定的可能回避的书记员实际上指法庭的担任记录的工作人员，可以译为 court secretaries。

3. 第四十三条："审判人员、检察人员、侦查人员必须依照法定程序，收集能够证实犯罪嫌疑人、被告人有罪或者无罪、<u>犯罪情节轻重</u>的各种证据。"英文本译为："Article 43 Judges, procurators and

investigators must, in accordance with the legally prescribed process, collect various kinds of evidence that can prove the criminal suspect's or defendant's guilt or innocence and the gravity of his crime."。

"犯罪情节轻重"对应的英文本译作 the gravity of his crime，意为"犯罪的严重性"，这属于比较典型的漏译现象。根据本条之规定，相关的公安司法人员应当收集的证据不仅包括"加重的犯罪情节"，还应该包括"减轻的犯罪情节"，这与我国刑事诉讼的基本理念相一致。《刑事诉讼法》的目的在于"准确及时地查明犯罪事实，正确适用法律，惩罚犯罪分子，保障无罪的人不受追究"，这就要求在职权主义模式下的诉讼程序中，公权力机关工作人员应当收集各种证据，无论此份证据是有利还是不利于犯罪嫌疑人或被告人。如果依英文本之理解，以上人员仅需要收集关于"犯罪的严重性"的证据，不仅削减了法律规定之义务，也不利于刑事诉讼"尊重与保障人权"之要求。在此处，"犯罪情节轻重"的对应英文翻译应体现出双层含义，宜翻译成为 "... collect various kinds of evidence that prove the criminal suspect's or defendant's guilt or innocence and indicate the mitigating and aggravating circumstances of the crime."。

4. 第一百六十五条第三款："由于当事人申请回避而不能进行审判的。"英文本译作："if the trial cannot proceed because a party applies for the withdrawal of a judicial officer."。

本条规定在《刑事诉讼法》第三部分"一审程序"中，主要涉及法庭审理过程中由于回避申请导致的延期审理问题。经过仔细对比可以发现，原文中的表述为"当事人申请回避"，并没有明确指出申请回避的对象，而英文本中却将回避的对象予以明确，这种方法能够让读者更加清楚、明了地认识到回避适用的范围，本身并无不妥，但是英文本在回避对象的表述上并不周全，仅有 judicial officer。

英文中 judicial 与"法院、法庭、法官"等有密切联系，译为"法院的；审判的；法庭上的"，比如 judicial action 指审判行为。① judicial 也含有"司法"的意思，但对应的仅仅是狭义审判意义上的司法，比如 judicial power 指法院和法官依法享有的审理和裁决案件，并作出有拘束力的判决的权力。② judicial officer 通常译为"（具有审判职权的）司法人员"，这种解释在英文本对第二百一十二条第四款"指挥执行的审判人员"（the judicial officer directing the execution）中可以得到印证。

从英文本的角度理解，在法庭审理过程中当事人申请回避的对象只能是"审判人员"，这不符合我国《刑事诉讼法》中关于回避制度的规定。回避适用于侦查人员、检察人员和审判人员（第二十八条），在法庭审理过程中，当事人及其法定代理人能够申请法官、人民陪审员、书记员进行回避（高法解释第二十六条），也可以申请检察人员进行回避（高法解释第三十一条）。很显然，judicial officer 无法涵盖上述法律规定的人员范围。

"回避"一词通常被译为 withdrawal③，withdrawal 的英文意思其实不能反映中文语境回避的全部含义。英文的 withdrawal 作为名词有"撤走，收回"的意思④，它的动词形式 withdraw 有"（使）退出"的含义⑤，在诉讼中指已经参与诉讼活动的人退出该诉讼。在中国的

---

① 李立，郭旭:《〈中国的司法改革〉英文本若干翻译问题之探讨》，《中国翻译》2013 年第 1 期。

② 薛波:《元照英美法词典》，法律出版社，2003 年 5 月第 1 版，第 750 页。

③ 中国刑事诉讼中的回避被译成 withdrawal 由来已久。全国人大法工委主编和法律出版社法规中心编写的《刑事诉讼法》英文本即是如此。

④ 〔英〕霍恩比:《牛津高阶英汉双解词典》，商务印书馆，2009 年第 7 版，第 2312 页。

⑤ 同上，第 2311 页。

刑事诉讼中，回避还指与案件有某种关系的人不得参与诉讼，即包括尚未参与诉讼的人不得参与该案件的诉讼活动。另外，从程序角度考察，回避分为主动回避、被动回避等不同情况。在英语中，不同情况的回避有不同的英语词组，将中文"回避"笼统地译为 withdrawal，不仅不能准确表达回避在各种语境下的含义，而且可能会引起误解。

在美国刑事诉讼中，法官回避分为主动回避和被动回避，都可以使用动词 recuse ①，其名词形式 recusal 指法官与案件有利害关系或对案件持有偏见、成见，当事人申请其（或法官主动）不参与案件审理的程序。② 主动回避可以表述为 voluntary recusal 或 self-recusal。被动回避则为 involuntary recusal。这两个说法似乎可以借鉴。

不过，英美法中的 voluntary recusal 虽也是法官主动要求退出诉讼活动，但是除某些将其纳入法律的法域外，大多是基于司法道德义务；而中国诉讼法中的自行回避则是由于出现了法定的回避情形。法官有可能被要求回避，即上文所说被动回避。针对法官的被动回避英语中还有 challenge of judges 一词 ③，与中国《刑事诉讼法》中申请审判人员回避的含义基本相同。英美法中要求回避包括 challenge for cause 和 peremptory challenge 两种形式，即有因回避和无因回避。根据词典中的解释，challenge for cause 是指申请陪审员回避时必须说明理由，诉讼双方均可提出，是否回避由法官裁决。④ 通常情况下 challenge for cause 针对的是候选陪审员，但是一些书中认为，同陪审员一样，审判法官也是有因回避的对象。

---

① Bryan A. Garner (ed.), *Black's Law Dictionary*, Eighth Edition, Minnesota: West, 2004. p.3996.

② 薛波：《元照英美法词典》，法律出版社，2003 年 5 月第 1 版，第 1161 页。

③ Wayne R. LaFave, Jerold H. Israel, Nancy J. King & Orin S. Kerr, *Criminal Procedure*, Fifth Edition, Minnesota: West, 2009, p.1096.

④ 薛波：《元照英美法词典》，法律出版社，2003 年 5 月第 1 版，第 210 页。

## 二、英文本中的误译问题

准确性是立法语言的灵魂和生命，因而是立法语言最基本的要求[①]。由于翻译人员对中外刑事诉讼制度的认识与理解无法做到面面俱到，在翻译的过程中难免会出现误译现象，主要表现在对本国的刑事制度把握不够深刻，译本与法条及立法原意不符。试析如下：

1. 第二十八条第四款："与本案当事人有其他关系，可能影响公正处理案件的。"英文本译作"（4）If he has any other relations with a party to the case that could affect the impartial handling of the case."。

在法律专业词汇中，party 有着特殊含义。根据《布莱克法律词典》，party 是指"在诉讼中起诉或者应诉的一方"[②]。在英美法系对抗制的刑事诉讼模式下，代表国家提起公诉的检察官与被告人作为诉讼双方，均可以用 party 表示，译作"当事人"并无不妥，但若作为中国刑事诉讼中的"当事人"，则会引起误解。

我国《刑事诉讼法》对"当事人"的概念作出了明确规定。"'当事人'是指被害人、自诉人、犯罪嫌疑人、被告人、附带民事诉讼的原告人和被告人"（第八十二条第二款），可见在中国法的语境下，出庭支持公诉的检察官并不是"当事人"。英文本翻译成 party，扩大了回避制度的适用范围，不符合法律文本的规定，也与诉讼逻辑与规律不符。例如，出庭支持公诉的检察官与法官关系很熟悉（在司法实践当中这种现象非常普遍），被告人不能以之为理由提出回避申请；若是被告人与法官熟识，则检察官可以提出回避之要求。

2. 第四十二条第二款"犯罪嫌疑人、被告人供述和辩解"，英

---

[①] 朱立宇：《立法学》，中国人民大学出版社，2006年。

[②] Bryan A. Garner (ed.), *Black's Law Dictionary*, Fourth Pocket Edition, Minnesota: West, 2009, p.3550.

文本译作 <u>statements</u> and <u>exculpations</u> of criminal suspects or defendants。

  从结构对应的角度上来看,"供述"对应单词 statements,"辩解"对应 exculpations,但这两个词均无法准确地表达原文的含义。第四十二条是关于证据种类的规定,犯罪嫌疑人、被告人供述和辩解是主要的证据来源,对于犯罪事实的认定起到至关重要的作用。"供述"是指被追诉人向公安司法人员作出的关于实施犯罪行为及其相关情况的口头或者书面的说明;"辩解"则是被追诉人提出的关于无罪、罪轻的申辩和解释。statement 的含义是"陈述",被追诉人关于案件情况的陈述,又称作"statement of accused",是指"被告人在预审法官面前对指控所作出的答辩……这种答辩在庭审时可用作证据"[1]。犯罪嫌疑人、被告人的陈述,既可能是供述,也可能是辩解,英文本中的 statement 比"供述"的范围更大。exculpations 的解释是"无罪"(free from blame or accusation)[2],相对于中文本中的"辩解"而言,不能涵盖"罪轻"的含义。相应的,"供述"在英文中宜译作 confession,而"辩解"则可以译为 explanations 或者 defence 或者 justifications。

  与此相关的还有第四十六条:"只有被告人供述,<u>没有其他证据</u>的,不能认定被告人有罪和处以刑罚。"英文本译作:"A defendant cannot be found guilty and sentenced to a criminal punishment if there is only his statement but <u>no evidence</u>."。第四十六条强调的是要重视证据之间的相互印证并形成证据链条,要求改变我国刑事诉讼中长期以来"重口供,轻调查"的司法状况。此处也将"供述"译成 statement,但从语境来看,本条中"供述"更有认罪的含义,应当用

---

  ①  薛波:《元照英美法词典》,法律出版社,2003年5月第1版,第1236页。

  ②  Bryan A. Garner (ed.), *Black's Law Dictionary*, Fourth Pocket Edition, Minnesota: West, 2009, p.1710.

confession 更准确一些。需要指出的另外一个问题是，法条中规定的是"没有其他证据"，而英文本翻译的是 no evidence，没有将"其他"这个词的含义表达出来。从英文本的角度理解，译者似乎将"供述"排除在证据之外，这不符合我国《刑事诉讼法》对证据的分类。第四十二条明确规定证据包括物证、书证等实物证据，也包括证人证言等言词证据，其中"犯罪嫌疑人、被告人供述和辩解"也是重要的证据类型。因此，本条宜译为："A defendant cannot be found guilty and sentenced to a criminal punishment if there is only his confession but no other evidence."。

3. 第四十五条第二款："有关单位和个人应当<u>如实提供证据</u>"，英文本译作："The units and individuals concerned shall <u>provide truthful evidence</u>."。

在英文本中，truthful 修饰的是名词 evidence，译回中文是"真实的证据"，但从中文法条上来看，"如实"修饰的应该是动词"提供"。根据语法结构，副词才能够修饰动词。无论从语义上还是语法上，英文本的翻译都存在问题。实际上，truthful evidence 的表达方式在刑事诉讼中也是不存在的。证据的含义是"证明案件事实的材料"，证据的基本特征是关联性、客观性与合法性。有关单位和个人提供的证据是否真实，是否能够成为判断案件的依据，并不是由该人的主观意思所决定，证据必须在法庭上经过质证后才能被认是否具有证明力。更何况，即便是定罪量刑中采用的证据，也有可能出于认识因素的限制，在二审或再审程序中被推翻。第四十五条强调的是单位和个人提供证据的"行为"，而不是"证据"本身的性质，英文本应为"The entity and individuals concerned shall provide evidence honestly."即把"如实"理解为"诚实地""诚信地"，有什么，给什么，不弄虚作假。

4. 第五十七条第六款："被监视居住的犯罪嫌疑人、被告人违反前款规定，<u>情节严重的</u>，予以逮捕。"英文本译为："If a criminal suspect or defendant under residential surveillance violates the provisions of the preceding paragraph and <u>if the case is serious</u>, he shall be arrested."。

本条是关于被监视居住人违反监视居住义务时所应受到的惩罚后果。从中文法条的表述来看，将监视居住变更为逮捕的前提条件是"违反规定"并"情节严重"，"情节严重"修饰的是犯罪嫌疑人、被告人违反规定的行为，而不是其涉嫌犯罪的严重程度。英文本译为 if the case is serious，容易产生歧义。译者的用意是将 case 指代"违反规定的行为"，但 case 在法律英语中是指"民事或者刑事的案件、诉讼"①，比如刑事案件（criminal case），民事案件（civil case）等。在阅读英文本时很有可能会将 if the case is serious 理解成为"如果属于重大刑事案件"，导致对我国逮捕适用条件出现不正确的认识。因此，本条宜译为"If a criminal suspect or defendant under residential surveillance violates the provisions of the preceding paragraph seriously, he shall be arrested (or remanded)."。

## 三、英文本中专业术语之探讨

文化因素、历史因素、政治因素、经济因素的不同会产生不同的法律制度。中外刑事诉讼法律制度存在着较大的差异，即使制度之间存在类似性，也不能完全进行套用，这使得一些专门术语的翻译确实也难以做到十分准确。笔者在本部分中着重对若干刑事诉讼专业术语的英文翻译进行探讨，希望能够起到抛砖引玉的作用，引起理论界

---

① Bryan A. Garner (ed.), *Black's Law Dictionary*, Fourth Pocket Edition, Minnesota: West, 2009, p.641.

及实务界的重视。

1. 关于取保候审

英文本中将"取保候审"译为 obtained a guarantor pending trial 或者 awaiting trial after obtaining a guarantor，将"保证人"翻译为 guarantor，"保证金"翻译为 guaranty money。《布莱克法律词典》和《元照英美法词典》中对于 guarantor 的解释基本一致，均为"对某项债务承担保证责任的保证人"①②，可见 guarantor 作为"保证人"只能用于民商事法律关系中。

取保候审是指在刑事诉讼过程中，公安机关、人民检察院、人民法院责令犯罪嫌疑人、被告人提出保证人或者缴纳保证金，保证犯罪嫌疑人、被告人不逃避或妨碍侦查、起诉和审判，并随传随到的一种强制方法。

有学者将其译作 bail pending trial ③。bail 在英美刑事诉讼中译作"保释"，是指受到犯罪指控而被逮捕或者拘押的犯罪嫌疑人或者被告人缴纳一定数额金钱或者提供保证人或者满足其他法律规定的条件，并保证在以后的诉讼中能够按照法庭传唤制定的时间和地点到案后，将其释放的制度。④ 从比较法律文化学的角度，不同法律文化中的各种术语、概念、意识等之所以能够进行比较、分析和沟通，在于人们从中可以找到相互间的"功能对应物"。⑤ 保释与取保候审因属

---

① Bryan A. Garner (ed.), *Black's Law Dictionary*, Fourth Pocket Edition, Minnesota: West, 2009, p.2071.

② 薛波:《元照英美法词典》，法律出版社，2003 年 5 月第 1 版，第 617 页。

③ Yi Yanyou, *Understanding China's Criminal Procedure*, Tsinghua University Press, 2011, p.102.

④ 薛波:《元照英美法词典》，法律出版社，2003 年 5 月第 1 版，第 127 页。

⑤ 林巍:《比较法律文化与法律翻译》，《中国翻译》，2006 年第 3 期。

于不同法律体系之内容，存在着一些差异，但是在功能和条件方面都具有实质性的相似性①，比如均可以减少审前羁押，要求被追诉人提供保证人或者保证金，具有暂时性的特点，能够保障刑事诉讼活动的顺利进行，等等。较 guarantor 而言，bail 更加便于国外学者对于我国取保候审特点的理解，"保证人"可以译为 bailor，"保证金"可以译为 bail money。必须指出的是，笔者并非完全赞同此种翻译方法，但囿于能力，无法给出更加精准的翻译，也在此求教于方家。

2. 关于撤销案件与撤销原判

《刑事诉讼法》中有三处涉及"撤销案件"，英文本译作 dismiss the case，三处涉及"撤销原判决或裁定"，译作 rescind。dismiss 是指"（尤指在法庭审理之前）终止诉讼"②，其用法通常是 the case is dismissed by judge 或者 judge dismissed the case。dismiss 确实有"撤销"的含义，但在英文语境下，只有法官才是撤销案件的主体，其作用在于终止案件进入法庭审判程序，与我国法律中的"不予受理、驳回起诉"相类似。法官在审理过程中终止案件也可以用 drop the case。在我国刑事诉讼中的"撤销案件"是指公安机关或者人民检察院在侦查过程中，发现案件有《刑事诉讼法》第十五条规定的法定不追究刑事责任的情形，则应当撤销立案不再进行刑事侦查活动的制度。此处撤销案件的主体是享有侦查权的公安机关、人民检察院，其目的在于终止侦查活动。基于以上不同，dismiss 并不能表达中文法条之内涵，宜改为 terminate 或者 cancel。rescind 是指"单方或者协商

---

① 宋英辉：《刑事诉讼法学研究述评》，北京师范大学出版社，2008年，第197、198页。

② Bryan A. Garner (ed.), *Black's Law Dictionary*, Fourth Pocket Edition, Minnesota: West, 2009, p. 1414.

取消终止（合同）"①。可见 rescind 也有"撤销"的含义，但主要适用在民商事法律领域中指合同的撤销。中文本的表述是"撤销刑事原判决或裁定"，翻译成 rescind 并不合适。在刑事司法领域，一审判决被上诉法院撤销，该专业术语为 reverse，含义为"通过上诉推翻（判决）"②。因此，对应的英文本应译作 reverse the judgment。

3. 关于起诉书

英文本中将起诉书译作 bill of prosecution，这种表达方式让人感到不理解。"起诉书"在英美法系中有专门的术语。

在美国刑事诉讼中，承担起诉职能的有两个专门机构，分别是大陪审团（grand jury）和检察官（prosecutor），向法院提起刑事指控时提交的起诉书分别称为 indictment 和 information。大陪审团通常由 23 位社区代表组成，决定是否起诉犯罪嫌疑人。美国《宪法第五修正案》规定，对可能判处死刑的犯罪和不名誉的指控，原则必须经由大陪审团进行。③ indictment 是指"大陪审团提交法院指控被告人罪行的正式起诉书"。在另外一些普通法系国家，indictment 专门用来指控重罪案件（indictable offence）。information 是指（在没有大陪审团的情况下）由检察官做出的正式指控。在美国，大多数州在指控轻罪时使用 information，大概一半左右的州也允许用 information 来指控重罪犯罪。information 又可以用 bill of information 来表示④。

---

① Bryan A. Garner (ed.), *Black's Law Dictionary*, Fourth Pocket Edition, Minnesota: West, 2009, p. 4075.

② 同上, p. 4111.

③ Wayne R. LaFave, Jerold H. Israel, Nancy J. King & Orin S. Kerr, *Criminal Procedure*, Fifth Edition, Minnesota: West, 2009, pp.770-777.

④ Bryan A. Garner (ed.), *Black's Law Dictionary*, Fourth Pocket Edition, Minnesota: West, 2009, p. 2281.

与起诉书相关的另外一个词汇是 complaint，它既可以用在刑事法中表示"对被告人犯罪行为的正式指控"，也可以用在民事诉讼中表示"提出民事诉讼、阐明法院管辖权、诉讼请求及损害赔偿的民事诉状"[①]。

我国刑事诉讼制度与美国并不相同，没有大陪审团的设置，刑事诉讼由检察官和自诉人提请。检察官指控较为严重的公诉案件，自诉人主要对告诉才处理的案件、有证据证明的轻微刑事案件向法院提起诉讼。符合法律规定的起诉书是审判程序启动的前提。"起诉书"的翻译应当分情况进行讨论，检察院提起公诉案件起诉书，可以统称为 information，如果要表现出指控犯罪的轻重程度，重罪起诉书可以用 indictment，轻罪起诉书可以用 information；至于自诉案件起诉书，由于在程序上与民事诉讼较为类似，可以用 complaint 来表示。

法律翻译要求译文严谨、准确，这需要精湛的语言能力及扎实的专业背景。一国法典的翻译，需要耗费大量的人力、物力和精力，需要政府相关部门高度重视，加大对法律翻译工作的投入力度，召集语言专家和相关法律领域内的专家学者进行初译，校对及反复讨论，并在广泛征求社会意见的基础上，公布于官方网站。《刑事诉讼法》是国家的基本法律，在惩罚犯罪与保障人权中发挥着重大作用。对刑事诉讼法英文本中翻译问题的探讨，有助于正确认识我国的刑事诉讼程序与制度设计，能够更好地促进国内外法律界的学习与交流，并通过借鉴国外类似制度及其先进经验，进一步深化我国的司法改革。

---

① Bryan A. Garner (ed.), *Black's Law Dictionary*, Fourth Pocket Edition, Minnesota: West, 2009, p. 858.

# 汉英索引

**A**

安全级别 security level 34
案件的实体（实质）问题 merits of the case 262-269
案例指导制度 case guidance system; guiding cases system 6, 26

**B**

保释 bail ix, 30, 31, 37, 54, 336
保释条件 bail conditions 31
报酬 remuneration 47, 121, 130, 134, 137, 185
暴力犯罪 violent crime 214
暴力侵害妇女行为 violence against women 208-210
被告（人） defendant; the accused 12
被告人最后陈述 final statement by the defendant 118, 119
被害人陈述 statements by the victim 68
被派遣劳工 dispatched worker/laborer 134
本证 positive evidence 68
避免双重危险原则 double jeopardy 52
避免自证其罪的特权 privilege against self-incrimination 66
编纂 codification 22, 24, 307-312

辩护人 counsel; defender viii, xi, 11, 12, 23, 32, 37, 38, 62, 94, 107, 108, 109, 110, 112, 118, 181, 185, 187, 188, 194, 227
辩解 justification 68, 114, 332-334
辩诉交易 plea bargaining 38, 59, 111, 250, 251
剥夺政治权利 deprivation of political rights 86, 141, 184
剥削 exploitation 209, 215, 289
驳回起诉 dismiss the case 31, 37, 257, 265, 337
驳回指控 dismiss the charge 37
补发工资 back pay 135
不成文法 unwritten law 16, 22
不定时就业 casual employment 129
不服管教 ungovernability 213
不顾陪审团裁决的裁判 judgment non obstante veredict; JNOV; judgment notwithstanding the verdict 8
不可抗力假 force majeure leave 136
不起诉 drop the charge; dismiss the charge; discontinue the case 36, 37, 43, 44
不同意见 dissenting opinion 262,
不争辩 nolo contendere 250, 251
不作为行为 act of omission 215

## C

财权 revenues 162, 164-166
财税法院 Court of Exchequer 17
裁决 verdict vii, 7, 8, 53, 88, 92, 94, 95, 97-99, 107, 115, 187, 197, 232, 239, 241, 258, 330, 331
裁决书 verdict form 95
采用（证据） admit 60, 62, 334
参审制度 assessors system 298, 301, 302
参议院 Senate 41, 237, 238
《残疾人权利公约》 Convention on the Rights of Persons with Disabilities; CRPD 200, 202
残疾养恤金 disability pension 136
操纵证言 tampering witness; tampering with the evidence 111
曾经定罪 autrefois convict 257
曾经开释 autrefois acquit 257
缠诉 endless petition vii, 7
长期雇员 long-term employee 125
常规就业/用工 regular employment 124
撤回指控 drop the charge 37
撤销假释 revocation 39
沉默权 right to silence 46, 49, 50, 114, 118
陈述 statement vii, x, xi, 7, 50, 63, 65, 68, 107-109, 115, 116, 118, 119, 333
成人监狱 adult jail 222
承认 recognition 197
惩罚改造 punishment and rehabilitation 46
程序法 procedure law 23, 243
持有武器 possession of a weapon 182
充足的证据 sufficient evidence 38

重审 retrial; new trial; trial *de novo* 89, 98, 236
抽象行政行为 abstract act 242, 243
初步听证 preliminary hearing 31, 37
初次到庭 initial appearance ix, 30, 37
初始罪 inchoate crimes 179
处罚 punishment; penalty; sanction 32-37, 39, 50, 51, 53, 105, 118, 138, 146, 147, 149, 178, 179, 182-184, 214, 242, 243
处置 disposition 36, 40, 220-222, 227
处置前报告 predisposition report 227
处置听证 disposition hearing 220, 221
传唤 summon xi, 38, 93, 109, 110, 112, 336
传来证据 secondary evidence 64, 67
传统文化表现形式 Traditional Cultural Expressions; TCEs 304, 314, 317
传统知识 Traditional Knowledge; TK 304, 305, 307, 309-317, 323
传闻证据 hearsay evidence x, 63, 64, 110
创造法律 create law 22
从犯 accessories; secondary participants in crime 178, 183
从重处罚 to aggravate punishment 147, 179, 182
存疑不起诉 non-prosecution for insufficient evidence 44
错案 miscarriage of justice 74-77

## D

大陆法系 continental law ix, 5, 10,

14-16, 21-27, 51, 53, 60, 88, 91, 105, 176, 177, 178, 186, 228, 231, 241, 252, 301, 302
大陪审团　grand jury　8, 31, 37, 38, 54, 101, 103, 104, 180, 298, 338, 339
逮捕　remand; detention; pre-trial detention　v, 30, 34, 36, 37, 46, 58, 86, 194, 335, 336
逮捕证　remand/detention warrant　30
带薪年假　annual leave　136
单方面　ex parte　xi, 65, 248, 249
单方面沟通　ex parte communication　249
单位受贿罪　giving of bribes by an institution　140
单位行贿罪　accepting of bribes by an institution　140
弹劾　impeach　237
当庭作证　live testimony　50, 109-111
到庭　appear in court　ix-xi, 30, 31, 37, 38, 63, 64, 93, 109, 112, 182
盗窃罪　theft　144, 182
敌对工作环境　hostile working environment　136
敌对证人　hostile witness　xii, 112
敌意环境型性骚扰　hostile environment sexual harassment　211
地方社区　local community　317, 318, 322-324
地方税　local taxes　158, 159
地区法院　district court　3, 4, 9, 236
地区公诉人办公室　District Attorney's Office　9
第二轮交叉询问　recross (examination)　xii, 113
第二轮直接询问　redirect (examination)　xii, 113
典型案例　typical case　6

典型用工　typical forms of employment　124
电话待命　on-call　132-134
电子监控　electronic monitoring　222
电子数据　electronic data　69
吊销执照　disbar　viii, 12
调查　investigation　viii, 5, 6, 12, 26, 30, 36, 38, 44, 65, 95, 102, 183, 197, 206, 227, 254, 316, 328, 333
调查取证权　right to investigate and collect evidence　viii, 12, 26
调卷令　writ of certiorari　39
定罪　conviction　12, 32, 38, 39, 43, 44, 48, 51, 53, 57, 58, 76, 91, 103, 175, 177, 220, 221, 238, 245, 252, 257, 334
定罪审判　adjudication　31
动机　motivation　175
动议　motion　60, 62, 99, 265
独立承揽者　independent contractor　124
独立行使审判权　independent exercise of judicial power　41-43
独任法官　single judge　6, 32, 42, 100
短期雇员　short-term employee　125
对案件的主张　theory of the case　107-109
对单位行贿罪　bribing an institution　140
对抗　contest　109
对抗制　adversary system　xii, 5, 23, 26, 113, 332
对抗制诉讼制度　adversarial/adversary system　23
对物管辖权　in rem jurisdiction　256
多数意见　majority opinion　239, 262
多样性管辖权　diversity jurisdiction　4

## E

儿童拐骗　child abduction　218-220
《儿童权利公约》　Convention on the Rights of the Child　200, 202
儿童性犯罪者　child sexual offender　214

## F

发现手段　discovery device　59
罚款　fine　32, 35, 54
法典编纂　codification　22
法典法系　codified law　21
法典化　codification　23, 24, 307-309, 312
法定不起诉　statutory non-prosecution　37, 44
法定从轻情节　statutory mitigating circumstances　33
法定归宿　statutory incidence　172
法定强奸　statutory rape　146, 147, 216, 217
法定证据主义　legalistic theory of evidence　67
法官　judge　vii, viii, ix, xii, 4-6, 7, 8, 9, 11, 13, 17, 18, 20, 22, 23, 26, 30-33, 37-39, 41, 42, 49, 50, 53, 57, 59, 60-62, 67, 73, 80, 91, 93, 95, 97-100, 102-104, 107-110, 112-116, 119, 183, 187, 193, 220, 221, 237-240, 249, 251, 259, 261, 264-266, 269, 297, 298, 301, 328, 330-333, 337
法官创造的法律　judge-made law　22, 187
法官独立　independence of judges　41
法官独任审判　bench trial; single-judge trial　119
法令　order of law　176
法律代理　attorney-at-law; legal representation　vii, viii, 11, 12, 269-272
法律的适用　application of law　119
法律服务所　legal service office　188, 193
法律解释　legal interpretation　22, 71
法律面前人人平等　equality before the law　196
法律认定者　finder of law　7, 9, 91
法律推理　legal reasoning　22
法律问题　question of law　39, 91, 99, 118, 229, 230, 232, 235, 301
法律渊源　sources of law　22, 24
法律援助　legal aid; legal assistance　xv, 185-197, 268
法律援助中心　Legal Aid Center　185, 187-190, 195
法律主张　legal theory of the case　108, 109, 118
法庭辩论　debates; argumentation　118
法庭会议　bench conference　115
法庭调查　court enquiry　118
法系　legal families; legal systems; legal traditions　vii, ix, xii, 2, 5, 6, 10, 14-27, 36, 40, 51, 53, 60, 88, 91, 105, 113, 175-180, 183, 186, 228-231, 240-242, 249, 252, 253, 261, 270, 298, 301-303, 328, 332, 338
法院　court　v, vi, vii, ix, x, 1-6, 8-12, 17-20, 23-26, 28, 30-32, 37-42, 44, 46, 48, 51, 57, 59-62, 68, 69, 72, 74, 77-80, 82-89, 93-95, 98-100, 103, 104, 106, 110, 116, 122, 126, 177, 182, 184, 185-188, 194, 197, 220, 221, 227, 228-243, 248-252, 257-259, 261, 262, 264-267, 269, 271, 283, 297, 308, 328, 330, 336, 338, 339

法院独立　independence of the court　41, 42
反驳　refutation　xi, 65, 115, 118, 253
反对　objection　63, 108, 114, 115, 239
反向歧视　reverse discrimination　131, 199
反证　negative evidence　56, 68, 135, 255
返还财物　restitution　32
犯人　convict　12, 34, 39, 282
犯罪　crime　x, xiii, 7, 30-37, 40, 43-46, 48, 50, 51, 53, 57, 58, 66, 76, 93, 95, 98, 100-102, 111, 138-155, 174-183, 213, 214, 218, 221, 224-227, 245, 249, 251, 252, 257, 282, 283, 284, 325, 327-329, 333, 335, 336, 338, 339
犯罪的客观方面　the objective side of a crime　175, 176
犯罪的客体　object　175
犯罪的严重性　seriousness of the case　43, 329
犯罪的主观方面　the subjective side of a crime　175
犯罪的主体　subject　175, 213
犯罪行为　*actus reus*; criminal act　7, 35, 36, 51, 58, 138, 139, 149, 175, 176, 181, 183, 214, 252, 333, 339
犯罪记录（前科）消灭　expungement　224, 225
犯罪既遂　completed crime　180
犯罪目的　purpose　175
犯罪前科　criminal record　44, 95, 226
犯罪未遂　attempt　180
犯罪未完成形态　uncompleted crime; incomplete crime　180
犯罪嫌疑人　suspect; criminal suspect　xiii, 12, 28, 44, 46, 52, 58, 68, 175, 194, 222, 328, 329, 332-336, 338
犯罪要件　elements of a crime　95, 174, 175
犯罪意图　*mens rea*; criminal intent　175
犯罪预备　preparation　180, 183
犯罪中止　voluntary abandonment　180
非常规就业　non-regular employment　124
非典型就业　atypical forms of employment　124
非法证据排除规则　exclusionary rules　61, 62
非监禁措施　non-incarceration　220, 222
非预谋故意杀人　voluntary manslaughter　153, 154
非预谋杀人　manslaughter　151, 153, 154, 182
非正式处置程序　informal processing　40
非正式就业　informal employment　124
诽谤　defamation　141-143, 226
分流　diversion　39, 40, 43, 182
"封闭性"问题　close-ended question　114
夫妻免证权　marital privilege　66
扶养费　spousal support　185, 186
福利模式　welfare model　291
抚养费　child support　185
辅助性　auxiliary　134, 328
父母拐骗儿童　parental child abduction　218
附加刑　accessory sanction/punishment; secondary sanction/punishment

184

附条件不起诉 conditional non-prosecution 37

附言 *obiter dicta* 262

## G

高等法院 High Court of Justice 19
高级人民法院 high people's court 5
高校学生志愿者 law student volunteer 193
个人劳动法 individual labor law 121
个人申诉 individual complaint 203
个人投诉程序 individual complaints procedure 206
工会 trade union 120, 135, 191
工会法 trade union law 120, 121
工伤事故 industrial accident 186
工时 working hours 120, 133, 134
工资 wage 41, 120, 121, 124, 133, 135, 136, 187, 191, 193, 237
工作时间 working time; hours worked 133, 136
工作条件 working conditions 133
公安机关 public security 1, 2, 30, 34, 37, 81, 86, 336, 337
公法 public law 23, 24
公检法分流 diversion by law enforcement, prosecutor, or court 39
《公民权利和政治权利国际公约》 International Covenant on Civil and Political Rights; ICCPR xii, 200, 201, 202
公平审判权 right to a fair trial 196
公设辩护人 public defender 37, 188-189, 227
公设辩护人办公室 Public Defenders Office 187
公诉机关 the prosecution service; the prosecutors' office 1, 12, 28, 43, 101, 249
公诉律师 prosecuting attorney viii, 11
公诉人 prosecutor viii, xi, 8-10, 11, 12, 36-38, 43-45, 57, 58, 62, 93, 94, 98, 99, 103, 107-110, 112, 118, 119, 175, 181, 185
公诉人办公室 State's Attorney's Office 9
公诉人可选程序的犯罪 Crown option offence 181
公诉书 indictment; information 38, 221
公益法律服务 *Pro Bono (Publico) Legal Services* 190, 193
公正司法 fair administration of justice 73, 74
共犯 accomplice 178, 222
共谋 conspiracy 179
《共有物业法》 Condominium Act 248
共同犯罪 complicity in an offence 174, 178, 179
共同主犯 joint principal 178
共享税 shared taxes 158, 159, 161
共有权 condominium 245, 247
共有物业 condominium 245, 247, 248
供述 admission; confession 58, 61, 67, 68, 332-334
固定期限合同 fixed term contract 124, 134
固定期限劳动合同 fixed/definite-term/period employment contract 124
故意 intentional; intent 94, 108, 149, 151-155, 174, 175, 177, 178, 179, 211, 214, 261

故意杀人　intentional homicide　94, 151-155, 177, 261
故意伤害罪　assault; intentionally causing injury　149, 179, 214
雇佣法　employment law　120, 135
雇用自由原则　Employment at Will Doctrine　135
拐卖　trafficking　215, 219, 220
关联性　relevancy　61, 334
管辖权　jurisdiction　4, 40, 98, 221, 231, 233, 237, 249, 256, 262, 339
管制　*guanzhi*; public surveillance　141, 181, 184, 319
归责　attribution　272-276
归责规则　attribution rule　274
《国际儿童拐骗事件的民事问题海牙公约》　The Hague Convention on the Civil Aspects of International Child Abduction　218
国际贸易法庭　the Court of International Trade　5
《国家公务员暂行条例》　Provisional Regulations on State Civil Servants　243
《国家赔偿法》　State Compensation Law　243
国家安全机关　national security agency; state security organ　1, 2, 30
国家赔偿　state compensation　36, 186, 243
过失　negligent; negligence　175, 177
过失杀人　involuntary manslaughter　151, 153-155
过失致人死亡　negligently causing death; negligent homicide　151, 155

## H

号衣　prison dress　47

合法性　legality　51, 61, 240, 252, 309, 334
合法性原则　legality principle　51, 252
合理根据　probable cause　x, 31, 37, 57, 103
合适成年人　appropriate adult　222-224
合宪性　constitutionality　240
合宪性审查　constitutional review; constitutionality review　242
合议庭　panel of judges; judicial panel　6, 38, 42, 118, 119, 227, 301
衡平　equity　16-20, 23, 24
衡平法　equity law　16-20, 23, 24
衡平法法院　courts of equity　18, 20
衡平法规则　rules of equity　19
后续观护　aftercare　40
候选陪审团　jury pool; *venire*　93
候选陪审员　venireman; prospective/potential juror; candidate　93, 331
护理假　carer's leave　136
会见当事人的权利　right to interview the client　viii, 12
贿赂犯罪　bribery　140, 213
还押　remand　ix, 30
婚内强奸　marital rape　146, 210
混合量刑　blended sentence　222
火审　ordeals by fire or hot iron　91
获得律师帮助权　right to counsel　196
获得司法救济的机会　access to justice　196

## J

积极歧视　positive discrimination　199
基层法律服务工作者　grassroots legal

service worker  193, 194
基层人民法院  basic-level people's court  5
基于人权的发展观  human rights-based approach to development  290-296
即决处决  summary execution  101, 182, 281-284, 287
集体劳动法  collective labor law  121
集体谈判  collective bargaining  120, 135
计件工资  piece rate  124
计件工作  piecework  124
计时工资  hourly rate  124
计时工作  hourly work  124
计税基础  tax basis; cost basis  172
既判事项  res judicata  256, 258
寄宿设施  residential facility  40
寄养照管  foster care  222
加班  overtime  133
加重罪行的情节  aggravating circumstance  182
家庭监禁/软禁  home confinement; house arrest  222
假释  parole  33, 34, 39, 221
间接证据  indirect/circumstantial evidence  67
监护人  guardian  13, 222
监禁  imprisonment  31-33, 188, 214, 220-222
监禁措施  incarceration  220, 222
监视居住  supervised residence; residential surveillance  38, 194, 335
监狱  prison  34, 39, 40, 81, 83, 86, 221, 222
检察官  procurator; public procurator  viii, 5, 6, 9, 10, 30, 80-82, 103, 115, 182, 193, 227, 250, 251, 297, 328, 332, 338, 339
检察院  procuracy; procuratorate; the prosecutors' office  v, vi, 1, 10, 11, 30, 36, 37, 42, 44, 59, 80, 82, 83, 85-87, 138, 182, 233, 328, 336, 337, 339
检察长  procurator general  10, 328
检警分立模式  separated operation model  28
检警一体化  integrated operation model  28
减轻罪行的情节  mitigating/extenuating circumstance/factors  182
减少起诉罪名  reduce charge  43
减时就业  part-time employment  129
减刑  goodtime; commutation; remission  34, 35
简易程序  summary procedure  99-102, 180-182, 283, 284
鉴定机构  forensic examination centers; forensic assessment centers; forensic laboratories  13
鉴定人  forensic examiner  13, 328
鉴定意见  forensic science opinion; forensic examiner's opinion  13, 68
交叉询问  cross-examination  vii, x-xiii, 7, 63, 65, 107, 111-114
交通事故  traffic accident  186
焦点  issue  23, 70, 78, 116
矫正  correction  34-35, 102, 220-222
矫正部门  corrections department  102
教唆  solicitation  178, 179
教唆犯  instigator; abettor  179
教唆他人犯罪  instigate the commission of crime by another person  178
结论性意见  concluding observation  202
解释和适用法律  interpreting and ap-

plying laws 41
介绍贿赂罪 intermediating bribery 140
戒毒 drug rehabilitation program 31
戒具 instrument of restraint 48
紧急避险 necessity 176, 177
进行认罪协商 negotiate guilty pleas; plea negotiation; plea bargaining 43
禁用 suppress 62
《禁止酷刑和其他残忍、不人道或有辱人格的待遇或处罚公约》 Convention against Torture and Other Cruel, Inhuman or Degrading Treatment or Punishment; CAT 200, 202
禁止竞争协议 noncompetition agreement 136
禁止类推适用 the interdiction of analogy 51
禁止溯及既往 non-retroactivity 51
经济法 economic law 23
经济归宿 economic incidence 172
经济合同 economic contract 121
《经济、社会及文化权利国际公约》 International Covenant on Economic, Social and Cultural Rights; ICESCR 200, 201
警察部门 police 1
纠问式诉讼制度 inquisitorial system 23
纠问制 inquisitorial system 5, 26
酒驾 driving under the influence of alcohol 7
就业歧视 employment discrimination 57, 120, 131
拘传 subpoena 194
拘留 custody; pre-charge detention ix, 30, 34, 36, 37, 46, 86, 194, 221, 222, 242, 245

拘留场所 detention center 194
拘留证 arrest warrant ix, 30
拘留中心 juvenile hall; juvenile detention facility 221, 222
拘役 *juyi*; criminal detention 12, 86, 141, 181, 183, 184
举证 production of evidence; presentation of evidence; present one's case 8, 46, 55, 56, 61, 95, 99, 108-111, 115, 118, 255, 283
举证责任 burden of proof; onus of proof; *onus probandi* 46, 55, 56, 99, 255
举证责任倒置 shift of burden of proof; reversing the burden of proof 46, 56
巨额财产来源不明罪 possessing huge amounts of assets of unknown origin / unaccounted assets 139
具体行政行为 specific act 242
决斗审 trials by battle/combat 92
绝对不起诉 statutory non-prosecution 44

## K

开场陈述 opening statement vii, 7, 107-109, 115, 116
开放性问题 open-ended question xii, 112, 114
开庭 opening the session 59, 95, 99, 108, 111, 118, 227, 328
看守所 jail 34, 46-48, 86, 221
考察人员 probation officer 34, 35
考验式审判 trial by ordeal 91-93
可扣除的费用 tax deductible expenses 168
可适用不同程序的犯罪 hybrid offence 181
可适用两种程序的犯罪 dual offence;

dual procedure offence 181
可适用任一程序的犯罪 either way offence 181
可退税抵免额 refundable tax credit 168
可信度 credibility 61, 67, 95, 114, 118
可选程序犯罪 wobbler 181
可用证据 admissible evidence 59, 60
控辩双方 the prosecution and the defense vii, viii, xii, 7, 11, 26, 31, 32, 50, 58, 59, 62, 69, 93-95, 102, 107-115, 118, 227
口头诽谤 slander 142, 143
口头警告 verbal warning 222
口头审理原则 orality principle xi, 65, 110, 111
口头作证 oral testimony xi, 65
宽大 clemency 35, 39
框架合同 framework agreement 133

**L**

来文 recommendation 206-208, 263, 267
栏边会议 side-bar conference 115
劳动报酬 remuneration 134, 185
劳动标准 labor standard 120
劳动法 labor law 23, 120, 121, 123, 125, 131, 211
《劳动法》 Labour Law 120, 121
劳动关系 labour/employment relationship 121, 122, 124
劳动合同 contract of service; contract of employment 120-126, 133, 134
《劳动合同法》 Labour Contract Law 120, 121
劳动力给付 delivery of service 134

劳动者 employee 121, 124, 125, 134
劳务合同 contract for services 121-126
劳务派遣 labor dispatch 124, 130, 134, 135
劳务派遣工人 dispatched worker 124
劳务派遣机构 labor dispatch agency; dispatched work agency 134
劳务派遣协议 labor dispatch agreement; business service agreement 134
类推 analogy 51, 252
冷暴力 cold violence 210
立法部门 legislature 1, 41, 71, 29
联邦地区法院 United States District Court 3, 4, 9
联邦公诉人 Federal Prosecutor 9
联邦律师 United States Attorney 9
联邦上诉法院 Federal Court of Appeals 3, 4, 9
联邦索赔法院 the Court of Federal Claims 5
联邦问题管辖权 Federal Question Jurisdiction 4
联邦最高法院 the Supreme Court of the United States 3, 9
联合国大会 General Assembly 75, 203
联合国日内瓦办事处 United Nations Office at Geneva; UNOG 281
两审终审制 two-instances system 39
量刑 sentencing 12, 32-34, 38-40, 44, 51, 91, 102, 103, 111, 183, 221, 222, 227, 251, 303, 334
量刑和制裁 sentencing and sanctions 32

量刑前报告　pre-sentencing report　33

量刑听证　sentencing hearing　32, 33, 102, 103, 221

量刑指南　sentencing guidelines　33, 102, 183

临时雇员　temporary employee　125

临时性　temporary　134

"零工时"合同　"zero hours" contract　133

令状　writ　17, 93

路标　sign post　107

路线图　road map　107

论证　argue　vii, 7, 107, 108, 113-116, 118

罗马法系　Roman law　ix, 21

罗马-日耳曼法系　Romano-Germanic law　21

履约报告　periodic report　202

律师　attorney-at-law; defense lawyer; attorney; private lawyer; practitioner　vii, viii, x, xi, xiii, 5-7, 9, 11, 12, 32, 37, 41, 44, 45, 50, 54, 58, 59, 63, 65, 66, 83, 93, 94, 113-115, 119, 185-196, 239, 249, 251, 265, 266, 271, 297, 298, 303

律师事务所　law firm　x, 65, 191, 193, 195

律师与当事人的保密特权　attorney-client privilege　44

律师执业技能　trial advocacy　119

律师执业证　Lawyer's Certificate of Practice　193

律师助理　paralegal; legal assistant　193

## M

满时就业　full-time employment　127

没有破案或没抓到人　unsolved or not arrested　36

美国军事上诉法院　the United States Court of Appeals for the Armed Forces　5

美国律师协会　American Bar Association　viii, 11, 191

美国司法统计局　the Bureau of Justice Statistics　28

美国退伍军人权利上诉法院　Court of Appeals for Veterans Claims　5

门槛动议　motion *in limine*　62

米兰达警告　Miranda warning　49

免除处罚　be exempted from punishment　178

免于起诉　exemption from prosecution　44

免证权　privilege　66

民法　civil law　ix, 1, 21, 23-25, 121, 143, 243, 247, 253, 308

民法法系　civil law　ix, 21

民间法律援助组织　civil society organization　193

民事法律援助　Civil Legal Aid　188

名义归宿　nominal incidence　172

名义用工单位　nominal employer　134

名誉侵权　reputation infringement　143

名誉权　right to reputation　143

没收财产　forfeiture of property　86, 184

谋杀　murder　150, 151, 153-155, 225, 252

## N

纳税抵免额　tax credit　167, 168

纳税申报表　tax return　170

闹访 aggressive petition vii, 7
内心确信原则 inner conviction 67
虐待儿童 maltreatment 214
虐待罪 misappropriation of public funds 214
挪用公款罪 child abuse; child maltreatment 139, 140

## O

殴击罪 battery 148, 179
欧洲性别平等研究院 the European Institute for Gender Equality; EIGE 210

## P

排除合理怀疑 beyond reasonable doubt x, 37, 57, 58, 103, 116, 175
排除合理怀疑标准 beyond (a) reasonable doubt 57, 352
判 sentencing 32
判决理由 *ratio decidendi* 24, 262
判例 precedent 6, 16, 22, 24, 26, 51, 187, 240, 258, 261, 271
判例法 case law 6, 16, 21, 22, 24, 187, 252
陪产假 paternity leave 136
陪审团 jury vi, vii, 6-9, 20, 31, 32, 37-39, 50, 53, 54, 57, 59-63, 91-109, 111, 113, 114-116, 118, 119, 180, 186, 298, 301, 338, 339
陪审团裁决 verdict vii, 8, 53, 97
陪审团团长 foreman 95
陪审团制度 jury system vii, 7, 8, 91, 97, 101, 104, 105, 301
赔偿 compensation 18, 36, 186, 259, 339
配偶之间的保密特权 spousal privilege; marital privilege; husband-wife privilege 45, 66
贫困被告人 indigent defendant 187, 188, 196
贫困当事人 indigent defendant 187, 188, 197
平权行动 affirmative action 131, 198, 199
评价证据 weighing the evidence 116
评议 deliberation 95, 97, 99, 107, 116, 118, 119
破产法庭 bankruptcy court 5
普遍定期审议 Universal Periodic Review 203
普通程序 regular procedure 101, 180-182, 284
普通程序简易化审理 simplified (regular) procedure 181
普通法法院 courts of law 20
普通法官 Associate Justice 237
普通法规则 rules of law 19
普通法系 common law ix, 5, 6, 15, 16, 22, 24, 180, 253, 338
普通法院 common law court; court of general jurisdiction 17, 18, 23, 88, 220, 230, 231, 237, 241, 242
普通民事法院 Court of Common Pleas 17

## Q

企图伤害罪 assault 148
起诉 bring criminal charge vi, 8, 9, 12, 17, 18, 28, 30, 31, 36, 37, 38, 43, 44, 50, 53, 59, 78, 101, 103, 104, 180, 190, 207, 242, 245, 249-252, 257, 259, 262, 265, 327, 332, 336-339
起诉书 indictment 38, 101, 103, 180, 338, 339

签订固定期限合同的工人 fixed-term worker 124
前置程序 pre-procedure 242
遣散费 severance pay 137
遣散协议 severance package 137
强奸 rape 146, 147, 209, 210, 216, 217
强制措施 compulsory measure 31, 46, 194
抢夺罪 snatch theft 143, 146
抢劫罪 robbery 144
敲门告知 knock-and-announce 6
亲权 parental right 214
亲属照管 kinship care 222
青少年处置 juvenile disposition 220
青少年犯罪/违法 juvenile delinquency/offending 214
青少年违法 juvenile delinquency 40, 220, 221, 225
青少年违法者 juvenile offender 40
轻伤 light injury 36, 214
轻微犯罪行为 less serious crimes 35, 36
轻罪 misdemeanor 35, 37, 39, 98, 101, 111, 148, 180, 284, 338, 339,
情感主张 persuasive/thematic theory of the case 108, 109
请求 motion; request 58-60, 72, 103, 115, 186, 221, 268, 339
请求排除 claim preclusion 259
驱逐出境 deportation 184
取保候审 bail 31, 37, 38, 194, 336, 337
取证 evidence taking viii, xi, 12, 23, 26, 59, 65
确定性原则 the principle of certainty 51

确认请求 request for admission 59

R

热忱的辩护 zealous defense viii, 12
人犯 criminal 28
人民陪审员 lay judge; assessor 104-106, 301, 302, 330
人民陪审员制度 assessors (lay judges) system 104-106, 301, 302
人民陪审制度 people's assessors system; lay judges system 8
人权理事会 Human Rights Council 202, 203, 245, 297
人权事务委员会 Human Rights Committee 202, 203
人权委员会 Commission on Human Rights; Human Rights Commission 201-203
人身保护令 *habeas corpus* 39
人身伤害 personal injury 186
认证 acceptance of evidence 61
认罪 plead guilty 32, 37, 38, 43, 46, 59, 102, 111, 251, 333
认罪程序 arraignment 38
认罪协商 plea bargaining 38, 43, 59, 102, 111

S

三阶（层）论 Three-Level Concept of Crime; Three-Pronged Concept of Crime 176
三权分立 separation of powers 1, 41, 80, 297
杀人罪 homicide 150, 151, 154, 177
赡养费 parental support 185
商法 commercial law 23-25
上访 petition 18, 39, 208
上诉 appeal 3-5, 9, 17, 39, 53, 88,

89, 102, 103, 115, 188, 228-232, 235-237, 249, 256, 338
上诉法院 appellate court; court of appeals 3-5, 9, 17, 39, 228-231, 235, 237, 338
设防的青少年设施 secured juvenile facilities; camps 222
社会法 social law 23
社会工作者 social worker 227
社会考察 probation 32, 35, 39, 214, 222
社会利益 public interest 43
社会调查报告 social investigation report 227
社会性别 gender 286-290
社会主义法系 Socialist Law 14, 25
社区服务 community service 35, 222
申诉 petition vii, 7, 23, 39, 203, 206-208, 233, 236, 255, 258, 268
身份盗窃 identity theft 214
身份违法/犯罪 Status Offence/Crime 213
身份诈骗 identity fraud 214
身体虐待 physical abuse 214
神判 *judicium Dei*; trial by ordeal 8, 91, 92
神职人员免证权 clergy-penitent privilege 66
审 trial 32, 38, 109
审查 review vi, 12, 28, 30, 31, 36, 39, 59, 78, 93, 95, 104, 116, 190, 195, 203, 229, 230, 232, 234, 238, 240-243, 253, 264, 308, 327
审理 hearing vii, xi, xii, 7, 17, 18, 23, 31, 32, 39, 42, 50, 53, 62, 65, 78, 79, 87, 89, 91, 93, 95, 98, 99, 110, 111, 118, 180, 181, 220, 221, 227, 233, 234,

237-239, 242, 268, 284, 303, 325, 327, 329-331, 337
审判法院 trial court 3
审判方式改革 trial method reform 26
审判分离 separation of trial and sentencing 32
审判委员会 adjudication committee 42, 297
审议 consider 202, 203, 268, 295
圣餐审 trials by Eucharist 92
十字架审 trials by the cross 92
实际用工单位 actual employer 134
实体法 substantive law vii, 7, 243
实物证据 real/physical evidence 67, 68
实刑 incarceration 34
市民法 civilian/citizens' law; *jus civile* ix, 21
事后条款 *ex post facto* clause 252
事权 spending responsibilities; functional responsibilities; mandates 162-167, 272
事权的划分 assignment of expenditure responsibilities 165
事实的认定 determination of facts 9, 119, 333
事实认定者 finder of fact 9, 91
事实问题 question of fact 91, 118, 229, 230, 301
事实主张 factual theory of the case 108, 109
事务代理 attorney-in-fact viii, 12
"事已决"原则 *res judicata* 256, 257
视听资料 audiovisual material 64, 69
适用法律 apply the law 22, 41, 71,

72, 102, 234, 301, 329
适用简易程序的犯罪 summary offence 180, 181, 284
适用普通程序的犯罪 indictable offence 180, 181, 284
释放 acquittal; release vi, 8, 36, 39, 49, 53, 99, 213
收回认罪 withdraw a guilty plea 102
收税救济 tax relief 169
收税照顾 tax relief 169
收养假 adoptive leave 136
首席大法官 Chief Justice 237-240
首要分子 ringleader; mastermind 178
受贿罪 accepting bribes 140
书面诽谤 libel 142, 143
书证 documentary evidence 58, 59, 64, 68, 69, 110, 113, 334
疏于照管/忽视 neglect of a child 215, 216
双重归责 dual attribution 274
（禁止）双重危险 prohibition against double jeopardy 249
谁主张，谁举证 *Ei incumbit probatio qui dicit, non qui negat*; the burden of proof rests on who asserts, not on who denies 46, 55
水审 ordeals by water 92
税额抵免 tax credit 167
税负 tax burden 172
税负归宿 tax incidence 172
税负转嫁 tax shifting 172
税基 tax base 170-172
税前扣除 tax deduction 168
税前列支 tax deduction 168
税收假日 tax holiday 169
税收减免 tax exemption 167, 169
税收优惠 tax break 167-169

税务法庭 the United States Tax Court 5
说服责任 burden of persuasion 55
司法部门 judiciary v, vi, 1, 41, 71, 82, 237, 242, 297
司法部 Department of Justice; Ministry of Justice v, vi, 1, 9, 34, 41, 71, 82, 83, 86, 187, 188, 237, 242, 297
司法部部长 Attorney General 9
司法部副部长 Solicitor General 9
司法独立 judicial independence 41-43
司法法 Judicature Acts 19
司法公正 judicial impartiality 74, 234
司法官 judicial officer xi, 6, 65, 84
司法行政机构 judicial administrative authorities 227
司法局 Bureau of Justice 82, 187
司法能动派 judicial activists 238
司法审查 judicial review 238, 240-243
司法所 Office of Justice 82, 188
司法厅 Department of Justice 82, 187
司法辖区 judicial district; jurisdiction 9, 33, 37, 146, 271
司法协助 judicial assistance 83, 197
私法 private law 23, 24
私分罚没财产罪 privately dividing up confiscated assets 140
私分国有资产罪 privately dividing up state-owned assets 140
私人律师 private attorney 187
私人侦探 private detective viii, 12
死刑 capital punishment; death sentence; death penalty 32, 39, 49, 86, 94, 151, 184, 185, 187, 259, 285, 338

诉答程序　pleading　99
诉讼程序法　procedure law　23
诉讼理由　cause of action　259
随附意见　*obiter dicta*　262

**T**

贪污贿赂罪　corruption crimes; crimes of embezzlement and bribery　139-141, 174
贪污罪　embezzlement　139-141
坦白从宽，抗拒从严　leniency for self-confession and severity for resistance　50
逃学　truancy　213
特赦　pardon　35, 39
体检请求　request for physical examination　59
替代性　replaceable; substitute　124, 134
替代性就业　alternative employment　124
挑选陪审员　jury selection　93, 98
条约机构　treaty body　131, 202, 206, 208
条约监测机构　treaty-monitoring body　202
调和　harmonization　276-280
听审　trial　38
庭审　trial　xii, 38, 50, 58, 59, 60, 61, 62, 69, 95, 99, 102, 106, 107-119, 180, 182, 190, 221, 232, 325, 327, 329, 330, 333, 337
庭外录取证言　deposition　x, 64, 65
庭外取证　deposition　xi, 59
同工同酬　equal pay for equal work　130
同值同酬　equal pay for work of equal value　130

土著人民　indigenous peoples　317-319, 323
推迟起诉　deferred prosecution　43
推定解雇　constructive dismissal　136
退回警察机关补充侦查　return the case to the police for more investigation　30
退税　tax refund; tax rebate　168, 170
吞噬审　trials by corsned　92

**W**

万民法　*jus gentium*　21
王座法院　Court of King's Bench　17
微罪　infraction　35
违法性意识　consciousness of wrongdoing　177
违法宣告　adjudication　220
违反信托关系　breach of trust　182
猥亵儿童　child sexual abuse; child molestation　214, 216
未成年保护委员会　Child Protection Committee　227
未成年人　minor　37, 146, 147, 183, 185, 212, 213, 217, 222-224, 227
未决陪审团　hung jury　98
未遂　attempt　179, 180, 183
文献编制　documentation　313, 314, 316, 317
无不利影响的特权　without prejudice privilege　66
无固定期限合同　indefinite-term contract　124, 130
无固定期限劳动合同　contract of indefinite duration/period/term; open-ended employment contract　124, 125
无期徒刑　non-fixed term imprisonment; life imprisonment (with parole)　33, 34, 86, 184

355　　汉英索引

无效审判　mistrial　98
无因排除　peremptory challenge　94
无罪　not-guilty　vii, 7, 8, 28, 32, 38, 39, 46-49, 53, 58, 75-77, 91, 92, 97, 99, 105, 249, 250, 257, 263, 266, 267, 328, 329, 333
无罪释放　acquitted　8, 39, 53, 99
无罪推定　innocent until proven guilty; presumption of innocence　28, 46, 48, 53
无罪推定原则　presumption of innocence　28, 46
物证　physical evidence　59, 62, 64, 67-69, 110, 113, 334

# X

习惯法　customary law　16, 17, 22, 51, 252, 308
习惯国际法　customary international law　252
先例　precedent　6, 16, 22, 24, 261-262
显然成立的　*prima facie*　56, 253-256
显然成立的证据　*prima facie* evidence　56, 256
现场待命　standby　132, 133
现场证人　live witness　110
现状　*status quo*　259, 260
宪法　constitution　3, 9, 20, 23-25, 38, 39, 41, 42, 49, 52, 54, 61, 63, 72, 101, 186-188, 231, 237-242, 338
相对不起诉　discretionary non-prosecution　44
《消除对妇女一切形式歧视公约》　Convention on the Elimination of All Forms of Discrimination against Women; CEDAW　131, 198, 200, 202
《消除一切形式种族歧视国际公约》　International Convention on the Elimination of All Forms of Racial Discrimination; ICERD　200, 202
宵禁　curfew　31
小陪审团　petit jury　8, 38, 103, 180, 298
小组之家　group home　222
协调　coordination　60, 128, 255, 276-280
胁从犯　forced accomplice; coerced accomplice; unwilling accomplice　178, 183
胁迫　coercion　38, 178
心理辅导　counseling　31, 222
心理虐待　psychological mistreatment　215
心理状态　state of mind　149, 153, 175
行贿罪　giving bribes　140
行为归属　attribution of conduct　275
行政　executive branch; administration　vi, 1-3, 23, 24, 31, 34, 41, 42, 71, 77-80, 82-85, 87, 88, 162, 185-187, 227, 230, 237, 238, 240-243, 254, 297, 320
行政处罚　administrative sanction　242
《行政处罚法》　Administrative Penalties Law　243
行政案件　administrative case　77-79, 88, 185
行政法　administrative law　23, 24, 243
行政法庭　administrative tribunal; administrative division　88, 241, 242
行政法院　administrative court　88, 230, 237, 241, 242

行政复议  administrative reconsideration; administrative review  88, 186, 241-243

《行政复议法》 Administrative Reconsideration Law  243

《行政监察法》 Administrative Supervision Law  243

行政检查  administrative inspection  242

行政强制执行  administrative enforcement  242

行政诉讼  administrative litigation  vi, 77, 78, 87, 88, 241-243

《行政诉讼法》 Administrative Litigation Law  242, 243

行政许可  administrative licensing  242

刑法  criminal law  ix, 12, 23-25, 34, 36, 50, 51, 81, 138-144, 147, 149, 151, 174-179, 184, 243, 249, 252, 253

刑事被告人  criminal defendant  12, 56

刑事法律援助  Criminal Legal Aid  188

刑事责任能力  capacity for criminal responsibility  177

刑事责任年龄  age of criminal responsibility  177

刑讯逼供  torture  46, 56

形式证据制度  formal theory of evidence  67

性别  sex; gender  57, 94, 135, 199, 203-205, 208, 210, 270, 286-290, 296

性暴力和社会性别暴力  sexual and gender based violence  286, 290

性别视角主流化  gender mainstreaming  203, 204

性骚扰  sexual harassment  136, 209-211

休假  leave  136

修正法院  Court of Revision  234, 235

续订  renew; extend  124

宣判  pronouncing sentence; sentencing  32, 118, 284

宣誓陈述  affidavit  xi, 65

宣誓证言  affidavit  95

巡回法官  *justiciae errantes*  17

巡回法院  circuit court  4, 17

巡回区  circuit  4

询问  examination; question  vii, x-xiii, 7, 13, 23, 63, 65, 93, 107, 109-114, 182, 197

# Y

严格解释派  strict constructionists  238

严重犯罪行为  serious crimes  36

言词证据  verbal evidence  67

养恤金  pension  136

要求查验  request for inspection  59

要求提供文件  request for production of documents  59

一审法院  court of first instance  3

一事不再理  *non bis in idem, ne bis in idem*  53, 249, 257, 258

伊斯兰法系  Islamic Law  14

医疗费用  medical costs  186

医疗事故  medical accident  186

医生免证权  medical professional privilege  66

疑罪从无  the benefit of the doubt  48, 49

以言语形式  verbal (in words)  304, 307

银盘理论  Silver Platter Doctrine  62

隐瞒境外存款罪　concealing overseas deposits　140
印度法系　Hindu Law　14
英美法系　Anglo-American Law　vii, ix, xii, 2, 5, 6, 14-27, 51, 53, 91, 105, 113, 175, 179, 183, 229, 240, 242, 249, 261, 298, 301, 303, 328, 332, 338
应纳税额　tax payable　167, 168, 170
永久雇员　permanent/regular employee　125
用工单位　user enterprise　121, 122, 134
用人单位　employer; user　121, 124, 125
优势证据标准　preponderance of evidence　57
有合理犯罪嫌疑　reasonable suspicion　x, 57
有期徒刑　fixed-term imprisonment　12, 33, 34, 36, 39, 86, 141, 181, 183, 184, 224
有因排除　challenge for cause; strike for cause; removal for cause　94
有责性　culpability; blameworthiness　176, 177
有组织犯罪　organized crime　182
有罪　guilty　vii, 7, 8, 28, 32, 38, 39, 44-46, 53, 58, 66, 75, 91, 92, 97, 102, 103, 105, 118, 151, 220, 221, 226, 227, 250-252, 257, 266, 303, 328, 333
有罪答辩　guilty plea　38, 251
有罪推定　the presumption of guilt　46
诱导性问题　leading question　xii, 112, 114
诱供　eliciting a confession　114
育儿假　parental leave　136
预扣税　withholding tax　170
御前会议　the *curia regis*　17

原告　plaintiff　12, 23, 56, 57, 78, 255, 256, 259, 271, 332
原始证据　original/primary evidence　64, 67
阅卷权　right to access case files　viii, 12, 59
孕产假　maternity leave　136

# Z

再审　reopen a case; extraordinary legal remedy; revision　88-90, 98, 228, 233-237, 334
再审法院　court of cassation; Cour de cassation　228, 234, 235
暂行特别措施　Temporary Special Measures　131, 198
责任归属　attribution of responsibility　275
责任能力　penal capacity　175, 177
展示性证据　demonstrative evidence　69
侦查　investigation　vi, 12, 28, 30, 31, 36, 37, 43, 45, 46, 62, 68, 81-83, 86, 183, 190, 327, 328, 330, 336, 337
侦查阶段　investigation stage　28, 327
真实性　truthfulness　x, 61, 63, 111
争点排除　issue preclusion　259
整理　codification　307, 312, 315, 328
正当程序　due process　26, 52-54, 62, 98, 101, 102, 284
正当防卫　self-defense　108, 150, 176, 177, 261
证据不足不起诉　non-prosecution for lack of evidence　37, 44
证据材料　evidentiary material　viii, 12
证据开示　disclosure; discovery　58, 59, 62, 99, 111

证据清楚可信 clear and convincing evidence 57
证据听证 evidentiary hearing 60, 61
证据显然成立的案件 prima facie case 56
证明标准 standards of proof x, 8, 57, 103, 116
证明力 probative value/weight 67, 118, 334
证明思路 theory of the case 58
证明责任 burden of proof; *onus of proof*; *onus probandi* 55-57, 107
证人证言 witness statement; testimonies by witnesses x, xi, 9, 38, 65, 68, 69, 110, 111, 114, 232, 234, 334
证物 exhibit 69, 110
政治论坛 political forum 203
执法机关 law enforcement agency 2, 71
执行 enforcement vi, 34, 35, 39, 41, 77-79, 82-87, 101, 104, 151, 174, 176, 177, 182, 197, 202, 242, 244, 248, 259, 327, 330
执行法律 enforcing laws 41
直接处决 summary execution 284, 290
直接雇用的减时/非全时工人 directly-employed part-time worker 124
直接询问 direct examination xii, 63, 107, 111-114
直接证据 direct evidence 67
值班律师 duty counsel 194, 195
职务犯罪 crimes committed in violation of public duties; crimes committed by public officers/officials 138, 139
指控 charge vi, x, 12, 31, 36-38, 45, 53, 54, 56, 58, 59, 63, 92, 94, 95, 97, 98, 101, 118, 181, 208, 221, 227, 238, 251, 282, 327, 333, 336, 338, 339
指令裁决 directed verdict 8, 99
指派律师 *ex officio* lawyer 189, 190, 196
指示陪审团 jury instruction 99, 107, 114, 116
志愿者 volunteer 193, 227
制定法 statutory law; statutes 6, 16, 22, 23, 41, 148, 151
制定法律 making laws 41
质询书 interrogatory 59
质证 contestation of evidence; challenge the evidence x, xi, 61, 65, 109, 113, 118, 334
中华法系 Chinese Law 14, 15, 25
中级人民法院 intermediate court 5, 20
中间性制裁 intermediate sanction 39
中央税 central taxes 158, 159
终身任职 life tenure 41, 237
终身监禁 life imprisonment; lifetime imprisonment 32, 33, 214
终审法院 court of final instance; court of final appeals 233, 237
仲裁人 arbitrator 23
众议院 Congress 41, 237, 238
《中华人民共和国未成年人保护法》 Law of the People's Republic of China on the Protection of Minors 213
重罪 felony 20, 35, 37, 98, 101, 154, 180, 187, 284, 338, 339
州法院 state court 3, 4, 94, 187, 237, 249, 250
主犯 principal 178
主询问 examination-in-chief xii, 112
主张 allegation; assertion; claim; theory 46, 55-57, 91, 92, 107-109, 112, 113, 115, 118, 253, 290, 294

助审员　assessor　297, 301, 303
抓捕　arrest　vi, 30, 176
专家证人　expert witness　13, 58
专门制度　*sui generis* system　304
专业合适成年人　professional appropriate adult　223, 224
追索　claim　185, 186
准备证人　witness preparation　111
酌定不起诉　discretionary non-prosecution　37
酌定从轻情节　discretionary mitigating circumstances　33
资格审查　*voir dire*　93, 195
自然公正　natural justice　20
自始　*ab initio*　244, 245
自我归罪　self-incrimination　46
自由裁量权　discretionary power; discretion　33, 43, 102
自由心证　principle of free evaluation of evidence; principle of unfettered consideration of evidence　66, 67
自证其罪　self-incrimination　49, 54, 61, 66

总结辩论　closing argument　vii, 7
最低证明标准　minimum standard of proof　8
"最多/最少工时"合同　"min/max" contract　133
最高法院　supreme court　3, 6, 9, 39, 95, 187, 188, 228-232, 235-241
最高人民法院　the Supreme People's Court　5, 11, 26, 51, 87, 227, 252
最后论证　closing argument; summation　108, 113, 115, 116
罪犯　criminal　12, 34, 62, 150, 220
罪刑法定　*nulla poena sine lege*; the principle of legality　50, 51, 251, 252,
罪刑相当　proportionality　51
罪责　culpability　44, 118, 217
醉驾　drunk driving　7
醉酒扰乱公共秩序罪　disorderly intoxication　95
遵循先例　*stare decisis*　22, 261
作为行为　act of commission　215
坐牢　serve their sentence in jail/prison　34, 245

# 英汉索引

## A

*ab initio* 自始 244, 245
abettor 教唆犯 179
abstract act 抽象行政行为 242
acceptance of evidence 认证 61
accepting bribes 受贿罪 140
accepting of bribes by an institution 单位受贿罪 140
access to justice 获得司法救济的机会 196
accessories 从犯 178
accessory sanction/punishment 附加刑 184
accomplice 共犯 178, 179
accused, the 被告（人） 12
acquittal 释放 49, 57, 99
acquitted 无罪释放 39, 53, 249, 257, 263
act of commission 作为行为 215
act of omission 不作为行为 215
actual employer 实际用工单位 134
*actus reus* 犯罪行为 174, 175
adjudication 违法宣告；定罪审判 31, 42, 220, 221
adjudication committee 审判委员会 42
administrative case 行政案件 88
administrative court 行政法院 241
administrative division 行政法庭 87, 241
administrative enforcement 行政强制执行 242
administrative inspection 行政检查 242
administrative law 行政法 23, 243
administrative licensing 行政许可 242
administrative litigation 行政诉讼 87, 88, 241-243
Administrative Litigation Law 《行政诉讼法》 243
Administrative Penalties Law 《行政处罚法》 243
administrative reconsideration 行政复议 88, 186, 241-243
Administrative Reconsideration Law 《行政复议法》 243
administrative review 行政复议 88, 186, 241-243
administrative sanction 行政处罚 34, 242
Administrative Supervision Law 《行政监察法》 243
administrative tribunal 行政法庭 88, 242
admissible evidence 可用证据 59, 60, 61
admission 供述 59, 60, 68, 96
admit 采用 60, 62, 64, 197

adoptive leave 收养假 136
adult jail 成人监狱 222
adversary system 对抗制；对抗制诉讼制度 5, 23, 25
affidavit 宣誓陈述；宣誓证言 xi, 65, 95, 99
affirmative action 平权行动 131, 198, 199
aftercare 后续观护 40, 221
age of criminal responsibility 刑事责任年龄 177
aggravate punichment 从重处罚 179
aggravating circumstance 加重罪行的情节 182, 329
aggressive petition 闹访 vii, 7
allegation 主张 55
allocation of revenues 财权的划分 165
alternative employment 替代性就业 124
American Bar Association 美国律师协会 viii, 11, 191
an integrated operation model 检警一体化 28
analogy 类推 51, 252
Anglo-American Law 英美法系 ix, 15
annual leave 带薪年假 128, 136
appeal 上诉 3-5, 39, 89, 90, 103, 228, 229, 232, 234-237, 240
appear in court 到庭 31
appellate court 上诉法院 3, 4, 89, 229
application of law 法律的适用 119
apply the law 适用法律 22
appropriate adult 合适成年人 222-224
arbitrator 仲裁人 23

argue 论证 207
argumentation 法庭辩论 118
arraignment 认罪程序 38
arrest 抓捕 ix, x, 30, 36, 46, 53, 57, 221, 222, 225, 226, 283, 335
arrest warrant 拘留证 ix, 30
assault 企图伤害罪；故意伤害罪 98, 148, 149, 179, 182, 216, 217
assertion 主张 55, 68
assessor 助审员；人民陪审员 8, 104, 297, 301-303
assessors (lay judges) system 人民陪审员制度 301, 302
assessors system 参审制度 8, 301
assignment of expenditure responsibilities 事权的划分 165
assignment of revenues 财权的划分 164
Associate Justice 普通法官 237
attempt 未遂；犯罪未遂 148, 157, 179, 180, 289
attorney 律师 vii, viii, 9, 11-13, 23, 44, 49, 50, 117, 181, 187, 192, 194, 239, 265, 270, 271
Attorney General 司法部部长 9
attorney-at-law 律师；法律代理 vii, viii, 11, 12, 23
attorney-client privilege 律师与当事人的保密特权 44
attorney-in-fact 事务代理 viii, 12
attribution 归责；归属 272-275
attribution of conduct 行为归属 273-275
attribution of responsibility 责任归属 274, 275
attribution rule 归责规则 274
atypical forms of employment 非典型就业 124

audiovisual material 视听资料 69
*autrefois acquit* 曾经开释 257
*autrefois convict* 曾经定罪 257
auxiliary 辅助性 134

## B

back pay 补发工资 135
bail 保释；取保候审 31, 37, 54, 194, 336, 337
bail conditions 保释条件 31
bankruptcy court 破产法庭 5
basic-level people's court 基层人民法院 5
battery 殴击罪 98, 148, 149, 179, 217
be exempted from punishment 免除处罚 178
bench conference 法庭会议 115
bench trial 法官独任审判 9, 91, 119
benefit of the doubt, the 疑罪从无 48, 49
beyond (a) reasonable doubt 排除合理怀疑标准 57
beyond reasonable doubt 排除合理怀疑 103, 116, 174
blameworthiness 有责性 177
blended sentence 混合量刑 222
breach of trust 违反信托关系 182
bribery 贿赂犯罪 139, 140
bribing an institution 对单位行贿罪 140
bring criminal charge 起诉 43
burden of persuasion 说服责任 55, 56
burden of proof 举证责任；证明责任 46, 55, 56, 107
Bureau of Justice 司法局 28, 187
Bureau of Justice Statistics, the 美国司法统计局 28
business service agreement 劳务派遣协议 134

## C

camps 设防的青少年设施 222
candidate 候选陪审员 93
capacity for criminal responsibility 刑事责任能力 177
capital punishment 死刑 32, 150
carer's leave 护理假 136
case guidance system 案例指导制度 6
case law 判例法 6, 16, 22, 187
casual employment 不定时就业 127, 129
CAT 《禁止酷刑和其他残忍、不人道或有辱人格的待遇或处罚公约》 200, 201
cause of action 诉讼理由 259
CEDAW 《消除对妇女一切形式歧视公约》 131, 200, 201
central taxes 中央税 159
challenge for cause 有因排除 94, 331
challenge the evidence 质证 113, 118
charge 指控 31, 36, 37, 43, 97, 98, 116, 142, 149, 174, 189, 190, 299
Chief Justice 首席大法官 237
child abduction 儿童拐骗 218
child abuse 虐待儿童 214, 215
child maltreatment 虐待儿童 214, 215
child molestation 猥亵儿童 216
Child Protection Committee 未成年保护委员会 213, 227
child sexual abuse 猥亵儿童 214, 216, 217

363

英汉索引

child sexual offender 儿童性犯罪者 214
child support 抚养费 185
Chinese Law 中华法系 14
circuit 巡回区 4, 17, 87
circuit court 巡回法院 4, 17, 87
circumstantial evidence 间接证据 67, 68
citizens' law 市民法 ix, 21
civil law 民法；民法法系 ix, 5, 21-23, 27, 104, 253
Civil Legal Aid 民事法律援助 188
civil society organization 民间法律援助组织 193
civilian law 市民法 ix, 21
claim 主张；追索 55, 185, 254, 259, 270
claim preclusion 请求排除 259
clear and convincing evidence 证据清楚可信 57
clemency 宽大 35, 39
clergy-penitent privilege 神职人员免证权 66
close-ended question "封闭性"问题 114
closing argument 总结辩论；最后论证 vii, 7, 107, 108, 115, 116, 118
codification 编纂；法典编纂；法典化；整理 22, 23, 307, 308, 312, 315
codified law 法典法系 16, 21
coerced accomplice 胁从犯 178
coercion 胁迫 39, 208
cold violence 冷暴力 210
collective bargaining 集体谈判 120, 135
collective labor law 集体劳动法 121
commercial law 商法 23
Commission on Human Rights 人权委员会 201, 203
common law 普通法系 ix, 6, 15-19, 21, 22, 27, 51, 252, 253, 311
common law court 普通法院 18
community service 社区服务 222
commutation 减刑 34, 35
compensation 赔偿 186, 243
completed crime 犯罪既遂 180
complicity in an offence 共同犯罪 178
compulsory measure 强制措施 31, 46, 194
concealing overseas deposits 隐瞒境外存款罪 140
concluding observation 结论性意见 202
conditional non-prosecution 附条件不起诉 37
condominium 共有权；共有物业 245-248
Condominium Act 《共有物业法》 246, 248
confession 供述 50, 67, 68, 114, 333, 334
Congress 众议院 70, 237
consciousness of wrongdoing 违法性意识 177
consider 审议 202, 268, 295
conspiracy 共谋 179
constitution 宪法 23, 72, 311
constitutional review 合宪性审查 242
constitutionality 合宪性 240, 242
constitutionality review 合宪性审查 242
constructive dismissal 推定解雇 136
contest 对抗 109, 181, 250, 251
contestation of evidence 质证 61

continental law 大陆法系 ix, 21
contract for services 劳务合同 121-123
contract of employment 劳动合同 123
contract of indefinite duration/period/term 无固定期限劳动合同 124, 125
contract of service 劳动合同 121-123
Convention against Torture and Other Cruel, Inhuman or Degrading Treatment or Punishment 《禁止酷刑和其他残忍、不人道或有辱人格的待遇或处罚公约》 200, 202
Convention on the Elimination of All Forms of Discrimination against Women 《消除对妇女一切形式歧视公约》 200
Convention on the Rights of Persons with Disabilities 《残疾人权利公约》 200
Convention on the Rights of the Child 《儿童权利公约》 200
convict 犯人 12, 34
conviction 定罪 32, 67, 76, 77, 102, 103, 174, 181, 220, 225, 226, 256
coordination 协调 276, 277, 279
correction 矫正 34, 102
corrections department 矫正部门 102
corruption crimes 贪污贿赂罪 139
cost basis 计税基础 172
counsel 辩护人 11, 54, 186, 189, 192, 194, 196, 268, 271
counseling 心理辅导 31, 222
Cour de Cassation 再审法院 228, 230-232, 235

court 法院 2-5, 15-19, 25, 28, 30, 31, 39-41, 49, 55, 56, 60, 64, 73, 75, 77, 78, 80-85, 87, 89, 95, 117, 118, 123, 126, 133, 189, 197, 224-226, 228-237, 239, 241, 254, 258, 264, 265, 269, 271, 281, 283, 297, 299, 300, 303, 327, 328
court enquiry 法庭调查 118
court of appeals 上诉法院 3-5, 232
Court of Appeals for Veterans Claims 美国退伍军人权利上诉法院 5
court of cassation 再审法院 228-234
Court of Common Pleas 普通民事法院 17
Court of Exchequer 财税法院 17
Court of Federal Claims, the 联邦索赔法院 5
court of final appeals 终审法院 237
court of final instance 终审法院 237
court of first instance 一审法院 3
court of general jurisdiction 普通法院 241
Court of International Trade, the 国际贸易法庭 5
Court of King's Bench 王座法院 17
Court of Revision 修正法院 234
courts of equity 衡平法法院 20
courts of law 普通法法院 20
create law 创造法律 22
credibility 可信度 61, 73, 74, 95, 114
crime 犯罪 viii, 12, 35, 36, 40, 50, 51, 68, 73, 76, 95-98, 117, 138, 139, 147-149, 152, 174-176, 178-180, 182, 186, 213, 214, 221, 225, 245, 251, 252, 281, 329
crimes committed by public officers/officials 职务犯罪 138, 139
crimes committed in violation of public duties 职务犯罪 138

crimes of embezzlement and bribery　贪污贿赂罪　139

criminal　人犯；罪犯；犯罪的；刑事的　9, 12, 27, 28, 34, 40, 43, 44, 51, 52, 68, 73, 83, 84, 86, 102, 141, 142, 145, 150, 154, 175-177, 179, 181, 184, 186, 188-190, 192, 193, 221, 223-226, 245, 253, 327, 329, 333-335

criminal act　犯罪行为　145, 150, 175

criminal defendant　刑事被告人　12, 52, 192

criminal detention　拘役　141, 142, 181, 184

criminal intent　犯罪意图　175

criminal law　刑法　23, 34, 58, 73, 253

Criminal Legal Aid　刑事法律援助　188

criminal record　犯罪前科　44, 95, 102, 224, 225

criminal suspect　犯罪嫌疑人　28, 52, 68, 329, 333, 335

cross-examination　交叉询问　vii, x, xi, xii, 7, 63, 107, 112, 113

Crown option offence　公诉人可选择序的犯罪　181

CRPD　《残疾人权利公约》　200, 201

culpability　罪责；有责性　44, 177

curfew　宵禁　31

*curia regi*, the　御前会议　17

custody　拘留　34, 194, 218, 221

customary international law　习惯国际法　252

customary law　习惯法　16, 22

# D

death penalty　死刑　184

death sentence　死刑　32

debates　法庭辩论　118

defamation　诽谤　141-143

defendant　被告（人）　12, 23, 28, 34, 43, 49, 52, 68, 96-98, 103, 118, 154, 178, 181, 188, 189, 192, 196, 256, 329, 333-335

defender　辩护人　12, 23, 37, 43, 187-189, 192, 227

defense lawyer　律师　13

deferred prosecution　推迟起诉　43

definite-term/period employment contract　固定期限劳动合同　124, 125

deliberation　评议　95, 107, 118, 119

delivery of service　劳动力给付　134

demonstrative evidence　展示性证据　69

Department of Justice　司法部；司法厅　9, 187

deportation　驱逐出境　184, 225

deposition　庭外取证；庭外录取证言　x, xi, 59, 64, 65

deprivation of political rights　剥夺政治权利　141, 184

detention　逮捕　30, 31, 34, 37, 141, 142, 181, 184, 194, 221, 222

detention center　拘留场所　34, 194, 221

detention warrant　逮捕证　30

determination of facts　事实的认定　119

directed verdict　指令裁决　8, 99

direct evidence　直接证据　67, 68

direct examination　直接询问　xi, 107, 112

directly-employed part-time worker　直接雇用的减时/非全时工人　124

disability pension　残疾养恤金　136

disbar　吊销执照　viii, 12

disclosure　证据开示　58, 138, 139
discontinue the case　不起诉　43
discovery　证据开示　58, 59, 65, 99
discovery device　发现手段　59
discretion　自由裁量权　33, 37, 43, 44, 157, 237
discretionary mitigating circumstances　酌定从轻情节　33
discretionary non-prosecution　相对不起诉；酌定不起诉　37, 44
discretionary power　自由裁量权　43
dismiss the case　驳回起诉　31, 265
dismiss the charge　驳回指控；不起诉　37, 43
disorderly intoxication　醉酒扰乱公共秩序罪　95, 96
dispatched work agency　劳务派遣机构　134
dispatched worker/laborer　劳务派遣工人；被派遣劳工　124
disposition　处置　30, 40, 59, 65, 220, 221, 227
disposition hearing　处置听证　220, 221
dissenting opinion　不同意见　262
District Attorney's Office　地区公诉人办公室　9
district court　地区法院　3, 4, 94, 96, 97
diversion　分流　39, 40, 43
diversion by law enforcement, prosecutor, or court　公检法分流　39
diversity jurisdiction　多样性管辖权　4
documentary evidence　书证　68, 110
documentation　文献编制　68, 313
double jeopardy　避免双重危险原则　52, 54, 249, 257

driving under the influence of alcohol　酒驾　7
drop the charge　撤回指控；不起诉　37, 43
drug rehabilitation program　戒毒　31
drunk driving　醉驾　7
dual attribution　双重归责　274
dual offence　可适用两种程序的犯罪　181
dual procedure offence　可适用两种程序的犯罪　181
due process　正当程序　52-54, 62, 98, 285
duty counsel　值班律师　194

# E

economic contract　经济合同　121
economic incidence　经济归宿　172
economic law　经济法　23
*Ei incumbit probatio qui dicit, non qui negat*　谁主张，谁举证　46
EIGE　欧洲性别平等研究院　210
either way offence　可适用任一程序的犯罪　181
electronic data　电子数据　69
electronic monitoring　电子监控　222
elements of a crime　犯罪要件　174, 176
eliciting a confession　诱供　114
embezzlement　贪污罪　139-141
employee　劳动者；雇员　120-129, 132-135
employer　用人单位　120, 122-124, 127, 132-134
Employment at Will Doctrine　雇用自由原则　135
employment discrimination　就业歧视　57, 120

employment law 雇佣法 120, 126
employment relationship 劳动关系 121-123, 126
endless petition 缠诉 vii, 7
enforcement 执行 2, 34, 39, 52, 82-87, 197, 224, 225, 242
enforcing laws 执行法律 41
equality before the law 法律面前人人平等 196
equal pay for equal work 同工同酬 130
equal pay for work of equal value 同值同酬 130
equity 衡平 16-20, 295
equity law 衡平法 16-18
European Institute for Gender Equality, the 欧洲性别平等研究院 210
evidence taking 取证 23, 65
evidentiary hearing 证据听证 60
evidentiary material 证据材料 viii, 12
ex officio lawyer 指派律师 189, 190
ex parte 单方面 248, 249
ex parte communication 单方面沟通 249
ex post facto clause 事后条款 252
examination 询问；鉴定；检查 vii, xi, xii, 7, 13, 59, 63, 107, 109, 113, 253
examination-in-chief 主询问 xii, 112
exclusionary rules 非法证据排除规则 61
executive branch 行政 1
exemption from prosecution 免于起诉 44
exhibit 证物 69, 110
expert witness 专家证人 13, 328
exploitation 剥削 209, 215, 289
expungement 犯罪记录（前科）消灭 224-226
extend 续订 124
extenuating circumstance/factors 减轻罪行的情节 182
extraordinary legal remedy 再审 88, 89, 99

F
factual theory of the case 事实主张 108
fair administration of justice 公正司法 73, 74
Federal Court of Appeals 联邦上诉法院 3, 4, 9
Federal Prosecutor 联邦公诉人 9
Federal Question Jurisdiction 联邦问题管辖权 4
felony 重罪 36, 101, 117, 154, 179, 180, 187
final statement by the defendant 被告人最后陈述 118
finder of fact 事实认定者 9, 91
finder of law 法律认定者 vii, 7, 9, 91
fine 罚款 32, 54, 132, 147, 181, 184, 222
fixed term contract 固定期限合同 124
fixed-term imprisonment 有期徒刑 141, 184
fixed-term/period employment contract 固定期限劳动合同 124, 125
fixed-term worker 签订固定期限合同的工人 124
forced accomplice 胁从犯 178
force majeure leave 不可抗力假 136
foreman 陪审团团长 95
forensic assessment centers 鉴定机构

13

forensic examination centers　鉴定机构　13

forensic examiner　鉴定人　13, 68

forensic examiner's opinion　鉴定意见　68

forensic laboratories　鉴定机构　13

forensic science opinion　鉴定意见　13

forfeiture of property　没收财产　184

formal theory of evidence　形式证据制度　67

foster care　寄养照管　222

framework agreement　框架合同　133

full-time employment　满时就业　127, 129

functional responsibilities　事权　164, 166

## G

gender　社会性别　57, 199, 203, 204, 208, 210, 270, 286-290, 296

gender mainstreaming　性别视角主流化　203, 204

General Assembly　联合国大会　122, 203, 307

giving bribes　行贿罪　140

giving of bribes by an institution　单位行贿罪　140

goodtime　减刑　34

grand jury　大陪审团　8, 37, 38, 54, 103, 298, 299, 338

grassroots legal service worker　基层法律服务工作者　193

group home　小组之家　222

guardian　监护人　218, 222, 223

guiding cases system　案例指导制度　26

guilty　有罪　vii, 7, 28, 32, 35, 38, 43, 46, 53, 59, 97, 98, 102, 175, 221, 251, 333, 334

guilty plea　有罪答辩　38, 43, 102, 251

## H

*habeas corpus*　人身保护令　39

harmonization　调和　255, 276-279

hearing　审；听证　31, 32, 37, 40, 52, 60, 62, 68, 77, 78, 87, 102, 220, 221

hearsay evidence　传闻证据　x, 63

High Court of Justice　高等法院　19

high people's court　高级人民法院　5

Hindu Law　印度法系　14

home confinement　家庭监禁/软禁　222

homicide　杀人罪　150, 151, 155

hostile environment sexual harassment　敌意环境型性骚扰　211

hostile witness　敌对证人　xii, 112

hostile working environment　敌对工作环境　136

hourly rate　计时工资　124

hourly work　计时工作　124

hours worked　工作时间　133

house arrest　家庭监禁/软禁　222

human rights-based approach to development　基于人权的发展观　290, 293-295

Human Rights Commission　人权委员会　202

Human Rights Committee　人权事务委员会　201-203

Human Rights Council　人权理事会　202

hung jury　未决陪审团　98

husband-wife privilege　配偶之间的保

密特权 45
hybrid offence 可适用不同程序的犯罪 181

I
ICCPR 《公民权利和政治权利国际公约》 200, 201
ICERD 《消除一切形式种族歧视国际公约》 200, 201
ICESCR 《经济、社会及文化权利国际公约》 200, 201
identity fraud 身份诈骗 214
identity theft 身份盗窃 214
impeach 弹劾 114, 237
imprisonment 监禁 32, 33, 98, 141, 147, 181, 184, 214
in rem jurisdiction 对物管辖权 256
incarceration 监禁措施；实刑 34, 220, 222
inchoate crimes 初始罪 179, 180
incomplete crime 犯罪未完成形态 179, 180
indefinite-term contract 无固定期限合同 124
independence of judges 法官独立 41, 297
independence of the court 法院独立 41
independent contractor 独立承揽者 122-124
independent exercise of judicial power 独立行使审判权 43
indictable offence 适用普通程序的犯罪 100, 101, 180, 181, 338
indictment 起诉书；公诉书 38, 54, 101, 103, 180, 221, 338, 339
indigenous peoples 土著人民 317-319, 322-324

indigent defendant 贫困被告人；贫困当事人 188, 196
indirect evidence 间接证据 67
individual complaint 个人申诉 203, 206
individual complaints procedure 个人投诉程序 206
individual labor law 个人劳动法 121
industrial accident 工伤事故 186
informal employment 非正式就业 124
informal processing 非正式处置程序 40
information 公诉书 38, 101, 103, 338, 339
infraction 微罪 35
initial appearance 初次到庭 ix, 30, 31, 37
inner conviction 内心确信原则 67
innocent until proven guilty 无罪推定 46, 53
inquisitorial system 纠问制；纠问式诉讼制度 5, 23, 25
instigate the commission of crime by another person 教唆他人犯罪 179
instigator 教唆犯 179
instrument of restraint 戒具 48
intent 故意 19, 145, 152, 153, 175, 177, 210
intentional 故意 142, 149, 150, 152, 153, 155, 175, 214
intentional homicide 故意杀人 155
interdiction of analogy, the 禁止类推适用 51
intermediate court 中级人民法院 5
intermediate sanction 中间性制裁 39

intermediating bribery 介绍贿赂罪 140

International Convention on the Elimination of All Forms of Racial Discrimination 《消除一切形式种族歧视国际公约》 131, 198, 200, 202

International Covenant on Civil and Political Rights 《公民权利和政治权利国际公约》 200-202

International Covenant on Economic, Social and Cultural Rights 《经济、社会及文化权利国际公约》 200

interpreting and applying laws 解释和适用法律 41

interrogatory 质询书 59

investigation 调查；侦查 28, 30, 36, 65, 73, 227, 254

investigation stage 侦查阶段 28

involuntary manslaughter 过失杀人 153, 154

Islamic Law 伊斯兰法系 14

issue 焦点；争点；问题 23, 64, 70, 99, 116, 123, 126, 259, 264-266, 268-271, 295, 323

issue preclusion 争点排除 259

## J

jail 看守所 34, 221, 222

joint principal 共同主犯 178

judge 法官 5, 6, 8, 22, 25, 32, 41, 60, 80, 87, 100, 104, 105, 116, 119, 139, 187, 264, 265, 288, 297, 301-303, 328, 331, 337

judge-made law 法官创造的法律 22, 187

judgment non obstante veredict 不顾陪审团裁决的裁判 8, 53

judgment notwithstanding the verdict 不顾陪审团裁决的裁判 8

Judicature Acts 司法法 19

judicial activists 司法能动派 238

judicial administrative authorities 司法行政机构 227

judicial assistance 司法协助 197

judicial district 司法辖区 9

judicial impartiality 司法公正 73, 74

judicial independence 司法独立 41, 43

judicial officer 司法官 6, 79-81, 329, 330

judicial panel 合议庭 38, 42, 119

judicial review 司法审查 18, 238, 240, 241

judiciary 司法部门 v, vi, 1, 2, 74, 79-81, 297, 303

*judicium Dei* 神判 91, 92

jurisdiction 司法辖区；管辖权 4, 5, 6, 33, 40, 80, 87-89, 98, 104, 150, 181, 197, 232, 237, 241, 253, 271

jury 陪审团 vi, vii, 7-9, 32, 37, 38, 54, 60, 89, 93-100, 103-107, 116, 298, 299, 301, 302, 338

jury instruction 指示陪审团 95, 107, 116

jury pool 候选陪审团 93

jury selection 挑选陪审员 93, 94, 96, 97

jury system 陪审团制度 301, 302

*jus civile* 市民法 21

*jus gentium* 万民法 21

*justiciae errantes* 巡回法官 17

justification 辩解 68, 149, 150, 152, 176, 177, 333

juvenile delinquency/offending 青少年犯罪/违法 214

juvenile detention facility 拘留中心

222
juvenile disposition　青少年处置　220
juvenile hall　拘留中心　221, 222
juvenile offender　青少年违法者　40, 52

**K**

kinship care　亲属照管　222
knock-and-announce　敲门告知　6

**L**

labor dispatch　劳务派遣　134
labor dispatch agency　劳务派遣机构　134
labor dispatch agreement　劳务派遣协议　134
labor law　劳动法　23, 120, 211
labor standard　劳动标准　120
Labour Contract Law　《劳动合同法》　121
Labour Law　《劳动法》　120, 121
labour relationship　劳动关系　121, 122, 124
law enforcement agency　执法机关　2
law firm　律师事务所　191-193
Law of the People's Republic of China on the Protection of Minors　《中华人民共和国未成年人保护法》　213
law student volunteer　高校学生志愿者　193
Lawyer's Certificate of Practice　律师执业证　193
lay judge　人民陪审员　8, 104, 105, 301-303
lay judges system　人民陪审制度　8
leading question　诱导性问题　xii, 112, 114

leave　休假　128, 136
legal aid　法律援助　185, 187-189, 192, 195-197
Legal Aid Center　法律援助中心　185, 187
legal assistance　法律援助　185, 189, 270
legal assistant　律师助理　193, 194
legal families　法系　14
legal interpretation　法律解释　22
legal reasoning　法律推理　22
legal representation　法律代理　192, 269-272
legal service office　法律服务所　189, 193
legal systems　法系；法律制度　14, 16, 27, 276
legal theory of the case　法律主张　108
legal traditions　法系　14
legalistic theory of evidence　法定证据主义　67
legality　合法性　50, 51, 61, 240, 252
legality principle　合法性原则　51, 252
legislature　立法部门　1, 166, 174
leniency for self-confession and severity for resistance　坦白从宽，抗拒从严　50
less serious crimes　轻微犯罪行为　36
libel　书面诽谤　142, 143
life imprisonment　终身监禁；无期徒刑　32, 33, 184
life tenure　终身任职　41
lifetime imprisonment　终身监禁　214
light injury　轻伤　214
live testimony　当庭作证　110

live witness 现场证人 110
local community 地方社区 317, 322-324
local taxes 地方税 159
long-term employee 长期雇员 125

## M

majority opinion 多数意见 262
making laws 制定法律 41
maltreatment 虐待罪 214, 215
mandates 事权 167
manslaughter 非预谋杀人 150-155, 182
marital privilege 夫妻免证权；配偶之间的保密特权 45, 66
marital rape 婚内强奸 146, 209, 210
mastermind 首要分子 178
maternity leave 孕产假 136
"min/max" contract "最多/最少工时"合同 133
medical accident 医疗事故 186
medical costs 医疗费用 186
medical professional privilege 医生免证权 66
*mens rea* 犯罪意图 174, 175
merits of the case 案件的实体（实质）问题 262-269
minimum standard of proof 最低证明标准 8
Ministry of Justice 司法部 187
minor 未成年人 146, 185, 212, 213, 217, 218
Miranda warning 米兰达警告 49
misappropriation of public funds 挪用公款罪 139
miscarriage of justice 错案 75, 76
misdemeanor 轻罪 35, 36, 39, 101, 179, 180

mistrial 无效审判 98, 99
mitigating circumstance/factors 减轻罪行的情节 182
motion 动议；请求 58, 60, 62, 89, 99, 265
motion *in limine* 门槛动议 62, 63
motivation 动机 175
murder 谋杀 94, 98, 150-154, 178, 282

## N

national security agency 国家安全机关 1
natural justice 自然公正 20
necessity 紧急避险 176, 177
negative evidence 反证 68
neglect of a child 疏于照管/忽视 215
negligence 过失 154, 177
negligent 过失 151, 155, 175, 215
negligent homicide 过失致人死亡 155
negligently causing death 过失致人死亡 155
negotiate guilty pleas 进行认罪协商 43
new trial 重审 89, 98
*nolo contendere* 不争辩 38, 250
nominal employer 名义用工单位 134
nominal incidence 名义归宿 172
*non bis in idem, ne bis in idem* 一事不再理 53, 249, 257, 258
noncompetition agreement 禁止竞争协议 136
non-fixed term imprisonment 无期徒刑 33, 184
non-incarceration 非监禁措施 220

non-prosecution for insufficient evidence 存疑不起诉 44
non-prosecution for lack of evidence 证据不足不起诉 37
non-regular employment 非常规就业 124
non-retroactivity 禁止溯及既往 51
not-guilty 无罪 vii, 7
*nulla poena sine lege* 罪刑法定 51, 251, 252

## O

*obiter dicta* 附言；随附意见 262
object 犯罪的客体 175
objection 反对 63, 108, 114, 115
objective side of a crime, the 犯罪的客观方面 175, 176
Office of Justice 司法所 188
on-call 电话待命 132-134
*onus of proof* 举证责任；证明责任 55
*onus probandi* 举证责任；证明责任 55
open-ended employment contract 无固定期限劳动合同 125
open-ended question 开放性问题 xii, 112
opening statement 开场陈述 vii, 7, 107
opening the session 开庭 118
orality principle 口头审理原则 xi, 65, 110
oral testimony 口头作证 xi, 65, 68
ordeals by fire or hot iron 火审 92
ordeals by water 水审 92
order of law 法令 176
organized crime 有组织犯罪 182
original evidence 原始证据 67

overtime 加班 133

## P

panel of judges 合议庭 6
paralegal 律师助理 193, 194
pardon 特赦 34, 35, 39
parental child abduction 父母拐骗儿童 218
parental leave 育儿假 136
parental right 亲权 212, 214
parental support 赡养费 185
parole 假释 33, 34, 184, 221
part-time employment 减时就业 127, 129
paternity leave 陪产假 136
penal capacity 责任能力 177
penalty 处罚 31, 32, 35, 50, 51, 182, 184, 251, 252
pension 养恤金 136, 163, 169, 186
people's assessors system 人民陪审制度 8
peremptory challenge 无因排除 94, 331
periodic report 履约报告 202
permanent employee 永久雇员 125
personal injury 人身伤害 186
persuasive theory of the case 情感主张 108, 109
petition 上访；申诉 vii, 7, 18, 39, 207, 221
petit jury 小陪审团 8, 38, 103
physical abuse 身体虐待 214
physical evidence 物证；实物证据 68, 110
piece rate 计件工资 124
piecework 计件工作 124
plaintiff 原告 12, 23, 256, 271
plea bargaining 辩诉交易；认罪协商

38, 43, 59, 102, 111
plea negotiation 认罪协商 43, 59
plead guilty 认罪 59, 251
pleading 诉答程序 99, 119
police 警察 1, 2, 30, 40, 50, 110, 184, 189, 223
political forum 政治论坛 203
positive discrimination 积极歧视 131, 198, 199
positive evidence 本证 68
possessing huge amounts of assets of unknown origin / unaccounted assets 139
possession of a weapon 持有武器 182
potential juror 候选陪审员 93
practitioner 律师 323
precedent 判例；先例 6, 16, 22, 261
pre-charge detention 拘留 194
predisposition report 处置前报告 227
preliminary hearing 初步听证 31, 37
preparation 犯罪预备 111, 180
preponderance of evidence 优势证据标准 57
pre-procedure 前置程序 242
present one's case 举案 109
presentation of evidence 举证 108
pre-sentencing report 量刑前报告 33, 227
presumption of guilt, the 有罪推定 46
presumption of innocence 无罪推定 28, 46, 53
pre-trial detention 逮捕 194
*prima facie* 显然成立的 56, 57, 99, 143, 253-256
*prima facie* case 证据显然成立的案件 56, 57, 253, 254, 256
*prima facie* evidence 显然成立的证据 56, 99
primary evidence 原始证据 64
principal 主犯 122, 178, 184
principle of certainty, the 确定性原则 51
principle of free evaluation of evidence 自由心证 66
principle of legality, the 罪刑法定原则 50, 51
principle of unfettered consideration of evidence 自由心证 66
prison 监狱 34, 47, 142, 221
prison dress 号衣 47
private attorney 私人律师 187, 192
private detective 私人侦探 viii, 12
private law 私法 23
private lawyer 律师 189, 190, 193
privately dividing up confiscated assets 私分罚没财产罪 140
privately dividing up state-owned assets 私分国有资产罪 140
privilege 免证权 44, 45, 66, 122
privilege against self-incrimination 避免自证其罪的特权 66
*Pro Bono (Publico)* Legal Services 公益法律服务 190
probable cause 合理根据 x, 31, 37, 57, 103
probation 社会考察 32-35, 39, 214, 222, 227
probation officer 考察人员 33, 34, 35, 227
probative value/weight 证明力 67, 118
procedure law 程序法；诉讼程序法 23, 243

procuracy 检察院 10, 11, 82
procurator 检察官 10, 11, 82, 83, 87, 328
procuratorate 检察院 10, 11, 82, 83, 87
procurator general 检察长 10
production of evidence 举证 61
professional appropriate adult 专业合适成年人 223
prohibition against double jeopardy （禁止）双重危险 249, 257
pronouncing sentence 宣判 32
proportionality 罪刑相当 51
prosecuting attorney 公诉律师 viii, 11
prosecution and the defense, the 控辩双方 32
prosecution service, the 公诉机关 1
prosecutor 公诉人 viii, 1, 2, 9-12, 39, 80-82, 189, 297, 338
prosecutors' office, the 检察院；公诉机关 1, 2, 11, 28, 80-82
prospective juror 候选陪审员 93, 331
Provisional Regulations on State Civil Servants 《国家公务员暂行条例》243
psychological mistreatment 心理虐待 215
public defender 公设辩护人 37, 187-189, 192, 227
Public Defenders Office 公设辩护人办公室 187
public interest 社会利益 43, 190, 192, 193
public law 公法 23
public procurator 检察官 10
public security 公安机关 30, 82

public surveillance 管制 141, 181
punishment 处罚 32-35, 46, 51, 54, 73, 76, 150, 152, 178, 179, 183, 184, 200, 251, 252, 333, 334
punishment and rehabilitation 惩罚改造 46

## Q

question 问题；询问 xii, 4, 23, 49, 50, 64, 91, 112, 114, 117, 239, 274
question of fact 事实问题 91
question of law 法律问题 91

## R

rape 强奸 146-148, 209, 210, 217
*ratio decidendi* 判决理由 261
real evidence 实物证据 68
reasonable suspicion 有合理犯罪嫌疑 x, 57
recognition 承认 197
recommendation 来文 131, 132, 206
recross (examination) 第二轮交叉询问 113
redirect (examination) 第二轮直接询问 113
reduce charge 减少起诉罪名 43
refundable tax credit 可退税抵免额 168
refutation 反驳 118
regular employee 永久雇员 125
regular employment 常规就业/用工 124
regular procedure 普通程序 101
relevancy 关联性 61
remand 还押；逮捕 ix, 30, 31, 194, 335
remand warrant 逮捕证 30
remission 减刑 35

removal for cause 有因排除 94
remuneration 报酬；劳动报酬 130, 134, 185
renew 续订 124
reopen a case 再审 99
replaceable 替代性 134
reprieve 缓期执行 35
reputation infringement 名誉侵权 143
request for admission 确认请求 59
request for inspection 要求查验 59
request for physical examination 体检请求 59
request for production of documents 要求提供文件 59
res judicata 既判事项；"事已决"原则 256-259
residential facility 寄宿设施 40
residential surveillance 监视居住 194
restitution 返还财物 33
retrial 重审 89, 98, 236
return the case to the police for more investigation 退回警察机关补充侦查 30
revenues 财权 163-165, 171
reverse discrimination 反向歧视 131, 198, 199
reversing the burden of proof 举证责任倒置 56
review 审查 18, 28, 30, 35, 89, 203, 232, 236, 238, 240-242, 264
revision 再审 72, 75, 234, 237, 311
revocation 撤销假释 39
right to access case files 阅卷权 viii, 12, 59
right to a fair trial 公平审判权 196
right to counsel 获得律师帮助权 54, 189, 196
right to interview the client 会见当事人的权利 viii, 12
right to investigate and collect evidence 调查取证权 viii, 12
right to reputation 名誉权 143
right to silence 沉默权 49
ringleader 首要分子 178
road map 路线图 107
robbery 抢劫罪 98, 144, 145, 178
Roman law 罗马法系 ix, 21, 212
Romano-Germanic law 罗马-日耳曼法系 21
rules of equity 衡平法规则 19
rules of law 普通法规则 19, 73, 308

## S

sanction 制裁；处罚 32, 34, 39, 83, 84, 86, 184, 242
secondary evidence 传来证据 64, 67
secondary participants in crime 从犯 178
secondary sanction/punishment 附加刑 184
secured juvenile facilities 设防的青少年设施 222
security level 安全级别 34
self-defense 正当防卫 150, 176, 177
self-incrimination 自我归罪；自证其罪 46, 49, 54, 61, 66
Senate 参议院 237
sentencing 量刑；宣判；判 30, 32, 33, 38, 40, 102, 103, 118, 183, 184, 225
sentencing and sanctions 量刑和制裁 32
sentencing guidelines 量刑指南 33, 102, 103, 183

sentencing hearing 量刑听证 32
separated operation model 检警分立模式 28
separation of powers 三权分立 41
separation of trial and sentencing 审判分离 32
serious crimes 严重犯罪行为 36, 179
seriousness of the case 犯罪的严重性 43
serve their sentence in jail/prison 坐牢 34
severance package 遣散协议 137
severance pay 遣散费 137
sex (sexual) 性 136, 146-148, 208-211, 214-217, 286-290
sexual and gender based violence 性暴力和社会性别暴力 286, 287
sexual harassment 性骚扰 136, 209-211
shared taxes 共享税 159, 161
shift of burden of proof 举证责任倒置 46
short-term employee 短期雇员 125
side-bar conference 栏边会议 115
sign post 路标 107
Silver Platter Doctrine 银盘理论 62
simplified (regular) procedure 普通程序简易化审理 181
single judge 独任法官 32
single-judge trial 法官独任审判 119
slander 口头诽谤 141-143
snatch theft 抢夺罪 143, 145
social investigation report 社会调查报告 227
social law 社会法 23
social worker 社会工作者 223, 227
Socialist Law 社会主义法系 14

solicitation 教唆 179
Solicitor General 司法部副部长 9
sources of law 法律渊源 22
specific act 具体行政行为 242
spending responsibilities 事权 163, 164
spousal privilege 配偶之间的保密特权 45
spousal support 扶养费 185, 186
standards of proof 证明标准 x, 57
standby 现场待命 132, 133
*stare decisis* 遵循先例 22, 261
state compensation 国家赔偿 243
State Compensation Law 《国家赔偿法》 243
state court 州法院 3
state of mind 心理状态 175
state security organ 国家安全机关 30
State's Attorney's Office 公诉人办公室 9
statement 陈述 vii, 7, 68, 107, 108, 110, 117, 118, 142, 333
statements by the victim 被害人陈述 68
Status Offence/Crime 身份违法/犯罪
*status quo* 现状 259-261
statutes 制定法 22, 271, 311
statutory incidence 法定归宿 172
statutory law 制定法 6, 16, 22
statutory mitigating circumstances 法定从轻情节 33
statutory non-prosecution 法定不起诉；绝对不起诉 37, 44
statutory rape 法定强奸 146, 147, 216, 217
strict constructionists 严格解释派 238

strike for cause 有因排除 94
subject 犯罪的主体 175
subjective side of a crime, the 犯罪的主观方面 175
subpoena 拘传 194
substantive law 实体法 73, 243
substitute 替代性 64, 134, 271
sufficient 充分 31, 38, 44, 58, 96, 103, 253
sufficient evidence 充足的证据 38, 44, 58, 103
*sui generis* system 专门制度 304
summary execution 即决处决；直接处决 101, 182, 281, 282, 284, 285, 287
summary offence 适用简易程序的犯罪 100, 101, 180, 181
summary procedure 简易程序 99, 101, 181
summation 最后论证 108, 115
summon 传唤 93, 189
supervised residence 监视居住 194
suppress 禁用 62
supreme court 最高法院 3, 55, 95, 228, 229, 231, 232, 235, 237
Supreme Court of the United States, the 联邦最高法院 3, 9
Supreme People's Court, the 最高人民法院 5, 11, 26, 51, 87, 227, 252
suspect 犯罪嫌疑人 12, 28, 52, 68, 329, 333, 335

T
tampering witness 操纵证言 111
tax base 税基 170-172
tax basis 计税基础 168, 170, 172
tax break 税收优惠 167-169
tax burden 税负 172

tax credit 税额抵免；纳税抵免额 167-169
tax deductible expenses 可扣除的费用 168
tax deduction 税前扣除；税前列支 167, 168
tax exemption 税收减免 167, 168
tax holiday 税收假日 167, 169
tax incidence 税负归宿 172
tax payable 应纳税额 168
tax rebate 退税 170
tax refund 退税 170
tax relief 收税救济；收税照顾 167, 169
tax return 纳税申报表 170
tax shifting 税负转嫁 172
TCEs 传统文化表现形式 304
temporary 临时性 125, 131, 132, 134, 169, 198
temporary employee 临时雇员 125
Temporary Special Measures 暂行特别措施 131, 132, 198
testimonies by witnesses 证人证言 68
The Hague Convention on the Civil Aspects of International Child Abduction 《国际儿童拐骗事件的民事问题海牙公约》 218
theft 盗窃；盗窃罪 143-145, 214, 218
thematic theory of the case 情感主张 109
theory of the case 对案件的主张；证明思路 58, 108, 109
Three-Level Concept of Crime 三阶（层）论 176
Three-Pronged Concept of Crime 三阶（层）论 176

TK 传统知识 304, 309, 310, 312, 314, 317
torture 刑讯逼供；酷刑 46, 200, 254, 284
trade union 工会 120
trade union law 工会法 120
Traditional Cultural Expressions 传统文化表现形式 304, 313
Traditional Knowledge 传统知识 304, 313, 323
traffic accident 交通事故 186
trafficking 拐卖；贩运 209, 215, 219, 220, 289, 296
treaty body 条约机构 131
treaty-monitoring body 条约监测机构 202
trial 审；庭审；听审 3, 8, 9, 26, 32, 34, 38, 39, 46, 54, 62, 73, 76, 87, 89, 91-93, 98-100, 102, 104, 107, 109, 118, 119, 181, 186, 196, 221, 281, 283, 284, 329, 336
trial advocacy 律师执业技能 108, 119
trial by ordeal 神判；考验式审判 8, 91-93
trial court 审判法院 3, 89
trial *de novo* 重审 98
trial method reform 审判方式改革 26
trials by battle/combat 决斗审 92
trials by corsned 吞噬审 92
trials by Eucharist 圣餐审 92
trials by the cross 十字架审 92
truancy 逃学 213
truthfulness 真实性 61
two-instances system 两审终审制 39
typical case 典型案例 6
typical forms of employment 典型用工 124

U

uncompleted crime 犯罪未完成形态 180
ungovernability 不服管教 213
United Nations Office at Geneva 联合国日内瓦办事处 281
United States Attorney 联邦律师 9
United States Court of Appeals for the Armed Forces, the 美国军事上诉法院 5
United States District Court 联邦地区法院 3, 4, 94, 96, 97
United States Tax Court, the 税务法庭 5
Universal Periodic Review 普遍定期审议 203
UNOG 联合国日内瓦办事处 281
unsolved or not arrested 没有破案或没抓到人 36
unwilling accomplice 胁从犯 178
unwritten law 不成文法 22
user 用人单位 124, 134
user enterprise 用工单位 134

V

*venire* 候选陪审团 93
*venireman* 候选陪审员 93
verbal evidence 言词证据 67
verbal (in words) 以言语形式 67
verbal warning 口头警告 222
verdict 裁决；陪审团裁决 vii, 7, 8, 53, 89, 95, 97-99, 107, 116, 264, 299
verdict form 裁决书 95
violence against women 暴力侵害妇女行为 208-210, 288, 289
violent crime 暴力犯罪 214

*voir dire* 资格审查 93
voluntary abandonment 犯罪中止 180
voluntary manslaughter 非预谋故意杀人 153-155
volunteer 志愿者 104, 193, 223, 227

# W

wage 工资 120
weighing the evidence 评价证据 116
welfare model 福利模式 291
withdraw a guilty plea 收回认罪 102
withholding tax 预扣税 170
without prejudice privilege 无不利影响的特权 66
witness preparation 准备证人 111
witness statement 证人证言 110
wobbler 可选程序犯罪 181
working conditions 工作条件 133
working hours 工时 120, 134
working time 工作时间 132, 133
writ 令状 39
*writ of certiorari* 调卷令 39

# Z

zealous defense 热忱的辩护 viii, 12
"zero hours" contract "零时工"合同 133